FINANCE
DICTIONARY

English-French
French-English

HARRAP

First published in Great Britain in 2000
by Chambers Harrap Publishers Ltd
7 Hopetoun Crescent
Edinburgh EH7 4AY

ISBN 0245 60671 8 (UK)
ISBN 0245 50405 2 (France)

Dépôt légal : février 2000

Designed and typeset by Chambers Harrap Publishers Ltd, Edinburgh
Printed and bound in France by IFC

Editor/Rédacteur
Gearóid Cronin

with/avec
Georges Pilard
Anna Stevenson

Publishing manager/Direction éditoriale
Patrick White

Specialist consultants/Consultants spécialistes

Nicole Génard
Université d'Angers

Peter Walton
Université de Genève

Marc Zagar
Financial Director
Chambers Harrap Publishers Ltd

iii

Copyright

Copyright for the draft euro banknote designs and for the common European side of the euro coins featured in the supplement on the single currency belongs to the European Community represented by the European Commission. Copyright for the national sides of the euro coins featured belongs to the ministries of finance in Belgium, Spain, France and Ireland.

Copyright

Le copyright des motifs des billets libellés en euros et des faces européennes des pièces qui apparaissent dans le supplément sur la monnaie unique est la propriété de la Communauté européenne représentée par la Commission européenne. Le copyright des faces nationales des pièces en euros est la propriété des ministères des Finances belge, espagnol, français et irlandais.

E-mail addresses

Please note that ''business@harrap.eng'' is not an e-mail address but simply a device to identify that the supplement is for English speakers.

Adresses électroniques

Remarque: ''business@harrap.fr'' est une adresse électronique factice dont le rôle est d'indiquer à l'utilisateur du dictionnaire qu'il s'agit du supplément destiné aux francophones.

Trademarks

Words considered to be trademarks have been designated in this dictionary by the symbol ®. However, no judgement is implied concerning the legal status of any trademark by virtue of the presence or absence of such a symbol.

Marques déposées

Les termes considérés comme des marques déposées sont signalés dans ce dictionnaire par le symbole ®. Cependant, la présence ou l'absence de ce symbole ne constitue nullement une indication quant à la valeur juridique de ces termes.

Contents
Table des Matières

T
1003085417

Preface

Developed and expanded from the databases used for the **Harrap Business Dictionary**, this new title aims to provide extensive coverage of terms from all the key areas of finance, covering the vocabulary of the stock exchange, banking, economics and accountancy as well as the language of everyday financial transactions. The dictionary will prove an invaluable resource for all business people, students and translators who require an in-depth knowledge of current financial terminology in their dealings with the French-speaking world.

Technology is dramatically changing the way in which financial transactions are conducted at the dawn of the new millennium, and this dictionary contains the latest new words linked to these developments: terms such as **e-broking, on-line banking** and **signature électronique** are all featured. Also included are many other topical financial terms such as **stakeholder pension, stockpicking, bancassurance** and **fiscalité écologique.** Given the importance of the new single currency in Europe vocabulary related to the euro is also widely covered.

Each side of the dictionary contains an illustrated **supplement** giving useful background and practical information about the euro and the European single market, and the implications of this major new development for the business communities in both Britain and France. Another supplement shows model financial statements in their variant UK, US and French formats with a brief explanation of the different accounting traditions in France, Britain and America.

As with other titles in the Harrap Business range, this dictionary aims to provide the user with **practical help** and to put financial terminology in clear **context**.

Practical help is provided in the form of panels integrated into the dictionary text which give information about the major banks in Britain and the US and in continental French-speaking countries, the main world stock exchanges and their indexes, and the pyramid of financial ratios.

Context is provided by the inclusion of quotations taken principally from the financial press in the English- and French-speaking worlds. These quotations are presented in boxes after the relevant entry and highlight the application of the term as it is used in the financial world.

Préface

Cet ouvrage entièrement nouveau a été conçu à partir des bases de données utilisées lors de l'élaboration du **Harrap's Business**. Il rassemble des termes et expressions issus de tous les domaines liés au monde de la finance, qu'il s'agisse de la Bourse, de la banque, de la comptabilité ou encore des transactions financières les plus courantes. Cet ouvrage sera l'outil idéal des hommes et des femmes d'affaires, des étudiants et des traducteurs pour qui une connaissance approfondie des termes financiers anglais et français est essentielle.

Les progrès de la technologie ont transformé radicalement la façon dont les transactions financières s'effectuent en ce début de troisième millénaire. Cet ouvrage contient tous les termes les plus récents liés à ces transformations, des termes tels que **e-broking, on-line banking** et **signature électronique**. Figurent également des termes d'actualité tels que **stakeholder pension, stockpicking, bancassurance, fonds de pension** et **fiscalité écologique**. Étant donné l'importance de la monnaie unique en Europe, tous les termes liés à l'euro trouvent leur place dans ce dictionnaire.

Chaque côté du dictionnaire contient un supplément illustré où figurent des informations sur l'euro et sur ses répercussions sur le monde des affaires en France et en Grande-Bretagne. L'autre partie du supplément présente des modèles de rapports financiers britanniques, américains et français ainsi que des informations sur les différences entre les systèmes comptables des trois pays.

Cet ouvrage, comme tous ceux de la collection **La vie des affaires** de Harrap, met l'accent sur **l'aide pratique** à l'utilisateur ainsi que sur **la mise en contexte** de la langue des affaires.

L'aide pratique à l'utilisateur est présentée sous forme d'encadrés intégrés au texte. Ces derniers renseignent l'utilisateur sur les principales banques de la Grande-Bretagne et de l'Irlande, des États-Unis et des pays francophones d'Europe ainsi que sur les principales places boursières et leurs indices. Enfin, un tableau présente les différents ratios de gestion.

Labels
Indications d'Usage

gloss	=	glose
[introduces an explanation]		[introduit une explication]
cultural equivalent	≃	équivalent culturel
[introduces a translation which has a roughly equivalent status in the target language]		[introduit une traduction dont les connotations dans la langue cible sont comparables]
abbreviation	*abbr, abrév*	abréviation
accounting	*Acct*	comptabilité
adjective	*adj*	adjectif
administration	*Admin*	administration
adverb	*adv*	adverbe
North American English	*Am*	anglais américain
banking	*Banking*	banque
banking	*Banque*	banque
stock exchange	*Bourse*	bourse
British English	*Br*	anglais britannique
Canadian French	*Can*	canadianisme
accountancy	*Compta*	comptabilité
computing	*Comptr*	informatique
economics	*Econ, Écon*	économie
European Union	*EU*	Union européenne
feminine	*f*	féminin
familiar	*Fam*	familier
law	*Jur*	droit
law	*Law*	droit
masculine	*m*	masculin
masculine and feminine noun	*mf*	nom masculin ou féminin
[same form for both genders, eg **actuary** actuaire *mf*]		[formes identiques]
masculine and feminine noun	*m,f*	nom masculin ou féminin
[different form in the feminine, eg **banker** banquier(ère) *m,f*]		[formes différentes]
noun	*n*	nom
feminine noun	*nf*	nom féminin

feminine plural noun	*nfpl*	nom féminin pluriel
masculine noun	*nm*	nom masculin
masculine and feminine noun	*nmf*	nom masculin ou féminin
[same form for both genders,		[formes identiques]
eg **actionnaire** *nmf*]		
masculine and feminine noun	*nm,f*	nom masculin ou féminin
[different form in the feminine,		[formes différentes]
eg **auditeur, -trice** *nm,f*]		
masculine plural noun	*nmpl*	nom masculin pluriel
computing	*Ordinat*	informatique
plural	*pl*	pluriel
stock exchange	*St Exch*	bourse
European Union	*UE*	Union européenne
intransitive verb	*vi*	verbe intransitif
reflexive verb	*vpr*	verbe pronominal
transitive verb	*vt*	verbe transitif
transitive verb used with	*vt ind*	verbe transitif indirect
a preposition		[par exemple : **souscrire à** :
[eg **souscrire à** (to apply for)		**souscrire à** des actions]
souscrire à des actions		
(to apply for shares)]		

inseparable transitive verb *vt insep* verbe transitif à particule
[phrasal verb where the verb inséparable [par exemple :
and the adverb or preposition **borrow against** (emprunter
cannot be separated, eg **borrow** sur) : to **borrow against** one's
against : to **borrow against** one's assets (emprunter de l'argent
salary] en utilisant son actif comme
garantie)]

separable transitive verb *vt sep* verbe transitif à particule
[phrasal verb where the verb séparable
and the adverb or preposition [par exemple : **bring forward**
can be separated, eg **bring** (reporter) : to **bring forward**
forward : to **bring forward** an an item, to **bring** an item
item, to **bring** an item **forward**] **forward** (reporter une
écriture)]

AA *n Banking, St Exch* (notation *f*) AA *f*

AAA *n Banking, St Exch* (notation *f*) AAA *f*

ABC *n Banking* (*abbr* **activity-based costing**) coûts *mpl* par activité

above-the-line *adj Acct* (*expenses*) au-dessus de la ligne
◇ *above-the-line* **accounts** comptes *mpl* de résultats courants
◇ *above-the-line costs, above-the-line expenditure* dépenses *fpl* au-dessus de la ligne, dépenses de création

absorption costing *n Acct* méthode *f* du coût de revient complet

accelerated depreciation *n Acct* amortissement *m* dégressif, amortissement accéléré

acceleration *n*
◇ *acceleration clause* clause *f* accélératrice
◇ *acceleration premium* prime *f* de rendement

accept *vt* (*bill*) accepter

acceptance *n* (*document*) effet *m* accepté, effet à payer; **to present a bill for acceptance** présenter un effet *ou* une traite à l'acceptation

◇ *Am* **acceptance bank** banque *f* d'acceptation, banque d'escompte d'effets étrangers
◇ *acceptance bill* effet *m* *ou* traite *f* contre acceptation
◇ *acceptance fee* commission *f* d'acceptation
◇ *Am* **acceptance house** banque *f* *ou* maison *f* d'acceptation

accepted *adj* (*written on accepted bill*) accepté, bon pour acceptation
◇ *accepted bill* effet *m* accepté, acceptation *f*

accepting house *n Br* banque *f* d'acceptation, maison *f* d'acceptation

acceptor *n* (*of bill*) accepteur *m*, tiré *m*

accommodation *n* (*of money*) avance *f*, prêt *m*
◇ *accommodation bill* traite *f* *ou* effet *m* de complaisance

account *n* (**a**) (*statement*) compte *m*, note *f*; **to pay a sum on account** payer une somme en acompte; **as per** *or* **to account rendered** (*on statement*) suivant compte *ou* relevé remis
(**b**) *Acct* **accounts** (*of company*) comptabilité *f*; **to keep the accounts** tenir les livres *ou* les écritures *ou* la comptabilité
(**c**) *Banking* compte *m*; **to**

open/close an account ouvrir/ fermer un compte; **to pay money into one's account** verser de l'argent sur son compte; **to pay sb's salary directly into his/ her account** verser le salaire de qn par virement direct sur son compte; **to overdraw an account** mettre un compte à découvert

(d) *(of expenses)* état *m*, note *f*; *(of transactions)* exposé *m*

(e) *St Exch* **the account** la liquidation (mensuelle)

◇ *Acct* **account balance** *(status)* situation *f* de compte; *(after audit)* reliquat *m* de compte

◇ *Acct* **account book** livre *m* de comptes, registre *m* de comptabilité

◇ *Banking* **account charges** frais *mpl* de tenue de compte

◇ *Acct* **accounts clerk** employé(e) *m,f* aux écritures

◇ *St Exch* **account day** (jour *m* de) règlement *m*

◇ *Acct* **accounts department** (service *m* de la) comptabilité *f*

◇ *Am St Exch* **account executive** agent *m* de change

◇ *Banking* **account fee** commission *f* de compte

◇ *Banking* **account handling fee** commission *f* de tenue de compte

◇ *Banking* **account holder** titulaire *mf*

◇ *Banking* **account manager** chargé *m* de compte

◇ *Banking* **account number** numéro *m* de compte

◇ *Acct* **account payable** compte *m* créditeur, dette *f* fournisseur

◇ *Acct* **accounts payable** dettes *fpl* passives, dettes *fpl* fournisseurs

◇ *Acct* **accounts payable ledger** livre *m* des créanciers

◇ *Acct* **account receivable** compte *m* client, compte *m* débiteur

◇ *Acct* **accounts receivable** dettes *fpl* actives, créances *fpl* (clients)

◇ *Acct* **accounts receivable ledger** livre *m* des débiteurs

◇ *Acct* **accounts receivable turnover** taux *m* de rotation des comptes clients

◇ *Banking* **account statement** relevé *m* ou état *m* ou bordereau *m* de compte

accountable receipt *n* quittance *f* comptable, reçu *m* certifié

accountancy *n Br* comptabilité *f*, expertise *f* comptable

accountant *n* comptable *mf*, agent *m* comptable; **he works as an accountant** il est comptable

accounting *n* comptabilité *f*, expertise *f* comptable

◇ **accounting clerk** commis *m* aux écritures

◇ **accounting control** contrôle *m* de la comptabilité

◇ **accounting day** journée *f* comptable

◇ **accounting entry** écriture *f* comptable

◇ **accounting entry sheet** bordereau *m* de saisie

◇ **accounting firm** cabinet *m* d'expert-comptable

◇ **accounting method** méthode *f* de comptabilité

◇ **accounting period** exercice *m* (financier), période *f* comptable

◇ **accounting procedure** pratique *f* comptable

◇ **accounting rate of return** taux *m* de rendement comptable

◇ **accounting system** système *m* ou plan *m* comptable

◇ **accounting year** exercice *m* (financier), période *f* comptable

accrual *n* (**a**) *(of interest, debt, cost)* accumulation *f* (**b**) *Acct* **accruals** *(expenses)* charges *fpl* à payer; *(income)* produits *mpl* à recevoir (**c**) *St Exch* **accrual of dividend** échéance *f* de dividende

◇ **accrual accounting** comptabilité *f* d'engagements

◇ **accruals concept** principe *m* d'indépendance des exercices ou de rattachement à l'exercice

◇ **accrual rate** taux *m* d'accumulation ou d'accroissement

accrue 1 *vt (interest)* produire; **to accrue interest** produire des intérêts

   2 *vi (of interest)* s'accumuler, courir; **interest accrues (as) from the 5th of the month** les intérêts courent à partir du 5 du mois; **accruing interest** intérêts *mpl* à échoir

accrued *adj*

◇ **accrued benefits** *(under pension scheme)* points *mpl* de retraite

◇ *Acct* **accrued charges** effets *mpl* à payer

◇ **accrued dividends** dividendes *mpl* accrus

◇ *Acct* **accrued expenses** frais *mpl* cumulés ou accumulés

◇ *Acct* **accrued income** effets *mpl* ou produit *m* à recevoir

◇ *St Exch* **accrued interest** intérêts *mpl* courus

> ❝
> Throughout this year building societies have faced strong competition from National Savings and throughout the summer months, new savings flowed away from building society accounts, although **accrued interest** of £8bn helped offset the immediate impact of this outflow.
> ❞

accumulated depreciation *n* amortissement *m* cumulé

ACH *n Banking (abbr* **automated clearing house)** chambre *f* de compensation automatisée

acid test ratio *n Acct* ratio *m* de liquidité immédiate

acquire *vt (other company)* prendre le contrôle de, racheter; *(shares)* acheter; **to acquire an interest in a company** prendre une participation dans une société

acquired surplus *n* surplus *m* acquis

acquisition *n (of company)* acquisition *f*, prise *f* de contrôle

◇ *Acct* **acquisition accounting** = base de préparation des comptes consolidés où une société a pris le contrôle d'une autre

◇ *Acct* **acquisition cost** coût *m* d'acquisition

acquit *vt (debt)* acquitter, s'acquitter de, régler

acquittance *n (of debt)* acquittement *m*, décharge *f*, quittance *f*

active *adj St Exch (shares)* actif(ive); *(market)* animé(e), actif;

there is an active demand for oils les valeurs pétrolières sont très recherchées, il y a une forte demande de valeurs pétrolières

◊ *Banking* **active money** monnaie *f* circulante

◊ **active partner** *(in company)* associé(e) *m,f* gérant(e), commandité(e) *m,f*

activity *adj Acct*

◊ **activity accounting** comptabilité *f* par centres de responsabilité

◊ **activity ratio** ratio *m ou* coefficient *m* d'activité, ratio de gestion

activity-based costing *n Acct* coûts *mpl* par activité

actual 1 *npl* **(a) actuals** *(real figures)* chiffres *mpl* réels; **to compare budgeted amounts with actuals** comparer les prévisions budgétaires et les résultats obtenus

(b) *St Exch* **actuals** livraisons *fpl* physiques, marchandises *fpl* livrées au comptant

2 *adj* réel(elle)

◊ **actual cost** prix *m* de revient *ou* d'achat

◊ **actual figures** chiffres *mpl* réels

◊ *St Exch* **actual quotations** cours *mpl* effectifs

◊ **actual value** valeur *f* réelle

actuarial *adj* actuariel(elle)

◊ **actuarial tables** tables *fpl* de mortalité

actuary *n* actuaire *mf*

added value *n Acct* valeur *f* ajoutée

additional *adj (investment, expenses)* supplémentaire

◊ **additional payment** supplément *m*

◊ **additional voluntary contribution** supplément *m* de cotisation retraite *(payé volontairement)*

adjust *vt (prices)* ajuster; *(figures, salaries)* rajuster, réajuster; *(accounts)* régulariser; **the figures have been seasonally adjusted** les chiffres sont les données corrigées des variations saisonnières; **pensions have been adjusted upwards/downwards** les pensions ont été revues à la hausse/à la baisse *ou* ont été augmentées/diminuées; **income adjusted for inflation** revenu réel compte tenu de l'inflation

adjusting entry *n Acct* écriture *f* de régularisation

adjustment *n (of prices)* ajustement *m*; *(of figures, salaries)* rajustement *m*, réajustement *m*; **no adjustment was made for seasonal variation** il n'y a pas eu de corrigé des variations saisonnières

◊ *Acct* **adjustment account** compte *m* collectif

administration *n* administration *f*

◊ *Acct* **administration costs, administration expenses** frais *mpl* d'administration *ou* de gestion

◊ *Banking* **administration fee** frais *mpl* de dossier

administrative *adj (work, skills)* administratif(ive); *(error)* d'administration

◊ *Acct* **administrative costs** frais *mpl* d'administration *ou* de gestion

ADR n (abbr **American Deposit-ary Receipt**) certificat m américain de dépôt

advance 1 n (of funds) avance f, acompte m; **he asked for an advance of £200 on his salary** il a demandé une avance de 200 livres sur son salaire; **advances on securities** or **against collateral** prêts mpl sur titres

  2 vt (money) avancer (**to** à); **sum advanced** avance f, acompte m; **we will advance him £500 before completion of the contract** nous lui verserons un acompte de 500 livres avant l'achèvement des travaux

  3 vi (of shares) augmenter (de prix), monter; **the stocks advanced to their highest point in May** les actions ont atteint leur valeur la plus haute au mois de mai

◇ **advance account** compte m d'avances

◇ **advance dividend** dividende m anticipé

◇ **advance payment** paiement m par anticipation

adverse adj (balance, budget) déficitaire

advice note n lettre f d'avis

advise vt Banking **to advise a draft** aviser d'une traite, donner avis d'une traite

advising bank n banque f notificatrice

advisory adj consultatif(ive)
◇ Banking **advisory committee** comité m de restructuration

affiliate n Am société f affiliée, filiale f

affiliated adj affilié(e)

◇ **affiliated company** société f affiliée, filiale f

affiliation n société f affiliée, filiale f

afloat adv **to keep bills afloat** faire circuler des effets

after-hours adj St Exch
◇ **after-hours dealing** transactions fpl hors Bourse
◇ **after-hours market** marché m hors Bourse
◇ **after-hours trading** transactions fpl hors Bourse

> **❝**
>
> The volume of orders thins dramatically after the market closes, which makes **after-hours trading** a riskier proposition for individual investors. Although the first day of widely accessible evening trading went relatively smoothly, some financial experts suggest that, for now at least, individual investors think twice before venturing into the **after-hours market**.
>
> **❞**

aftermarket n St Exch marché m secondaire

after-tax adj
◇ **after-tax profit** bénéfices mpl après impôts
◇ **after-tax salary** salaire m après impôts

aged debtors n Acct balance f âgée

agency fee n Banking commission f de gestion

aggregate adj
◇ **aggregate amount** montant m global
◇ **aggregate figure** chiffre m global

◇ *aggregate net increment* accroissement *m* global net

agio *n* (a) *(price)* agio *m*, prix *m* du change (b) *(business)* commerce *m* du change

◇ *agio account* compte *m* d'agio

agiotage *n* agiotage *m*

AGM *n* (*abbr* **annual general meeting**) AGA*f*

AIM *n Br St Exch* (*abbr* **Alternative Investment Market**) = marché hors-cote rattaché à la Bourse de Londres.

> **"**
>
> Several billion pounds have been raised on the Alternative Investment Market (**AIM**) over the last four years, following the billion-plus invested on its predecessor, the Unlisted Securities Market, over a much longer period. Another half billion has flowed into venture capital trusts (VCTs) which offer 20% income tax relief and other incentives to invest in very small companies. So far subscribers have seen scant reward, though, as it takes five years to qualify permanently for the reliefs.
>
> **"**

align *vt (currency)* aligner (**on** sur)

alignment *n (of currencies)* alignement *m*

allocate *vt (resources, money, capital)* affecter, attribuer (**to** à); *St Exch (shares)* attribuer, allouer (**to** à); **10% of profits were allocated to investment/advertising** 10% des bénéfices ont été affectés aux investissements/à la publicité

allocation *n (of resources,*
money, capital) affectation*f*, attribution *f*; *St Exch (of shares)* attribution*f*, allocation*f*

allot *vt St Exch (shares)* attribuer, allouer

allotment *n St Exch (of shares)* attribution*f*, allocation*f*

◇ *allotment letter* avis *m* d'attribution

◇ *allotment right* droit *m* d'attribution

allow *vt (give)* **to allow sb a discount** faire un escompte *ou* une remise à qn; **the bank allows 5% interest on deposits** la banque alloue *ou* attribue 5% d'intérêt sur les dépôts

allowance *n (discount)* déduction *f*, concession *f*; *(for tax)* abattement *m*

All-Share Index *n Br* = indice du *Financial Times* et de l'Institut des actuaires britannique

alpha stocks *npl St Exch* valeurs *fpl* de père de famille *ou* de premier ordre

Alternative Investment Market *n Br St Exch* = marché hors-cote rattaché à la Bourse de Londres.

American depositary receipt *n* certificat *m* américain de dépôt

> **"**
>
> Trintech will be aggressively pitching to investors in the German market, with an advertising and awareness campaign already under way there… This is the first time an Irish company has chosen to list on the German Neuer Markt and it is also the first time **American de-**

positary receipts** have been simultaneously issued on the German and US Nasdaq exchanges.

,,

American Express® n American Express®; **to pay by American Express®** payer par American Express®

◊ **American Express® card** carte *f* American Express®

American-style option n *St Exch* option *f* américaine

Amex n (**a**) (*abbr* **American Stock Exchange**) = deuxième place boursière des États-Unis (**b**) (*abbr* **American Express®**) American Express®

amortizable *adj* (*debt*) amortissable

amortization n (*of debt*) amortissement *m*

amortize *vt* (*debt*) amortir

amount n (*sum of money*) somme *f*; (*total*) montant *m*, total *m*; **amount due** montant dû, somme due; *Acct* **amount brought forward** montant *m* à reporter; **she billed us for the amount of £50** elle nous a présenté une facture d'un montant de 50 livres; **you're in credit to the amount of £100** vous avez un crédit de 100 livres; **please find enclosed a cheque to the amount of $100** veuillez trouver ci-joint un chèque de 100 dollars

analysis ledger n journal *m* analytique

angel n bailleur(eresse) *m,f* de fonds

annual *adj* annuel(elle)

◊ *Acct* **annual accounts** bilan *m* annuel, comptes *mpl* de clôture *ou* de fin d'exercice

◊ **annual budget** budget *m* annuel

◊ **annual contribution** (*to pension scheme*) cotisation *f* annuelle

◊ *Acct* **annual depreciation** dépréciation *f* annuelle, amortissement *m* annuel

◊ **annual earnings** (*of company*) recette(s) *f(pl)* annuelle(s); (*of person*) revenu *m* annuel

◊ **annual general meeting** assemblée *f* générale (annuelle)

◊ **annual income** revenu *m* annuel

◊ **annual instalment** annuité *f*

◊ **annual percentage rate** taux *m* effectif global

◊ **annual profit** profit *m* annuel

◊ **annual report** rapport *m* annuel de gestion

◊ **annual returns** déclarations *fpl* annuelles

◊ *Acct* **annual statement of results** déclaration *f* annuelle de résultats

◊ **annual turnover** chiffre *m* d'affaires annuel

◊ *Acct* **annual writedown** dépréciation *f* annuelle, amortissement *m* annuel

annualize *vt* annualiser; **the annualized figures** le montant total pour un an

◊ **annualized percentage rate** taux *m* effectif global

annuity n (*regular income*) rente *f* (annuelle); (*for life*) viager *m*, rente viagère; (*investment*) viager *m*; **to invest money in an annuity, to buy an annuity** placer son argent en viager; **to pay sb an annuity** servir *ou* faire une rente à qn

anticipated profit n profit m espéré

antitrust law n Econ loi f antitrust

application n (a) (for loan) demande f (**for** de); **to submit an application** faire une demande (b) St Exch **application for shares** demande f de titres en souscription, souscription f d'actions; **to make an application for shares** souscrire (à) des actions; **payable on application** payable à la souscription

◊ **application form** (for shares) bulletin m de souscription

apply vi (a) **to apply for a loan** demander un prêt (b) St Exch **to apply for shares** souscrire (à) des actions

apportion vt (costs, taxes, shares) répartir; (funds) affecter

apportionment n (of costs, taxes, shares) répartition f; (of funds) affectation f

appreciate vi (of goods, investment, shares) prendre de la valeur; (of value, price) augmenter; (of currency) s'apprécier

appreciation n (of goods, investment, shares) augmentation f de la valeur; (of value, price) augmentation; (of currency) appréciation f

appropriate vt (funds) affecter (**to** or **for** à); **£4,000 has been appropriated to upgrading computers** 4000 livres ont été affectées à l'augmentation de mémoire des ordinateurs

appropriation n (of funds) affectation f; (of payment) imputation f; **appropriation to the**

reserve dotation f au compte de provisions

◊ Acct, Econ **appropriation account** compte m d'affectation

APR n (abbr **annual** or **annualized percentage rate**) TEG m

APT n (abbr **arbitrage pricing theory**) théorie f de l'évaluation arbitrage

arbitrage n St Exch arbitrage m

◊ **arbitrage pricing theory** théorie f de l'évaluation arbitrage

> **"**
>
> They had been playing in a high stakes financial game known as risk **arbitrage**, hoping to get ahead of the rapid run-up in a company's share price when it became the object of a takeover (or the reversal of fortune that occurred when a takeover fell apart).
>
> **"**

arbitrageur n St Exch arbitragiste mf

arbitration of exchange n arbitrage m de change

Ariel n St Exch = système informatique qui rend possible les operations boursières entre souscripteurs sans passer par la Bourse de Londres

ARR n (abbr **accounting rate of return**) taux m de rendement comptable

arrangement n (understanding, agreement) arrangement m; (with creditors) accommodement m; **he came to an arrangement with the bank** il est parvenu à un accord avec la banque

arrears *npl* arriéré *m*; **we're three months in arrears on the loan payments** nous devons trois mois de traites; **to get into arrears** s'arriérer; **interest on arrears** intérêts *mpl* moratoires; **arrears of interest** intérêts *mpl* non payés

A-share *n St Exch* action *f* ordinaire sans droit de vote

> **"**
>
> Turnover on the local-currency **A-share** markets in Shanghai and Shenzhen, which are restricted to Chinese investors, has more than trebled, to a daily $6 billion–8 billion, and prices have soared…. The hard-currency B-share markets, supposedly reserved for foreigners but in fact havens for hot Chinese money, have almost doubled from their all-time lows earlier this year.
>
> **"**

asked price, asking price *n Am St Exch* cours *m* offert, cours vendeur

assessable income *n* assiette *f* de l'impôt

assessed income *n* revenu *m* imposable

assessor of taxes *n* inspecteur(trice) *m,f* des contributions directes

asset *n* assets *(of company)* actif *m*; *(personal)* patrimoine *m*; **assets and liabilities** actif et passif; **total assets** total de l'actif; **excess of assets over liabilities** excédent *m* de l'actif sur le passif

◇ **asset allocation** répartition *f* des actifs

◇ **asset management** gestion *f* de capital

◇ **asset stripper** dépeceur *m* d'entreprise

◇ **asset stripping** démantèlement *m* d'entreprise

◇ **asset swap** swap *m* d'actifs

◇ **asset turnover** rotation *f* des capitaux

◇ *Acct* **asset utilization ratio** taux *m* d'utilisation des actifs

◇ *Acct* **asset valuation** réserve *f*, provision *f* pour évaluation d'actif

◇ *Acct* **asset value** valeur *f* de l'actif

assign *vt (funds)* affecter (**to** à); *(debts)* céder, transférer (**to** à); *(shares)* attribuer (**to** à)

assignment *n (of funds)* affectation *f*; *(of shares)* attribution *f*; *Acct* **assignment of accounts receivable, assignment of debts** transfert *m* de créances

ATM *n Banking (abbr* **automated teller machine)** DAB *m*

at-the-money option *n St Exch* option *f* au cours, option à la monnaie

attributable profit *n Acct* bénéfices *mpl* nets

attribute *vt Acct* attribuer

attribution *n Acct* attribution *f*

audit 1 *n* vérification *f* des comptes, audit *m*
2 *vt (accounts)* vérifier, apurer, examiner

◇ **audit manager** directeur (trice) *m,f* du service d'audit

◇ *Admin* **Audit office** ≃ Cour *f* des Comptes

◇ **audit trail** vérification *f* à rebours

auditing *n* vérification *f* des comptes, audit *m*

auditor n *(of company)* audit m, auditeur(trice) m,f; *(officially appointed)* commissaire m aux comptes; **firm of auditors** cabinet m d'audit, cabinet comptable
◇ **auditor's report** rapport m du commissaire aux comptes

auditorship n commissariat m aux comptes

AUR n *(abbr* **asset utilization ratio)** taux m d'utilisation des actifs

authorized adj autorisé(e)
◇ *St Exch* **authorized capital** capital m autorisé ou social ou nominal
◇ *Banking* **authorized overdraft facility** autorisation f de découvert
◇ *St Exch* **authorized share capital** capital m autorisé
◇ *St Exch* **authorized unit trust** = SICAV autorisée par la commission britannique des opérations de Bourse

automated adj automatisé(e)
◇ *Banking* **automated clearing house** chambre f de compensation automatisée
◇ **automated teller machine** distributeur m automatique de billets
◇ **automated withdrawal** retrait m automatique

automatic adj automatique
◇ **automatic accounting** comptabilité f mécanographique
◇ **automatic transfer** virement m automatique

available adj disponible; **sum available for dividend** affectation f aux actions
◇ **available assets** actif m disponible ou liquide
◇ **available balance** solde m disponible

◇ **available capital** capitaux mpl disponibles
◇ **available cash flow** cash-flow m disponible
◇ **available funds** fonds mpl liquides ou disponibles, disponibilités fpl
◇ **available market** marché m effectif

AVC n *(abbr* **additional voluntary contribution)** supplément m de cotisation retraite *(payé volontairement)*

> **"**
>
> AVCs are additional voluntary contributions – extra payments made from your salary or other net relevant earnings to top up your company pension. You can pay **AVCs** into a scheme run by your company, known as an in-house **AVC** scheme, or into a free-standing (FSAVC) policy run by another company, or you can pay **AVCs** to buy extra years of service in a final-salary company pension scheme.
>
> **"**

AVCO n *(abbr* **average cost)** coût m moyen

average 1 n *St Exch* indice m
2 adj moyen(enne)
◇ **average cost** coût m moyen
◇ **average due date** échéance f moyenne
◇ **average revenue** produit m moyen
◇ *Am* **average tax rate** taux m d'imposition effectif ou moyen
◇ **average yield** rendement m moyen

avoidable costs npl *Acct* coûts mpl évitables

back 1 *n (of cheque)* dos *m*, verso *m*

2 *vt* **(a)** *(support financially)* financer **(b)** *(bill)* avaliser, endosser, donner son aval à

◇ *back door* financement *m* déguisé

◇ *back interest* arrérages *mpl*, intérêts *mpl* arriérés

◇ *Banking* **back office** back-office *m*

◇ *back pay* rappel *m* de salaire

◇ *back tax* arriéré *m* d'impôt

back-end load *n Am St Exch* frais *mpl* de sortie

backer *n* **(a)** *(financial supporter)* bailleur(eresse) *m,f* de fonds **(b)** *(of bill)* donneur *m* d'aval, avaliseur *m*

backhander *n Br Fam (bribe)* pot-de-vin *m*, dessous-de-table *m*

backing *n (financial support)* financement *m*; **to give financial backing to sth** financer qch

back-to-back *adj Banking*
◇ *back-to-back credit* crédit *m* dos-à-dos
◇ *back-to-back loan, back-to-back operation* opération *f* de face à face

backwardation *n Br* déport *m*

◇ *backwardation rate* taux *m* de déport

BACS *n (abbr* **Bankers' Automated Clearing System)** = système électronique de paiement; **to pay by BACS** payer par virement électronique

bad 1 *n* **he is £5,000 to the bad** *(overdrawn)* il a un découvert de 5000 livres; *(after a deal)* il a perdu 5000 livres

2 *adj*

◇ *bad cheque* chèque *m* sans provision

◇ *bad debt* créance *f* irrécouvrable *ou* douteuse

◇ *bad debtor* créance *f* irrécouvrable *ou* douteuse

◇ *bad debt provision* provision *f* pour créances douteuses

◇ *bad debts reserve* réserve *f* pour créances douteuses

> A deterioration in loans to mainland-related companies has forced the Bank of China's local operations to drastically increase **bad debt provisions** in the six months to June 30, causing a 46.74 per cent plunge in pretax profit to $3 billion.

balance 1 *n (of account)* solde *m*; *Acct* balance *f*, bilan *m*; **balance in hand** solde en caisse; **balance carried forward** solde à reporter; *(on balance sheet)* report *m* à nouveau; **balance brought forward** solde reporté; *(on balance sheet)* report; **balance due** solde débiteur *ou* dû; **to pay the balance** régler le solde; **off the balance sheet** hors de bilan

2 *vt (account)* équilibrer, balancer; *(debt)* compenser; *(budget)* équilibrer; **to balance the books** dresser *ou* établir le bilan, arrêter les comptes; **to balance the budget** équilibrer le budget; **to balance an adverse budget** rétablir un budget déficitaire; **balanced budget** budget équilibré

3 *vi (of accounts)* s'équilibrer, balancer; **I can't get the accounts to balance** je n'arrive pas à équilibrer les comptes

◇ *Acct* **balance book** livre *m* d'inventaire

◇ *Econ* **balance of payments** balance *f* des paiements

◇ *Econ* **balance of payments deficit** déficit *m* de la balance des paiements, déficit extérieur

◇ *Acct* **balance sheet** bilan *m*

◇ *Acct* **balance sheet auditing** contrôle *m* du bilan

◇ *Acct* **balance sheet consolidation** consolidation *f* de bilan

◇ *Acct* **balance sheet item** poste *m* de bilan

◇ *Acct* **balance sheet value** valeur *f* bilantielle *ou* d'inventaire

◇ *Econ* **balance of trade** balance *f* commerciale

balancing *n (of accounts)* solde *m*, alignement *m*, arrêté *m*

ballot *n St Exch (when shares are oversubscribed)* allocation *f* d'actions par tirage au sort

bancassurance *n Banking* bancassurance *f*

> **"**
>
> The term imported from the Continent is **bancassurance**. In essence, it is meant to describe the business model that uses a bank's high street branches to sell insurance products.
>
> **"**

bang *vt St Exch* **to bang the market** faire baisser les prix, écraser le marché

bank 1 *n* banque *f*; **the High Street banks** les grandes banques centrales; **the Bank of England/France** la Banque d'Angleterre/de France

2 *vt (cheque, money)* mettre *ou* déposer à la banque

3 *vi* **to bank with sb** avoir un compte (bancaire) chez qn; **where do you bank?, who do you bank with?** à quelle banque êtes-vous *ou* avez-vous votre compte?, quelle est votre banque?

◇ **bank account** compte *m* en banque, compte bancaire; **to open/close a bank account** ouvrir/fermer un compte bancaire

◇ **bank advance** avance *f* bancaire

◇ **bank advice** avis *m* de la banque

◇ **bank balance** solde *m* (en banque)

Banks – UK, Ireland & the US

Les grandes banques de la Royaume-Uni, de l'Irlande et des États-Unis

Major banks in the UK/Les grandes banques de la Grande Bretagne

Abbey National PLC www.abbeynational.co.uk

Alliance & Leicester
  www.alliance-leicester.co.uk*

Bank of Scotland www.bankofscotland.co.uk

Barclays Bank PLC www.barclays.com

Bristol & West www.baw.avonibp.co.uk*

Cheltenham & Gloucester
  www.cheltglos.co.uk*

Co-Operative Bank www.co-opbank.co.uk

First Direct www.firstdirect.co.uk

The Halifax www.halifax.co.uk*

Lloyds Bank www.lloydsbank.co.uk

Lombard Bank www.lombank.co.uk

Midland Bank www.midlandbank.co.uk

National Westminster (NatWest)
  www.natwest.co.uk

Royal Bank of Scotland www.rbos.co.uk

TSB www.tsb.co.uk

Woolwich www.woolwich.co.uk*

UK building societies/Sociétés de crédit immobilier britanniques

Bradford & Bingley Building Society
  www.bradford-bingley.co.uk

The Nationwide Building Society
  www.nationwide.co.uk

The Yorkshire Building Society www.ybs.co.uk

* In Britain many leading building societies
  have recently demutualized to become banks

* Au cours des dernières années de nombreuses
  sociétés de crédit immobilier britanniques ont
  abandonné leur statut de sociétés mutuelles
  pour devenir des banques cotées en Bourse

Major banks in Ireland/Les grandes banques de l'Irlande

Allied Irish Bank www.aib.ie

Bank of Ireland www.boi.ie

Ulster Bank www.ulsterbank.com

Major US banks/Les grandes banques américaines

Bank of America www.bankamerica.com

Bank Boston www.bankboston.com

Bank One www.bankone.com

Bankers Trust www.bankerstrust.com

Chase Manhattan Bank www.chase.com

Citibank/Citicorp www.citicorp.com

First Union www.firstunion.com

J. P. Morgan www.jpmorgan.com

Nations Bank www.nationsbank.com

Norwest Corporation www.norwest.com

* America's banking system differs
  fundamentally from the British banking
  system in that there is no nationwide high-
  street banking structure, but instead a more
  decentralised network of banks based in the
  different US states.

* Le système bancaire américain est très
  différent du système britannique. En effet,
  chaque état américain possède son propre
  réseau bancaire et les grandes banques sont
  beaucoup moins présentes au niveau local
  qu'en Grande-Bretagne.

⋄ *bank base rate* taux *m* de base bancaire

⋄ *bank bill* effet *m* *(tiré par une banque sur une autre)*

⋄ *bank book* livret *m* de caisse d'épargne, carnet *m* de banque

⋄ *bank borrowings* emprunts *mpl* bancaires, concours *m* bancaire

⋄ *bank branch code* code *m* guichet

⋄ *bank buying rate* taux *m* de change à l'achat

⋄ *bank card* carte *f* (d'identité) bancaire

⋄ *bank charges* frais *mpl* bancaires *ou* de banque

⋄ *bank clerk* employé(e) *m,f* de banque

⋄ *bank commitment* engagement *m* bancaire

⋄ *bank credit* avoir *m* en banque, crédit *m* bancaire

⋄ *bank debts* dettes *fpl* bancaires

⋄ *bank deposit* dépôt *m* bancaire *ou* en banque

⋄ *bank details* relevé *m* d'identité bancaire, RIB *m*

⋄ *bank discount* escompte *m* de banque *ou* en dehors

⋄ *bank discount rate* escompte *m* officiel

⋄ *bank draft* traite *f* bancaire

⋄ *bank guarantee* garantie *f* bancaire, caution *f* de banque

⋄ *Br* *bank holiday* jour *m* férié

⋄ *bank interest* intérêt *m* bancaire

⋄ *bank lending* concours *m* bancaire

⋄ *bank loan* prêt *m* bancaire

⋄ *bank manager* directeur (trice) *m,f* de banque

⋄ *bank money* monnaie *f* de banque, monnaie scripturale

⋄ *bank notification* avis *m* de la banque

⋄ *bank overdraft* découvert *m* bancaire

⋄ *bank rate* taux *m* bancaire

⋄ *Acct* *bank reconciliation* rapprochement *m* bancaire

⋄ *bank reserves* réserves *fpl* bancaires

⋄ *bank selling rate* taux *m* de change à la vente

⋄ *bank shares* valeurs *fpl* bancaires

⋄ *bank sort code* code *m* guichet

⋄ *bank statement* relevé *m* de compte

⋄ *bank teller* guichetier(ère) *m,f*

⋄ *bank transactions* transactions *fpl* bancaires

⋄ *bank transfer* virement *m* bancaire

⋄ *bank transfer advice* avis *m* de virement

⋄ *bank treasurer* trésorier(ère) *m,f* de banque

bankable *adj* bancable

⋄ *bankable paper* papier *m* bancable

banker *n* banquier(ère) *m,f*

⋄ *banker's acceptance* acceptation *f* bancaire

⋄ *Bankers' Automated Clearing System* = système électronique de compensation de chèques

⋄ *banker's card* carte *f* d'identité bancaire

⋄ *banker's cheque, banker's draft* traite *f* bancaire

⋄ *banker's order* ordre *m* de virement bancaire

banking *n* *(activity)* opérations

fpl bancaires, activité *f* bancaire ; *(profession)* profession *f* de banquier ; **she's in banking** elle travaille dans la banque

◇ *Am* **banking account** compte *m* en banque, compte bancaire

◇ **banking business** trafic *m* bancaire

◇ **banking controls** contrôle *m* bancaire

◇ **banking hours** heures *fpl* d'ouverture de la banque

◇ **banking house** maison *f* de banque, établissement *m* bancaire

◇ **banking mechanism** mécanisme *m* bancaire

◇ **banking product** produit *m* bancaire

◇ **banking system** système *m* banciare

banknote *n* billet *m* de banque

bankroll *Am* **1** *n* fonds *mpl*, finances *fpl*

2 *vt (deal, project)* financer

bankrupt **1** *n* failli(e) *m,f*

◇ **bankrupt's certificate** concordat *m*

2 *adj* failli(e) ; **to go bankrupt** faire faillite ; **to be bankrupt** être en faillite ; **to adjudicate** *or* **declare sb bankrupt** déclarer qn en faillite

3 *vt (company, person)* mettre en faillite ; **the deal bankrupted the business** la transaction a mis l'entreprise en faillite

bankruptcy *n* faillite *f* ; **to present** *or* **file one's petition for bankruptcy** déposer son bilan

◇ *Br* **bankruptcy court** ≃ tribunal *m* de commerce

◇ **bankruptcy proceedings** procédure *f* de faillite

base *n Banking*

◇ **base date** date *f* de base

◇ **base rate** taux *m* de base (bancaire)

◇ **base year** année *f* de référence

basket of currencies *n* panier *m* de devises, panier de monnaies

BE *n (abbr* **Bank of England**) Banque *f* d'Angleterre

b/e *n (abbr* **bill of exchange**) lettre *f* de change

bear *St Exch* **1** *n* baissier(ère) *m,f*, spéculateur(trice) *m,f* à la baisse ; **to go a bear** spéculer *ou* jouer à la baisse

2 *vt* **to bear the market** chercher à faire baisser les cours

3 *vi* spéculer à la baisse

◇ **bear closing** arbitrage *m* à la baisse

◇ **bear market** marché *m* à la baisse *ou* baissier

◇ **bear position** position *f* vendeur *ou* baissière

◇ **bear sale** vente *f* à découvert

◇ **bear speculation** spéculation *f* à la baisse

◇ **bear trading** spéculation *f* à la baisse

◇ **bear transaction** transaction *f* à la baisse

bearer *n (of cheque)* porteur (euse) *m,f* ; **cheque made payable to bearer** chèque *m* (payable) au porteur

◇ **bearer bill** effet *m ou* billet *m* au porteur

◇ *St Exch* **bearer bond** titre *m ou* obligation *f* au porteur

◇ **bearer cheque** chèque *m* au porteur

◇ Banking **bearer paper** papier *m* au porteur

◇ St Exch **bearer share** action *f* au porteur

bearish *adj* St Exch *(market, trend)* à la baisse, baissier(ère); **to be bearish** *(person)* spéculer *ou* jouer à la baisse

◇ **bearish tendency** tendance *f* à la baisse

bed and breakfasting *n* St Exch aller et retour *m*

Belgian franc *n* franc *m* belge

belly-up *n* Fam **to go belly up** *(of company)* faire faillite

below-the-line *adj* Acct *(expenses)* au-dessous de la ligne

◇ **below-the-line accounts** comptes *mpl* de résultats exceptionnels

benchmark *n* point *m* de repère

◇ **benchmark market** marché *m* de référence

beneficiary *n* bénéficiaire *mf*; **beneficiary under a trust** bénéficiaire d'une fiducie

b/f Acct *(abbr* **brought forward)** reporté

bid *n* Am St Exch **the bid and asked** les cours *mpl* d'achat et de vente

◇ **bid bond** caution *f* d'adjudication *ou* de soumission

◇ **bid price** cours *m* acheteur

bidding price *n* Am St Exch cours *m* acheteur

big *adj*

◇ Br Fam St Exch **Big Bang** = déréglementation de la Bourse de Londres en octobre 1986

◇ Am **the big board** la Bourse de New York

◇ Br Formerly **the Big Four** = les quatre grandes banques anglaises *(Lloyds, National Westminster, Barclays, Midland)*

bill 1 *n* **(a)** *(notice of payment due)* facture *f*; *(for gas, electricity)* facture, note *f*; *(in hotel)* note; *Br (in restaurant)* addition *f*; **to make out a bill** dresser *ou* rédiger une facture; **to pay a bill** payer *ou* régler une facture; **to foot the bill** payer la note *ou* les dépenses

(b) *Am (banknote)* billet *m* de banque; **five-dollar bill** billet de cinq dollars

(c) *(promissory note)* effet *m* (de commerce), traite *f*; **bills for collection** effets à l'encaissement; **bills in hand** effets en portefeuille

2 *vt* facturer

◇ **bill book** livre *m* d'échéance

◇ **bill broker, bill discounter** courtier(ère) *m,f* de change

◇ **bill of exchange** lettre *f* de change, effet *m* de commerce

◇ **bills of exchange statement** lettre *f* de change relevé

◇ Acct **bills payable** effets *mpl* à payer; **bill payable at sight** effet payable à vue *ou* à présentation

◇ Acct **bills payable ledger** journal *m* ou livre *m* des effets à payer

◇ Acct **bills receivable** effets *mpl* à recevoir

◇ Acct **bills receivable ledger** journal *m* ou livre *m* des effets à recevoir

◇ **bill of sale** acte *m* ou contrat *m* de vente

billing date *n* date *f* de facturation

black 1 *n* **to be in the black** *(of person)* être solvable; *(of account)* être créditeur(trice)
2 *adj*
◇ *St Exch* **black knight** chevalier *m* noir
◇ **black market** marché *m* noir
◇ *St Exch* **Black Monday** jour *m* du krach (boursier) *(le lundi 19 octobre 1987)*

blank *adj*
◇ **blank cheque** chèque *m* en blanc
◇ **blank credit** crédit *m* en blanc
◇ **blank endorsement** endossement *m* en blanc

block 1 *n* **(a)** *(of shares)* paquet *m* **(b)** **to put a block on sth** *(cheque, account, prices, imports)* bloquer qch
2 *vt* *(cheque, account, prices, imports)* bloquer; **blocked currency** monnaie *f* bloquée *ou* non convertible
◇ *St Exch* **block issue** émission *f* par série
◇ *St Exch* **block trading** négociations *fpl* de bloc

blue chip *n St Exch* valeur *f* de père de famille *ou* de premier ordre

blue-chip *adj St Exch*
◇ **blue-chip company** affaire *f* de premier ordre
◇ **blue-chip shares, blue-chip stocks** valeurs *fpl* de père de famille *ou* de premier ordre

blue-sky security *n St Exch* titre *m* hautement speculatif *ou* à haut risque

board of directors *n* conseil *m* d'administration

boiler room *n Am Fam* = organisation qui vend illégalement au public des produits financiers très spéculatifs ou sans valeur

bolster *vt* *(currency, economy)* soutenir

> **"**
>
> On the positive side, interest rates are low, which is **bolstering** consumer demand and easing the debt burden of companies.
>
> **"**

bond *n* obligation *f*; **long/medium/short bond** obligation longue/moyenne/courte
◇ **bond equivalent yield** = rendement équivalent à celui d'une obligation
◇ **bond investment** placement *m* obligataire
◇ **bond issue** émission *f* obligataire *ou* d'obligations, emprunt *m* obligataire; **to make a bond issue** émettre un emprunt
◇ **bond market** marché *m* obligataire *ou* des obligations
◇ **bond note** titre *m* d'obligation
◇ **bond yield** rendement *m* de l'obligation

bondholder *n* obligataire *mf*, détenteur(trice) *m,f ou* porteur(euse) *m,f* d'obligations

bonus *n St Exch (on shares)* dividende *m* supplémentaire, bonification *f*
◇ **bonus issue** émission *f* d'actions gratuites
◇ **bonus scheme** système *m* de primes
◇ **bonus share** action *f* gratuite *ou* donnée en prime

book n Acct **the books** (of company) les comptes mpl; **to keep the books** tenir la comptabilité ou les comptes

◇ **book debts** comptes mpl fournisseurs, dettes fpl compte

◇ **book entry** écriture f comptable

◇ **book entry transfer** transfert m de compte à compte

◇ **book value** valeur f comptable, valeur de bilan

bookkeeper n Acct comptable mf, teneur m de comptes

bookkeeping n Acct tenue f de(s) livres, comptabilité f

boom n Econ boom m, période f d'essor

◇ **boom and bust (cycle)** cycle m expansion-récession

> **"**
>
> Some praised the Bank. Higher rates improve the prospects for stability in the property sector and reduce the possibility of a repeat of the 1980s **boom and bust cycle**, said Milan Khatri, chief economist at the Royal Institution of Chartered Surveyors.
>
> **"**

borrow 1 vt emprunter; **to borrow money from sb** emprunter de l'argent à qn

2 vi emprunter (**from** à); **to borrow on** or **at interest** emprunter à intérêt

▸ **borrow against** vt insep (salary, property) emprunter sur; **the company borrowed against its assets** l'entreprise a emprunté de l'argent en utilisant son actif comme garantie

borrowed adj emprunté(e), d'emprunt

◇ **borrowed capital** capitaux mpl empruntés ou d'emprunt

borrowing n emprunts mpl; **financed by borrowing** financé(e) par des emprunts

◇ **borrowing power** capacité f d'emprunt ou d'endettement

◇ **borrowing rate** taux m d'emprunt

◇ **borrowing requirements** besoins mpl de crédit

bottom 1 n **the bottom has fallen out of the market** le marché s'est effondré

2 adj

◇ **bottom line** solde m final, résultat m financier; **black bottom line** solde créditeur; **red bottom line** solde débiteur

bought ledger n Acct cahier m ou livre m des achats

bounce Fam 1 vt (cheque) refuser d'honorer

2 vi (of cheque) être refusé(e) pour non-provision; **I hope this cheque won't bounce** j'espère que ce chèque ne sera pas refusé

branch n (of company) agence f, succursale f, filiale f; (of bank) agence

◇ **branch banking** banque f à réseau

◇ **branch manager** directeur (trice) m,f de succursale

◇ **branch office** agence f

▸ **break down** vt sep (account, figures, expenses) décomposer, ventiler; (statistics) analyser; (bill, estimate) détailler

▸ **break even** vi (of person, company) rentrer dans ses frais

▸ **break up 1** *vt sep (conglomerate, trust)* scinder, diviser; *(company)* scinder; *(coalition)* rompre

2 *vi (of meeting)* se terminer, prendre fin; *(of partnership)* cesser, prendre fin; *(of talks, negotiations)* cesser

breakdown *n (of account, figures, expenses)* décomposition *f*, ventilation *f*; *(of statistics)* analyse *f*; *(of bill, estimate)* détail *m*; *Banking (of charges, interest)* décompte *m*

break-even 1 *n* seuil *m* de rentabilité; *Acct* point *m* mort, point *m* d'équilibre; **to reach break-even** atteindre le seuil de rentabilité

2 *adj*
◇ **break-even analysis** analyse *f* du point mort
◇ **break-even point** seuil *m* de rentabilité; *Acct* point *m* mort
◇ **break-even price** prix *m* minimum rentable

break-up *n (of company)* scission *f*
◇ **break-up price** prix *m* de liquidation
◇ *Acct* **break-up value** valeur *f* à la casse

bridge loan *n Am* prêt-relais *m*

bridging *adj Br*
◇ **bridging loan** prêt-relais *m*
◇ **bridging value** valeur *f* de récupération

▸ **bring forward** *vt sep Acct (item)* reporter; **brought forward** reporté(e)

▸ **bring out** *vt sep (shares)* émettre; **to bring out new shares** émettre de nouvelles actions

broker *n* (**a**) *(for insurance, goods)* courtier(ère) *m,f* (de commerce) (**b**) *St Exch* agent *m* de change, courtier(ère) *m,f* (en Bourse)
◇ **broker's commission** (frais *mpl* de) courtage *m*
◇ **broker's contract** courtage *m*

brokerage *n* (**a**) *(profession of broker)* courtage *m* (**b**) *(fee)* (frais *mpl* de) courtage *m*
◇ **brokerage house** maison *f* de courtage

broking *n (profession)* courtage *m*

B-share *n St Exch* action *f* ordinaire avec droit de vote, action à dividende prioritaire

bt/fwd *adj Acct* (*abbr* **brought forward**) reporté(e)

bucket shop *n Fam* bureau *m* de courtier marron

budget 1 *n (financial plan)* budget *m*; *(allocated ceiling)* enveloppe *f* budgétaire; **to balance the budget** équilibrer le budget
2 *vi* budgétiser
◇ **budget account** compte *m* permanent
◇ **budget allocation** enveloppe *f* budgétaire
◇ **budget constraint** contrainte *f* budgétaire
◇ **budget cuts** coupes *fpl* budgétaires
◇ **budget deficit** déficit *m* budgétaire
◇ **budget estimates** prévisions *fpl* budgétaires
◇ **budget forecast** prévisions *fpl* budgétaires
◇ **budget planning** planification *f* budgétaire

◇ **budget surplus** excédent *m* budgétaire

budgetary *adj* budgétaire

◇ **budgetary control** gestion *f* budgétaire

◇ **budgetary limit** plafond *m* des charges budgétaires

◇ **budgetary policy** politique *f* budgétaire

◇ **budgetary variance** écart *m* budgétaire

◇ **budgetary year** exercice *m* budgétaire

budgeting *n* (**a**) *(of person, company)* budgétisation *f*, planification *f* budgétaire (**b**) *Acct* comptabilité *f* budgétaire

building society *n Br* ≃ société *f* de crédit immobilier

◇ **building society passbook** livret *m* d'épargne logement

bull **1** *n St Exch* haussier(ère) *m, f*, spéculateur(trice) *m,f* à la hausse

2 *vt* **to bull the market** chercher à faire hausser les cours

3 *vi (of person)* spéculer ou jouer à la hausse; *(of stocks)* être en hausse

◇ **bull market** marché *m* à la hausse *ou* haussier

◇ **bull position** position *f* acheteur

◇ **bull purchase** achat *m* à la hausse

◇ **bull speculation, bull trading** spéculation *f* à la hausse

◇ **bull transaction** opération *f* à la hausse

"

INVESCO is expecting a **bull market** in Asia on the back of corporate restructuring. Sam Lau, director of investment at INVESCO Asia, says: 'Economic recovery is on its way. It is in its early stages and is still fragile, but key indicators show an improvement in demand'. Lau adds that corporate restructuring will provide better returns to shareholders and share prices will rise to reflect that.

"

---

bulldog bond *n* obligation *f* bulldog

bullet *n Am* remboursement *m* in fine

◇ *Am St Exch* **bullet bond** obligation *f* remboursable en une seule fois

bullion *n* encaisse-or *f*, or *m* en barres *ou* en lingots

◇ **bullion reserve** réserve *f* métallique

bullish *adj St Exch (market, trend)* à la hausse, haussier (ère); **to be bullish** *(of person)* spéculer *ou* jouer à la hausse

◇ **bullish tendency** tendance *f* à la hausse

buoyancy *n St Exch (of market)* fermeté *f*; *(of prices, currency)* stabilité *f*

buoyant *adj St Exch (market)* ferme; *(prices, currency)* stable

bureau de change *n* bureau *m* de change

business *n* (**a**) *(trade)* affaires *fpl*; *(commerce)* commerce *m*; **to set up in business** ouvrir un commerce; **to go out of business** faire faillite; **to do business with sb** faire affaire *ou* des affaires avec qn

(**b**) *(company, firm)* affaire *f*, entreprise *f*

◇ *business account* compte *m* professionnel *ou* commercial
◇ *business accounting* comptabilité *f* commerciale
◇ *business bank* banque *f* d'affaires
◇ *business banking* opérations *fpl* des banques d'affaires
◇ *business expenses* frais *mpl* professionnels
◇ *business failure* défaillance *f* d'entreprise
◇ *business plan* projet *m* commercial
◇ *business portfolio* portefeuille *m* d'activités
◇ *business transaction* transaction *f* commerciale

buy 1 *vt* acheter; **to buy sth from sb** acheter qch à qn; **to buy earnings** investir en valeurs de croissance
2 *vi St Exch* **to buy spot** acheter au comptant; **to buy on credit** acheter à crédit *ou* à terme; **to buy on margin** acheter à découvert
◇ *St Exch* **buy order** ordre *m* d'achat; **to give a buy order** donner un ordre d'achat
▸ **buy in** *St Exch* 1 *vt sep* acheter, acquérir
2 *vi* **to buy in against a client** exécuter un client

buy-back *n St Exch* rachat *m* d'actions

buyer *n* acheteur(euse) *m,f*
◇ *buyer credit* crédit-acheteur *m*
◇ *buyer's market* marché *m* à la baisse, marché demandeur
◇ *buyer's option* prime *f* acheteur

buy-in *n St Exch* exécution *f*

buying *n St Exch* exécution *f*
◇ *buying quotation, buying rate* (*of shares*) cours *m* d'achat

buy-sell agreement *n* protocole *m ou* accord *m* d'achat et de vente

CA *n Br (abbr* **chartered accountant)** expert *m* comptable

C/A, c/a *n Banking (abbr Br* **current** *or* **cheque** *or Am* **checking account)** C/C *m*, CCB *m*

CAC 40 index *n St Exch* indice *m* CAC 40

CAD *n (abbr* **cash against documents)** comptant *m* contre documents

calendar year *n* année *f* civile

call 1 *n* (a) *(claim)* demande *f* (d'argent); **call (up)** appel *m* de fonds, appel de versement; **call for capital** appel de fonds; **payable at call** payable sur demande *ou* à présentation *ou* à vue (b) *St Exch* **call (option)** option *f* d'achat, call *m*; **call of more** option du double; **call on a hundred shares** option de cent actions

2 *vt* **to call a loan** demander le remboursement d'un prêt

◇ *St Exch* **call feature** = clause de remboursement anticipé au gré de l'émetteur

◇ **call letter** avis *m* d'appel de fonds

◇ **call loan** prêt *m* à vue, prêt remboursable sur demande

◇ **call money** argent *m* au jour le jour

◇ *St Exch* **call option** option *f* d'achat

◇ *St Exch* **call price** cours *m* du dont

◇ *St Exch* **call warrant** warrant *m* à l'achat

▸ **call in** *vt sep* (a) **to call in one's money** faire rentrer ses fonds; **to call in a loan** demander le remboursement d'un prêt (b) *(currency)* retirer de la circulation

callable *adj (bond, debt)* remboursable avant échéance; *(loan)* (à terme) révocable

called-up capital *n* capital *m* appelé

calling in *n* (a) *(of debt, loan)* demande *f* de remboursement immédiat (b) *(of currency)* retrait *m*

cancel *vt* (a) *(debt)* faire remise à; *(cheque)* faire opposition à (b) *Acct* contrepasser; **to cancel each other** *(of two entries)* s'annuler

cap 1 *n (limit)* taux *m* plafonné

2 *vt (spending)* plafonner, fixer un plafond à; **these measures have been effective in capping overall expenditure** ces mesures ont permis de limiter les dépenses globales

capital *n* capital *m*, capitaux *mpl*, fonds *mpl*; *(assets)* avoir *m*; **to put up capital** faire une mise de fonds; **to live on one's capital** vivre sur son capital

◇ *capital account* compte *m* de capital

◇ *capital accumulation* accumulation *f* de capital

◇ *capital adequacy* adéquation *f* des fonds propres

◇ *capital allowances* déductions *fpl* (fiscales) sur frais d'établissement

◇ *capital asset pricing model* modèle *m* d'évaluation des actifs

◇ *capital assets* actif *m* immobilisé, immobilisations *fpl* corporelles

◇ *capital bond* obligation *f* à coupon zéro

◇ *capital budget* budget *m* d'investissement

◇ *capital budgeting* gestion *f* des investissements

◇ *capital charge* intérêt *m* des capitaux (investis)

◇ *capital clause (in memorandum of association)* constitution *f* du capital social

◇ *capital contribution* apport *m* ou dotation *f* en capital

◇ *capital cost* coût *m* du capital

◇ *Acct capital employed* capital *m* engagé, capitaux *mpl* permanents

◇ *capital equipment* biens *mpl* d'équipement, capitaux *mpl* fixes

◇ *capital expenditure* mise *f* de fonds, investissements *mpl* (en immobilisations), dépenses *fpl* d'équipement

◇ *capital gains* plus-value *f*

◇ *capital gains distribution* distribution *f* de plus-values

◇ *capital gains tax* impôt *m* sur les plus-values

◇ *capital goods* biens *mpl* d'équipement

◇ *capital goods market* marché *m* d'équipement

◇ *capital grants* subventions *fpl* en capital

◇ *capital growth* croissance *f* du capital

◇ *capital inflow* afflux *m* de capitaux *ou* de fonds

◇ *capital injection* injection *f* de capital *ou* de capitaux

◇ *capital investment* investissement *m* de capitaux

◇ *Acct capital items* biens *mpl* capitaux

◇ *capital levy* prélèvement *m* sur le capital

◇ *capital loss* moins-value *f*

◇ *capital market* marché *m* financier *ou* des capitaux

◇ *capital movements* mouvements *mpl* des capitaux

◇ *capital outlay* dépenses *fpl* en capital

◇ *capital profits* plus-value *f*

◇ *capital reserves* profits *mpl* mis en réserve, réserves *fpl* non distribuées

◇ *Acct capital and reserves* capitaux *mpl* propres

◇ *capital share* part *f* sociale

◇ *St Exch capital shares* actions *fpl* de capitalisation

◇ *capital shortfall* manque *m* de capitaux

◇ *Am capital stock* capital *m* social, capital-actions *m*

◇ *capital structure* plan *m* financier

◇ *capital tax* impôt *m* sur le capital

◇ *capital transaction* opération *f* en capital

◇ *capital transfer tax* droits *mpl* de mutation

◇ *capital turnover* rotation *f* des capitaux

> **❝**
>
> **Capital gains tax** is not a huge issue for most people, as few people surpass the CGT allowance each year. In the 1999/2000 tax year, the individual CGT threshold, which applies to children as well as adults, is £6,800. This means a couple would have to realise gains from the sale of investments of more than £14,200 to save tax by putting some of their assets in their child's name.
>
> **❞**

capitalization *n* capitalisation *f*

◇ *capitalization issue* attribution *f* d'actions gratuites

◇ *capitalization ratio* ratio *m* de capitalisation

◇ *capitalization of reserves* incorporation *f* de réserves au capital

capitalize *vt* (**a**) *(convert into capital)* capitaliser; *(raise capital from)* constituer le capital social de *(par émission d'actions)*; *(provide with capital)* pourvoir de capital *ou* de fonds (**b**) *(estimate value of)* capitaliser; **they capitalized her investments at £50,000** ils ont capitalisé ses investissements à 50 000 livres; **the company is capitalized at £100,000** la société dispose d'un capital de 100 000 livres

◇ *capitalized value* valeur *f* capitalisée

capital-labour ratio *n* ratio *m* capital-travail

capital-output ratio *n* ratio *m* capital-travail

CAPM *n* (*abbr* **capital asset pricing model**) MÉDAF *m*

captive fund *n* fonds *m* de capital-risque maison

card *n* carte *f*

◇ *card payment* paiement *m* par carte

◇ *card transaction* transaction *f* par carte

▸ **carry forward** *vt sep Acct (item)* reporter; **carried forward** report, à reporter; **carried forward from the previous financial year** report de l'exercice précédent

▸ **carry over** *vt sep* (**a**) *Acct (balance)* faire un report de, reporter; **to carry over a loss to the following year** reporter une perte sur l'année suivante (**b**) *St Exch (shares)* reporter, prendre en report; **carried over** *(stock)* en report

carrying *n*

◇ *carrying amount* valeur *f* nette comptable

◇ *Am Acct carrying cost, carrying value* valeur *f* comptable

cascade taxation *n* imposition *f* en cascade

cash *n (coins, banknotes)* liquide *m*, espèces *fpl*; *Fam (money in general)* argent *m*; **to pay (in) cash** *(not credit)* payer comptant; *(money as opposed to cheque)* payer en liquide *ou* en espèces; **cash against documents** comptant contre documents; **cash in hand** argent *m* liquide *ou* en caisse ; *Acct* **cash at bank** avoir *m* en banque ; *Acct* **cash in till** encaisse *f*, fonds *mpl* de caisse

2 *vt (cheque)* toucher, encaisser ; *(bill)* encaisser, escompter

◇ **cash account** compte *m* de caisse

◇ **cash advance** avance *m* de trésorerie *ou* en numéraire

◇ **cash balance** *(status)* situation *f* de caisse ; *(amount remaining)* solde *m* actif, solde de caisse *ou* de trésorerie

◇ *Acct* **cash basis accounting** comptabilité *f* de caisse *ou* de gestion

◇ **cash benefits** avantages *mpl* en espèces

◇ **cash bonus** prime *f* en espèces

◇ **cash book** livre *m* de caisse

◇ **cash box** caisse *f*

◇ **cash budget** budget *m* de trésorerie

◇ *St Exch* **cash and carry arbitrage** arbitrage *m* comptant-terme

◇ *Acct* **cash contribution** apport *m* en numéraire *ou* en espèces

◇ **cash deal** marché *m* au comptant

◇ **cash debit** débit *m* de caisse

◇ **cash deficit** déficit *m* de trésorerie

◇ **cash deposit** versement *m* d'espèces, dépôt *m* d'espèces

◇ **cash discount** escompte *m* de caisse, remise *f* sur paiement (au) comptant

◇ **cash dispenser** distributeur *m* (automatique) de billets

◇ **cash dividend** dividende *m* en espèces

◇ **cash equivalents** quasi-espèces *fpl*, actifs *mpl* facilement réalisables

◇ *Acct* **cash expenditure** dépenses *fpl* de caisse

◇ **cash flow** cash-flow *m*, trésorerie *f* ; *Acct (in cash flow statement)* marge *f* brute d'autofinancement ; **to have cash flow problems** avoir des problèmes de trésorerie

◇ *Acct* **cash flow accounting** comptabilité *f* de caisse

◇ **cash flow forecast** prévision *f* *ou* plan *m* de trésorerie

◇ **cash flow management** gestion *f* de trésorerie

◇ **cash flow rate** taux *m* d'autofinancement

◇ **cash flow situation** situation *f* de trésorerie

◇ *Acct* **cash flow statement** tableau *m* de financement, tableau des flux de trésorerie

◇ **cash incentive** stimulation *f* financière

◇ *Acct* **cash inflow** encaissements *mpl*, rentrée *f* de fonds

◇ **cash inflows and outflows** encaissements *mpl* et décaissements *mpl*

◇ *Acct* **cash item** article *m* de caisse

◇ **cash management** gestion *f* de trésorerie

◇ *Acct* **cash order** ordre *m* au comptant

◇ *Acct* **cash outflow** sorties *fpl* de trésorerie

◇ **cash outgoings** sorties *fpl* de trésorerie

◇ **cash overs** excédent *m* de caisse

◇ **cash payment** paiement *m* (au) comptant, paiement en espèces

◇ **cash price** prix *m* au comptant

◇ **cash purchase** achat *m* au

comptant, achat contre espèces

◇ *Acct* **cash ratio** ratio *m* ou coefficient *m* de trésorerie

◇ *Acct* **cash receipt** reçu *m* pour paiement en espèces

◇ **cash receipts and payments** rentrées *fpl* et sorties *fpl* de caisse

◇ *Acct* **cash received** *(balance sheet item)* entrée *f* d'argent

◇ *Acct* **cash report (form)** situation *f* de caisse

◇ **cash reserves** réserves *fpl* en espèces

◇ **cash sale** vente *f* au comptant

◇ **cash settlement** règlement *m* ou liquidation *f* en espèces

◇ **cash shortage** insuffisance *f* d'espèces

◇ *Acct* **cash statement** état *m* ou relevé *m* de caisse

◇ *Acct* **cash surplus** restant *m* en caisse

◇ **cash terms** conditions *fpl* au comptant

◇ **cash transaction** mouvement *m* d'espèces, transaction *f* au comptant

◇ **cash unders** manque *m* de caisse

◇ **cash value** valeur *f* au comptant, valeur de rachat

◇ *Acct* **cash voucher** pièce *f* de caisse, PC *f*, bon *m* de caisse

◇ **cash withdrawal** retrait *m* d'espèces

▸ **cash in** *vt sep (bond, savings certificate)* se faire rembourser, réaliser

cashback *n* (a) *(in mortgage lending)* = prime versée par une société de crédit immobilier au souscripteur d'un emprunt (b) *(in supermarket)* = espèces retirées à la caisse d'un supermarché lors d'un paiement par carte

cash-based accounting *n Compta* comptabilité *f* de caisse

cashier *n* caissier(ère) *m,f*

cashless society *n* société *f* sans argent *(où toutes les transactions sont effectuées en argent électronique)*

cashpoint *n* point *m* retrait, distributeur *m* (automatique) de billets

catch *vt Fam St Exch* **to catch a cold** *(dealer)* perdre de l'argent lors d'une transaction; *(share)* perdre de la valeur

CBOE *n* (*abbr* **Chicago Board Options Exchange**) marché *m* des options de Chicago, ≃ MATIF *m*

CCA *n* (*abbr* **current cost accounting**) comptabilité *f* en coûts actuels

cd/fwd *Acct* (*abbr* **carried forward**) reporté(e)

ceiling *n Econ* plafond *m*; **to reach a ceiling** *(of prices, interest rates)* plafonner; **to have a ceiling of** être plafonné(e) à; **to set a 3% ceiling on wage rises** limiter les augmentations de salaire à 3%

◇ **ceiling price** prix *m* plafond

central *adj* central(e)

◇ *Banking* **central account** compte *m* centralisateur

◇ *Banking* **central bank** banque *f* centrale

◇ *Banking, St Exch* **Central Securities Depository** dépositaire *m* national de titres

certificate *n* certificat *m*

◇ **certificate of deposit** bon *m* de caisse

certified *adj* (*cheque*) certifié(e)

◇ **certified accounts** comptes *mpl* approuvés

◇ *Am* **certified public accountant** expert *m* comptable

CFO *n Am* (*abbr* **Chief Financial Officer**) chef *m* comptable, chef de la comptabilité

CGT *n* (*abbr* **capital gains tax**) impôt *m* sur les plus-values

chaebol *n Econ* chaebol *m*

> **"**
>
> The Fair Trade Commission (FTC), the nation's antitrust watchdog, has begun to use its scalpel to root out unfair business practices by the nation's five largest business groups in the initial stages of an operation which will later be applied to 24 other groups or **chaebol**. The punitive action by the government agency is expected to serve as a key means to press **chaebol** groups to expedite their restructuring work in compliance with the government call.
>
> **"**

chain bank *n US Banking* banque *f* à succursales multiples

Chancellor of the Exchequer *n Br* Chancelier *m* de l'Échiquier, ≃ ministre *m* des finances

change 1 *n* (**small**) **change** (petite) monnaie *f*; **to give change for £20** donner *ou* rendre la monnaie de 20 livres

2 *vt* (*money*) changer; **to change dollars into francs** changer des dollars en francs

CHAPS *n Br Banking* (*abbr* **clearing house automated payment system**) = système de télécompensation interbancaire, ≃ SIT *m*

charge 1 *n* (*cost*) frais *mpl*, prix *m*; (*to an account*) imputation *f*; **to make a charge for sth** compter qch, faire payer qch; **what's the charge?** combien est-ce que ça coûte?; **at a small charge** moyennant une faible rétribution; *Am* **will that be cash or charge?** vous payez comptant ou vous le portez à votre compte?

2 *vt* (**a**) (*defer payment of*) **charge it** mettez-le sur mon compte; **charge it to the company's account** mettez-le sur le compte de l'entreprise; **I charged all my expenses to the company** j'ai mis tous mes frais sur le compte de la société

(**b**) (*person*) faire payer; (*sum*) faire payer, prendre; (*commission*) prélever; **they charged us $50 for delivery** ils nous ont fait payer 50 dollars pour la livraison; **how much will you charge for the lot?** combien demandez-vous pour le tout?; **you will be charged for postage** les frais postaux seront à votre charge

3 *vi* (*demand payment*) faire payer; **they don't charge for postage and packing** ils ne font pas payer le port et l'emballage

◇ *Am* **charge account** compte *m* crédit d'achats, compte accréditif

◊ *charge card* carte *f* de paiement, carte accréditive

▶**charge off** *vt Am (capital)* réduire, amortir

▶**charge up** *vt sep* **to charge sth up to sb's account** mettre qch sur le compte de qn

chargeable *adj* (**a**) *(to an account)* imputable; **to be chargeable to sb** *(payable by)* être à la charge de qn, être pris(e) en charge par qn; **who is it chargeable to?** c'est à la charge de qui?; **could you make that chargeable to Crown Ltd?** est-ce que vous pourriez facturer Crown Ltd? (**b**) *(subject to tax)* imposable

◊ *chargeable asset* actif *m* imposable sur les plus-values

◊ *chargeable expenses* frais *mpl* facturables

◊ *chargeable gain* bénéfice *m* imposable

chart *n (diagram)* graphique *m*

◊ *Acct* **chart of accounts** plan *m* comptable général

◊ *chart analyst* analyste *mf* sur graphiques

chartered *adj*

◊ *Br* **chartered accountant** expert *m* comptable, *Can* comptable *mf* agréé(e)

◊ *Br* **chartered bank** banque *f* privilégiée

cheap *adj* bon marché, pas cher (chère)

◊ *cheap money* argent *m* à bon marché

◊ *cheap rate* tarif *m* réduit

check 1 *n Am* = **cheque**

2 *vt* (**a**) *(price increases, inflation)* enrayer

(**b**) *(verify, examine) (accounts, figures)* vérifier; *(document)* examiner; **to check the books** pointer les écritures

checkbook *Am* = **chequebook**

checking account *n Am* compte *m* courant

checkless society *Am* = **chequeless society**

cheque, *Am* **check** *n* chèque *m*; **a cheque for ten pounds** un chèque de dix livres; **cheque to order** chèque à ordre; **cheque to bearer** chèque au porteur; **to cash a cheque** toucher un chèque; **to endorse a cheque** endosser un chèque; **to make out a cheque (to sb)** établir *ou* faire un chèque (à l'ordre de qn); **who should I make the cheque out to?** à quel ordre dois-je faire *ou* écrire le chèque?; **will you take a cheque?** est-ce que vous acceptez les chèques?; **to pay by cheque** régler par chèque; **to pay a cheque into the bank** déposer un chèque à la banque; **to stop a cheque** faire opposition à un chèque

◊ *cheque account* compte *m* (de) chèques

◊ *cheque counterfoil* talon *m* de chèque, souche *f*

◊ *cheque form* formule *f* de chèque

◊ *Br* **cheque (guarantee) card** carte *f* bancaire *(sans laquelle un chéquier n'est pas valable)*

◊ *cheque number* numéro *m* de chèque

◊ *cheque stub* talon *m* de chèque, souche *f*

chequebook, *Am* **checkbook** *n* carnet *m* de chèques, chéquier *m*

◇ *chequebook account* compte *m* (de) chèques

chequeless society, *Am* **checkless society** *n* société *f* sans chèques

chief *adj*
◇ *Br* **chief accountant** chef *m* comptable, chef de la comptabilité
◇ *chief clerk* commis *m* principal
◇ *Am* **Chief Financial Officer** chef *m* comptable, chef de la comptabilité

Chinese walls *npl* = murs imaginaires qui symbolisent la confidentialité indispensable dans certains milieux financiers et séparent des services qui, par ailleurs, travaillent côte à côte

CHIPS *n Am Banking* (*abbr* **Clearing House Interbank Payment System**) SIT *m*

churn *vt Fam St Exch* (*portfolio*) faire tourner

churning *n Fam St Exch* rotation *f* de portefeuille

> **"**
>
> In August 1990, the Securities Association, the self-regulatory body covering share dealers and advisers, acted for the first time against a broker found guilty of '**churning**' his clients' portfolios. This involves brokers generating income by constantly and needlessly buying and selling investments for their clients in order to collect the heavy commissions which accrue. It is virtually impossible to prove because guilty brokers tend to '**churn**' the portfolios of inexperienced clients.
>
> **"**

circular letter of credit *n* lettre *f* de crédit circulaire

circulate 1 *vt* (*banknotes*) mettre en circulation, émettre
2 *vi* (*of money*) circuler; **to circulate freely** circuler librement, rouler

circulating *adj* circulant(e)
◇ *Acct* **circulating assets** actif *m* circulant
◇ *circulating capital* capitaux *mpl* circulants

circulation *n* (**a**) (*of capital*) roulement *m*, circulation *f* (**b**) **to be in circulation** (*of money*) circuler; **notes in circulation** billets *mpl* en circulation

City *n* **the City** la Cité *ou* City (de Londres) (*centre des affaires*); **he's in the City** il est dans la finance (*dans la Cité de Londres*); **the City Companies** les corporations *fpl* de la Cité de Londres

▸ **claw back** *vt sep* (*expenditure, tax relief, stock relief*) récupérer

clawback *n* (*of expenditure, tax relief, stock relief*) récupération *f*

clean *adj*
◇ *clean bill* effet *m* libre, traite *m* libre
◇ *St Exch* **clean float** taux *mpl* de change libres *ou* flottants

clear 1 *adj* (**a**) (*net*) net (nette); **clear of taxes** net d'impôt
(**b**) (*accounts*) en règle
2 *vt* (**a**) (*debt*) liquider, acquitter; (*mortgage*) purger; (*account*) solder
(**b**) (*make profit of*) **she cleared 10% on the deal** l'affaire lui a rapporté 10% tous frais payés *ou* 10% net; **I clear a thousand pounds monthly** je fais un bénéfice net de mille livres par mois

(**c**) *Banking (cheque)* compenser, virer; *(bill)* régler

3 *vi (of cheque)* être encaissé(e); **it takes three working days for cheques to clear** il y a trois jours ouvrables de délai d'encaissement

◊ *clear loss* perte *f* sèche

◊ *clear profit* bénéfice *m* net

cleared *adj Banking*

◊ *cleared cheque* chèque *m* compensé

◊ *cleared value* valeur *f* compensée

clearing *n (of cheque)* compensation *f*; *(of account)* liquidation *f*, solde *m*; *(of debt)* acquittement *m*; **general clearing** compensation de chèques en dehors de Londres; **under the clearing procedure** par voie de compensation

◊ *clearing account* compte *m* de compensation

◊ *clearing agreement* accord *m* de clearing

◊ *clearing bank* banque *f* compensatrice *ou* de clearing

◊ *clearing house* chambre *f* de compensation *ou* de clearing; **to pass a cheque through the clearing house** compenser un chèque

◊ *clearing system* système *m* de compensation

◊ *clearing transaction* opération *f* de clearing

client *n (of bank)* client(e) *m,f*

◊ *Banking client account* compte *m* client

close 1 *n St Exch (on financial futures market)* clôture *f*; *(closing price)* cours *m* de clôture; **at close of business** à la *ou* en clôture

2 *vt* (**a**) *Acct* **to close the books**

balancer les comptes, régler les livres; **to close the yearly accounts** arrêter les comptes de l'exercice (**b**) *(bank account)* fermer (**c**) *St Exch (operation)* liquider; **to close a position** couvrir une position

3 *vi St Exch* clôturer; **the shares closed at 420p** les actions ont clôturé *ou* terminé à 420 pence; **the share index closed two points down** l'indice (boursier) a clôturé en baisse de deux points

▶ **close off** *vt sep (account)* arrêter

closed-end *adj*

◊ *closed-end (investment) fund* société *f* d'investissement à capital fixe

◊ *closed-end mortgage* prêt *m* hypothécaire à montant fixe

closing 1 *n* (**a**) *(of bank account)* fermeture *f* (**b**) *St Exch (of position)* clôture *f*

2 *adj*

◊ *closing account balance* quittance *f* pour solde de tout compte

◊ *Acct closing entry* écriture *f* d'inventaire *ou* de clôture

◊ *St Exch closing prices* cours *mpl* de clôture

◊ *closing quotations* cotes *fpl* en clôture

◊ *closing session* séance *f* de clôture

◊ *Acct closing stock* stock *m* final

◊ *closing trade* transactions *fpl* de clôture

closing-down costs *npl* frais *mpl* de liquidation

closing-off *n Acct (of accounts)* arrêt *m*

closure n St Exch **closure by repurchase** clôture f par rachat

CMO n Am (abbr **collateralized mortgage obligation**) obligation f garantie par une hypothèque

coefficient tax n impôt m de quotité

COGS n Acct (abbr **cost of goods sold**) coût m des produits vendus

coinage n (a) (monetary system) système m monétaire (b) (coins) monnaie f

collateral 1 n nantissement m; **to lodge sth as collateral** déposer qch en nantissement; **the bank prefers not to lend without collateral** de préférence, la banque ne prête pas sans nantissement
   2 adj subsidiaire
◊ **collateral loan** prêt m avec garantie
◊ **collateral security** nantissement m, garantie f accessoire

collateralize vt Am garantir

collateralized mortgage obligation n Am obligation f garantie par une hypothèque

collect vt (salary) toucher; (debt) recouvrer; (taxes) percevoir, lever

collecting adj
◊ **collecting agency, collecting bank** banque f de recouvrement
◊ **collecting banker** banquier m encaisseur
◊ **collecting department** service m de recouvrement

collection n (a) (of debts) recouvrement m; (of taxes) perception f, levée f (b) (of bill) encaissement m; **to hand sth in for collection** donner qch à l'encaissement; **a bill for collection** un effet à l'encaissement
◊ **collection bank** banque f d'encaissement
◊ **collection charges, collection fees** frais mpl d'encaissement ou de recouvrement
◊ **collection rate** tarif m d'encaissement

column n Acct colonne f

combine n cartel m, trust m

commercial 1 n (advertisement) publicité f
   2 adj commercial(e)
◊ **commercial agency** agence f commerciale
◊ **commercial bank** banque f commerciale
◊ **commercial bill** titre m commercial
◊ **commercial broker** courtier m de marchandises
◊ **commercial contract** contrat m commercial
◊ **commercial loan** prêt m commercial
◊ **commercial paper** effet m commercial, billet m de trésorerie
◊ **commercial value** valeur f marchande

commission 1 n (payment) commission f; **to get 3% commission** toucher 3% de commission; **to work on a commission basis** travailler à la commission
   2 vt (order) commander; **to commission sb to do sth** charger qn de faire qch
◊ **commission agent** commissionnaire mf, courtier m à la commission
◊ Acct **commission note** note f de commission

◇ *commission sale* vente *f* à (la) commission

Commissioner of the Inland Revenue *n Br* ≃ Inspecteur *m* des impôts

commitment *n* engagement *m* financier
◇ *commitment fee* commission *f* d'engagement
◇ *commitment of funds* engagement *m* de dépenses

committed costs *npl Acct* coûts *mpl* engagés

commodity *n St Exch* matière *f* première ; **to trade commodities** spéculer sur les marchés à terme des matières premières
◇ *commodity broker, commodity dealer* courtier(ère) *m,f* en matières premières
◇ *commodities exchange, commodity exchange* marché *m* des matières premières
◇ *commodity futures* opérations *fpl* à terme sur matières premières
◇ *commodity market* marché *m* des matières premières
◇ *commodity money* monnaie *f* de marchandise

He says the main reasons why the recovery will continue is to do with **commodity** prices and capital flows, which he says have yet to recover. We are at the bottom˙of the **commodity** price market – these countries produce raw materials and so it is a very important part of their economy, he says. And people have stopped pulling their money dramatically out of emerging markets.

common *adj*
◇ *Am St Exch* **common equities** actions *fpl* ordinaires
◇ *Acct* **common fixed costs** coûts *mpl* fixes communs
◇ *Am St Exch* **common stock** actions *fpl* ordinaires

company *n* entreprise *f*
◇ *company accounts* comptes *mpl* sociaux
◇ *company funds* fonds *m* social
◇ *company reserves* épargne *f* des entreprises
◇ *company savings scheme* plan *m* d'épargne entreprise

compensatory amounts *npl EU* montants *mpl* compensatoires

composite index *n St Exch* indice *m* composé, indice composite

Last week's rally in software and computer service stocks continued yesterday, with investors encouraged by the 4% rise in Wall Street's technology-laden Nasdaq **composite index** on Friday.

compound 1 *vt (debt)* régler à l'amiable
2 *adj*
◇ *compound interest* intérêts *mpl* composés
◇ *compound (net) annual return* annuités *fpl* composées

comptroller *n Am* contrôleur (euse) *m,f* ; *(of accounts)* vérificateur(trice) *m,f*

computerized *adj*
◇ *Acct* **computerized accounts** comptabilité *f* informatisée

⋄ *St Exch* **computerized trading system** système *m* informatique de cotation

conceal *vt (assets)* dissimuler

concealment *n*
⋄ **concealment of assets** dissimulation *f* d'actif

concession *n (discount)* réduction *f*

confirming *adj* Banking
⋄ **confirming bank** banque *f* confirmatrice
⋄ **confirming house** organisme *m* confirmateur

conservatism concept *n Acct* principe *m* de prudence

consistency concept *n Acct* principe *m* de la permanence (des méthodes)

consolidate *vt (companies)* fusionner, réunir; *(shares)* regrouper; *(debts, funds, loans)* consolider, unifier; **the company has consolidated its position as the market leader** la société a conforté sa position de leader sur le marché

consolidated *adj*
⋄ *Acct* **consolidated accounts** comptes *mpl* consolidés *ou* intégrés
⋄ **consolidated annuities** fonds *mpl* consolidés
⋄ *Acct* **consolidated balance sheet** bilan *m* consolidé
⋄ **consolidated debt** dette *f* consolidée *ou* inscrite
⋄ **consolidated funds** fonds *mpl* consolidés
⋄ **consolidated loan** emprunt *m* consolidé
⋄ *Acct* **consolidated profit and loss account** bilan *m* consolidé
⋄ **consolidated statement of net income** résultat *m* net consolidé
⋄ **consolidated stock** fonds *mpl* consolidés

consolidation *n (of debts, funds, loans)* consolidation *f*, unification *f*

consols *npl Br* (fonds *mpl*) consolidés *mpl*

consortium *n* consortium *m*

consumer *n* consommateur (trice) *m,f*
⋄ **consumer credit** crédit *m* à la consommation *ou* au consommateur
⋄ **consumer debt** endettement *m* des consommateurs
⋄ **consumer expenditure** dépenses *fpl* de consommation
⋄ **consumer loan** prêt *m* à la consommation

contango *St Exch* **1** *n* report *m*; *(percentage)* taux *m* de report; **money on contango** capitaux *mpl* en report; **contangoes are low** les reports sont bon marché
2 *vt* reporter
3 *vi* reporter une position
⋄ **contango day** jour *m* des reports
⋄ **contango rate** taux *m* de report

contingency *n* éventualité *f*
⋄ **contingency fund** fonds *mpl* de prévoyance
⋄ **contingency and loss provision** provision *f* pour risques et charges
⋄ *Acct* **contingency theory** théorie *f* de la contingence

contingent *adj (possible)* éventuel(elle)
⋄ **contingent liabilities, contingent liability** passif *m* éventuel

◊ *contingent profit* profit *m* aléatoire

◊ *St Exch* *contingent value right* certificat *m* de valeur garantie

continuous budget *n Acct* budget *m* renouvelable

contra *Acct* **1** *n* **per contra** par contre ; **as per contra** en contrepartie, porté ci-contre
   2 *vt* contrepasser

◊ *contra account* compte *m* de contrepartie *ou* d'autre part

◊ *contra entry* article *m ou* écriture *f* inverse, contre-passation *f*

contract *n (agreement)* contrat *m*

◊ *St Exch* *contract bond* garantie *f* d'exécution

◊ *St Exch* *contract note* avis *m* d'exécution, avis d'opération sur titres

contribute *vt* donner, verser ; **she contributes 10% of her salary to the pension scheme** elle verse 10% de son salaire dans son plan de retraite

contribution *n* (**a**) *(payment)* contribution *f*, cotisation *f* ; **employer's and employee's contributions** cotisations *fpl* patronales et ouvrières (**b**) *Acct (in management accounting)* marge *f* (brute) (**c**) *(made to share capital by new shareholder)* apport *m*

◊ *Acct* *contribution margin* marge *f* sur les coûts variables

◊ *Acct* *contribution ratio* ratio *m* de marge brute

contributory **1** *n St Exch* = actionnaire responsable proportionnellement à son apport
   2 *adj*

◊ *contributory pension plan*

système *m* de retraite par répartition

control **1** *n (of exchange rates, prices)* contrôle *m* ; **to impose controls on sth** contrôler qch ; **there are to be new government controls on financial practices** il y aura de nouvelles réglementations gouvernementales sur les pratiques financières
   2 *vt (exchange rates, prices)* contrôler ; *(inflation)* maîtriser, juguler ; **to control the rise in the cost of living** enrayer la hausse du coût de la vie

◊ *control commission* commission *f* de contrôle

controllable costs *npl Acct* coûts *mpl* maîtrisables

controller *n* contrôleur(euse) *m,f*

◊ *controller in bankruptcy* contrôleur *m* aux liquidations

conversion *n (of securities)* conversion *f*

◊ *Acct* *conversion cost* coût *m* de transformation

◊ *St Exch* *conversion issue* émission *f* de conversion

◊ *conversion loan* emprunt *m* de conversion

◊ *conversion premium* prime *f* de conversion

◊ *St Exch* *conversion price* prix *m* de conversion

◊ *conversion rate* taux *m* de conversion

convert **1** *n Am* obligation *f* convertible (en actions)
   2 *vt* convertir ; **to convert pounds into francs** *(as calculation)* convertir des livres en francs ; *(by exchanging them)* changer des livres en francs

convertibility *n* convertibilité *f*

convertible *adj (loan, security)* convertible

◇ *convertible bond* obligation *f* convertible (en actions)

◇ *convertible currency* monnaie *f* ou devise *f* convertible

◇ *St Exch* **convertible loan stock** obligation *f* convertible (en actions), emprunt *m* obligataire convertible

◇ *convertible money of account* monnaie *f* de compte convertible

> **"**
>
> The Clerical Medical Equity High Income fund has doubled its weightings in **convertibles** to 11%. **Convertibles** are bonds which can be converted into shares. William Claxton-Smith, the fund manager, has bought **convertibles** to gain exposure to growth areas in the market such as media and banking services. Shares in these types of companies tend to offer low yields, while a higher yield is available through **convertibles.**
>
> **"**

cooperative *n* société *f* coopérative

corporate *adj* corporatif(ive), d'entreprise

◇ *corporate assets* biens *mpl* sociaux

◇ *corporate banking* banque *f* d'entreprise

◇ *corporate bond* obligation *f* de sociétés

◇ *corporate finance* finance *f* d'entreprise

◇ *corporate finance manager* financier *m* d'entreprise

◇ *corporate income* revenu *m* de société

◇ *corporate income tax* impôt *m* sur les bénéfices des sociétés

corporation *n* société *f*, compagnie *f*

◇ *Am* **corporation income tax** impôt *m* sur les sociétés

◇ *Br* **corporation tax** impôt *m* sur les sociétés

correct *vt Acct* rectifier; **corrected for inflation** corrigé de l'inflation, ajusté pour l'inflation

corrected entry *n Acct* écriture *f* d'ajustement, écriture rectificative

corresponding entry *n Acct* écriture *f* conforme

cost 1 *n (price)* coût *m*, frais *mpl*
2 *vt* (a) *(be priced at)* coûter; **how much does it cost?** combien cela coûte-t-il?; **it costs \$25** ça coûte 25 dollars -
(b) *(estimate cost of) (article)* établir le prix de revient de; *(job)* évaluer le coût de; **how much was it costed at?** *(of job)* à combien est-ce que le coût a été évalué?

◇ *Acct* **cost accounting** comptabilité *f* analytique, comptabilité *f* de prix de revient

◇ *Acct* **cost allocation** imputation *f* des charges

◇ *cost analysis* analyse *f* des coûts, analyse du prix de revient

◇ *cost assessment* évaluation *f* de coût

◇ *Acct* **cost centre** centre *m* de coût

◇ *cost curve* courbe *f* des coûts

◇ *cost equation* équation *f* de coût

◇ *cost factor* facteur *m* coût

◇ *cost of goods purchased* coût *m* d'achat

◇ *Acct* **cost of goods sold** coût *m* des ventes, coût des marchandises vendues

◇ *cost of living* coût *m* de la vie

◇ *cost management* gestion *f* des coûts

◇ *cost overrun* dépassement *m* de coût

◇ *cost price* prix *m* coûtant *ou* de revient

◇ *cost pricing* méthode *f* des coûts marginaux

◇ *Acct* **cost of sales** coût *m* de revient des produits vendus

◇ *cost unit* unité *f* de coût

◇ *cost variance* écart *m* des coûts

cost-benefit *adj*

◇ *cost-benefit analysis* analyse *f* coûts-bénéfices *ou* coût-profit

◇ *cost-benefit ratio* rapport *m* coût-profit

cost-effective *adj* rentable

cost-effectiveness *n* rentabilité *f*

◇ *cost-effectiveness analysis* analyse *f* de coût et d'efficacité

cost-of-living *adj*

◇ *cost-of-living allowance* indemnité *f* de vie chère

◇ *cost-of-living increase* (in *salary*) augmentation *f* de salaire indexée sur le coût de la vie

◇ *cost-of-living index* indice *m* du coût de la vie

cost-push inflation *n Econ* inflation *f* par les coûts

cost-volume-profit analysis *n Acct* étude *f* de coût-efficacité

council tax *n Br* impôts *mpl* locaux

counter *n* (in bank) guichet *m*; **to buy/sell sth under the counter** acheter/vendre qch sous le manteau; *St Exch* **to buy shares over the counter** acheter des actions sur le marché hors cote

◇ *counter cash book* main *f* courante de caisse

◇ *Banking* **counter services** services *mpl* de caisse

◇ *Banking* **counter transactions** opérations *fpl* de caisse

counterbid *n* suroffre *f*, surenchère *f*

> **❝**
>
> There is the possibility of a **counterbid**. Barclays, Aegon, Generali, Allianz and AXA could all be interested. But analysts are sceptical of a serious bidding war. A counterbidder would have to increase the price and at this level it looks hard to justify, says banking analyst John Kirk of broker Fox-Pitt Kelton.
>
> **❞**

counterbidder *n* surenchérisseur(euse) *m,f*

counterfoil *n* (of cheque) talon *m*, souche *f*

◇ *counterfoil book* carnet *m* à souche

counter-guarantee *n St Exch* contre-garantie *f*

counterparty risk *n Banking* risque *m* de contrepartie

coupon *n* (on bearer bond) coupon *m*

◇ *coupon bond* obligation *f* au porteur

◇ *coupon yield* rendement *m* coupon

cover 1 *n* marge *f* de sécurité; **to operate with/without cover** opérer avec couverture/à découvert

2 *vt* (**a**) *Acct* **to cover a bill** faire la provision d'une lettre de change; **to cover a loss** couvrir un déficit (**b**) *St Exch* **to cover a position** couvrir une position

covered *adj St Exch (position)* couvert(e)

◇ *covered (short) position* position *f* (courte) couverte

covering purchases *npl St Exch* rachats *mpl*

CPA *n Am (abbr* **Certified Public Accountant)** expert *m* comptable

crash 1 *n (financial)* krach *m*

2 *vi (of business)* faire faillite; *(of prices, shares, economy, stock market)* s'effondrer, s'écrouler; **shares crashed from 75p to 11p** le cours des actions s'est effondré: de 75 pence il est passé à 11 pence

crawling peg *n St Exch* parité *f* rampante

▸**cream off** *vt sep (money, profits)* écrémer

creative accounting *n* manipulations *fpl* comptables

credit *n* (**a**) *(for future payment)* crédit *m*; **to give sb credit** faire crédit à qn; **to buy/sell sth on credit** acheter/vendre qch à crédit

(**b**) **to be in credit** *(of person)* avoir un compte créditeur; *(of account)* être créditeur(trice);

Acct **debit and credit** doit *m* et avoir *m*

2 *vt (account)* créditer; **to credit an account with £200, to credit £200 to an account** créditer un compte de 200 livres

◇ *Acct* **credit account** compte *m* crédit d'achats

◇ *credit advice* avis *m* de crédit

◇ *credit agency* agence *f* de notation

◇ *credit agreement* accord *m ou* convention *f* de crédit

◇ *Acct, Banking* **credit balance** solde *m* créditeur

◇ *credit bank* banque *f* de crédit

◇ *Am* **credit bureau** agence *f* de notation

◇ *credit card* carte *f* de crédit

◇ *credit ceiling* plafond *m* de crédit

◇ *Acct* **credit column** colonne *f* créditrice

◇ *credit control* encadrement *m* du crédit

◇ *credit controller* contrôleur *m* du crédit

◇ *credit creation* création *f* de crédit

◇ *credit crunch* resserrement *m* de crédit

◇ *credit enquiry* renseignements *mpl* de crédit, enquête *f* de solvabilité

◇ *Banking* **credit entry** *Acct* écriture *f* passée au crédit; *Banking* article *m* porté au crédit d'un compte

◇ *credit facilities* facilités *fpl* de paiement *ou* de crédit; **to give sb credit facilities** accréditer qn (auprès d'une banque)

◇ *credit freeze* blocage *m* du crédit, gel *m* des crédits

◇ *credit history* profil *m* crédit; **to obtain information on sb's**

credit history établir des renseignements de solvabilité sur qn

◇ **credit institution** établissement *m* de crédit

◇ *Acct* **credit item** poste *m* créditeur

◇ **credit limit** limite *f* de crédit, plafond *m* de crédit

◇ **credit line** ligne *f* de crédit, autorisation *f* de crédit

◇ **credit management** direction *f* des crédits

◇ **credit manager** directeur *m* du crédit

◇ **credit margin** marge *f* de crédit

◇ **credit memo** bulletin *m* de versement

◇ *Banking* **credit note** note *f* d'avoir

◇ **credit options** formules *fpl* de crédit

◇ **credit purchase** achat *m* à crédit

◇ **credit rating** *(of person, company)* degré *m* de solvabilité; *(awarded by credit reference agency)* notation *f*

◇ **credit rating agency, credit reference agency** agence *f* de notation (financière)

◇ **credit risk** risque *m* de contrepartie

◇ **credit scoring** méthode *f* d'évaluation de la solvabilité, crédit-scoring *m*

◇ **credit side** *(of account)* avoir *m*

◇ **credit squeeze** restriction *f* ou reserrement *m* du crédit

◇ **credit transaction** transaction *f* à crédit

◇ **credit transfer** virement *m*

◇ **credit union** caisse *f* populaire

◇ **credit voucher** chèque *m* de caisse

> 66
>
> The Money Store, which has 140 employees at branches in Glasgow, Birmingham, Bristol, Manchester, Newcastle and Warrington, is focused on customers such as the self-employed and divorced who can suffer difficulties in getting a **credit rating** from high street lenders.
>
> 99

creditor *n* créancier(ère) *m,f*

◇ **creditors' meeting** réunion *f* des créanciers

◇ *Acct* **creditors' turnover** rotation *f* des fournisseurs

creditworthiness *n* solvabilité *f*

creditworthy *adj* solvable

cross *vt (cheque)* barrer

◇ **crossed cheque** chèque *m* barré

cross-currency *adj*

◇ **cross-currency interest rate** taux *m* d'intérêt croisé

◇ *St Exch* **cross-currency swap** crédit *m* croisé

cross-holding *n* participation *f* croisée

> 66
>
> This did not satisfy Mr Pébereau, who had made compromises which included BNP retaining its 37% stake in SocGen but reducing its voting rights to less than 20%. He also offered SocGen a **cross-holding** in BNP which would make it his bank's biggest shareholder.
>
> 99

CSD *n Banking, St Exch* (*abbr* **Central Securities Depository**) dépositaire *m* national de titres

cumulative *adj*
◇ **cumulative balance** solde *m* cumulé
◇ **cumulative interest** intérêts *mpl* cumulatifs
◇ *St Exch* **cumulative preference share** action *f* privilégiée cumulative
◇ **cumulative profit** bénéfice *m* cumulé
◇ *St Exch* **cumulative share** action *f* à dividende cumulatif

currency *n* monnaie *f*; *(foreign)* devise *f*
◇ **currency conversion** conversion *f* de monnaies
◇ **currency dealer** cambiste *mf*
◇ **currency exposure** risque *m* de change
◇ **currency fluctuation** mouvement *m* des devises
◇ **currency interest-rate swap** échange *m* d'intérêts et de monnaies
◇ **currency pool** pool *m* de monnaies
◇ **currency risk** risque *m* de change
◇ **currency speculator** spéculateur(trice) *m,f* sur devises
◇ **currency swap** échange *m* de devises
◇ **currency transfer** transfert *m* de devises

current *adj*
◇ **current account** *(in bank)* compte *m* courant; *St Exch* liquidation *f* courante
◇ **current assets** actif *m* de roulement, actif circulant

◇ **current cost** prix *m* courant *ou* du marché; *St Exch* cours *m* instantané
◇ *Acct* **current cost accounting** comptabilité *f* en coûts actuels
◇ **current earnings** bénéfices *mpl* de l'exercice, revenus *mpl* actuels
◇ **current expenditure** dépenses *fpl* courantes
◇ **current** *Br* **financial** *or Am* **fiscal year** exercice *m* en cours
◇ **current income** *(in accounts)* produits *mpl* courants; *(actual earnings)* revenu *m* actuel
◇ **current liabilities** passif *m* exigible *ou* circulant
◇ **current net value** valeur *f* actuelle nette
◇ **current rate of exchange** taux *m* de change en cours
◇ *Acct* **current ratio** coefficient *m* de liquidité
◇ **current value** valeur *f* actuelle
◇ *Acct* **current value accounting** comptabilité *f* en valeur actuelle
◇ **current year** exercice *m* en cours
◇ **current yield** taux *m* de rendement courant

custodian *n St Exch* dépositaire *mf*, conservateur *m* de titres

custody account *n Am* compte *m* de garde

CVP *n* (*abbr* **cost-volume-profit**) étude *f* de coût-efficacité

CVR *n St Exch* (*abbr* **contingent value right**) CVG *m*

cyclical stocks *npl St Exch* valeurs *fpl* cycliques

D/A *npl* (*abbr* **documents against acceptance**) documents *mpl* contre acceptation

daily *adj* quotidien(enne)
◇ *St Exch* **Daily Official List** cours *mpl* de clôture quotidiens
◇ *daily trading report* rapport *m* de situation journalière

damages *npl* dommages et intérêts *mpl*, dommages-intérêts *mpl*; **to be awarded damages** obtenir des dommages et intérêts *ou* des dommages-intérêts

date *n* (a) *(of week, month)* **to date** à ce jour; **interest to date** intérêts *mpl* à ce jour; **date of invoice** date *f* de facturation; **date of issue** date *f* d'émission (b) *(of bill)* terme *m*, échéance *f*; **three months after date, at three months' date** à trois mois de date *ou* d'échéance; **date of maturity** (date *f* d')échéance

dawn *n St Exch*
◇ *dawn raid* raid *m*
◇ *dawn raider* raider *m*

Dax *n St Exch* **the Dax index** l'indice *m* Dax

day *n St Exch*
◇ *day order* ordre *m* valable pour la journée
◇ *day trade* opération *f* de journée

◇ *day trader* spéculateur(trice) *m,f* à la journée
◇ *day trading* spéculation *f* à la journée

daybook *n Acct* brouillard *m*

DCF *n Acct* (*abbr* **discounted cash flow**) cash-flow *m* actualisé, flux *mpl* de trésorerie actualisés

dead *adj*
◇ *dead account* compte *m* inactif
◇ *Fam St Exch* **dead cat bounce** = reprise de courte durée lors de l'effondrement des cours de la Bourse
◇ *dead loss* perte *f* sèche
◇ *dead market* marché *m* mort
◇ *dead money* argent *m* mort, argent qui dort

deadline *n* *(day)* date *f* limite; *(time)* heure *f* limite; **deadline for payment** date limite de paiement

deal 1 *n* affaire *f*, marché *m*; **to do** *or* **make a deal with sb** conclure une affaire *ou* un marché avec qn
2 *vi* négocier, traiter; **to deal on the Stock Exchange** faire des opérations *ou* des transactions en Bourse; *St Exch* **to deal in options** faire le commerce des primes

dealer *n* *(on Stock Exchange)*

courtier(ère) *m,f*; *(in foreign exchange)* cambiste *mf*; *St Exch* **dealer in securities** négociant *m* en titres

dealing *n St Exch* opérations *fpl*, transactions *fpl*

◇ **dealing room** salle *f* des changes *ou* de marchés

dear money *n* argent *m* cher

death *n*

◇ **death duties** droits *mpl* de succession

◇ **death in service (benefit)** capital-décès *m*

◇ *Am* **death tax** droits *mpl* de succession

debenture *n* obligation *f*

◇ **debenture bond** obligation *f*

◇ **debenture holder** porteur (euse) *m,f* d'obligations, obligataire *mf*

◇ **debenture issue** émission *f* d'obligations

◇ **debenture loan** emprunt *m* obligataire

◇ **debenture stock** obligations (sans garantie) *fpl*

> **"**
>
> A **debenture** includes **debenture stock**, bonds and other securities of a company, whether amounting to a charge on the assets or not. It is a document which sets out the terms of a loan and is usually issued under authority of a company's seal. Repayment is provided for at some future date. Payment of interest is made to the **debenture holder** at a specified rate and at clearly defined intervals.
>
> **"**

debit 1 *n* débit *m*; *Acct* **debit and credit** doit *m* et avoir *m*

2 *vt (account)* débiter; **to debit an account with £200, to debit £200 to an account** débiter un compte de 200 livres; **has this cheque been debited to my account?** est-ce que ce chèque a été débité de mon compte?

◇ **debit account** compte *m* débiteur

◇ **debit advice** avis *m* de débit

◇ **debit balance** solde *m* débiteur *ou* déficitaire

◇ **debit card** carte *f* de débit

◇ *Acct* **debit column** colonne *f* débitrice *ou* des débits

◇ **debit entry** *Acct* écriture *f* passée au débit; *Banking* article *m* porté au débit d'un compte

◇ **debit interest** intérêts *mpl* débiteurs

◇ *Acct* **debit item** poste *m* débiteur

◇ **debit note** facture *f ou* note *f ou* bordereau *m* de débit

◇ **debit side** *(of account)* débit *m*

debt *n* dette *f*; *(to be recovered)* créance *f*; **to be in debt** être endetté(e); avoir des dettes; **to be £12,000 in debt** avoir 12 000 livres de dettes; **to be in debt to sb** être en dette envers qn; **to pay off a debt** rembourser *ou* payer une dette; **to be out of debt** n'avoir plus de dettes; **to get** *or* **run into debt** s'endetter, faire des dettes; **to reschedule** *or* **restructure a debt** rééchelonner une dette; **debt owed by us** dette passive; **debt owed to us** dette active

◇ **debt capacity** capacité *f* d'endettement

◇ **debt collection** recouvrement *m* de créances

◇ **debt collection agency** agence *f* de recouvrements

◊ *debt collector* agent *m* de recouvrements
◊ *debt due* créance *f* exigible
◊ *debt financing* financement *m* par endettement *ou* emprunt
◊ *debt of honour* dette *f* d'honneur
◊ *debt instrument* titre *m* de créance
◊ *debt limit* limite *f* d'endettement
◊ *debt ratio* ratio *m* d'endettement
◊ *debt rescheduling, debt restructuring* rééchelonnement *m* des dettes
◊ *Am debt service* service *m* de la dette
◊ *Br debt servicing* service *m* de la dette
◊ *debt swap* échange *m* de créances

debt-equity *adj*
◊ *debt-equity ratio* rapport *m* dettes-actions
◊ *debt-equity swap* échange *m* de créances contre actifs

> **"**
> However, while the idea of spinning off debt in this way is sound in principle…it suffers in practice from a number of problems… Firstly, the amount that will be dealt with in the **debt-equity swaps** will total only about one trillion yuan. This compares with as much as four trillion yuan worth of red ink that currently swamps the state banks, and even greater amounts of debt within the state sector itself.
> **"**

debtor *n* débiteur(trice) *m,f*;

Acct **debtors** comptes *mpl* clients, créances *fpl*
◊ *Acct debtor account* compte *m* débiteur
◊ *debtor side* (of account) débit *m*, doit *m*
◊ *Acct debtors' turnover* rotation *f* des clients

declaration *n* déclaration *f*
◊ *declaration of bankruptcy* déclaration *f* de faillite
◊ *St Exch declaration of dividend* déclaration *f* de dividende
◊ *declaration of income* déclaration *f* de revenu
◊ *St Exch declaration of options* réponse *f* des primes
◊ *declaration of solvency* déclaration *f* de solvabilité
◊ *declaration of value* déclaration *f* de valeur

declare *vt* to declare sb bankrupt constater *ou* prononcer la faillite de qn; *St Exch* to declare a dividend of 10% déclarer un dividende de 10%

declared value *n* valeur *f* déclarée

declining *adj Acct*
◊ *declining balance depreciation* amortissement *m* dégressif
◊ *declining balance method* méthode *f* de l'amortissement dégressif

decrease a *n* baisse *f*
2 *vi* diminuer, baisser

decreasing *adj* en baisse; (number, value) décroissant(e)
◊ *decreasing costs* frais *mpl* dégressifs
◊ *Acct decreasing rate* taux *m* dégressif

deduct *vt* déduire; *(tax)* prélever; **to deduct £10 from the price** déduire 10 livres du prix; **to be deducted at source** *(of tax)* être prélevé(e) à la source

deduction *n* déduction *f* (**from** sur); *(from salary)* prélèvement *m*, retenue *f*; **after deduction of taxes** après déduction des impôts; **deduction (of income tax) at source** retenue à la source, prélèvement de l'impôt à la source; **after deductions, I'm left with a salary of £20,000** une fois les prélèvements *ou* les retenues décompté(e)s, il me reste un salaire de 20 000 livres

deep-discount bond *n* obligation *f* à forte décote

> **"**
>
> **Deep-discount bonds** are bonds which carry a low nominal rate of interest and accordingly are issued at a discount to the value at which they will be redeemed. In the extreme case where no interest at all is payable they are sometimes referred to as zero coupon bonds.
>
> **"**

defalcation *n* détournement *m* de fonds

default 1 *n* **in default of payment** à défaut de paiement
2 *vi* manquer à ses engagements; **to default on a payment** ne pas honorer un paiement
◇ **default interest** intérêts *mpl* moratoires

defaulter *n* débiteur(trice) *m,f* défaillant(e)

defensive stocks *npl St Exch*

titres *mpl* de placement, valeurs *fpl* d'investissement

deferred *adj* différé(e)
◇ **deferred annuity** annuité *f* différée
◇ **deferred asset** actif *m* différé
◇ **deferred charges** frais *mpl* différés
◇ **deferred credit** crédit *m* ou paiement *m* différé
◇ **deferred debit** débit *m* différé
◇ **deferred income** produit *m* constaté d'avance
◇ **deferred liabilities** passif *m* reporté
◇ **deferred payment** paiement *m* différé
◇ **deferred rebate** rabais *m* différé
◇ **deferred results** résultats *mpl* à longue échéance
◇ **deferred taxation** impôts *mpl* différés

deficit *n* déficit *m*; **to be in deficit** être en déficit; **the balance of payments shows a deficit of £800 million** la balance des paiements indique un déficit de 800 millions de livres

deflate *vt Econ (prices)* faire baisser; **to deflate the economy** pratiquer une politique déflationniste; **this measure is intended to deflate the economy** cette mesure est destinée à faire de la déflation

deflation *n Econ* déflation *f*

deflationary *adj Econ (measures)* déflationniste; *(policy)* de désinflation

degressive taxation *n* impôt *m* dégressif

delay 1 *n* délai *m*; **delay in pay-**

ment délai de paiement
   2 vt (payment) différer

delinquent adj (debt, loan)
échu, en souffrance

> Foremost among these steps
> has been the introduction of a
> framework to relieve state
> banks of at least part of their
> crippling burden of bad debt –
> owed almost entirely by state
> firms – by transferring some
> **delinquent loans** to four
> asset management companies
> (AMCs) … The idea, according
> to details released last week …
> is that Cinda and its brethren will
> assume the **delinquent debt**
> in return for equity shares of
> debtor companies.

delist vt St Exch radier de la cote

delisting n St Exch radiation f
de la cote

deliver vt St Exch (shares) déli-
vrer

delivery n St Exch livraison f
◊ **delivery month** mois m de livraison

demand adj Am
◊ **demand deposit** dépôt m à vue
◊ **demand deposit account**
compte m à vue

dematerialization n St Exch
(of securities) dématérialisation f

dematerialized adj St Exch
(securities) dématérialisé(e)

demonetization n (of currency) démonétisation f

demonetize vt (currency) démonétiser

demutualization n = transformation d'une société mutuelle en société par actions

demutualize vi = passer d'un
statut de société mutuelle à un
statut de société par actions

> Introductory rates have been as
> low as 2% for the first year, and
> it would seem unfair on the len-
> der if it could not recoup the loss
> on lending at that rate by tying
> the borrower to a standard rate
> mortgage for an agreed period
> afterwards. However, if the len-
> der is allowed to increase sales
> arbitrarily, it effectively has a
> blank cheque to draw on the
> borrower's money. … People
> who borrow from a building so-
> ciety which **demutualizes** are
> particularly vulnerable to this.
> Building societies, theoretically
> at least, act solely in their mem-
> bers' interests and have no in-
> terest in overcharging.

denomination n valeur f; (of
share, banknote) coupure f;
coins of all denominations
pièces fpl de toutes valeurs;
small/large denominations peti-
tes/grosses coupures

deposit n (a) Banking dépôt m;
to make a deposit déposer de
l'argent; **to make a deposit of
£500** déposer 500 livres en
banque; **on deposit** en dépôt
   (b) (down payment) acompte
m; (not returnable, for contract)
arrhes fpl; (against damage)
caution f; **to pay** or **put down a
deposit on sth** verser un
acompte/des arrhes sur qch;
he left £10 as a deposit il a versé

un acompte de 10 livres

2 *vt (money)* déposer; *(document) (with a bank)* mettre en dépôt (**with** dans); *(with a solicitor)* confier (**with** à); **to deposit sth as security** nantir qch, gager qch

◇ *Br Banking* **deposit account** compte *m* livret, compte de dépôt; *(when notice has to be given before withdrawal)* compte à terme

◇ *Banking* **deposit bank** banque *f* de dépôt

◇ *Banking* **deposit book** livret *m* ou carnet *m* de dépôt

◇ **deposit money** monnaie *f* de banque, monnaie scripturale

◇ **deposit receipt** récépissé *m* de dépôt

◇ *Banking* **deposit slip** bordereau *m* ou bulletin *m* de versement

depositor *n Banking* déposant(e) *m,f*

depreciable base *n Am* assiette *f* de l'amortissement

depreciate 1 *vt* (**a**) *(value)* déprécier, rabaisser; *(goods)* faire perdre de la valeur à (**b**) *Acct (property, equipment)* amortir

2 *vi (of goods, money, currency, property, equipment)* se déprécier, se dévaloriser; *(of shares)* baisser; **the pound has depreciated against the dollar** la livre a reculé par rapport au dollar

depreciated *adj Acct* amorti(e); *(currency)* déprécié(e)

depreciation *n* (**a**) *(of goods, money, currency)* dépréciation *f*, dévalorisation *f*; *(amount)* moins-value *f*; *(of shares)* moins-value, décote *f* (**b**) *Acct*

(of property, equipment) amortissement *m*

◇ *Acct* **depreciation accounting** comptabilité *f* de la dépréciation

◇ *Acct* **depreciation charges** frais *mpl* d'amortissement

◇ *Acct* **depreciation period** période *f* d'amortissement

◇ *Acct* **depreciation provision** dotation *f* aux amortissements

◇ *Acct* **depreciation rate** taux *m* d'amortissement

◇ *Acct* **depreciation schedule** plan *m* d'amortissement

derivative *n St Exch* produit *m* dérivé; **to deal in derivatives** faire le commerce des produits dérivés

◇ **derivative market, derivatives market** marché *m* à terme des instruments financiers

devaluation *n Econ* dévaluation *f*

devalue *vt Econ* dévaluer; **the franc has been devalued by 3%** le franc a été dévalué de 3%

development loans *npl* crédits *mpl* de développement

diagnostic audit *n* diagnostic *m* financier

digital signature *n Comptr* signature *f* électronique

> E-commerce transactions are encrypted, but it is hard to verify that buyers and merchants are who they say they are. That is why Visa is urging a swifter adoption of the Secure Electronic Transaction (SET) protocol and a rapid move towards **digital signatures**.

diluted adj St Exch
◇ **fully diluted earnings per share** bénéfice m net dilué par action

dilution n St Exch dilution f
◇ **dilution of equity** dilution f du bénéfice par action
◇ **dilution of shareholding** dilution f des actions

diminishing adj décroissant(e); (price, quality, value) en baisse
◇ Acct **diminishing balance (method)** amortissement m linéaire
◇ **diminishing marginal product** produit m marginal décroissant
◇ **diminishing returns** rendements mpl décroissants; **law of diminishing returns** loi f des rendements décroissants

dip 1 n (in prices, value, figures) baisse f; **the winter months saw a sharp dip in profits** les bénéfices ont fortement baissé pendant l'hiver
2 vi (of prices, value, figures) baisser; **shares dipped on the London Stock Market yesterday** les actions ont baissé à la Bourse des valeurs de Londres hier

direct adj
◇ **direct banking** banque f à distance
◇ **direct costs** charges fpl directes, frais mpl directs
◇ Acct **direct cost accounting** (méthode f de) comptabilité f des coûts variables
◇ **direct costing** méthode f des coûts variables ou proportionnels
◇ Br Banking **direct debit** prélè-

vement m (bancaire) automatique; **to pay by direct debit** payer par prélèvement automatique
◇ Br Banking **direct debit advice** avis m de prélèvement
◇ Br Banking **direct debit mandate** autorisation f de prélèvement
◇ **direct fixed costs** coûts mpl fixes directs ou attribuables
◇ **direct investment** investissement m direct
◇ **direct labour** main d'œuvre f directe
◇ **direct labour cost** prix m de la main-d'œuvre directe
◇ **direct letter of credit** lettre f de crédit directe
◇ **direct tax** impôt m direct
◇ **direct taxation** contributions fpl directes

dirty adj
◇ St Exch **dirty float** taux mpl de change concertés
◇ **dirty money** argent m mal acquis ou sale

disburse vt (funds, loan) débourser

disbursement n (of funds, loan) déboursement m

discharge 1 n (a) (of bankrupt) réhabilitation f; **discharge in bankruptcy** (b) (of debt) liquidation f, acquittement m; (of account, obligation) paiement m, apurement m; **in full discharge** (on bill) pour acquit
2 vt (a) (bankrupt) réhabiliter, décharger; **discharged bankrupt** failli déchargé ou réhabilité
(b) (debt) liquider, acquitter; (fine) payer; (account, obliga-

tion) apurer, payer, faire l'apurement de

disclosure *n St Exch* information *f* aux actionnaires
◇ *Acct* **disclosure of accounts** publication *f* des comptes
◇ *St Exch* **disclosure threshold** seuil *m* d'annonce obligatoire

discount 1 *n* escompte *m*; **discounts and allowances** remise, rabais, ristourne, RRR
2 *vt (bill)* escompter
◇ *Banking* **discount bank** banque *f* d'escompte
◇ *St Exch* **discount bond** obligation *f* émise au-dessous du pair
◇ **discount card** carte *f* de réduction
◇ **discount house** comptoir *m* ou maison *f* d'escompte
◇ **discount loan** prêt *m* escompté
◇ **discount market** marché *m* de l'escompte
◇ **discount mechanism** mécanisme *m* de l'escompte
◇ **discount rate** taux *m* d'escompte

discountable *adj* escomptable

discounted *adj*
◇ **discounted bill** effet *m* escompté
◇ *Acct* **discounted cash flow** cash-flow *m* actualisé, flux *mpl* de trésorerie actualisés
◇ **discounted rate** taux *m* d'escompte
◇ **discounted value** valeur *f* actualisée

discounting *n* escompte *m*
◇ **discounting bank** banque *f* ou maison *f* d'escompte

discretionary *adj*
◇ *Banking* **discretionary account** compte *m* avec procuration, compte sous mandat de gestion
◇ **discretionary costs** coûts *mpl* discrétionnaires
◇ **discretionary fund** compte *m* sous mandat de gestion
◇ *St Exch* **discretionary order** ordre *m* à appréciation
◇ **discretionary portfolio** portefeuille *m* avec mandat

dishonour, *Am* **dishonor** *vt (bill, cheque)* ne pas accepter, ne pas honorer, refuser de payer; **dishonoured cheque** chèque *m* impayé *ou* non honoré

dispenser *n (for cash)* distributeur *m*

displaced share *n St Exch* action *f* déclassée

displacement *n St Exch* déclassement *m*

disposable 1 *n* **disposables** biens *mpl* de consommation non durables
2 *adj (available)* disponible
◇ **disposable funds** disponibilités *fpl*, fonds *mpl* disponibles
◇ **disposable income** surplus *m*, revenu *m* disponible

distributable *adj (profits, reserves)* distribuable

distribution *n* distribution *f*
◇ **distribution costs** frais *mpl* de distribution, coût *m* de la distribution
◇ **distribution ratio** ratio *m* de distribution

disturbed *adj St Exch (market)* agité(e)

div *n (abbr* **dividend)** div.

diversification *n* diversification *f*

diversify **1** *vt (portfolio)* diversifier

2 *vi (of company)* se diversifier

> First, contrary to popular belief, high yield does not necessarily equate with high risk – as a well-**diversified** portfolio of high yield bonds has shown to deliver higher income with reduced volatility over longer periods of time.

divestment *n (of assets)* scission *f*

dividend *n* dividende *m*; *(from cooperative society)* ristourne *f*; **the company has declared a dividend of 10%** la société a déclaré un dividende de 10%; **cum dividend,** *Am* **dividend on** avec le dividende attaché; **ex dividend,** *Am* **dividend off** ex-dividende

◇ **dividend announcement** déclaration *f* de dividende

◇ **dividend cover** taux *m* de couverture du dividende

◇ **dividend mandate** ordonnance *f* de paiement

◇ **dividend per share** dividende *m* par action

◇ **dividend tax** impôt *m* sur les dividendes

◇ **dividend warrant** chèque-dividende *m*, coupon *m* d'arrérages

◇ **dividend yield** taux *m* de rendement des actions *(en dividendes)*

dividend-price ratio *n Am St Exch* ratio *m* cours-bénéfice

document *n* document *m*; **documents against acceptance** documents contre acceptation; **documents against payment** documents contre paiement

documentary *adj*

◇ **documentary bill** traite *m* documentaire

◇ **documentary letter of credit** lettre *f* de crédit documentaire

dollar *n* dollar *m*

◇ *Econ* **dollar area** zone *f* dollar

◇ **dollar balances** soldes *mpl* en dollars

◇ *Am* **dollar cost averaging** = calcul du coût moyen en dollars; *St Exch* = coût moyen des actions achetées par sommes fixes

◇ **dollar crisis** crise *f* du dollar

◇ **dollar premium** prime *f* sur le dollar

◇ **dollar rate** cours *m* du dollar

◇ **dollar sign** signe *m* dollar

> At one level the Ministry of Defence argument about the dollar costs of overseas expenditure was not absurd. Most of the expenditure was outside the **dollar area**, and did not give rise to immediate dollar payments. But, other things being equal, such financial transfers would ultimately lead to a real transfer of resources to the recipients of expenditure.

domicile *vt* domicilier

◇ **domiciled bill** effet *m* domicilié, traite *f* domiciliée

dormant *adj Banking (account)* sans mouvement

double *adj*
◊ *St Exch* **double option** stellage *m*, option *f* du double
◊ *double taxation* double imposition *f*
◊ *double taxation agreement* convention *f* de double imposition

double-A rating *n St Exch* notation *f* AA

double-digit *adj (salary, profit, inflation)* à deux chiffres

double-entry bookkeeping *n Acct* comptabilité *f* en partie double

doubtful *adj*
◊ *doubtful debt* créance *f* douteuse
◊ *doubtful loan* prêt *m* douteux

Dow-Jones *n St Exch* **Dow Jones (Industrial) Average** *or* **Index** indice *m* Dow Jones

down 1 *adv (reduced, lower)* **the price of gold is down** le prix de l'or a baissé; **the pound is down two cents against the dollar** la livre a baissé de deux cents par rapport au dollar; **to be down 12% as against last year** être en baisse de 12% par rapport à l'année précédente
2 *adj*
◊ *down payment* acompte *m*; **to make a down payment on sth** verser un acompte sur qch; **he made a down payment of £500** il a versé un acompte de 500 livres

downside *adj St Exch*
◊ *downside potential* potentiel *m* de baisse
◊ *downside risk* risque *m* de baisse

downward *adj* **the economy is on a downward path** l'économie est sur une mauvaise pente
◊ *Econ* **downward movement** mouvement *m* de baisse
◊ *Econ, St Exch* **downward trend** tendance *f* à la baisse

drachma *n* drachme *f*

draft *n* traite *f*; **to make a draft on sb** tirer sur qn

draw 1 *vt* (**a**) *(salary)* toucher; **to draw money from the bank** retirer de l'argent de la banque (**b**) *(cheque, bill)* tirer; **to draw a cheque on one's account** tirer un chèque sur son compte (**c**) *(interest)* produire
2 *vi* **to draw at sight** tirer à vue

▸ **draw out** *vt sep (money)* retirer

drawdown *n* tirage *m*

> Until now, anyone wanting to take advantage of **drawdown** had first to make the costly transfer into a personal pension plan. The new rules aim to make this unnecessary by extending **drawdown** to occupational money purchase schemes … small, self-administered schemes … executive pension plans … additional voluntary contributions … and individual or free-standing AVCs.

drawee *n (of bill)* tiré *m*, payeur *m*

drawer *n* tireur *m*; *(of bill)* souscripteur *m*; **to refer a cheque to**

drawer refuser d'honorer un chèque

drawing n (a) *(of sum)* prélèvement m, retrait m (b) *(of cheque, bill)* traite f

◇ **drawing account** compte m courant, compte de dépôt à vue

◇ **drawing rights** droits mpl de tirage

drop vi *(of prices, inflation)* baisser; **interest rates have dropped by 1%** les taux d'intérêt ont baissé de 1%; St Exch **shares dropped a point** les actions ont reculé d'un point; **the pound dropped three points against the dollar** la livre a reculé de *ou* a perdu trois points par rapport au dollar

drop-dead adj

◇ **drop-dead fee** commission f de désintéressement

◇ **drop-dead rate** taux m de désintéressement

dual adj

◇ EU **dual circulation** *(of currencies)* double circulation f

◇ EU **dual dirculation period** période f de double circulation

◇ **dual currency** deux monnaies fpl

◇ St Exch **dual exchange market** double marché m des changes

◇ St Exch **dual listing** cotation f sur deux Bourses

◇ **dual pricing** régime m du double prix; *(showing prices in national currency and in euros)* double affichage m (des prix)

> **"**
>
> The brothers who founded software company Trintech could be worth £37–75 million ($50–100 million) when their company takes a **dual listing** on German and US stock markets next month. … Mr McGuire said the dual listing had taken a great deal of planning, particularly given recent hits taken by Irish technology companies on the Nasdaq exchange.
>
> **"**

dual-currency adj *(system)* bimonétaire

dud adj *(banknote, coin)* faux (fausse); *(cheque)* sans provision

due adj *(owed)* dû (due); *(debt)* exigible; *(bill)* payable

◇ **due date** date f d'échéance, date d'exigibilité

dummy company n société f fictive

duplication n Acct **duplication (of entry)** double emploi m

E & OE *Br Acct (abbr* **errors and omissions excepted**) SEO

earmark *vt (funds)* assigner, affecter (**for** à); **this money has been earmarked for research** cet argent a été affecté à la recherche

earn *vt (money)* gagner; *(interest)* rapporter; **how much do you earn?** combien gagnez-vous?; **their money is earning a high rate of interest** leur argent est rémunéré à un taux élevé

earned *adj*

◊ *earned income* revenus *mpl* salariaux

◊ *earned income allowance* = déduction au titre de revenus salariaux ou professionnels

◊ *earned interest* revenu *m* des intérêts

◊ *Acct* *earned surplus* bénéfices *mpl* non distribués

> A dependent wife's pension is included in her husband's income and is offset against the married man's tax allowance. A pension in your own right is automatically offset against the wife's **earned income allowance**.

earnings *npl (of person)* salaire *m*, revenus *mpl*; *(of company)* revenus; **earnings before interest and tax** bénéfices *mpl* avant impôts et charges

◊ *earnings forecast* résultats *mpl* prévisionnels

◊ *earnings growth* accroissement *m* des bénéfices, augmentation *f* des bénéfices

◊ *earnings per share* bénéfice *m* par action

◊ *earnings retained* bénéfices *mpl* non distribués

earnings-related *adj* proportionnel(elle) au revenu

◊ *earnings-related pension* retraite *f* indexée sur le revenu

earnout *n* = supplément de prix payable éventuellement en fonction des bénéfices futurs (dans le cadre de l'acquisition d'une entreprise)

easy *adj* **by easy payments, on easy terms** avec facilités de paiement

EBIT *npl (abbr* **earnings before interest and tax**) bénéfices *mpl* avant impôts et charges

EBRD *n (abbr* **European Bank of Reconstruction and Development**) BERD *f*

"

Representatives of 40 countries met at the Elysée Palace in Paris on May 29 to sign the founding charter of the European Bank for Reconstruction and Development (**EBRD** or, by its French acronym, BERD), a new international organization intended to finance industrial and economic development in the countries of Eastern Europe, using loans, guarantees, equity investment and underwriting to promote the transition to free-market economic systems in those countries.

"

e-broker n St Exch courtier (ère) m,f électronique

e-broking n St Exch courtage m électronique

"

The emergence of **e-broking** has had a huge impact on the cost of trading. The average commission for each online trade is around $15 (though Schwab, the market leader, charges $30), compared with $100–300 at full-service brokerages, which, as well as executing trades, offer research, advice and a personal broker. These traditional firms have been slow to respond to the online challenge.

"

e-cash n Comptr argent m électronique, argent virtuel, e-cash m

ECB n (abbr **European Central Bank**) BCE f

ECN n St Exch (abbr **electronic communications network**) marché m électronique privé

ECOFIN n EU (abbr **Economic and Financial Council of Ministers**) Conseil m Ecofin

economic adj (a) (relating to the economy) économique (b) Br (profitable) rentable; **to make sth economic** rentabiliser qch

◇ **economic climate** climat m économique

◇ **economic cost** coût m économique

◇ **economic growth rate** taux m d'expansion économique

◇ **economic indicators** indicateurs mpl économiques

◇ **economic life** (of machinery, product) durée f économique

◇ EU **Economic and Monetary Union** union f économique et monétaire

◇ **economic situation** conjoncture f économique

◇ **economic trend** tendance f économique, conjoncture f économique

◇ Acct **economic value added** valeur f ajoutée économique

economics 1 n (science) économie f

2 npl (profitability) rentabilité f; (financial aspects) aspects mpl financiers; **we must consider the economics of the project before making any decisions** nous devons considérer l'aspect financier du projet avant de prendre une décision

economy n économie f; **economies of scale** économies fpl d'échelle

ECP n EU (abbr **eurocommercial paper**) billet m de trésorerie (émis sur le marché des eurodevises)

ECSDA n EU (abbr **European Central Securities Depositories Association**) association f européenne des déspositaires cenraux de titres

ECU, ecu n EU (abbr **European Currency Unit**) ÉCU m, écu m

EDGAR n (abbr **electronic data gathering, analysis and retrieval**) = banque de données créée par la commission américaine des opérations de Bourse (le SEC), qui contient toutes sortes d'informations sur de nombreux fonds communs de placement et entreprises publiques

EDI n Comptr (abbr **European Data Interchange**) EED m

effective adj Econ (yield, return, production) effectif(ive); (value) réel(elle)

◇ **effective annual rate** taux m annuel effectif

◇ **effective tax rate** taux m d'imposition effectif

EFT n (abbr **electronic funds transfer**) transfert m de fonds électronique

EFTPOS n (abbr **electronic funds transfer at point of sale**) transfert m de fonds électronique au point de vente

80/20 rule n règle f 80/20

electronic adj électronique

◇ **electronic banking** bancatique f

◇ St Exch **electronic communi-** cations network marché m électronique privé

◇ Comptr **Electronic Data Interchange** Échange m Électronique de Données

◇ **electronic funds transfer** transfert m de fonds électronique

◇ **electronic funds transfer at point of sale** transfert m de fonds électronique au point de vente

◇ **electronic money** argent m électronique, argent virtuel

◇ **electronic payment** paiement m électronique

◇ **electronic payment terminal** terminal m électronique de paiement

◇ St Exch **electronic trading** transactions fpl boursières electroniques

◇ **electronic transfer** transfert m de fonds électronique

❝

Today, information about the demand, supply and price of capital moves freely around the world, increasingly over networked computers. Computers themselves are becoming ever better at bringing together buyers and sellers and matching their trades automatically. Now that the London Stock Exchange has introduced **electronic trading**, every major stockmarket in Europe uses computers for a task that was once handled by braying traders.

❞

eligible adj

◇ Br **eligible bill** effet m escomptable

◇ Br **eligible list** effet m bancable

◇ Am **eligible paper** effet m escomptable

EMA n (abbr **European Monetary Agreement**) AME m

embezzle 1 vt (money, funds) détourner

2 vi commettre des détournements de fonds; **to embezzle from a company** détourner les fonds d'une société

embezzlement n **embezzlement (of funds)** détournement m de fonds

embezzler n auteur m d'un détournement de fonds

emergency tax n impôt m extraordinaire

emerging market n Econ marché m émergeant

EMI n (abbr **European Monetary Institute**) IME m

e-money n Comptr argent m électronique, argent virtuel

employee n employé(e) m,f

◇ **employee's contribution** (to benefits) cotisation f des salariés

◇ **employee incentive scheme** système m de rémunération au rendement

◇ **employee shareholding** actionnariat m ouvrier

◇ Br **employee share ownership plan,** Am **employee stock ownership plan** plan m d'actionnariat des salariés, plan d'épargne entreprise

employer n employeur(euse) m,f

◇ **employer's contribution** cotisation f patronale

EMS n (abbr **European Monetary System**) SME m

EMU n (abbr **Economic and Monetary Union**) UME f

encash vt Br (cheque) encaisser

encashment n Br (of cheque) encaissement m

end n (of month, year) fin f; **at the end of the month/of the year** à la fin du mois/de l'année; **end of the financial year** clôture f de l'exercice

end-of-month adj de fin de mois

◇ **end-of-month balance** solde m de fin de mois

◇ **end-of-month payments** échéances fpl de fin de mois

◇ **end-of-month settlement** liquidation f de fin de mois

◇ **end-of-month statement** relevé m de fin de mois

end-of-year adj de fin d'année; Acct de fin d'exercice

◇ Acct **end-of-year balance sheet** bilan m de l'exercice

endorse vt (document, cheque) endosser; (bill of exchange) avaliser, endosser, donner son aval à

endorsee n endossataire mf

endorsement n (of document, cheque) endossement m, endos m; (of bill of exchange) aval m

◇ **endorsement fee** commission f d'endos

endorser n (of document, cheque) endosseur m, cessionnaire mf; (of bill of exchange) avaliste mf, avaliseur m

endow vt (person, company) doter (**with** de)

endowment n (action, fund) dotation f

◇ **endowment assurance** assurance *f* en cas de vie, assurance à dotation

◊ *endowment fund* fonds *m* de dotation

◊ *endowment mortgage* prêt-logement *m* lié à une assurance-vie

◊ *endowment policy* assurance *f* en cas de vie, assurance à dotation

"

Paying £35 a month into the average investment trust over 20 years would produce a fund of almost £8,000, whereas the average with-profits **endowment policy** would return £6,800. But as long as you are aware of the pitfalls, **endowment policies** do have some benefits. This includes the ability to withdraw money free of all taxes, provided you hold the policy for a specified period.

"

enhance *vt (pension, value)* augmenter

enhanced *adj (pension, value)* augmenté(e)

enhancement *n (of pension, value)* augmentation *f*

enter *vt Acct (item)* comptabiliser; **to enter an item/figures in the ledger** porter un article/des chiffres sur le livre de comptes

▸ **enter up** *vt sep Acct* **to enter up an item/figures in the ledger** porter un article/des chiffres sur le livre de comptes

entrant *n (on market)* acteur *m*; **stocks in two new entrants to**

the market performed well les actions de deux sociétés nouvellement introduites en Bourse se sont bien comportées

entry *n Acct (action)* passation *f* d'écriture, inscription *f*; *(item)* article *m*, écriture *f*; **to make an entry** passer une écriture, porter un article à compte

EONIA *n (abbr* **Euro Overnight Index Average)** EONIA *m*, TEMPÉ *m*

EPS *n (abbr* **earnings per share)** BPA *m*

equalization *n (of dividends)* régularisation *f*

◊ *equalization fund* fonds *m* de parité

◊ *equalization payment* soulte *f*

equalize *vt (dividends)* régulariser

equity *n (of shareholders)* capitaux *mpl* propres, fonds *mpl* propres; *(of company)* capital *m* actions; **equities** actions *fpl* ordinaires

◊ *equity capital* capital *m* actions

◊ *equity dilution* dilution *f* du capital

◊ *equity financing* financement *m* par actions, financement par capitaux propres

◊ *equity investment* placement *m* en actions

◊ *equity issue* augmentation *f* du capital par émission d'actions

◊ *equity leader* valeur *f* vedette

◊ *equity loan* prêt *m* participatif

◊ *equity market, equities market* marché *m* des actions (ordinaires)

◇ *equity risk premium* prime *f* de risque de variation du prix des actions

◇ *equity share* action *f* ordinaire

◇ *equity share capital* capital *m* en actions ordinaires

◇ *equities trader* courtier(ère) *m,f* sur actions

◇ *equity trading* courtage *m* sur actions

◇ *equity warrant* bon *m* de souscription d'actions

> Savers won't necessarily benefit from lower inflation if they have **equity investments**, because of the adverse effect that low inflation has on the **equity risk premium** – the extra returns investors demand above cash for taking on extra risk.

equity-based unit trust *n* SICAV *f* actions

equity-linked *adj (policy)* libellé(e), investi(e) en actions

equivalences of exchange *npl* parités *fpl* de change

erase *vt (debt)* effacer

ERM *n (abbr* **Exchange Rate Mechanism)** mécanisme *m* de change

error *n* erreur *f*; *Acct* **errors and omissions excepted** sauf erreur ou omission

escrow *n* **in escrow** en dépôt fiduciaire

◇ *Am Banking* **escrow account** compte *m* bloqué

escudo *n* escudo *m*

ESOP *n (abbr* **employee** *Br* **share**

or *Am* **stock ownership plan)** plan *m* d'actionnariat des salariés, plan d'épargne entreprise

estate tax *n Am* droits *mpl* de succession

estimate 1 *n (calculation)* évaluation *f*; *(of cost)* devis *m*
   2 *vt (cost)* évaluer, estimer

ethical *adj* éthique

◇ *ethical investment* investissement *m* éthique

◇ *ethical investment fund* fonds *m* d'investissement éthique, SICAV *f* éthique

EURIBOR *n (abbr* **Euro Interbank Offered Rate)** EURIBOR *m*, TIBEUR *m*

euro *n EU* euro *m*; **in euro** en euros

◇ *euro zone* zone *f* euro

> French growth exceeded expectations in the second quarter, providing fresh evidence that the **euro zone** is beginning to pull strongly out of the slowdown triggered last year by the crises in Asia, Russia and Latin America.
>
> According to figures from Insee, the national statistics institute, the gross domestic product (GDP) of the **euro zone**'s second biggest economy grew by 0.6 per cent in the second quarter, after rising 0.4 per cent in the first three months.

Eurobank *n EU* eurobanque *f*

eurobond *n* euro-obligation *f*

eurocard *n* eurocarte *f*

eurocheque *n* eurochèque *m*

euro-commercial paper *n* *EU* billet *m* de trésorerie *(émis sur le marché des eurodevises)*

eurocredit *n* eurocrédit *m*

euro-currency *n* eurodevise *f*, euromonnaie *f*

◇ **euro-currency market** marché *m* des eurodevises

> **"**
>
> The **euro-currency markets** have altered the structure and operations of most major banks by encouraging overseas representation and making them innovative and adaptable to changing economic circumstances and customer needs.
>
> **"**

eurodollar *n* eurodollar *m*

Euroland *n* *EU* Eurolande *f*

euromarket *n* euromarché *m*

European *adj* européen (enne)

◇ **European Bank of Reconstruction and Development** Banque *f* européenne de reconstruction et de développement

◇ **European Central Bank** banque *f* centrale européenne

◇ **European currency snake** serpent *m* monétaire européen

◇ **European Currency Unit** unité *f* monétaire européenne

◇ **European Exchange Rate Mechanism** mécanisme *m* de change européen

◇ **European Investment Bank** Banque *f* européenne d'investissement

◇ **European monetary agreement** accord *m* monétaire européen

◇ Formerly **European Monetary Cooperation Fund** Fonds *m* européen de coopération monétaire

◇ **European Monetary Institute** Institut *m* monétaire européen

◇ **European Monetary System** système *m* monétaire européen

◇ **European Social Fund** Fonds *m* social européen

European-style option *n* *St Exch* option *f* européenne

eurosterling *n* eurosterling *m*

Euro Stoxx *n* *St Exch* Euro Stoxx *m*; **the Euro Stoxx 50 (index)** l'Euro Stoxx 50

euroyen *n* euroyen *m*

EVA *n* (*abbr* **economic value added**) VAE *f*

evade *vt* **to evade tax** frauder le fisc

evergreen *adj*

◇ **evergreen facility** possibilité *f* de crédit permanent

◇ **evergreen fund** fonds *m* de crédit permanent non confirmé

ex *prep* (*without*) **ex all, ex allotment** ex-répartition *f*; **ex bonus** ex-capitalisation *f*; **ex cap, ex capitalisation** ex-capitalisation *f*; **ex coupon** ex-coupon *m*, coupon *m* détaché; **this stock goes ex coupon on 1 August** le coupon de cette action se détache le 1 août; **ex dividend** ex-dividende *m*, dividende *m* détaché, coupon *m* échu; **ex new, ex rights** ex-droit *m*; **ex scrip** ex-répartition *f*

exceptional item n Acct poste m extraordinaire

excess n excédent m; **there has been an excess of expenditure over revenue** les dépenses ont excédé les recettes

◇ **excess profits** surplus m des bénéfices; (unexpected) bénéfices mpl exceptionnels, bénéfices mpl extraordinaires

◇ Banking **excess reserves** réserves fpl excédentaires

exchange 1 n (a) (of currency) change m
(b) (of goods, shares, commodities) échange m
(c) Am **exchanges** (bills) lettres fpl de change, traites fpl
2 vt (goods, shares, commodities) échanger

◇ **exchange broker** agent m ou courtier m de change, cambiste mf

◇ **exchange control** contrôle m des changes

◇ **exchange cross rate** taux m de change entre devises tierces

◇ **exchange dealer** agent m de change, cambiste mf

◇ **exchange equalization account** fonds m de stabilisation des changes

◇ **exchange index** indice m boursier

◇ **exchange loss** perte f de change

◇ **exchange market** marché m des changes

◇ **exchange offer** offre f publique d'échange

◇ **exchange premium** prime f de change

◇ **exchange rate** cours m de change, taux m de change; **at the current exchange rate** au cours du jour

◇ EU **Exchange Rate Mechanism** mécanisme m de change

◇ **exchange rate parity** parité f du change

◇ **exchange reserves** réserves fpl en devises (étrangères)

◇ **exchange restrictions** contrôle m des changes

◇ **exchange transaction** opération f de change

◇ **exchange value** valeur f d'échange

exchequer n Br Admin **the Exchequer** (money) le Trésor public; (government department) ≃ le Ministère des Finances

◇ **exchequer bill** bon m du Trésor

execute vt (transfer) effectuer

exempt 1 adj exempté(e), dispensé(e) (**from** de); **exempt from taxes** exonéré(e) d'impôt, exempt(e) d'impôt
2 vt exempter, dispenser (**from** de); (from taxes) exonérer, exempter (**from** de)

exemption n exemption f, dispense f; (from tax) exonération f, exemption f

exercise St Exch 1 n (of option) levée f
2 vt **to exercise an option** lever une prime

◇ **exercise date** date f d'échéance

◇ **exercise notion** assignation f

◇ **exercise price** cours m de base, prix m d'exercice

ex gratia adj (payment) à titre de faveur

exit charge(s) *n(pl)* frais *mpl* de sortie

> However, fund managers must make money somewhere. Annual fees range from 0.5% to 1.5% a year, and you will pay other charges, such as legal or audit costs, on top of that … Groups that have abolished the initial charge will usually impose an **exit charge** which is in force long enough to ensure they can turn a profit from a customer – usually five years.

expected *adj* attendu(e)
◇ *expected monetary value* valeur *f* monétaire escomptée
◇ *expected value* valeur *f* attendue

expenditure *n* (a) *(spending)* dépense *f* (b) *(amount spent)* dépenses *fpl*; **it entails heavy expenditure** cela entraîne de fortes dépenses

expense *n* (a) *(cost)* dépense *f*, frais *mpl*; **at great expense** à grands frais

(b) **expenses** frais *mpl*; **to meet / cover sb's expenses** rembourser/couvrir les frais de qn; **to put sth on expenses** mettre qch sur la note de frais; **it's on expenses** c'est la société qui paie, ça va sur la note de frais; **to cut down on expenses** réduire les frais; **to have all expenses paid** être défrayé de tout

◇ *expense account* note *f* de frais; **to put sth on the expense account** mettre qch sur la note de frais

◇ *expense budget* budget *m* des dépenses
◇ *expenses claim form* note *f* de frais

expiration *n* échéance *f*

expire *vi* expirer

expiry *n* échéance *f*
◇ *expiry date* date *f* d'échéance

extension *n Acct (of balance)* transport *m*, report *m*

external *adj (trade, debt)* extérieur(e)
◇ *external account* compte *m* étranger, *Can* compte *m* de non-résident
◇ *external auditing* audit *m ou* vérification *f* externe
◇ *external auditor* auditeur (trice) *m,f ou* vérificateur (trice) *m,f* externe
◇ *external deficit* déficit *m* extérieur
◇ *external financing* fonds *mpl* extérieurs

extraordinary *adj* extraordinaire
◇ *Acct extraordinary expenses* frais *mpl or* dépenses *fpl* extraordinaies
◇ *extraordinary general meeting* assemblée *f* générale extraordinaire; **to call an extraordinary general meeting of the shareholders** convoquer d'urgence les actionnaires
◇ *extraordinary income* produits *mpl* exceptionnels
◇ *extraordinary item* poste *m* extraordinaire
◇ *extraordinary profit or loss* résultat *m* exceptionnel

extrinsic value *n* valeur *f* extrinsèque

face value, *Am* **face amount**
n (of banknote, traveller's cheque)
valeur *f* nominale; *(d'une action)*
valeur faciale

factor *n (factoring company)* société *f* d'affacturage

factorage *n (charge)* commission *f* d'affacturage

factoring *n* affacturage *m*, factoring *m*
◇ **factoring agent** agent *m* d'affacturage
◇ **factoring charges** commission *f* d'affacturage
◇ **factoring company** société *f*
d'affacturage

"

The more we expanded, the
worse our cashflow got till, in
the end, our very success
threatened us with bankruptcy.
The simple answer is **factoring**.
We get paid up front, we've got
credit protection, and we save a
huge amount of work chasing
payments.

"
---

failure investment *n* investissement *m* en valeurs de redressement *ou* de retournement

fair market value *n* valeur *f*
vénale

fallen angel *n St Exch* ange *m*
déchu

false *adj*
◇ **false bill** fausse facture *f*
◇ **false entry** fausse écriture *f*

fat cat *n Fam (in industry)* =
personne touchant un salaire
extrêmement élevé de façon
injustifiée

Fed *n Am* (**a**) *(abbr Federal*
Reserve Board) banque *f* centrale (des États-Unis)
(**b**) *(abbr Federal Reserve (Sys-*
tem)) (système *m* de) Réserve *f*
fédérale
◇ **Fed funds** fonds *mpl* fédéraux

"

City economists said yesterday
that the American decision to
cut the **Fed funds** rate by $\frac{1}{4}$
point to 33/4 p.c. may have
been taken with the international as well as the domestic situation in mind.

"
---

federal *adj Am*
◇ **Federal Debt** dette *f* publique
ou de l'État
◇ **Federal funds** fonds *mpl* fédé-
raux
◇ **Federal Reserve Bank** banque
f membre de la Réserve fédérale
◇ **Federal Reserve Board** conseil

m d'administration des banques centrales américaines

◇ *Federal Reserve (System)* (système *m* de) Réserve *f* fédérale

◇ *Federal Trade Commission* = commission fédérale chargée de veiller au respect de la concurrence sur le marché

> ❝
>
> Wall Street soared yesterday after the **Federal Reserve Board**, the nation's central bank, lowered short-term interest rates to prevent the economic recovery from stalling.
>
> ❞

fiat money *n Am* monnaie *f* fiduciaire

> ❝
>
> In most of the models of temporary equilibrium the only financial asset which is explicitly modelled is the stock of **fiat money** – effectively notes and coins in circulation. Other financial assets – bonds, equities, inside money – scarcely feature at all.
>
> ❞

fictitious *adj*

◇ *fictitious assets* actif *m* fictif

◇ *fictitious cost* charge *f* fictive

◇ *fictitious person* personne *f* fictive

fiduciary 1 *n (trustee)* dépositaire *mf*

  2 *adj* fiduciaire

◇ *fiduciary account* compte *m* fiduciaire

◇ *fiduciary issue* émission *f* fiduciaire

FIFO *Acct (abbr* **first in, first out**) PEPS

figure *n* chiffre *m*; **to find a mistake in the figures** trouver une erreur de calcul

file *vt* **to file one's petition in bankruptcy, to file for bankruptcy** déposer son bilan; *Am* **to file one's tax return** remplir sa déclaration d'impôts

▸ **fill in** *vt sep (cheque stub, form)* remplir

▸ **fill out** *vt sep (cheque stub, form)* remplir

final *adj* dernier(ère)

◇ *final accounts* compte *m* définitif

◇ *final date (for payment)* date *f* limite

◇ *final demand (for payment of bill)* dernier rappel *m*

◇ *St Exch* **final dividend** dividende *m* définitif *ou* final

◇ *final instalment* dernier versement *m*, versement libératoire

◇ *final offer* dernier prix *m*

◇ *final settlement* solde *m* de tout compte

finance 1 *n* (a) *(money, field)* finance *f*; **we don't have the necessary finance** nous n'avons pas les fonds nécessaires

  (b) **finances** *(funds)* finances *fpl*; **the company's finances are a bit low just now** les finances de l'entreprise sont un peu basses en ce moment

  2 *vt (project)* financer; *(person, company)* financer, commanditer; **to finance staff training** financer la formation du personnel

◇ *Finance Act* loi *f* de Finances

◇ *finance charges* frais *mpl* financiers

◇ *finance company* société *f* financière

◇ *finance costs* frais *mpl* financiers *ou* de trésorerie

◇ *finance department* direction *f* financière

◇ *Br finance house* société *f* financière

◇ *Finance Minister* ministre *m* de l'Économie et des Finances

financial *adj* financier(ère)

◇ *Acct financial accountant* comptable *mf* financier(ère)

◇ *Acct financial accounting* comptabilité *f* générale *ou* financière

◇ *financial administration* gestion *f* financière

◇ *financial adviser* conseiller (ère) *m,f* financier(ère)

◇ *financial aid* aide *f* financière

◇ *financial analyst* analyste *mf* financier(ère)

◇ *financial appraisal* évaluation *f* financière

◇ *financial assistance* appui *m* financier, aide *f* financière

◇ *financial backer* bailleur (eresse) *m,f* de fonds

◇ *financial backing* financement *m*, aide *f* financière

◇ *financial centre* place *f* financière

◇ *financial consultant* conseiller(ère) *m,f* financier(ère), conseil *m* financier

◇ *financial control* contrôle *m* financier

◇ *financial controller* contrôleur *m* financier

◇ *financial costs* frais *mpl* financiers

◇ *financial deal* opération *f* financière

◇ *financial director* directeur (trice) *m,f* financier(ère)

◇ *financial expenses* charges *fpl* financières

◇ *St Exch financial future* instrument *m* financier à terme

◇ *St Exch financial futures exchange* Bourse *f* d'instruments financiers à terme

◇ *St Exch financial futures market* marché *m* à terme d'instruments financiers

◇ *financial gearing* effet *m* de levier financier

◇ *financial healthcheck* diagnostic *m* financier

◇ *financial institution* établissement *m* financier

◇ *financial instrument* instrument *m* financier

◇ *financial intermediary* intermédiaire *mf* financier(ère)

◇ *financial management* direction *f ou* gestion *f* financière

◇ *financial manager* directeur (trice) *m,f* financier(ère)

◇ *St Exch financial market* marché *m* financier

◇ *financial ombudsman* arbitre *m* financier

◇ *financial partner* partenaire *m,f* financier(ère)

◇ *financial period* période *f* comptable

◇ *financial plan* plan *m* de financement

◇ *financial planning* planification *f* financière

◇ *financial position* position *f ou* situation *f* financière

◇ *financial pressure* problèmes *mpl* financiers

◇ *financial product* produit *m* financier

◇ *Acct financial ratio* ratio *m* de gestion

◇ *Acct financial report* rapport *m* financier

◇ *Acct* **financial reporting** communication *f* de l'information financière

◇ *Br* **Financial Reporting Council** = commission de contrôle de la qualité de l'information financière publiée par les entreprises

◇ **financial resources** ressources *fpl*

◇ **financial services** services *mpl* financiers

◇ **Financial Services Authority** = organisme gouvernemental britannique chargé de contrôler les activités du secteur financier

◇ **financial situation** situation *f* financière

◇ *Acct* **financial statement** état *m* financier, déclaration *f* de résultats

◇ **financial syndicate** syndicat *m* financier

◇ *Br St Exch* **Financial Times All-Share Index** = indice boursier du *Financial Times* basé sur la valeur de 700 actions cotées à la Bourse de Londres

◇ *Br St Exch* **Financial Times (Industrial) Ordinary Share Index** = indice boursier du *Financial Times* basé sur la valeur de 30 actions cotées à la Bourse de Londres

◇ *Br St Exch* **Financial Times-Stock Exchange 100 Share Index** = principal indice boursier du *Financial Times* basé sur la valeur de 100 actions cotées à la Bourse de Londres

◇ **financial transaction** opération *f* financière

◇ *Br* **financial year** exercice *m* (comptable *ou* financier), année *f* d'exercice

financially *adv* financièrement; **financially sound** solvable

financier *n* financier *m*

financing *n* financement *m*

◇ **financing terms** modalités *fpl* de financement

fine *adj*

◇ **fine bill** beau papier *m*

◇ **fine trade bill** papier *m* de haut commerce *ou* de première catégorie

finish *n St Exch* **price at the finish** prix *m* de clôture; **trading at the finish** opérations *fpl* de clôture; **shares were up at the finish** les actions étaient en hausse à la clôture

firm *adj* (market, offer, sale, deal) ferme; (contango rates) tendu(e); **oil shares remain firm at $20** les valeurs pétrolières se maintiennent à 20 dollars

◇ **firm currency** devise *f* soutenue

first *adj Acct* **first in, first out** premier entré, premier sorti

◇ *Banking* **first of exchange** première *f* de change

◇ **first quarter** (of financial year) premier trimestre *m*

first-class paper *n* effet *m* de première catégorie

first-notice day *n St Exch* premier jour *m* de notification

first-time buyer *n* (of property) = personne achetant un logement pour la première fois

fiscal *adj* fiscal(e)

◇ **fiscal agent** représentant(e) *m,f* fiscal(e)

◇ **fiscal policy** politique *f* budgétaire

◇ *Am* **fiscal year** exercice *m* (financier), année *f* fiscale *ou* d'exercice

fixed *adj (price, rate)* fixe
⋄ *Acct* **fixed asset** actif *m* immobilisé
⋄ *Acct* **fixed assets** immobilisations *fpl*, actif *m* immobilisé
⋄ **fixed capital** capital *m* fixe
⋄ **fixed charge** frais *mpl* fixes
⋄ **fixed cost** coût *m* fixe *ou* constant, charge *f* fixe
⋄ **fixed deposit** dépôt *m* à terme (fixe) *ou* à échéance fixe
⋄ **fixed exchange rate** taux *m* de change fixe
⋄ **fixed income** revenu *m* fixe
⋄ *Banking* **fixed interest** intérêt *m* fixe
⋄ **fixed investment** immobilisations *fpl*
⋄ **fixed maturity** échéance *f* fixe
⋄ **fixed parity** parité *f* fixe
⋄ *Banking, Econ* **fixed rate** taux *m* fixe
⋄ **fixed salary, fixed wage** salaire *m* fixe
⋄ **fixed yield** rendement *m* constant

fixed-income *adj*
⋄ **fixed-income investment** placement *m* à revenu fixe
⋄ **fixed-income securities** valeurs *fpl* à revenu fixe

fixed-interest *adj (investments)* à intérêt fixe
⋄ **fixed-interest market** marché *m* des obligations
⋄ **fixed-interest securities** valeurs *fpl* à intérêt fixe

fixed-rate *adj (loan, mortgage)* à taux fixe ; *(investment)* à revenu fixe
⋄ **fixed-rate assessment system** régime *m* du forfait

⋄ **fixed-rate bond** obligation *f* à taux *ou* à revenu fixe
⋄ **fixed-rate borrowing** emprunts *mpl* à taux fixe
⋄ **fixed-rate securities** titres *mpl* à revenu fixe

fixed-term *adj* à date fixe
⋄ **fixed-term bill** effet *m* à date fixe
⋄ **fixed-term deposit** dépôt *m* à terme fixe *ou* à échéance fixe

fixing *n St Exch* fixage *m*

fixture *n* installation *f* fixe
⋄ **fixtures and fittings** reprise *f* ; '**fixtures and fittings £2,000**' 'reprise 2 000 livres'

flexible budget *n Acct* budget *m* variable, budget flexible

flight *n* flight of capital évasion *f* des capitaux
⋄ **flight capital** capitaux *mpl* flottants *ou* fébriles

float 1 *n St Exch* flottant *m*
2 *vt* (**a**) *St Exch (company)* introduire en Bourse ; *(loan, bonds, share issue)* émettre, lancer (**b**) *(currency)* laisser flotter
3 *vi (currency)* flotter

floatation = flotation

floater *n* effet *m* à taux flottant

floating 1 *n* (**a**) *St Exch (of company)* introduction *f* en Bourse ; *(of loan, bonds, share issue)* émission *f*, lancement *m* (**b**) *(of currency)* flottement *m*
2 *adj (currency, exchange rate)* flottant(e)
⋄ *Acct* **floating assets** actif *m* circulant
⋄ *Acct* **floating capital** capital *m* circulant
⋄ *Banking* **floating charge** nantissement *m* général

◇ Econ **floating currency** monnaie f flottante

◇ **floating debt** dette f flottante ou non consolidée

◇ Econ **floating exchange rate** taux m de change flottant

◇ **floating rate** taux m flottant

floating-rate adj à taux flottant

◇ St Exch **floating-rate bond** obligation f à taux flottant ou variable

◇ Banking **floating-rate certificate of deposit** certificat m de dépôt à taux flottant

◇ **floating-rate interest** intérêt m à taux flottant

◇ **floating-rate investment** investissement m à taux flottant ou variable

◇ **floating-rate note** effet m à taux flottant

◇ St Exch **floating-rate securities** titres mpl à taux flottant ou variable

floor n (of Stock Exchange) parquet m; **trading on the floor was quiet today** la journée n'a pas été très animée à la Bourse

◇ **floor price** prix m seuil

◇ **floor trader** commis m

◇ **floor trading** cotation f à la corbeille

"

Floor price funds quote three prices … and a **floor price** (a price below which the bid price cannot fall). This **floor price** is adjusted annually, or after any significant market movement, to give a new **floor price** which is valid for a year. So no matter what happens to the market, the value of your units will not fall below the **floor price**.

"

flotation n (**a**) St Exch (of company) introduction f en Bourse, lancement m; (of loan, bonds, share issue) émission f, lancement m (**b**) (of currency) flottement m

flow 1 n (of capital) mouvement m; (of information) circulation f; **flow of funds** mouvement m de fonds; **flow of money** flux m monétaire

2 vi (of capital, money) circuler

◇ Acct **flow sheet** feuille f d'avancement

flow-through method n Am Acct méthode f de l'impôt exigible

fluctuate vi (of exchange rate, share prices) fluctuer

fluctuation n (of currency) fluctuation f

◇ **fluctuation band, fluctuation margin** marge f de fluctuation

flutter n Br Fam St Exch **to have a flutter on the stock market** boursicoter

folio n Acct (sheet) folio m, feuillet m; (book) (livre m) in-folio m

FOOTSIE, Footsie n St Exch (abbr **Financial Times-Stock Exchange 100 Index**) = principal indice boursier du Financial Times basé sur la valeur de 100 actions cotées à la Bourse de Londres

forced adj

◇ **forced currency** cours m forcé

◇ **forced loan** emprunt m forcé

forecast balance sheet n Acct bilan m prévisionnel

foreign adj étranger(ère)

◊ *foreign account* compte *m* étranger

◊ *foreign bill* effet *m* ou traite *f* sur l'extérieur

◊ *foreign currency* devises *fpl* étrangères

◊ *foreign currency account* compte *m* en devises étrangères

◊ *foreign currency assets* avoirs *mpl* en devises étrangères

◊ *foreign currency loan* prêt *m* en devises étrangères

◊ *foreign currency option* option *f* de change

◊ *foreign currency reserves* réserves *fpl* de change, réserves en devises

◊ *foreign debt* dette *f* extérieure

◊ *foreign exchange* devises *fpl* étrangères

◊ *foreign exchange broker, foreign exchange dealer* cambiste *mf*, courtier(ère) *m,f* en devises

◊ *foreign exchange market* marché *m* des changes

◊ *foreign exchange option* option *f* sur devises

◊ *foreign exchange rate* cours *m* des devises

◊ *foreign exchange reserves* réserves *fpl* de change, réserves en devises

◊ *foreign exchange transfer* transfert *m* de devises

◊ *foreign investments* investissements *mpl* à l'étranger

◊ *foreign market* marché *m* extérieur

> It is important for the reader to realise that no physical **foreign exchange market** exists. Instead it consists of telephones, telexes, visual display units and other electronic gadgetry which link together the **foreign exchange** departments of banks in London and overseas. Modern communications have created a truly worldwide market for major currencies.

forex *n* (*abbr* **foreign currency**) devises *fpl* étrangères

◊ *forex trading* transactions *fpl* en devises étrangères

> On the world's adrenaline-charged foreign exchange markets, \$1.5 trilllion changes hands every day. To set that figure in context, the global trade in merchandise and commercial services last year was \$6.5 trillion — or 4.3 days of **forex trading**.

forfaiting *n Banking* forfaitage *m*, forfaitisation *f*

forfeit **1** *n St Exch* **to relinquish the forfeit** abandonner la prime **2** *vt* **to forfeit a deposit** perdre les arrhes

forfeiture *n St Exch* (*of shares*) déchéance *f*, forfaiture *f*

forge *vt* (*banknotes*) contrefaire

forged *adj* (*banknote*) faux (fausse)

forgery *n* (**a**) (*banknote*) contrefaçon (**b**) *Acct* faux *m* en écritures

forward **1** *adj St Exch* à terme **2** *adv Acct* **to carry the balance forward** reporter le solde à nouveau; **(carried) forward** report *m*

◇ *St Exch* **forward account** compte *m* à terme

◇ *St Exch* **forward buying** achat *m* à terme

◇ *St Exch* **forward contract** contrat *m* à terme

◇ *St Exch* **forward dealing** opérations *fpl* à terme

◇ *St Exch* **forward delivery** livraison *f* à terme

◇ *St Exch* **forward exchange market** marché *m* des changes à terme

◇ *St Exch* **forward exchange transaction** opération *f* de change à terme

◇ *St Exch* **forward market** marché *m* à terme

◇ *St Exch* **forward price** prix *m* à terme

◇ *St Exch* **forward purchase** achat *m* à terme

◇ *St Exch* **forward rate** cours *m* à terme, taux *m* pour les opérations à terme

◇ *St Exch* **Forward Rate Agreement** accord *m* de taux à terme

◇ *St Exch* **Forward sale** vente *f* à terme

◇ *St Exch* **forward trading** opérations *fpl* à terme

fourth quarter *n (of financial year)* quatrième trimestre *m*

Fr *(abbr* franc*)* F

FRA *n (abbr* Future Rate Agreement, Forward Rate Agreement*)* ATF *m*

fraction *n (of share)* fraction *f*

fractional money *n* monnaie *f* divisionnaire, monnaie d'appoint

franc *n* franc *m*

◇ **franc area** zone *f* franc

fraudulent *adj* frauduleux (euse)

◇ *Acct* **fraudulent balance sheet** faux bilan *m*

◇ **fraudulent bankruptcy** faillite *f* frauduleuse

◇ **fraudulent trading** commerce *m* frauduleux

◇ **fraudulent transaction** transaction *f* frauduleuse

FRB *n (abbr* Federal Reserve Board*)* conseil *m* d'administration des banques centrales américaines

FRCD *n Banking (abbr* floating-rate certificate of deposit*)* certificat *m* de dépôt à taux flottant

free *adj*

◇ *St Exch* **free float** actions *fpl* disponibles (au marché)

◇ *St Exch* **free issue** attribution *f* d'actions gratuites

◇ *Econ* **free market** marché *m* libre

◇ **free movement of capital** libre circulation *f* des capitaux

◇ *Econ* **free trade** libre-échange *m*

> **❝**
>
> FTSE International said weightings for individual stocks would be restricted where the **free float** of shares was less than 75 per cent. … Companies with a **free float** of 15 per cent or less will be ineligible for inclusion in FTSE indexes. Companies with 15–25 per cent will have a 25 per cent weighting, 25–50 per cent a 50 per cent weighting and 50–75 per cent a 75 per cent weighting. … Any company with **free float** exceeding 75% will gain a 100 per cent weighting.
>
> **❞**

free-flowing adj (capital) flottant(e)

freeze 1 n (of credit, wages) blocage m, gel m; (of currency, prices, assets) gel
  2 vt (credit, wages) geler, bloquer; (currency, prices, assets) geler

freezing n (of credit, wages) blocage m, gel m; (of currency, prices, assets) gel

French franc n franc m français

friendly adj
◇ Br **friendly society** société f de mutualité
◇ **friendly takeover bid** OPA f amicale

FRN n Banking (abbr **floating-rate note**) effet m à taux flottant

front n Fam **to pay up front** payer d'avance; **they want £5,000 up front** ils veulent 5 000 livres d'avance
◇ Banking **front office** front-office m

front-end adj
◇ **front-end fee** frais mpl d'entrée
◇ **front-end loading** = système de prélèvement des frais sur les premiers versements

> **"**
> The charges for buying into a trust are usually at the standard rate. Dunedin, however, has no **front-end fee** for its share plan other than stamp duty.
> **"**

frozen adj (credit, wages) gelé(e), bloqué(e); (currency, prices, assets) gelé

◇ **frozen account** compte m bloqué
◇ **frozen assets** capitaux mpl gelés

FSA n (abbr **Financial Services Authority**) = organisme gouvernemental britannique chargé de contrôler les activités du secteur financier

FT index n Br St Exch (a) (abbr **Financial Times-(Industrial) Ordinary Share Index**) = indice boursier du Financial Times basé sur la valeur de 30 actions cotées à la Bourse de Londres (b) (abbr **Financial Times-Stock Exchange 100 Index**) = principal indice boursier du Financial Times basé sur la valeur de 100 actions cotées à la Bourse de Londres

FT-SE index n Br St Exch (abbr **Financial Times-Stock Exchange 100 Index**) = principal indice boursier du Financial Times basé sur la valeur de 100 actions cotées à la Bourse de Londres

full 1 n **to pay in full** payer intégralement; **we paid the bill in full** nous avons payé la facture dans son intégralité; **they refunded my money in full** ils m'ont entièrement remboursé
  2 adj
◇ Acct **full consolidation** intégration f globale
◇ Acct **full cost accounting (method)** méthode f de capitalisation du coût entier
◇ **full costing** méthode f du coût complet
◇ **full discharge** quitus m
◇ **full payment** paiement m intégral

fully-paid capital n capital m entièrement versé

fund 1 n (**a**) (reserve of money) fonds m, caisse f; **fund of funds** fonds de fonds

(**b**) **funds** (cash resources) fonds mpl; (of government) fonds publics; **to be short of** or **low on funds** être à court d'argent; Br **the Funds** les bons mpl du Trésor; **to make a call for funds** faire un appel de fonds

2 vt (project) financer; (company) pourvoir de fonds; (public debt) consolider; **to fund money** placer de l'argent dans les fonds publics

◇ **fund management** gestion f de fonds

◇ **fund manager** gestionnaire mf de fonds

◇ **funds flow statement** tableau m des emplois et ressources

funded adj (assets) en rentes

◇ **funded capital** capitaux mpl investis

◇ **funded debt** dette f consolidée

◇ **funded pension scheme** régime m de retraite par capitalisation

fundholder n rentier(ère) m,f

funding n (of project) financement m; (of debt) consolidation f; (of income) assiette f; **BP will put up half of the funding** BP financera le projet à 50%

◇ **funding loan** emprunt m de consolidation

◇ **funding operation** opération f de financement

◇ **funding plan** plan m de financement

fungible St Exch **1** n **fungibles**

fongibles mpl

2 adj fongible

◇ **fungible securities** titres mpl en suspens

future adj St Exch (delivery) à terme

◇ **Future Rate Agreement** accord m de taux à terme

◇ **future value** valeur f capitalisée

futures npl St Exch (financial instruments, contracts) contrats mpl à terme; (transactions) opérations fpl à terme; (securities) titres mpl ou valeurs fpl à terme

◇ **futures contract** contrat m à terme

◇ **futures exchange** marché m à terme

◇ **futures market** marché m à terme

◇ **futures option** option f sur contrats à terme

◇ **futures and options** contrats mpl à terme et options

◇ **futures and options fund** fonds m investissant dans des contrats à terme et des options

◇ **futures order** ordre m à terme

◇ **futures trading** négociations fpl à terme

◇ **futures transaction** opération f à terme

FX n (abbr **foreign exchange**) devises fpl étrangères

◇ **FX broker, FX dealer** cambiste mf, courtier(ère) m,f en devises

◇ **FX market** marché m des changes

◇ **FX option** option f sur devises

◇ **FX transfer** transfert m de devises

GAAP *npl Acct* (*abbr* **generally-accepted accounting principles**) PCGR *mpl*

gain 1 *n* (*increase*) accroissement *m*, augmentation *f*; **gain in value** plus-value *f*; **there has been a net gain in profits this year** il y a eu une augmentation nette des bénéfices cette année; **there has been a gain of 100 points on the Dow Jones** l'indice Dow Jones a gagné 100 points

2 *vt* gagner, bénéficier de; **the share index has gained two points** l'indice des actions a gagné deux points

gamble *vi* **to gamble on the Stock Exchange** boursicoter, jouer à la Bourse

GATT *n* (*abbr* **General Agreement on Tariffs and Trade**) Agétac *m*

gazump *vt* = revenir sur une promesse de vente de maison pour accepter l'offre plus élevée d'une tierce personne

gear *vt* (*link*) indexer; **salaries are geared to the cost of living** les salaires sont indexés au coût de la vie

gearing *n* (*leverage*) effet *m* de levier; (*as percentage*) ratio *m* d'endettement

◇ **gearing adjustment** redressement *m* financier

GEMM *n* (*abbr* **gilt-edged market maker**) teneur *m* de marché de premier ordre

general *adj*
◇ *Acct* **general accounts** comptabilité *f* générale
◇ *Banking* **general account manager** chargé(e) *m,f* de clientèle grand public
◇ **general and administrative expenses** frais *mpl* généraux et frais de gestion
◇ *Econ* **General Agreement on Tariffs and Trade** Accord *m* Général sur les Tarifs Douaniers et le Commerce
◇ **general expenses** frais *mpl* généraux
◇ *Acct* **general ledger** grand livre *m*
◇ *Am St Exch* **general obligation bond** emprunt *m* de collectivité locale
◇ *Br* **general overheads,** *Am*

general overhead frais *mpl* d'administration générale

gift *n*
◊ *gift inter vivos* donation *f* inter vivos
◊ *gift tax* impôt *m* sur les donations

gifts tax *n* impôt *m* sur les donations

gilt *n St Exch* fonds *m* d'État, valeur *f* de premier ordre *ou* de père de famille
◊ *gilts market* marché *m* des valeurs de premier ordre
◊ *gilt switching* rotation *f* de portefeuille-obligation

gilt-edged *adj St Exch*
◊ *Am gilt-edged bond* valeur *f* du Trésor américain
◊ *gilt-edged market* marché *m* des valeurs de premier ordre
◊ *gilt-edged market maker* teneur *m* de marché des valeurs de premier ordre
◊ *gilt-edged securities, gilt-edged stock* valeurs *fpl* de premier ordre *ou* de père de famille

"

The Chancellor is expected to modify the Government's policy of buying in enough long-dated **gilt-edged stock** in a single fiscal year to offset the financial drain on the economy created by the budget surplus and foreign exchange intervention to support the pound – the so-called full funding rule.

"

giro *n Br (system)* = système de virement interbancaire introduit par la Poste britannique

◊ *giro account* compte *m* chèque postal, CCP *m*
◊ *giro cheque* chèque *m* de virement
◊ *giro transfer* transfert *m* par CCP

Girobank *n Br* service *m* de chèques postaux

glamour stock *n St Exch* valeur *f* vedette

global *adj (worldwide)* mondial(e); *(comprehensive)* global(e)
◊ *Banking global banking* banque *f* universelle
◊ *global bond* obligation *f* multimarchés
◊ *St Exch global equities market* marché *m* mondial des actions
◊ *global finance* financement *m* aux entreprises
◊ *global market* marché *m* global *ou* international

glut 1 *n (on market)* encombrement *m*; *(of commodity)* surabondance *f*; **glut of money** pléthore *f* de capitaux
2 *vt (market, economy)* encombrer, inonder

gnome *n Fam* **the gnomes of Zurich** les grands banquiers *mpl* suisses

go-go stock *n St Exch* action *f* hautement spéculative

"

In a distinctly lack-lustre sector, Iceland, bizarrely, has gained a reputation as something of a **go-go stock**. And the share price has tripled. In the world of food retailing, Iceland is hot.

"

going concern n affaire f qui marche ; **for sale as a going concern** à vendre avec fonds

going-concern adj Acct

◇ **going-concern concept, going-concern convention** principe m de la continuité de l'exploitation

◇ **going-concern status** continuité f d'exploitation

gold n or m

◇ **gold bond** obligation f or

◇ **gold bullion** encaisse f or

◇ **gold bullion standard** étalon m or-lingot

◇ **gold card** carte f de crédit illimitée

◇ **gold currency** monnaie f d'or

◇ Econ **gold exchange standard** étalon m de change-or

◇ **gold ingot** lingot m d'or

◇ **gold market** marché m de l'or

◇ **gold reserves** réserve f d'or

◇ **gold share** valeur f aurifère

◇ Econ **gold standard** étalon-or m

good-till-cancelled order n ordre m à révocation

goodwill n fonds m de commerce, biens mpl incorporels

> **❝**
>
> Much of the concern is levelled at agency balance sheets which have been weakened by the sector's lust for acquisitions. Quoted advertising agencies wrote off **goodwill** totalling £1.7bn in the year to November 1988, leaving aggregate shareholders' funds in the sector below £39m.
>
> **❞**

government n gouvernement m

◇ **government auditor** commissaire m aux comptes

◇ **government bonds** obligations fpl d'État

◇ **government borrowings** emprunts mpl de l'État

◇ Br **government broker** agent m du Trésor

◇ **government developmental grant, government developmental subsidy** prime f de développement

◇ **government loan** emprunt m public ou d'État

◇ **government securities, government stock** effets mpl publics, fonds mpl publics ou d'État

grace period n délai m de grâce

graduated adj (tax) progressif (ive)

graduated-payment mortgage n Am hypothèque f à paiements échelonnés

granny bond n Br Fam = type d'obligation visant le marché des retraités

grant 1 n (financial aid) subvention f, allocation f

2 vt (subsidy, loan, overdraft) accorder ; **to grant a loan to sb** accorder un prêt à qn

grantor n concédant m

gray adj Am = grey

green adj

◇ EU **green currency** monnaie f verte

◇ EU **green pound** livre f verte

◇ Econ **green rate** taux m vert

◇ **green taxation** fiscalité f écologique

greenback n Am Fam billet m vert

greenmail n greenmail m

grey, Am **gray** adj St Exch
◇ **grey knight** chevalier m gris
◇ **grey market** marché m gris

gross adj (price, profit, interest, salary, value) brut(e)
◇ **gross amount** montant m brut
◇ **gross assets** actif m brut
◇ **gross dividend** dividende m brut
◇ **gross income** (in accounts) produit m brut; (of individual) revenu m brut
◇ **gross margin** marge f brute
◇ Econ **gross national income** revenu m national brut
◇ **gross profit** bénéfice m brut
◇ **gross profit margin** marge f commerciale brute
◇ **gross receipts** recettes fpl brutes
◇ **gross redemption yield** rendement m actuarial brut
◇ **gross return, gross yield** rendement m brut

grossed-up dividend n dividende m majoré

group n (of people, companies) groupe m; **the Shell Group** le Groupe Shell
◇ **group turnover** chiffre m d'affaires consolidé ou du groupe

growing-equity mortgage n Am hypothèque f à capital croissant

growth n croissance f
◇ Econ **growth rate** taux m de croissance
◇ St Exch **growth shares, growth stock** actions fpl d'avenir ou de croissance

guarantee 1 n (a) (security) garantie f, caution f, cautionnement m; **to secure all guarantees** s'assurer toutes les garanties nécessaires
(b) (person) garant(e) m,f, caution f; **to act as guarantee (for sb)** se porter garant (de qn)
2 vt (loan, cheque, debt) garantir, cautionner
◇ **guarantee company** société f de sécurité
◇ **guarantee fund** fonds m de garantie

guaranteed adj (bond, stocks) garanti(e)
◇ **guaranteed bill** traite f avalisée
◇ **guaranteed loan** prêt m garanti

guarantor n garant(e) m,f; **to stand as guarantor for sb** se porter garant de qn

guilder n florin m

haircut *n Fam St Exch* marge *f* de sécurité

hammered *adj St Exch (stockbroker)* déclaré(e) insolvable

Hang Seng index *n St Exch* indice *m* Hang Seng, indice Hong Kong

hard *adj (stock, rates)* soutenu(e), ferme
◇ **hard commodities** minerais *mpl*
◇ **hard currency** devise *f ou* monnaie *f* forte
◇ **hard loan** prêt *m* aux conditions du marché

hedge 1 *vt (shares)* arbitrer; *(transactions)* couvrir
2 *vi* se couvrir; **to hedge against currency fluctuations** se couvrir contre les fluctuations monétaires
◇ *St Exch* **hedge fund** société *f* d'investissement

hedger *n St Exch* opérateur (trice) *m,f* en couverture

hedging *n St Exch* opérations *fpl* de couverture

hidden *adj (cost)* caché
◇ **hidden extras** dépenses *fpl* supplémentaires inattendues
◇ **hidden tax** impôt *m* déguisé

high 1 *n (peak)* haut *m*, sommet *m*; **the Stock Market reached a new high** la Bourse a atteint un nouveau record *ou* maximum; *St Exch* **the highs and lows** les hauts et les bas
2 *adj (cost, price, interest rate)* élevé(e); *(salary)* élevé, gros (grosse); **to fetch a high price** se vendre cher

highly-geared *adj* à ratio d'endettement élevé

> An aura of mystique surrounds **hedge funds**, based on a general perception that they offer rather exclusive investment opportunities run by financial whizz kids who invest their own money in the fund and who have the skill and expertise to exploit investment opportunities to produce absolute returns.

> The attractions of ordinary shares can often depend upon the economic environment and the company's potential for growth. In periods of rising profits a company which is geared at a low level may not have the growth potential to give ordinary shareholders the returns expected from a more **highly-geared** company.

high-street bank n Br the **high-street banks** les grandes banques fpl

high-yield adj (bond, security) à rendement élevé

historical cost n Acct coût m historique, coût à l'origine
◇ **historical cost accounting** comptabilité f par coûts historiques

holder n (of bonds, bill) porteur (euse) m,f

holding n (shares in company) participation f; **he has holdings in several companies** il est actionnaire de plusieurs sociétés
◇ **holding company** (société f en) holding m, société à portefeuille
◇ **holding costs** coûts mpl de détention

> A preferable alternative for both sides would be a merger. One way would be to form a **holding company** to which both banks would issue shares in proportion to their shareholders' funds. This would enable Hongkong Bank to avoid paying a packet for goodwill and for it to remain a Hongkong bank while Midland remained British.

hole-in-the-wall machine n Fam Banking distributeur m (de billets)

home n
◇ **home banking** banque f à domicile
◇ Am **home equity loan** prêt m sur valeur nette de la propriété
◇ **home loan** prêt m immobilier, prêt d'épargne-logement

honour, Am **honor** vt (cheque, bill of exchange) honorer, payer

horizontal adj
◇ **horizontal equity** équité f horizontale
◇ **horizontal spread** écart m horizontal

hostile takeover bid n OPA f hostile

> The board of directors of the target company have to give their opinion on the offer and make it clear whether or not they recommend it. However, restrictions are placed on the power of management to combat a **hostile takeover bid**, for fear that they might act only in their own interests rather than for those of the company or its shareholders.

hot money n capitaux mpl fébriles, capitaux flottants

house n St Exch the **House** la Bourse (de Londres)

IASC *n* (*abbr* **International Accounting Standards Committee**) comité *m* international des normes comptables

IBOR *n* (*abbr* **interbank offered rate**) taux *m* interbancaire offert

IBRD *n* (*abbr* **International Bank for Reconstruction and Development**) BIRD *f*

IDB *n* (*abbr* **inter-dealer broker**) courtier *m* intermédiaire

idle *adj* **to lie idle** *(of money)* dormir; **to let one's money lie idle** laisser dormir son argent

IFA *n* (*abbr* **independent financial adviser**) conseiller(ère) *m,f* financier(ère) indépendant(e)

> If you're considering making an investment, it's nearly always better to talk to an independent financial adviser (**IFA**). A company representative or agent will only tell you about his own firm's plans and so his advice will be limited. But an **IFA** can shop around for the best deals.

illiquid *adj* non liquide
◇ **illiquid assets** actif *m* non-disponible *ou* immobilisé

illiquidity *n* illiquidité *f*
◇ **illiquidity premium** prime *f* d'illiquidité

IMF *n* *Econ* (*abbr* **International Monetary Fund**) FMI *m*

> The European Investment Bank will make available up to Ecu 1bn (£685m) for loans to Poland and Hungary – another first. The traditional multilateral institutions, **IMF** and World Bank, are gearing up for a major contribution.

immobilization *n* *(of capital)* immobilisation *f*

immobilize *vt* *(capital)* immobiliser

impact day *n* *St Exch* = jour où l'on annonce une nouvelle émission d'actions

impersonal accounts *npl* *Acct* comptes *mpl* impersonnels

imprest *n* avance *f*
◇ **imprest account** compte *m* d'avances (à montant fixe)
◇ **imprest fund** fonds *m* de caisse à montant fixe
◇ **imprest system** comptabilité *f* de prévision

> **"**
>
> In most businesses it is usual to keep a petty cash book for the payment of small expenses. This petty cash is kept on the **imprest system**, whereby the petty cashier is entrusted with a fixed sum of money. This is called the **imprest**, and out of this he or she makes all small payments.
>
> **"**

inactive *adj (money, bank account)* inactif(ive)

incidental **1** *n* **incidentals** faux frais *mpl*
  2 *adj*
◊ **incidental costs, incidental expenses** faux frais *mpl*

in-clearing book *n Banking* livre *m* du dedans, registre *m* des chèques à rembourser

inclusive *adj (price, sum)* net (nette); **inclusive of all taxes** toutes taxes comprises; **inclusive of VAT** TVA comprise

income *n* **(a)** *(of person)* revenu *m*; **to be on a low/high income** avoir un faible revenu/un revenu élevé; **their combined income totals $200,000** leurs revenus additionnés s'élèvent à 200 000 dollars; **the income from her investments** les revenus provenant de ses placements
  (b) *(of company)* recettes *fpl*, revenus *mpl*; *Acct* **income from operations** produits *mpl* de gestion courante *ou* d'exploitation
◊ *Acct* **income account** compte *m* de produits
◊ **income bond** obligation *f* à intérêt conditionnel

◊ **income bracket** tranche *f* de salaire *ou* de revenu
◊ *Acct* **income and expenditure account** compte *m* de dépenses et recettes
◊ **income group** tranche *f* de salaire *ou* de revenu
◊ **income smoothing** manipulations *fpl* comptables
◊ *Am Acct* **income statement** compte *m* de résultat
◊ *Am St Exch* **income stocks** valeurs *fpl* de rendement
◊ **income stream** flux *m* de revenus
◊ **income support** ≃ revenu *m* minimum d'insertion
◊ **income tax** impôt *m* sur le revenu
◊ **income tax allowance** déduction *f* avant impôt, déduction fiscale
◊ **income tax return** déclaration *f* de revenu; *(form)* feuille *f* d'impôt
◊ **income velocity of capital** vitesse *f* de circulation du capital en revenus
◊ **income velocity of circulation** vitesse *f* de circulation de la monnaie en revenus

incomings *npl* recettes *fpl*, revenus *mpl*; **incomings and outgoings** dépenses *fpl* et recettes

inconvertible *adj* inconvertible

incorporated company *n Am* société *f* par actions

incremental *adj*
◊ **incremental cash flow** cashflow *m* marginal
◊ **incremental cost** coût *m* marginal

incur *vt (expenses)* engager; *(debts)* contracter

incurred *adj Acct*
◊ *incurred expenditure, incurred expenses* dépenses *fpl* engagées

independent *adj* indépendant(e)
◊ *independent financial adviser* conseiller(ère) *m,f* financier(ère) indépendant(e)
◊ *independent income* revenus *mpl* indépendants

index 1 *vt* indexer (**to** sur)
2 *n St Exch* indice *m*
◊ *Am St Exch* **index arbitrage** arbitrage *m* sur indice
◊ *St Exch* **index fund** fonds *m* à gestion indicielle, fonds indiciel
◊ *St Exch* **index option** option *f* sur indice

66

Trading in the final hour in both Dublin and London was frantic as **index funds** bid the shares up to a close of euro 5.00 (£3.94) with bids for stock at euro 4.98. … Whether the magical euro 5.00 will trigger more selling by private investors remains to be seen but the shares are well-supported.

99

indexation *n* indexation *f*
◊ *indexation clause* clause *f* d'indexation

index-linked *adj (bond, certificate, portfolio, pension)* indexé(e)
◊ *index-linked fund* fonds *m* à gestion indicielle, fonds indiciel

index-linking *n* indexation *f*

indirect *adj* indirect(e)
◊ *indirect costs* coûts *mpl* indirects
◊ *indirect investment* investissement *m* indirect
◊ *indirect tax* impôt *m* indirect
◊ *indirect taxation* contributions *fpl* indirectes

individual *adj*
◊ *individual company accounts* comptes *mpl* sociaux, comptes d'entreprise individuelle
◊ *Am* **individual retirement account** plan *m* d'épargne retraite personnel
◊ *individual savings account* plan *m* d'épargne en actions

industrial 1 *n St Exch* **industrials** valeurs *fpl* industrielles
2 *adj* industriel(elle)
◊ *industrial bank* banque *f* industrielle
◊ *industrial monopoly* trust *m* industriel
◊ *St Exch* **industrial shares** valeurs *fpl* industrielles

inflation *n* inflation *f*; **inflation is down/up on last year** l'inflation est en baisse/en hausse par rapport à l'année dernière; **inflation now stands at 5%** l'inflation est maintenant à 5%
◊ *inflation tax* impôt *m* à la production

inflow *n* afflux *m*; **the inflow of capital** l'afflux de capitaux

ingot *n* lingot *m*

inheritance *n* héritage *m*
◊ *inheritance tax* droits *mpl* de succession

initial *adj* initial(e)

Main stock market indexes

Principaux indices boursiers

Europe

France — CAC-40
(= *Compagnie des Agents de Change 40 Index*)

Germany — DAX
(= *Deutscher Aktienindex*)

Italy — MIB 30
(= *Milano Italia Borsa Index 30*)

Switzerland — SMI
(= *Swiss Market Index*)

United Kingdom — FT-SE 100
(= *Financial Times Stock Exchange 100 Index*)

USA

DJIA (= *Dow-Jones Industrial Average*)

NASDAQ
(= *National Association of Securities Dealers Automated Quotation Composite Index*)

Canada

TSE 300 index
(= *Toronto Stock Exchange Index*)

Australia/Australie

All Ordinaries index
(= *Sydney Stock Exchange Index*)

Far East/Extrême Orient

Hang Seng index
(= *Hong Kong Stock Exchange Index*)

Nikkei (Average)
(= *Tokyo Stock Exchange Index*)

* London's FT-SE, or "Footsie", index is the leading European stock exchange index. It is comprised of the top 100 listed companies on the London Stock Exchange, and is compiled jointly by the Financial Times and the London Stock Exchange Ltd. The FT-SE index is complemented by the FT 30 share index which focuses on the leading 30 listed companies.

The Dow Jones Industrial Average, or DJIA, is America's main stock exchange index and is based on the New York Stock Exchange.

The FT-SE and Dow Jones indices, as well as the Japanese Nikkei index, dominate the world of international finance.

* L'indice FT-SE ou Footsie 100 est le principal indice boursier européen. Il est composé des 100 valeurs les plus importantes de la Bourse de Londres et il est établi par le Financial Times en collaboration avec la Bourse de Londres. Il existe un autre indice, le FT 30, composé des 30 valeurs les plus importantes.

Le Dow Jones Industrial Average, ou DJIA, est le principal indice boursier américain; il est établi à la Bourse de New York.

Le Footsie 100 et le Dow Jones ainsi que l'indice boursier japonais Nikkei dominent la scène financière internationale.

◇ *initial capital* capital *m* initial ou d'apport

◇ *initial cost* coût *m* initial; *(of manufactured product)* prix *m* de revient

◇ *initial expenditure* frais *mpl* de premier établissement

◇ *initial investment* investissements *mpl* initiaux

◇ St Exch *initial margin* dépôt *m* initial ou de marge

◇ Am St Exch *initial public offering* introduction *f* en Bourse

◇ *initial value* valeur *f* de départ

inject *vt (money)* injecter (**into** dans)

injection *n (of money)* injection *f* (**into** dans); **an injection of capital** une injection de capitaux

Inland Revenue *n Br* **the Inland Revenue** ≃ le fisc, la Direction Générale des Impôts

input tax *n Acct* TVA *f* récupérée

insider *n St Exch* **the insiders** les initiés *mpl*

◇ *insider dealing, insider trading* délit *m* ou opération *f* d'initié

> **❝**
>
> National Westminster, a British bank that has offered £10.75 billion ($17.4 billion) for Legal & General, a British insurance company, said that there may have been **insider dealing** in L&G shares. It was forced to announce prematurely that talks were taking place, after unusual volumes of shares changed hands.
>
> **❞**

insolvency *n (of person)* insolvabilité *f*; *(of company)* faillite *f*

insolvent *adj (person)* insolvable; *(company)* en faillite; **to declare oneself insolvent** *(of person)* se déclarer insolvable; *(of company)* déposer son bilan

instalment, *Am* **installment** *n (part payment)* acompte *m*, versement *m*; **to pay in** or **by instalments** payer par versements échelonnés

◇ *instalment loan* prêt *m* à tempérament ou à remboursements échelonnés

instant-access *adj (bank account)* à accès immédiat

> **❝**
>
> The distinction between sight and time deposits has become increasingly blurred in recent years, with interest being paid on current accounts and with **instant-access**, no-penalty, high-interest accounts.
>
> **❞**

institution *n (financial)* établissement *m*

institutional *adj*

◇ *institutional buying* achats *mpl* institutionnels

◇ *institutional investment* investissement *m* institutionnel

◇ *institutional investors* investisseurs *mpl* institutionnels

◇ *institutional savings* épargne *f* institutionnelle

instrument *n* effet *m*, titre *m*

◇ *instrument of incorporation* statut *m*, acte *m* de constitution

◇ *instrument to order* papier *m* à ordre

insufficient *adj*
◇ *insufficient capital* insuffisance *f* de capitaux
◇ *Banking* *insufficient funds* provision *f* insuffisante, insuffisance *f* de provision

insurance *n* assurance *f*; *(cover)* garantie *f* (d'assurance), couverture *f*; *(premium)* prime *f* (d'assurance)
◇ *insurance broker* courtier (ère) *m,f* d'assurances
◇ *insurance policy* police *f* d'assurance
◇ *insurance portfolio* portefeuille *m* d'assurances
◇ *insurance premium* prime *f* d'assurance

intangible *n* intangibles valeurs *fpl* immatérielles, actif *m* incorporel
◇ *Acct* *intangible asset* valeur *f* immatérielle, actif *m* incorporel
◇ *intangible fixed assets* immobilisations *fpl* incorporelles

interbank *adj* interbancaire
◇ *interbank deposit* dépôt *m* interbancaire
◇ *interbank loan* prêt *m* de banque à banque *ou* entre banques
◇ *interbank market* marché *m* interbancaire
◇ *interbank offered rate* taux *m* interbancaire offert
◇ *interbank transfer* virement *m* interbancaire

inter-dealer broker *n* courtier(ère) *m,f* intermédiaire

interest *n* *(on loan, investment)* intérêt(s) *m(pl)* **(on** sur); **interest paid** intérêts versés; **interest payable** intérêt exigible; **inter-**

est received produits *mpl* financiers, intérêts *mpl* perçus; **to bear** *or* **yield interest** porter intérêt, rapporter; **to bear** *or* **yield 5% interest** rapporter du 5% *ou* un intérêt de 5%; **to pay interest** payer des intérêts
◇ *interest charges* intérêts *mpl* (à payer); *(on overdraft)* agios *mpl*
◇ *interest days* jours *mpl* d'intérêt
◇ *interest and dividend income* produits *mpl* financiers
◇ *interest payment date* date *f* d'échéance des intérêts
◇ *interest rate* taux *m* d'intérêt; **the interest rate is 4%** le taux d'intérêt est de 4%
◇ *St Exch* *interest rate differential* différentiel *m* de taux
◇ *St Exch* *interest rate swap* échange *m* de taux d'intérêt

interest-bearing *adj* productif(ive) d'intérêts
◇ *Banking* *interest-bearing account* compte *m* rémunéré
◇ *interest-bearing capital* capital *m* productif d'intérêts
◇ *interest-bearing loan* prêt *m* à intérêt
◇ *St Exch* *interest-bearing securities* titres *mpl* qui produisent des intérêts

interest-free *adj* sans intérêt
◇ *Acct* *interest-free credit* crédit *m* gratuit
◇ *interest-free loan* prêt *m* sans intérêt

interim *adj* intérimaire
◇ *Acct* *interim accounts* comptes *mpl* semestriels
◇ *interim dividend* dividende *m* intérimaire

◇ *interim payment* paiement *m* provisoire

◇ *Acct* *interim profit and loss statement* compte *m* de résultat prévisionnel

◇ *Acct* *interim statement* bilan *m* intérimaire

❝

Shares in Dixons, the UK retailer, jumped 2.88 per cent to £12.50 after the company declared a special **interim dividend** of 7.5p per ordinary share to be paid on December 13. Sir Stanley Kalms, Dixons' chairman, said total retail sales for the 18 weeks to September 4 were up 20 per cent over the same period last year and 9 per cent higher on a like-for-like basis.

❞

intermediate *adj*

◇ *intermediate broker* intermédiaire *mf*, remisier *m* (en Bourse)

◇ *intermediate credit* crédit *m* à moyen terme

internal *adj*

◇ *internal audit* audit *m* interne

◇ *internal auditing* vérification *f* ou audit *m* interne

◇ *internal auditor* audit *m* ou auditeur(trice) *m,f* interne

◇ *internal check* contrôle *m* interne

◇ *internal debt* endettement *m* intérieur

◇ *internal rate of return* taux *m* de rentabilité interne

◇ *internal revenue* recettes *fpl* fiscales

◇ *Am* **the Internal Revenue**

Service ≃ le fisc, la Direction Générale des Impôts

international *adj* international(e)

◇ *International Accounting Standards Committee* comité *m* international des normes comptables

◇ *International Bank for Reconstruction and Development* Banque *f* internationale pour la reconstruction et le développement

◇ *international currency* devise *f* internationale

◇ *International Monetary Fund* Fonds *m* monétaire international

◇ *international monetary reserves* réserves *fpl* monétaires internationales

◇ *international money market* marché *m* monétaire international

◇ *international money order* mandat *m* international

Internet *n* *Comptr* Internet *m*

◇ *Internet banking* opérations *fpl* bancaires par l'Internet

intervention rate *n* taux *m* d'intervention

in-the-money option *n* *St Exch* option *f* en dedans

intrinsic value *n* *St Exch* valeur *f* intrinsèque

introduce *vt* *St Exch* (shares) introduire

introduction *n* *St Exch* introduction *f* au marché hors cote

inventory *n* (list) inventaire *m*; (stock) stock(s) *m(pl)*

◇ *inventory account* compte *m* de stock

◊ *inventory turnover* rotation *f* des stocks

◊ *inventory valuation* valorisation *f* des stocks

◊ *inventory value* valeur *f* d'inventaire

invest 1 *vt (money)* placer, investir; *(capital)* investir; **to invest money in a business** mettre de l'argent *ou* placer des fonds dans un commerce

  2 *vi* investir, faire des placements; **to invest in shares/in the oil industry** investir en actions/dans l'industrie pétrolière; **to invest in property** faire des placements dans l'immobilier; **to invest on the Stock Market** investir en Bourse

investment *n* placement *m*, investissement *m*; *(money invested)* investissement, mise *f* de fonds; **are these shares a good investment?** ces actions sont-elles un bon placement?; **property is no longer such a safe investment** l'immobilier n'est plus un placement aussi sûr; **investment in industry/real estate** investissement industriel/immobilier; **I'd prefer a better return on investment** je préférerais un investissement plus rentable; **the company has investments all over the world** la société a des capitaux investis dans le monde entier

◊ *investment account* compte *m* d'investissement

◊ *investment advice* conseil *m* en placements

◊ *investment adviser* conseiller (ère) *m,f* en placements

◊ *investment analyst* analyste *mf* en placements

◊ *investment appraisal* appréciation *f* des investissements

◊ *Am investment bank* banque *f* d'affaires

◊ *Am investment banker* banquier *m* d'affaires

◊ *Am investment banking* banque *f* d'affaires

◊ *investment boom* boom *m* des investissements

◊ *investment certificate* certificat *m* d'investissement

◊ *investment company* société *f* d'investissement

◊ *investment consultancy* société *f* de conseil en investissement

◊ *investment curve* courbe *f* d'investissement

◊ *investment fund* fonds *m* commun de placement, fonds d'investissement

◊ *investment grant* subvention *f* d'investissement

◊ *investment income* revenu *m* provenant d'investissements

◊ *investment institution* société *f* d'investissements

◊ *investment instrument* instrument *m* de placement

◊ *investment management* gestion *f* des investissements

◊ *investment market* marché *m* des capitaux

◊ *investment objectives* objectifs *mpl* de placement

◊ *investment plan* plan *m* d'investissement

◊ *investment policy* politique *f* d'investissement

◊ *investment portfolio* portefeuille *m* d'investissements

◊ *investment programme* programme *m* d'investissement

◊ *investment return* retour *m* sur investissements

◇ *investment securities* valeurs *fpl* en portefeuille *ou* de placement

◇ *investment services* services *mpl* d'investissement

◇ *investment stock* valeurs *fpl* en portefeuille *ou* de placement

◇ *investment subsidy* prime *f* à l'investissement

◇ *investment trust* société *f* de placement, trust *m* de placement

investor *n* investisseur *m*; *(shareholder)* actionnaire *mf*

invisible *n Econ* invisibles invisibles *mpl*

◇ *invisible asset* actif *m* incorporel, immobilisation *f* (incorporelle)

◇ *invisible earnings* gains *mpl* invisibles

invoice 1 *n* facture *f*; **to make out an invoice** établir *ou* faire une facture; **to settle an invoice** régler une facture; **as per invoice** conformément à la facture; **payable against invoice** à payer à réception de la facture

2 *vt (goods)* facturer, porter sur une facture; *(person, company)* envoyer la facture à; **to invoice sb for sth** facturer qch à qn

◇ *invoice discounting* escompte *m* de créances *ou* de traites

◇ *invoice value* valeur *f* de facture

invoicing *n (of goods)* facturation *f*

inward *adj*

◇ *inward investment* investissements *mpl* étrangers

◇ *Acct* **inward payment** paiement *m* reçu

IOU *n (abbr* **I owe you)** reconnaissance *f* de dette

IPO *n Am St Exch (abbr* **initial public offering)** introduction *f* en Bourse

❝

Over in the US, Wit Capital appeared to be on to a good thing. It offered Internet subscribers first bite of the cherry on **IPOs**, as Americans call flotations. This would allow them to get the share of a float usually reserved for institutional investors and, as Wit had access to all those lovely technology **IPOs**, which appear to go to an astonishing premium, this would be lucrative for all concerned.

❞

IRA *n Am (abbr* **individual retirement account)** plan *m* d'épargne retraite personnel

Irish pound *n* livre *f* irlandaise

IRR *n (abbr* **internal rate of return)** taux *m* de rentabilité interne

irrecoverable *adj (debt)* irrécouvrable

irredeemable 1 *n* **irredeemables** obligations *fpl* non amortissables

2 *adj (funds, share)* non remboursable; *(bill)* non convertible

◇ *irredeemable bond* obligation *f* non amortissable

irrevocable *adj Banking (letter of credit)* irrévocable

IRS *n Am* (*abbr* **Internal Revenue Service**) **the IRS** ≃ le fisc

ISA *n Br* (*abbr* **individual savings account**) ≃ PEA *m*, plan *m* d'épargne en actions

> **"**
>
> **ISAs** should be the first investments you consider because they are the next most tax-efficient, after pensions. They allow you to hold up to £5,000 a year … in three types of investment: cash, life insurance and stockmarket investments, such as shares and unit trusts.
>
> **"**

issue 1 *n* (*of banknotes, money orders*) émission *f*

2 *vt* (*banknotes, money orders*) émettre; (*letter of credit*) fournir; **to issue a draft on sb** fournir une traite sur qn

◊ *issue department* service *m* des émissions

◊ *issue premium* prime *f* d'émission

◊ *issue price* prix *m* d'émission, valeur *f* d'émission

issued *adj St Exch*

◊ *issued capital* capital *m* émis

◊ *issued securities* titres *mpl* émis

issuing *adj* émetteur(trice)

◊ *issuing bank* banque *f* émettrice, banque d'émission

◊ *issuing company* société *f* émettrice

◊ *issuing house* banque *f* émettrice, banque d'émission

item *n Acct* article *m*, écriture *f*; **item of expenditure** article *m* de dépense

itemize *vt* (*bill, account*) détailler

◊ *itemized bill* facture *f* détaillée

◊ *itemized billing, itemized invoicing* facturation *f* détaillée

J/A, j/a *n Banking* (*abbr* **joint account**) compte *m* joint, compte conjoint

joint *adj*
⋄ *Banking* **joint account** compte *m* joint, compte conjoint
⋄ *joint beneficiary* bénéficiaire *mf* conjoint(e)
⋄ *joint creditor* cocréancier (ère) *m,f*
⋄ *joint debtor* codébiteur(trice) *m,f*
⋄ *joint stock* capital *m* social
⋄ *joint venture* (*undertaking*) opération *f* en commun; (*company*) société *f* commune, société en participation
⋄ *joint venture company* société *f* commune, société en participation

joint-stock *adj Br*
⋄ *joint-stock bank* banque *f* de dépôt
⋄ *joint-stock company* société *f* (anonyme) par actions

journal *n Acct* (*for transactions*) livre *m* de comptes, (livre) journal *m*
⋄ *journal entry* écriture *f* comptable, passation *f* d'écriture

jumbo *adj Am* (*loan*) géant(e)
⋄ *jumbo certificate of deposit* certificat *m* de très grand dépôt

junk bond *n St Exch* obligation *f* à haut rendement mais à haut risque, junk bond *m*

> Corporate restructuring on a large scale began with the development of the **junk bond** market in the USA in the 1980s. **Junk bonds** were used to finance leveraged buyouts and takeovers, with the aim of extracting value from existing bondholders and shareholders.

K *n* (*abbr* **thousand, thousand pounds**) **he earns 30K** il gagne 30 000 livres

kaffir *n Fam St Exch* valeur-or *f* sud-africaine

kangaroo *n Fam St Exch* valeur *f* australienne

kerb *n Fam St Exch* **to buy/sell on the kerb** acheter/vendre après la clôture officielle de la Bourse; **business done on the kerb** opérations *fpl* effectuées en coulisse *ou* après clôture de Bourse
⋄ *kerb broker* coulissier *m*,

courtier(ère) *m,f* hors Bourse, courtier(ère) des valeurs hors cote

◇ *kerb market* marché *m* hors cote, coulisse *f*

kerbstone market *n Fam St Exch* marché *m* hors cote, coulisse *f*

key-escrow *n Comptr* système *m* du tiers de confiance *(principe selon lequel l'utilisateur confie sa clé privée de cryptage à un tiers de confiance agréé)*

"

Under **key-escrow**, your private key would be held in trust by a third party, and if you came under suspicion it would be made available to the authorities. … Where can we find a suitably trustworthy third party, anyway? In some countries where **key-escrow** has

been mooted, the banking institutions have been seen as the logical TTP. People trust them with their money, so why not with a crypto key?

"

kickback *n Fam* dessous-de-table *m*, pot-de-vin *m*

kite *n Fam* traite *f* en l'air, billet *m* de complaisance; **to fly** *or* **to send up a kite** tirer en l'air *ou* à découvert

◇ *kite flyer* tireur *m* en l'air *ou* à découvert

◇ *kite flying* tirage *m* en l'air *ou* à découvert

kiting *n Fam* tirage *m* en l'air, tirage à découvert

krona *n* couronne *f* (suédoise)

krone *n (in Norway)* couronne *f* (norvégienne); *(in Denmark)* couronne (danoise)

labour costs *npl* frais *mpl* de main-d'œuvre

laddered portfolio *n Am* portefeuille *m* d'obligations à rendement échelonné

landed costs *npl Acct* coûts *mpl* fonciers

land tax *n* impôt *m* foncier, contribution *f* foncière

lapsed *adj (fund)* périmé
◇ *St Exch* **lapsed option** option *f* expirée

last *adj Acct* **last in, first out** dernier entré premier sorti
◇ *St Exch* **last trading day** dernier jour *m* de cotation

late *adj*
◇ **late payment** retard *m* de paiement
◇ **late payment penalty** pénalité *f* de retard
◇ *St Exch* **late trading** opérations *fpl* de clôture

launch 1 *n (of product, project)* lancement *m*
2 *vt* **(a)** *(product, project)* lancer; **to launch a £3m cash bid** lancer une offre au comptant de 3 millions de livres **(b)** *St Exch (company)* introduire en Bourse; *(shares)* émettre

launder *vt (money)* blanchir

laundering *n (of money)* blanchiment *m*

LBO *n (abbr* **leveraged buy-out**) rachat *m* d'entreprise financé par l'endettement

L/C *n (abbr* **letter of credit**) l/c *f*

leader *n St Exch* valeur *f* vedette

leading share *n St Exch* valeur *f* vedette

lead manager *n Banking, St Exch* (banque *f*) chef *m* de file

lease 1 *n (of property)* bail *m*; *(document)* (contrat *m* de) bail; **the lease runs out in May** le bail expire en mai; **to sign a lease** signer un bail
2 *vt* **(a)** *(of owner) (property)* louer *ou* céder à bail; *(equipment)* louer; *(land)* affermer

(**b**) *(of leaseholder) (property)* prendre à bail, louer; *(equipment)* louer; *(land)* prendre en fermage

◇ Acct **lease charges** charges *fpl* locatives

◇ **lease contract** *(for property)* contrat *m* de bail; *(for equipment)* contrat en location

◇ **lease financing** leasing *m*, location *f* avec option d'achat

◇ Acct **lease revenue** loyers *mpl*

▸ **lease back** *vt sep* = louer dans le cadre d'une cession-bail

▸ **lease out** *vt sep (property)* louer *ou* céder à bail; *(equipment)* louer; *(land)* affermer

lease-back *n* cession-bail *f*

leasehold 1 *n (contract)* bail *m*; *(property)* location *f* à bail
2 *adj* loué(e) à bail

leaseholder *n* locataire *mf*

leasing *n (of property)* location *f* à bail; *(of equipment)* location; *(of land)* affermage *m*; *(system)* crédit-bail *m*, leasing *m*

◇ **leasing company** société *f* de leasing

ledger *n* Acct grand-livre *m*, livre *m* de comptabilité *ou* de comptes

legal *adj*

◇ **legal currency** monnaie *f* courante

◇ **legal tender** cours *m* légal; **to be legal tender** avoir cours (légal)

legal-tender value *n* valeur *f* numéraire

lend 1 *vt* prêter; **to lend money at interest** prêter de l'argent à intérêt; **to lend money against security** prêter de l'argent sur

titres
2 *vi* prêter; **to lend at 12%** prêter à 12%

lender *n (person)* prêteur(euse) *m,f*; *(institution)* organisme *m* de crédit; **lender of last resort** prêteur *m* en dernier ressort

lending *n* prêt *m*; **bank lending has increased** le volume des prêts bancaires a augmenté

◇ **lending bank** banque *f* de crédit

◇ **lending banker** banquier *m* prêteur

◇ **lending limit** plafond *m* de crédit

◇ **lending rate** taux *m* de prêt

letter *n*

◇ Banking **letter of advice** lettre *f* d'avis

◇ St Exch **letter of allotment** avis *m* d'attribution *ou* de répartition, lettre *f* d'allocation

◇ St Exch **letter of application** *(for shares)* lettre *f* de souscription

◇ **letter of credit** lettre *f* de crédit *ou* de créance

◇ **letter of exchange** lettre *f* de change

◇ **letter of guaranty** lettre *f* d'aval

◇ **letter of indemnity** cautionnement *m*, lettre *f* de garantie (d'indemnité)

◇ **letter of intent** lettre *f* d'intention

leverage *n (gearing)* effet *m* de levier; *(as percentage)* ratio *m* d'endettement, ratio de levier

leveraged *adj* **the company is highly leveraged** la société est fortement endettée

◇ **leveraged buy-out** rachat *m*

d'entreprise financé par l'endettement

◊ **leveraged management buy-out** rachat m d'entreprise par les salariés

> **"**
>
> AMI is 65 per cent owned by American Healthcare International, the US group. The parent company is subject of a £1.3bn **leveraged buy-out** from IMA, an investor group.
>
> **"**

levy n **1** n (a) *(activity)* prélèvement m ; **a capital levy of 10%** un prélèvement de 10% sur le capital (b) *(tax)* impôt m, droit m ; **to impose a levy on imports** taxer les importations ; **special levy** taxe f exceptionnelle

2 vt *(tax)* prélever ; **to levy a duty on goods** imposer des marchandises, prélever une taxe sur les marchandises

liability n Acct **liabilities** *(debts)* passif m, dettes fpl ; **assets and liabilities** actif et passif ; **to meet one's liabilities** rembourser ses dettes

liable adj **to be liable to pay tax** être assujetti à l'impôt ; **to be liable for sb's debts** répondre des dettes de qn

LIBOR n Br *(abbr* **London Inter-Bank Offer Rate)** ≃ TIOP m

lien n privilège m, droit m de rétention ; **lien on shares** nantissement m d'actions

life n *(of loan)* durée f

◊ **life annuity** rente f viagère

LIFFE n *(abbr* **London International Financial Futures Exchange)** = marché à terme

d'instruments financiers, ≃ MATIF m

> **"**
>
> In the UK, all financial futures contracts are traded on the London International Financial Futures Exchange (**LIFFE**) which opened in 1982. Members of **LIFFE** include banks, member firms of the ISE, money and commodity brokers, discount houses and individual traders (known as locals) who trade on their own account.
>
> **"**

LIFO Acct *(abbr* **last in, first out)** DEPS

limited adj

◊ **limited company** ≃ société f à responsabilité limitée

◊ **limited liability** responsabilité f limitée

◊ **limited liability company** ≃ société f à responsabilité limitée

◊ **limited partner** commanditaire m

◊ **limited partnership** société f en commandite (simple)

limit order n St Exch ordre m limite

line of credit n ligne f de crédit, ligne de découvert

liquid adj liquide

◊ **liquid assets, liquid capital** actif m liquide, liquidités fpl

◊ **liquid debt** dette f liquide

◊ **liquid securities** valeurs fpl liquides

liquidate vt *(company, debt)* liquider ; *(capital)* mobiliser ; St Exch **to liquidate a position** liquider une position

liquidation n *(of company, debt)* liquidation f ; *(of capital)* mobilisation f ; **to go into liquidation** *(of company)* entrer en liquidation, déposer son bilan

liquidator n *(of company)* liquidateur(trice) m,f

liquidity n *(of company, debt)* liquidité f

◇ Banking **liquidity ratio** ratio m de liquidité, coéfficient m de liquidité

❝

The ratio of an institution's liquid assets to illiquid assets is known as its **liquidity ratio**. For example, if a bank had £100 million of assets, of which £10 million were liquid and £90 million were illiquid, the bank would have a 10 per cent **liquidity ratio**. If a financial institution's **liquidity ratio** is too high, it will make too little profit. If the ratio is too low, there will be the risk that customers' demands may not be able to be met.

❞

lira n lire f

LISA n *(abbr* **long-term individual savings account**) plan m de retraite en actions

list n **(a)** *(of bills, assets, liabilities)* liste f ; St Exch **list of applicants** or **applications** *(for loan, shares)* liste des souscripteurs ; St Exch **list of quotations** bulletin m des cours
(b) Banking **list of investments** (bordereau m de) portefeuille m ; **list of bills for collection/for discount** bordereau d'effets à l'encaissement/à l'escompte

listed adj **to be listed on the Stock Exchange** être coté en Bourse

◇ St Exch **listed company** société f cotée en Bourse

◇ St Exch **listed securities, listed stock** valeurs fpl admises ou inscrites à la cote officielle

listing n St Exch admission f à la cote officielle ; **to have a listing** être coté(e) en Bourse

◇ **listing agreement** dossier m de demande d'introduction en Bourse

living expenses npl indemnité f de séjour

LMBO n *(abbr* **leveraged management buy-out**) rachat m d'entreprise par les salariés

load n St Exch frais mpl d'achat ou d'acquisition

loan n *(money lent)* prêt m ; *(money borrowed)* emprunt m ; **to take out a loan** faire un emprunt ; **to apply for a loan** demander un prêt ; **to repay a loan** rembourser un emprunt ; Acct **loans and advances to customers** créances fpl clients ; Acct **loans outstanding** encours m ; **loan at interest** prêt à intérêt ; **loan at reduced rate of interest** prêt bonifié ; **loan at call, loan repayable on demand** prêt remboursable sur demande ; **loan at notice** prêt à terme ; **loan on collateral** prêt sur gage ou sur nantissement ; **loan on mortgage** prêt hypothécaire ou sur hypothèque ; **loan on overdraft** prêt à découvert ; **loan on** or **against securities** emprunt sur titre ; **loan against security** prêt sur gage; **loan without security** prêt à fonds perdus; **loan on trust** prêt d'honneur

2 vt prêter

◇ Banking **loan account** compte m de prêt

◇ **loan agreement** contrat m de prêt

◇ Acct **loan capital** capital m sur prêt ou d'emprunt

◇ **loan certificate** titre m de prêt

◇ **loan charges** frais mpl financiers

◇ **loan company** société f de crédit, maison f de prêt

◇ **loan department** service m des crédits

◇ **loan guarantee scheme** prêts mpl bonifiés d'aide au développement des entreprises

◇ **loan market** marché m des prêts

◇ **loan maturity** échéance f emprunt

◇ **loan note** titre m d'obligation ou de créance

◇ **loan office** organisme m de crédit, maison f de prêt

◇ **loan origination fee** commission f de montage

◇ **loan repayment insurance** assurance f crédit

◇ **loan risk cover** couverture f du risque de crédit

◇ **loan stock** emprunt m obligataire

◇ **loan transaction** opération f de prêt

loan-back, loanback n cession-bail f

◇ **loanback pension** retraite f par capitalisation

local taxes npl Am impôts mpl locaux

lodge vt (money) consigner, déposer; **to lodge securities with a bank** déposer des titres dans une banque

Lombard rate n Br Banking taux m Lombard

long **1** n St Exch **longs** titres mpl longs, obligations fpl longues

2 adv St Exch **to go long** acheter à la hausse, prendre une position longue; **to buy long** acheter à long terme

◇ **long credit** crédit m à long terme

◇ **long hedge** couverture f longue, achat m par couverture

◇ St Exch **long position** position f acheteur ou longue; **to take a long position** acheter à la hausse, prendre une position longue

long-dated adj à longue échéance

◇ **long-dated bill** effet m ou traite f à longue échéance

◇ **long-dated securities** titres mpl longs, obligations fpl longues

long-lived assets npl Acct actifs mpl à long terme, actifs à longue durée de vie

longstanding adj de longue date

◇ **longstanding accounts** vieux comptes mpl

long-term adj (loan, policy) à long terme

◇ **long-term bond** obligation f à long terme

◇ **long-term bond rate** taux m long obligataire

◇ Acct **long-term borrowings** emprunts mpl à long terme

◊ *Acct **long-term capital*** capitaux *mpl* permanents

◊ ***long-term credit*** crédit *m* (à) long terme

◊ ***long-term debt*** dette *f* à long terme

◊ ***long-term financing*** financement *m* à long terme

◊ ***long-term interest rate*** taux *m* d'intérêt à long terme

◊ ***long-term investments*** placements *mpl* à long terme

◊ ***long-term liabilities*** dettes *fpl* ou passif *m* à long terme

◊ ***long-term loan*** prêt *m* à long terme

◊ ***long-term maturity*** échéance *f* à long terme

lose 1 *vt (custom, market share, job, money)* perdre; **his shop is losing money** son magasin perd de l'argent

2 *vi* perdre; **the dollar is losing in value** le dollar baisse

▸ **lose out** *vi* perdre; **to lose out on a deal** être perdant(e) dans une affaire

loser *n St Exch* valeur *f* en baisse

loss *n (financial)* déficit *m*; **to make a loss** perdre de l'argent, être déficitaire; **to run at a loss** *(of business)* tourner à perte; **to sell sth at a loss** vendre qch à perte; **the company announced losses** *or* **a loss of £4m** la société a annoncé un déficit de 4 millions de livres; **we made a loss of 10% on the deal** nous avons perdu 10% dans l'affaire; *Acct* **loss attributable** perte *f* supportée; **loss carry back** report *m* déficitaire sur les exercices précédents; **loss carry forward** déficit reportable, report *m* déficitaire sur les exercices ulté-

rieurs; **loss transferred** perte *f* transférée

loss-making *adj* déficitaire

lot *n (of bonds)* paquet *m*; **in lots** par lots; **to buy/sell in one lot** acheter/vendre en bloc

◊ ***lot number*** numéro *m* de lot

◊ ***lot size*** unité *f* de transaction

lottery *n*

◊ *St Exch **lottery bonds*** valeurs *fpl* à lot

◊ *Br **lottery funding*** *(from National Lottery)* = fonds provenant de la loterie nationale

◊ ***lottery loan*** emprunt *m* à lots

◊ ***lottery loan bond*** titre *m* à lots

low 1 *n* niveau *m* bas; **the share index has reached a new low** l'indice des actions est descendu à son plus bas niveau; **inflation is at an all-time low** l'inflation est à son niveau le plus bas; *St Exch* **the highs and lows** les hauts *mpl* et les bas *mpl*

2 *adj (interest rate, cost)* bas (basse), faible; *(salary)* peu élevé(e)

lower *vt (interest rate, prices)* baisser

low-interest loan *n* crédit *m* à taux réduit, prêt *m* à taux réduit

LSE *n St Exch (abbr* **London Stock Exchange***)* = la Bourse de Londres

lump sum *n* somme *f* forfaitaire, montant *m* forfaitaire; **to be paid in a lump sum** être payé(e) en une seule fois

Luxembourg franc *n* franc *m* luxembourgeois

luxury tax *n* taxe *f* de luxe

machine-hour *n Acct* heure *f* machine

MACRS *n Am Acct* (*abbr* **modified accelerated cost recovery system**) = méthode d'amortissement accéléré

MAD *n Acct* (*abbr* **mean absolute deviation**) écart *m* moyen absolu

M&A *n* (*abbr* **mergers and acquisitions**) fusions et acquisitions *fpl*

MAI *n* (*abbr* **multilateral agreement on investment**) AMI *m*

mail transfer *n* virement *m* par courrier

main *adj* principal(e)

◇ **main branch** (*of bank*) établissement *m* principal

◇ *Acct* **main cost centre** centre *m* d'analyse principal

◇ *St Exch* **main market** = marché principal de la Bourse de Londres

◇ **main office** bureau *m* principal; (*headquarters*) siège *m* (social)

majority *n* majorité *f*

◇ **majority holding, majority interest** participation *f* majoritaire

◇ *Br* **majority shareholder,** *Am*

majority stockholder actionnaire *mf* majoritaire

major shareholder *n* actionnaire *mf* de référence

▸ **make out** *vt sep* to make out a cheque (to sb) faire un chèque (à l'ordre de qn)

making-up *n St Exch*

◇ **making-up day** jour *m* de liquidation

◇ **making-up price** cours *m* de compensation

manage *vt* (a) (*company, bank*) diriger (b) (*economy, money, resources*) gérer; **to manage sb's affairs** gérer les affaires de qn

managed *adj*

◇ *Acct* **managed costs** coûts *mpl* maîtrisables

◇ **managed currency** devise *f* contrôlée, monnaie *f* dirigée

◇ **managed fund** fonds *m* géré

◇ **managed unit trust** fonds *m* commun de placement géré

management *n* (a) (*action*) (*of company, bank*) gestion *f*, direction *f*; (*of economy, money, resources*) gestion (b) (*managers, employers*) administration *f*, direction *f*

◇ **management accountant** contrôleur *m* de gestion

◇ *management accounting* comptabilité *f* de gestion

◇ *management accounts* comptes *mpl* de gestion

◇ *management audit* contrôle *m* de gestion

◇ *management buy-in* apport *m* de gestion

◇ *management buy-out* rachat *m* d'une société par la direction

◇ *management by exception* direction *f* par exceptions

◇ *management by objectives* gestion *f ou* direction *f* par objectifs

manager *n (of company, bank)* directeur(trice) *m,f*; *(of funds, money)* gestionnaire *mf*; *(of assets)* administrateur(trice) *m,f*

manageress *n (of company, bank)* directrice *f*

mandate *n* mandat *m*

◇ *Banking mandate form* lettre *f* de signatures autorisées

mandatory *adj* obligatoire

◇ *Banking mandatory liquid assets* liquidités *fpl* obligatoires

◇ *St Exch mandatory quote period* période *f* de cotation obligatoire

man-hour *n Acct* heure *f* homme

manipulate *vt* to manipulate **the accounts** trafiquer les comptes; *St Exch* to manipulate **the market** agir sur le marché

manufacturing account *n Acct* compte *m* de production

margin *n* (a) *(profit)* marge *f*; **they want more margin** ils veulent augmenter leur marge bénéficiaire; **the margins are**

very tight les marges sont très réduites

(b) *St Exch* marge *f* de garantie

◇ *margin call* appel *m* de couverture *ou* de marge *ou* de garantie

◇ *St Exch margin dealing (method of dealing commodities or financial futures)* cotation *f* par appel de marge; *(high-gear dealing)* arbitrage *m* à la marge *ou* marginal; *(transactions on margin of loan)* arbitrage sur dépôt de titres de garantie

◇ *margin of fluctuation (of a currency)* marge *f* de fluctuation

◇ *margin of interest* marge *f* d'intérêt

◇ *St Exch margin requirement* couverture *f* (boursière) obligatoire

◇ *margin of safety* marge *f* de sécurité

marginal *adj (business, profit)* marginal(e)

◇ *marginal cost* coût *m* marginal

◇ *marginal costing* méthode *f* des coûts marginaux

◇ *marginal cost pricing* méthode *f* des coûts marginaux

◇ *marginal disinvestment* désinvestissement *m* marginal

◇ *marginal profit* bénéfice *m* marginal

◇ *marginal relief* dégrèvement *m* marginal

◇ *marginal return on capital* rendement *m* marginal du capital

◇ *marginal revenue* revenu *m* marginal

◇ *marginal value* valeur *f* marginale

“
Another duty of the accounts department is that of recording the costs incurred in company activities such as manufacturing. One method of doing this is the system of **marginal costing**. **Marginal cost** is defined as 'prime cost plus variable overheads'.
”

mark n (currency) mark m, Deutschmark m

▸**mark down** vt sep St Exch **prices have been marked down** les cours sont en baisse

▸**mark up** vt sep St Exch **prices have been marked up** les cours sont en hausse

market n St Exch marché m; **to play the market** spéculer

◇ *market analyst* analyste mf du marché

◇ *market capitalization* capitalisation f boursière

◇ *market commentator* chroniqueur m boursier

◇ *market crisis* choc m boursier

◇ *market economy* économie f de marché

◇ *market fluctuation* mouvement m du marché

◇ *market indicator* indicateur m de marché

◇ *market maker* intermédiaire mf

◇ *market order* ordre m au mieux

◇ *market price* cours m (de la Bourse)

◇ *market price list* mercuriale f

◇ *market quotation* cotation f au cours du marché

◇ *market rating* cours m en Bourse

◇ *market risk* risque m du marché

◇ *market trend* conjoncture f boursière

◇ *market value* valeur f boursière

“
A **market maker** does not have complete control over his portfolio because he is always required to make a market. We are therefore left with the unsatisfactory position that the **market maker** may well be harmed but be the very person who is unable to prove that this was caused by the inside trade.
”

marketable adj St Exch (shares, securities) négociable

marking n St Exch (of shares) cotation f

markka n mark m finlandais

master budget n budget m global

Mastercard® n carte f Mastercard®

matched adj St Exch

◇ *matched bargain* mariage m

◇ Am *matched orders* ordres mpl couplés d'achat et de vente (pour stimuler le marché)

matching n (a) Acct rapprochement m, rattachement m (b) Am St Exch application f

◇ Acct *matching principle* principe m du rapprochement ou rattachement des produits et des charges

mature 1 adj (bill, investment, insurance policy) échu(e)
2 vi (of bill, investment, insu-

rance policy) échoir, arriver à échéance

◇ *mature economy* économie *f* en pleine maturité

maturity *n (of bill, investment, insurance policy)* échéance *f*

◇ *maturity date* date *f* d'échéance

◇ *maturity value* valeur *f* à l'échéance

MBI *n (abbr* management buy-in) apport *m* de gestion

❝

In the last few months, we have seen more managers taking advantage of the bottom of the economic cycle to buy into businesses. As companies continue to dispose of non-core subsidiaries, this next generation of **MBI** managers will have golden opportunities to acquire companies at realistic prices.

❞

MBO *n (***a***) (abbr* management buy-out) rachat *m* d'une société par la direction (**b**) *(abbr* management by objectives) gestion *f ou* direction *f* par objectifs

MBS *n (abbr* mortgage-backed security) titre *m* garanti par des créances hypothécaires

medium-dated *adj (gilts, securities)* à échéance moyenne

medium-term *adj (forecast, loan)* à moyen terme (négociable)

◇ *medium-term credit* crédit *m* (à) moyen terme

◇ *EU medium-term financial assistance* aide *f* financière à moyen terme

◇ *medium-term liabilities* dettes *fpl* à moyen terme

◇ *medium-term maturity* échéance *f* à moyen terme

◇ *medium-term note* billet *m* à moyen terme (négociable)

megamerger *n* méga-fusion *f*

member *n* membre *m*

◇ *Am member bank* banque *f* membre de la Réserve fédérale

◇ *St Exch member firm* société *f* membre

memo account *n Acct* poste *m* de mémoire

mercantile *adj* commercial(e)

◇ *mercantile agency* agence *f* commerciale

◇ *mercantile agent* agent *m* commercial

◇ *mercantile bank* banque *f* de commerce

◇ *mercantile broker* agent *m* de change

◇ *mercantile operations* opérations *fpl* mercantiles

◇ *mercantile paper* papier *m* commercial *ou* de commerce

❝

The seller must be a **mercantile agent**, i.e. a factor. Broadly, a **mercantile agent** is an independent agent acting in a way of business to whom someone else entrusts his goods and upon whom is conferred authority.

❞

mercantilism *n* mercantilisme *m*

merchant *n (trader)* négociant(e) *m,f; (shopkeeper)* marchand(e) *m,f*

◇ *Br merchant bank* banque *f* d'affaires *f ou* d'investissement

◇ *merchant banker* banquier (ère) *m,f* d'affaires

merge 1 *vt (banks, companies)* amalgamer, fusionner
    2 *vi (of banks, companies)* s'amalgamer, fusionner

merger *n (of banks, companies)* (absorption-)fusion *f*, unification *f*

◇ *Acct* **merger accounting** = bases de préparation des comptes consolidés où deux sociétés se sont unifiées

◇ *mergers and acquisitions* fusions et acquisitions *fpl*

◇ *merger premium* prime *f* de fusion

◇ *merger talks* discussions *fpl* en vue d'une fusion

method *n* méthode *f*

◇ *method of payment* mode *m* *ou* modalité *f* de paiement, mode *ou* modalité de règlement

mezzanine *n*

◇ *mezzanine debt* dette *f* subordonnée *ou* mezzanine

◇ *mezzanine finance* = méthode de financement d'une partie du capital nécessaire pour acheter une entreprise *(utilisée principalement par ses employés)*

> **"**
>
> The money will be raised in a mixture of straightforward borrowing and long-term, high-interest bearing **mezzanine finance** often referred to as junk bonds. The existing equity holders may also be asked to participate in a further round of equity raising, for around 10 per cent of the total.
>
> **"**

MidCap *n St Exch* = indice boursier américain composé d'actions de sociétés à moyenne capitalisation, ≃ MidCAC *m*

middle price *n St Exch* cours *m* moyen

mid-month account *n St Exch* liquidation *f* de quinzaine

minimum 1 *n* minimum *m*
    2 *adj* minimum, minimal(e)

◇ *minimum charge* tarif *m* minimum

◇ *minimum deposit* acompte *m* minimum

◇ *Br* **minimum lending rate** taux *m* de base, taux officiel d'escompte

◇ *minimum payment* paiement *m* minimum

◇ *minimum rate* taux *m* minimum

◇ *minimum wage* salaire *m* minimum

minority *n* minorité *f*

◇ *minority holding, minority interest* participation *f* minoritaire

◇ *minority investor* investisseur *m* minoritaire

◇ *Br* **minority shareholder,** *Am* **minority stockholder** actionnaire *mf* minoritaire

minor shareholder *n* actionnaire *mf* minoritaire

mint 1 *n Br* **the (Royal) Mint** ≃ (l'hôtel *m* de) la Monnaie
    2 *vt (coins)* frapper, battre

◇ *mint par* pair *m* intrinsèque

MIRAS *n (abbr* **Mortgage Interest Relief at Source)** = système par lequel les intérêts dus à une société de crédit immobilier sont déductibles des impôts

> **❝**
>
> The appropriate tax rates are then applied to calculate the total income tax due and it is only at this stage that the **MIRAS** system is introduced into the assessment. The income tax relief already given under **MIRAS** should be offset against PAYE deductions, income tax deducted from dividends etc in order to arrive at the net income tax already suffered.
>
> **❞**

misapplication n (of money) détournement m

misapply vt (money) détourner

misappropriate vt (money) détourner

misappropriation n (of money) détournement m

◇ **misappropriation of funds** détournement m de fonds, abus m de biens sociaux

misentry n Acct contre-position f

MLR n Br (abbr **minimum lending rate**) taux m de base

MMF n St Exch (abbr **money market fund**) ≃ SICAV f monétaire

mobilization n (of capital, resources) mobilisation f; **mobilization of capital** mobilisation des capitaux ou des fonds

mobilize vt (capital, resources) mobiliser

monetary adj monétaire

◇ Acct **monetary adjustment, monetary alignment** alignement m monétaire

◇ **monetary area** zone f monétaire

◇ **monetary assets** liquidités fpl

◇ **monetary bloc** bloc m monétaire

◇ EU **monetary compensatory amounts** montants mpl compensatoires monétaires

◇ **monetary control** contrôle m monétaire

◇ **monetary convention** convention f monétaire

◇ **monetary parity** parité f des monnaies

◇ **monetary policy** politique f monétaire

◇ Br **monetary policy committee** = comité formé de quatre membres de la Banque d'Angleterre et de quatre économistes nommés par le gouvernement, dont l'un des rôles est de fixer les taux d'intérêt

◇ **monetary reform** réforme f monétaire

◇ **monetary reserves** réserves fpl de change

◇ **monetary standard** étalon m monétaire

◇ **monetary surplus** surplus m monétaire

◇ **monetary system** système m monétaire

◇ **monetary unit** unité f monétaire

money n argent m; (currency) monnaie f; **to make money** (of person) gagner de l'argent; (of business) rapporter de l'argent; **to be worth a lot of money** (of thing) valoir cher; (of person) être riche; **the deal is worth a lot of money** c'est un contrat qui porte sur de très grosses sommes; **to get one's money back** (get reimbursed) se faire rembourser; (recover one's expenses) rentrer dans ses fonds

◇ **money broker** prêteur(euse) m,f sur titre

◇ Banking **money at call** argent m au jour le jour, argent à vue

◇ **money laundering** blanchiment m d'argent

◇ Am **money manager** gestionnaire mf de portefeuille

◇ **money market** marché m monétaire ou financier

◇ **money market fund** ≃ SICAV f monétaire

◇ **money market rate** taux m moyen du marché monétaire

◇ **money measurement** estimation f monétaire

◇ **money order** mandat m (postal)

◇ **money rate** taux m de l'argent

◇ Banking **money at short notice** argent m à court terme

◇ **money supply** masse f monétaire

◇ **money trader** cambiste mf

> **"**
>
> But these problems, together with those seen in the euro switchover, do post a warning. We now know that the far simpler changeover to the euro resulted in large bank payments going astray and a serious liquidity problem in the Euroland **money markets**, which required large injections of cash.
>
> **"**

moneychanger n (**a**) (person) courtier(ère) m,f de change (**b**) Am (machine) distributeur m de monnaie

moneylender n prêteur(euse) m,f

Monopoly money n Fam monnaie f de singe

monthly 1 adj mensuel(elle)
2 adv tous les mois; (pay) mensuellement

◇ **monthly instalment** mensualité f

◇ **monthly investment plan** plan m d'investissement mensuel

◇ **monthly payment** mensualité f

◇ **monthly statement** relevé m de fin de mois

moratorium n moratoire m; **to declare a moratorium** décréter un moratoire

mortgage 1 n (for house purchase) crédit m immobilier, prêt m immobilier; (raised on property) hypothèque f; **to take out a mortgage** prendre un crédit ou un prêt immobilier; **to secure a debt by mortgage** hypothéquer une créance; **to pay off a mortgage** purger une hypothèque
2 vt (land, building, title deeds) hypothéquer

◇ **mortgage bank** banque f hypothécaire

◇ **mortgage bond** obligation f hypothécaire

◇ **mortgage charge** affectation f hypothécaire

◇ **mortgage debenture** obligation f hypothécaire

◇ **mortgage deed** acte m hypothécaire

◇ **mortgage lender** prêteur m hypothécaire

◇ **mortgage loan** prêt m hypothécaire, prêt sur hypothèque

◇ **mortgage market** marché m hypothécaire

◇ *mortgage rate* taux *m* de crédit immobilier

◇ *mortgage registrar* conservateur(trice) *m,f* des hypothèques

◇ *mortgage repayment* remboursement *m* d'emprunt

◇ *mortgage security* garantie *f* hypothécaire

> A number of big banks quickly increased their base rates, including Halifax, the UK's largest **mortgage lender**. But the momentum of the housing market in recent months is likely to be too powerful to be halted by a single rate rise. Nationwide, the largest building society lender, announced that it would leave its rates unchanged.

mortgageable *adj* hypothécable

mortgage-backed security *n* titre *m* garanti par des créances hypothécaires

mortgagee *n* créancier(ère) *m,f* hypothécaire

mortgagor *n* débiteur(trice) *m,f* hypothécaire

▸ **move up** *vi St Exch (of shares)* se relever, reprendre; **shares moved up three points today** les actions ont gagné trois points aujourd'hui

movement *n (of capital)* circulation *f*; *(of share prices)* mouvement *m*; *(of market)* activité *f*

MPC *n Br (abbr* **monetary policy committee)** = comité formé de quatre membres de la Banque d'Angleterre et de quatre économistes nommés par le gouvernement, dont l'un des rôles est de fixer les taux d'intérêt

> Most City economists believe the Bank of England monetary policy committee will leave base rates on hold at 5 per cent at their two-day meeting tomorrow…. It is believed the **MPC** will feel economic indicators show overall inflationary pressures are under control, despite concerns about last week's statement from Halifax, Britain's biggest mortgage lender, that house prices had risen 9.4 per cent in the year to August.

MTFA *n EU (abbr* **medium-term financial assistance)** aide *f* financière à moyen terme

MTN *n (abbr* **medium-term note)** bon *m* à moyen terme (négociable)

multicurrency *adj EU* multidevise

multifunctional card *n Banking* carte *f* multifonctions

multilateral *adj* multilatéral(e)

◇ *multilateral agreement on investment* accord *m* multilatéral sur l'investissement

multiple *adj* multiple

◇ *St Exch* **multiple application** application *f* multiple

◇ *multiple exchange rate* taux *m* de change multiple

◇ *St Exch* **multiple options facility** ligne *f* de crédit à options multiples

municipal bond *n Am* obligation *f* de collectivité locale

mutual *adj* mutuel(elle), réciproque

◇ *mutual benefit society* société *f* de secours mutuel

◇ *Am mutual fund* fonds *m* commun de placement

◇ *mutual insurance company* société *f* de crédit mutuel, société de mutualité

naked *adj* sans garantie

◇ *St Exch* **naked debenture** obligation *f* chirographaire *ou* sans garantie

◇ *St Exch* **naked option** option *f* d'achat vendue à découvert

◇ **naked sale** vente *f* nue

name *n (of person)* nom *m*; *(of company)* raison *f* sociale; *(of account)* intitulé *m*; **the shares are in my name** les actions sont à mon nom

◇ *St Exch* **name day** deuxième jour *m* de liquidation

narration, narrative *n Acct* = note explicative dans un livre de commerce justifiant une écriture

narrow *adj (market)* étroit(e)

◇ **narrow money** = ensemble des billets et pièces de monnaie en circulation

Nasdaq *n St Exch (abbr* **National Association of Securities Dealers Automated Quotation**) le Nasdaq *(Bourse américaine des valeurs technologiques)*

national *adj* national(e)

◇ *Econ* **national debt** dette *f* publique, dette de l'État

◇ *Banking* **National Giro** = service britannique de chèques postaux

◇ **national income** revenu *m* national

◇ **National Insurance** = système britannique de sécurité sociale

◇ *Br* **National Insurance contributions** cotisations *fpl* à la Sécurité sociale

◇ **national product** produit *m* national

◇ *Br* **National Savings Bank** ≃ Caisse *f* nationale d'épargne

NAV *n (abbr* **net asset value**) valeur *f* d'actif net

NBV *n Acct (abbr* **net book value**) valeur *f* comptable nette

NDP *n Acct (abbr* **net domestic product**) produit *m* intérieur net

near month *n St Exch* échéance *f* proche

negative *adj* négatif(ive)

◇ **negative amortization** amortissement *m* négatif

◇ **negative amortization loan** prêt *m* à amortissement négatif

◇ **negative equity** plus-value *f* immobilière négative

◇ *Br* **negative income tax** impôt *m* négatif sur le revenu

◇ **negative interest** intérêt *m* négatif

◇ **negative pledge** clause *f* de nantissement négative

◇ *negative prescription* prescription *f* extinctive

> **44**
>
> For homeowners who have **negative equity** – where the value of their house is less than the mortgage – the Chancellor ratified earlier proposals to make it easier for them to trade down.
>
> **77**

neglected *adj St Exch (shares)* négligé(e)

negotiability *n* négociabilité *f*

negotiable *adj (salary, fee)* négociable, à débattre; *(bill, document)* négociable; **not negotiable** *(on cheque)* non à ordre

◇ *negotiable instrument* instrument *m* négociable

◇ *negotiable paper* papier *m* négociable

◇ *negotiable stock* titres *mpl* négociables

negotiate 1 *vt* (a) *(business deal)* négocier, traiter; *(loan, treaty, fee)* négocier; *(bill, document)* négocier, trafiquer
  2 *vi* négocier

nest egg *n* bas *m* de laine, pécule *m*

net 1 *adj (price, profit, interest)* net (nette)
  2 *n* net *m*; **net payable** net à payer
  3 *vt (of person, company)* gagner net; *(of sale)* produire net; **he nets £20,000 a year** il gagne 20 000 livres net par an
  4 *adv* **net of tax** net d'impôt; **net of VAT** hors TVA

◇ *net amount* montant *m* net

◇ *net assets* actif *m* net

◇ *Acct* **net asset value** valeur *f* d'actif net

◇ *Acct* **net book value** valeur *f* comptable nette

◇ *net capital expenditure* mise *f* de fonds nette, dépenses *fpl* nettes d'investissement

◇ *Acct* **net cash flow** cash-flow *m* net

◇ *net change* écart *m* net

◇ *net cost* prix *m* de revient

◇ *Acct* **net current assets** actif *m* circulant net

◇ *Acct* **net discounted cash-flow** cash-flow *m* actualisé net, flux *mpl* de trésorerie actualisés nets

◇ *net dividend* dividende *m* net

◇ *Econ* **net domestic product** produit *m* intérieur net

◇ *net earnings (of company)* bénéfices *mpl* nets; *(of worker)* salaire *m* net

◇ *net income (in accounts)* produit *m* net; *(of individual)* revenu *m* net

◇ *net interest income* net *m* financier

◇ *net loss* perte *f* nette

◇ *net margin* marge *f* nette

◇ *Econ* **net national income** revenu *m* national net

◇ *Econ* **net national product** produit *m* national net

◇ *net operating profit* rentabilité *f* nette d'exploitation

◇ *net present value* valeur *f* actuelle nette

◇ *Acct* **net present value rate** taux *m* d'actualisation

◇ *net profit* bénéfice *m* net, net *m* commercial

◇ *net profit ratio* ratio *m* de rentabilité nette, taux *m* de profit net

◇ Acct **net realizable value** valeur f réalisable nette

◇ **net receipts** recettes fpl nettes

◇ Acct **net residual value** valeur f résiduelle nette

◇ **net result** résultat m final

◇ **net return** rendement m net, résultat m net

◇ **net salary** salaire m net

◇ **net tangible assets** actif m corporel net

◇ **net total** montant m net

◇ Acct **net variance** écart m net

◇ **net working capital** fonds m de roulement net

◇ **net worth** situation f nette, valeur f nette

> **"**
>
> **Net asset value** (NAV), worked out by dividing the value of the portfolio, less borrowings, by the number of shares in issue, tells you how much each share can claim of the trust's assets. Discount or premium to NAV, the gap between the share price and the asset value, helps measure a trust's popularity.
>
> **"**

new adj nouveau(elle); (not used) neuf (neuve)

◇ **new borrowings** nouveaux emprunts mpl

◇ **new capital** capitaux mpl frais

◇ St Exch **new issue** nouvelle émission f

◇ St Exch **new issue market** marché m des nouvelles émissions, marché primaire

◇ Banking, St Exch **new money** crédit m de restructuration

◇ **new shares** actions fpl nouvelles

NI n (abbr **National Insurance**) = système britannique de sécurité sociale

NIC n Br (abbr **National Insurance contributions**) cotisations fpl à la Sécurité sociale

NIF n Banking (abbr **note issuance facility**) autorisation f d'émettre les billets de banque

night n nuit f

◇ **night rate** tarif m de nuit

◇ Banking **night safe** coffre (-fort) m de nuit

Nikkei Index n St Exch indice m Nikkei

nil 1 n néant m, zéro m; **the balance is nil** le solde est nul **2** adj nul (nulle), zéro

◇ **nil profit** bénéfice m nul

◇ **nil return** état m néant

no-load fund n St Exch fonds m sans frais d'acquisition, fonds qui ne prélève pas une commission

nominal adj (neglible) nominal(e); (rent) insignifiant(e); (damages) symbolique

◇ Acct **nominal account** compte m d'exploitation générale

◇ **nominal capital** capital m nominal

◇ **nominal interest rate** taux m d'intérêt nominal

◇ **nominal ledger** grand-livre m général

◇ **nominal partner** associé(e) m,f fictif(ive)

◇ **nominal price** prix m nominal

◇ **nominal value** valeur f nominale

◇ **nominal wages** salaire m nominal

◇ **nominal yield** taux m nominal

nominee n St Exch

◇ *nominee account* compte *m* d'intermédiaire

◇ *nominee company* prête-nom *m*

◇ *nominee name* nom *m* de l'intermédiaire

◇ *nominee shareholder* actionnaire *mf* intermédiaire

◇ *nominee shareholding* actionnariat *m* intermédiaire

non-acceptance *n (of bill of exchange)* non-acceptation *f*

non-accruing loan *n* emprunt *m* à risques

non-contributory pension *n* caisse *f* de retraite sans versements de la part des bénéficiaires

44

Although 70% of the 135 individuals questioned said they would prefer an equivalent salary increase to most benefits, given a choice of perks, the **non-contributory pension** narrowly defeated a company car as favourite.

77

non-convertible *adj (currency)* non convertible

non-cumulative *adj (shares)* non cumulatif(ive)

non-current liabilities *npl* Acct passif *m* non exigible

non-equity share *n* St Exch action *f* sans privilège de participation

non-participating *adj* St Exch *(share)* sans droit de participation

non-payment *n* non-paiement *m*; **in case of non-payment** en cas de non-paiement

non-performing loan *n* Banking prêt *m* en souffrance

non-recourse finance *n* financement *m* sans recours

non-recurring expenditure *n* dépenses *fpl* extraordinaires

non-taxable *adj (revenue)* non imposable

non-voting *adj* St Exch *(share)* sans droit de vote

normal *adj (profit)* normal(e)

note *n (banknote)* billet *m*; **a ten-pound note** un billet de dix livres

◇ *note of hand* billet *m* à ordre

◇ Banking *note issue* émission *f* fiduciaire

◇ Banking *note issue facility* autorisation *f* d'émettre les billets de banque

notice *n* (a) *(notification)* avis *m*, notification *f*; **until further notice** jusqu'à nouvel ordre (b) *(warning)* avertissement *m*; Banking **deposit at seven days' notice** dépôt *m* à sept jours de préavis

◇ *notice of receipt* accusé *m* de réception

◇ *notice of withdrawal* avis *m* de retrait de fonds

notional *adj (income)* fictif(ive)

NPV *n* Acct *(abbr* **net present value**) VAN *f*

◇ *NPV rate* taux *m* d'actualisation

NYMEX *n* St Exch *(abbr* **New York Mercantile Exchange**) = marché à terme des produits pétroliers de New York

NYSE *n* St Exch *(abbr* **New York Stock Exchange**) = la Bourse de New York

objectivity n Acct objectivité f

obligate vt Am (funds, credits) affecter

occupational pension scheme n caisse f de retraite maison

> Generally, an individual cannot be a member of an **occupational pension scheme** and make contributions to a personal pension scheme or retirement annuity policy in respect of the same source of income.

OD n (abbr **overdraft**) découvert m

odd lot n St Exch (of shares) lot m de moins de cent actions

odd-lot adj St Exch
◇ **odd-lot order** ordre m de moins de cent actions
◇ **odd-lot trading** achats mpl et ventes fpl de lots de moins de cent actions

off-balance sheet adj Acct (transaction) hors bilan
◇ **off-balance sheet item** poste m ou élément m hors bilan

offer n offre f; **to make sb an offer (for sth)** faire une offre à qn (pour qch)

◇ **offer price** cours m ou prix m vendeur
◇ **offer by prospectus** offre f publique de vente
◇ **offer to purchase** offre f publique d'achat
◇ **offer for sale** mise f sur le marché

offering n (of new shares) mise f sur le marché
◇ Am **offering circular** note f d'information

off-exchange adj St Exch (transaction, contract, market) hors Bourse, hors cote

office account n Acct, Banking compte m commercial

official 1 n fonctionnaire mf
2 adj officiel(elle)
◇ **official exchange rate** cours m officiel
◇ St Exch **Official List** cote f officielle
◇ **official market** marché m officiel
◇ St Exch **official quotation** cours m officiel
◇ Banking **official rate** taux m officiel d'escompte
◇ **official receiver** administrateur(trice) m,f judiciaire
◇ **official receivership** liquidation f judiciaire

offset 1 n Acct compensation f,

dédommagement *m*

2 *vt (compensate for)* compenser; **to offset sth against tax** déduire le montant de qch de ses impôts

◊ *offset agreement* accord *m* de compensation

offsetting entry *n Acct* écriture *f* de compensation

offshore 1 *adv* **to keep sth offshore** garder qch off-shore

2 *adj*

◊ *offshore banking* opérations *fpl* bancaires off-shore

◊ *offshore company* société *f* off-shore

◊ *offshore fund* fonds *m* off-shore

◊ *offshore investment* placement *m* off-shore

44

For UK residents, the reason for considering **offshore funds**, other than if they have some special appeal … will be possible tax advantages. If an **offshore fund** does not acquire distributor status from the Inland Revenue then any gain will be taxed as income when realised.

77

OID *n (abbr* **original issue discount bond)** obligation *f* à prime d'émission

oil royalty *n* redevance *f* pétrolière

omnium *n St Exch* omnium *m*

one *n St Exch* unité *f*; **to issue shares in ones** émettre des actions en unités

on-line *adj Comptr* en ligne

◊ *on-line bank* banque *f* en ligne

◊ *on-line banking* transactions *fpl* bancaires en ligne

◊ *St Exch* *on-line broker* courtier(ère) *m,f* électronique

◊ *on-line investor* investisseur *m* en ligne

◊ *on-line investing* investissement *m* en ligne

◊ *St Exch* *on-line trading* transactions *fpl* boursières électroniques

44

The explosion of **on-line trading** so far has done little to keep Merrill's bosses awake at night. After all, discount brokerages, including Schwab, have been around offline for years, but have not stopped Merrill and other full-service firms from earning a good living. E-broking is fiercely competitive. Although average prices have stopped falling, the more expensive firms such as Schwab and Fidelity are under huge pressure to offer their more active online traders a better deal.

77

OPEIC *n (abbr* **open-ended investment company)** SICAV *f*, société *f* d'investissement à capital variable

open 1 *adj* ouvert(e)

2 *vt* ouvrir; *(negotiations, conversation, debate)* entamer; **to open a line of credit** ouvrir un crédit; **to open a loan** ouvrir un emprunt

3 *vi St Exch* coter à l'ouverture; **the FTSE opened at 1083** l'indice FTA ouvert à 1083

◊ *open account* compte *m* ouvert

◇ *open cheque* chèque *m* ouvert *ou* non barré

◇ *St Exch* *open contract* position *f* ouverte

◇ *open credit* crédit *m* à découvert

◇ *Econ* *open market* marché *m* libre; *St Exch* **to buy shares on the open market** acheter des actions en Bourse

◇ *open money market* marché *m* libre des capitaux

◇ *St Exch* *open outcry* criée *f*

◇ *St Exch* *open position* position *f* ouverte

open-ended *adj (mortgage)* sans date limite

◇ *open-ended investment company*, *open-ended trust* société *f* d'investissement à capital variable, SICAV *f*

opening *n (of account, credit)* ouverture *f*

◇ *Acct* *opening balance* solde *m* d'ouverture

◇ *Acct* *opening balance sheet* bilan *m* d'ouverture

◇ *St Exch* *opening day* jour *m* d'ouverture

◇ *Acct* *opening entry* écriture *f* d'ouverture

◇ *St Exch* *opening price (at start of trading)* cours *m* d'ouverture, premier cours *m*; *(of new shares)* cours *m* d'introduction

◇ *opening session* séance *f* d'ouverture

◇ *Acct* *opening stock* stock *m* initial *ou* d'ouverture

operating *adj*

◇ *Am Acct* *operating account* compte *m* d'exploitation

◇ *operating assets* actif *m* d'exploitation

◇ *operating budget* budget *m* d'exploitation *ou* de fonctionnement

◇ *Am* *operating capital* capital *m* d'exploitation *ou* de roulement

◇ *operating cost* charge *f* opérationnelle

◇ *operation cash flow* cash-flow *m* disponible

◇ *operating costs* frais *mpl ou* coûts *mpl* d'exploitation

◇ *Acct* *operating costs analysis* comptabilité *f* analytique d'exploitation

◇ *operating deficit* déficit *m* d'exploitation

◇ *operating expenses* frais *mpl* d'exploitation

◇ *operating income* produits *mpl* d'exploitation

◇ *operating leverage* levier *m* d'exploitation

◇ *operating loss* perte *f* d'exploitation

◇ *operating margin* marge *f* (nette) d'exploitation

◇ *operating profit* bénéfice *m* d'exploitation

◇ *Acct* *operating ratio* coefficient *m ou* ratio *m* d'exploitation

◇ *Acct* *operating statement* compte *m ou* rapport *m* d'exploitation

operational *adj* opérationnel(elle)

◇ *operational audit* audit *m* opérationnel

◇ *operational costs* coûts *mpl* opérationnels

◇ *Acct* *operational cost accounting* comptabilité *f* analytique d'exploitation

◇ *Acct* *operational cost ac-*

counts comptes *mpl* analytiques d'exploitation

◇ Acct **operational cost centre** centre *m* d'analyse opérationnel

operator *n* St Exch opérateur *m*; **operator for a fall/rise** opérateur *m* à la baisse/hausse

opportunity cost *n* Acct coût *m* d'opportunité

option *n* St Exch option *f*, (marché *m* à) prime *f*; **to take an option (on sth)** prendre une option (sur qch); **to declare an option** répondre à une option; **option on shares** option sur actions; **option to double** option du double

◇ **option date** jour *m* d'option

◇ **option day** (jour *m* de la) réponse *f* des primes

◇ **option deal** opération *f* à prime

◇ **options desk** desk *m* d'options

◇ **options market** marché *m* à options *ou* à primes

◇ **option money** (montant *m* de la) prime *f*

◇ **option price** prix *m* de l'option

◇ **option spread** écart *m* de prime

◇ **options trading** négociations *fpl* à prime, opérations *fpl* à option

optionee *n* St Exch bénéficiaire *mf* d'options

order *n* (document) mandat *m*; **pay to the order of J. Martin** payez à l'ordre de J. Martin; **pay J. Martin or order** payez à J. Martin ou à son ordre; **by order and for account of J. Martin** d'ordre et pour compte de J. Martin

◇ **order form** bon *m* de commande

◇ **order to pay** mandat *m* ou ordonnance *f* de paiement

◇ **order to sell** ordre *m* de vente

order-driven *adj* St Exch (market) dirigé(e) par les ordres

ordinary *adj*

◇ Acct **ordinary activities** (balance sheet item) opérations *fpl* courantes

◇ **ordinary creditor** créancier (ère) *m,f* ordinaire

◇ Br St Exch **ordinary share** action *f* ordinaire

◇ Br St Exch **ordinary share capital** capital *m* en actions ordinaires

original 1 *n* (of document) original *m*; (of bill of exchange) primata *m*

2 *adj* original(e)

◇ **original capital** capital *m* d'origine

◇ **original cost** coût *m* initial

◇ Acct **original document** pièce *f* comptable

◇ St Exch **original issue discount bond** obligation *f* à prime d'émission

◇ **original value** valeur *f* initiale *ou* d'origine

OTC *adj* St Exch (abbr **over-the-counter**) hors cote

out book *n* Acct livre *m* du dehors

outflow *n* (of gold, currency) sortie *f*; **outflow per hour** débit *m* par heure

outgoings *npl* dépenses *fpl*, décaissements *mpl*; **the outgoings exceed the incomings** les dépenses excèdent les recettes

outlay *n* frais *mpl*, dépenses *fpl*

out-of-pocket expenses *npl* menues dépenses *fpl*

out-of-the-money option *n St Exch* option *f* en dehors

output *n*
◇ *Acct* **output ratio** coefficient *m* de capital
◇ **output tax** *n* TVA *f* encaissée, impôt *m* à la consommation

outside *adj St Exch*
◇ **outside broker** courtier(ère) *m,f* marron *ou* libre
◇ **outside brokerage** affaires *fpl* de banque
◇ **outside market** marché *m* hors cote *ou* en coulisse
◇ **outside price** prix *m* maximum

outsider *n St Exch* courtier (ère) *m,f* marron

outstanding *adj (amount, account)* impayé(e), dû (due); *(payment)* en retard; *(invoice)* en souffrance; *(interest)* échu(e)
◇ *Banking* **outstanding balance** solde *m* à découvert
◇ *Banking* **outstanding cheque** chèque *m* en circulation
◇ **outstanding credits** encours *m* de crédit
◇ **outstanding debts** créances *fpl* (à recouvrer)
◇ *St Exch* **outstanding shares** actions *fpl* en cours *ou* en circulation

outward investment *n* investissement *m* à l'étranger

overall budget *n* budget *m* global

overassess *vt (for tax)* surimposer

overassessment *n (for tax)* surimposition *f*

overborrow *vi (of company)* emprunter de façon excessive

overborrowed *adj (of company)* surendetté(e)

overborrowing *n (of company)* surendettement *m*

overbought *adj St Exch (market)* surévalué(e), suracheté(e)

> Mr Greenspan's dilemma is that he would probably like to raise interest rates – inflation indicators from the labour market are mixed but the productivity miracle cannot continue for ever while signals from the energy sector are less equivocal. He would also like to see the US stock markets down from their current **overbought** levels. But he must achieve both without causing a nervous market to panic.

overcapitalization *n* surcapitalisation *f*

overcapitalize *vt* surcapitaliser

overdraft *n Banking* découvert *m*; **to have an overdraft** avoir un découvert; **to allow sb an overdraft** accorder à qn un découvert; **to pay off one's overdraft** rembourser son découvert
◇ **overdraft facility** autorisation *f* de découvert, facilités *fpl* de caisse
◇ **overdraft limit** plafond *m* de découvert

◇ *overdraft loan* prêt *m* à découvert

> **"**
>
> A company can borrow from its clearing bank via an **overdraft facility** attached to its current account. Large corporate customers pay interest on overdrafts at the bank's base rate plus 1%. Smaller companies will pay a higher margin.
>
> **"**

overdraw *Banking* **1** *vt (account)* mettre à découvert; **to be overdrawn** avoir un découvert, être à découvert; **your account is overdrawn** votre compte est débiteur *ou* à découvert; **I'm £100 overdrawn** j'ai un découvert de 100 livres

2 *vi* tirer à découvert; **to overdraw on one's account** mettre son compte à découvert

overdue *adj (account, payment)* en retard, impayé(e); *(bill)* en souffrance; **our repayments are two months overdue** nous avons un retard de deux mois dans nos remboursements

over-gear *vt (company)* surendetter; **to be over-geared** être surendetté

over-gearing *n* surendettement *m*

overhead *n* charge *f* opérationnelle; *Br* **overheads,** *Am* **overhead** frais *mpl* généraux; **to reduce overheads** réduire les frais généraux

◇ *Acct* **overhead absorption rate** taux *m* d'amortissement des frais généraux

◇ *overhead budget* budget *m* des charges

◇ *overhead costs, overhead expenses* frais *mpl* généraux

◇ *overhead variance* variance *f* des frais généraux

overinvest 1 *vt* trop investir
2 *vi* trop investir (**in** dans)

overinvestment *n* surinvestissement *m*

overissue 1 *n (of paper money)* surémission *f*
2 *vt (paper money)* faire une surémission de

overnight *adj*

◇ *overnight loan* prêt *m* du jour au lendemain

◇ *overnight rate* taux *m* de l'argent au jour le jour

overperform *vi St Exch (of shares)* avoir un cours anormalement élevé

over-riding commission *n* commission *f* d'arrangement

oversold *adj St Exch (market)* sousévalué(e)

overspend 1 *n* dépenses *fpl* excessives
2 *vt (money)* dépenser trop de
3 *vi* dépasser le budget, dépenser trop d'argent

overspending *n* dépassement *m* budgétaire

oversubscribe *vt St Exch (loan, share issue)* sursouscrire; **the share issue was oversubscribed** la demande d'achats a dépassé le nombre de titres émis

oversubscription *n St Exch (of loan, share issue)* sursouscription *f*

overtax *vt (goods)* surtaxer; *(person)* surtaxer, surimposer

over-the-counter *adj St Exch* hors cote

◇ *Am* **over-the-counter market** marché *m* hors cote, marché des transactions hors séance

"

Some companies will transfer from the Third market to the USM, some will go to the **over-the-counter market** (OTC), which is an informal market that consists of trading in small business shares by a group of brokers and licensed dealers to the public.

"

owing *adj* dû (due); **all the money owing to me** tout l'argent qui m'est dû

owner *n* propriétaire *mf*

◇ *Acct* **owner's capital account** compte *m* de l'exploitant

paid *adj* (**a**) *(goods, bill)* payé(e); **paid** *(on bill)* pour acquit (**b**) *(person, work)* payé(e), rémunéré(e)

paid-up *adj*

◇ **paid-up capital** capital *m* versé

◇ **paid-up shares** actions *fpl* libérées

> A member's liability is limited to the amount, if any, which remains unpaid upon the member's shares. Since normal practice is for a member to be issued with **paid-up shares**, the member's liability is limited to the extent that the shares which he or she has in the company are rendered valueless.

P & L *n* (**a**) *(abbr* **profit and loss**) pertes *fpl* et profits *mpl* (**b**) *(abbr* **profit and loss account, profit and loss statement**) compte *m* de résultat; **we can see from the P & L that developing the product is not a viable option** le compte de résultat montre clairement qu'il ne serait pas rentable de développer ce produit

◇ **P & L statement** compte *m* de résultat

panic *n St Exch*

◇ **panic buying** achats *mpl* de précaution

◇ **panic selling** ventes *fpl* de précaution

paper *n (banknotes)* billets *mpl* (de banque)

◇ **paper company** société *f* d'investissement

◇ **paper loss** moins-value *f*

◇ **paper money** papier-monnaie *m*, monnaie *f* fiduciaire

◇ **paper profit** profit *m* fictif

◇ **paper securities** titres *mpl* fiduciaires, papiers *mpl* valeurs

◇ **paper transaction** jeu *m* d'écritures

> Wall Street's rapid rise has meant many Americans feel richer and they have been prepared to spend their **paper profits** from the US equity markets by borrowing against them or running down their savings. If Mr Greenspan's policy decisions spark a crisis of confidence, Wall Street could nose dive with a consequent impact on consumer spending.

paperless trading *n St Exch* marché *m* électronique, cotation *f* électronique

par n (of bills, shares) pair m; **at par** au pair; **to issue shares at par** émettre des actions au pair; **above par** au-dessus du pair; **below par** au-dessous du pair

◇ St Exch **par bond** obligation f émise au pair

◇ **par of exchange** pair m du change

◇ St Exch **par value** valeur f au pair ou nominale

parallel adj

◇ **parallel market** marché m parallèle

◇ **parallel rate of exchange** cours m parallèle

parcel n St Exch (of shares) paquet m

parent company n société f mère

pari passu adj St Exch pari passu (**with** avec)

parity n parité f; **the two currencies were at parity** les deux monnaies étaient à parité; **franc-dollar parity** parité franc-dollar

◇ **parity of exchange** parité f de change

◇ **parity ratio** rapport m de parité

◇ **parity table** table f des parités

◇ **parity value** valeur f au pair

park vt St Exch mettre en attente

parking n St Exch mise f en attente

partial adj partiel(elle)

◇ Banking **partial acceptance** (of bill) acceptation f partielle

◇ **partial payment** paiement m partiel

participating interest n intérêt m de participation; **to hold a participating interest in a company** avoir un intérêt de participation dans une société

participation n St Exch

◇ **participation certificate** titre m ou bon m de participation

◇ **participation rate** taux m d'activité

particular lien n privilège m spécial

partly adv partiellement, en partie

◇ **partly paid-up capital** capital m non entièrement versé

◇ **partly paid-up shares** actions fpl non entièrement libérées

◇ **partly secured creditor** créancier(ère) m,f partiellement nanti(e)

partner n associé(e) m,f

partnership n (association) association f; (company) ≃ société f en nom collectif

◇ **partnership share** part f d'association

part payment n paiement m partiel

pass book n livret m de banque, carnet m de banque

pass-through *adj Am*

◇ *pass-through tax entity* = société fiscalement opaque

◇ *pass-through securities* titres *mpl* garantis par des créances hypothécaires

pay 1 *n (wages)* salaire *m*, paie *f*
  2 *vt (bill, debt)* payer, régler; *(dividend)* distribuer; *(taxes)* payer; **to pay cash** payer (argent) comptant, payer en espèces; **to pay a cheque into the bank** déposer un chèque à la banque
  3 *vi* payer, régler; **how would you like to pay?** comment souhaitez-vous régler?; **to pay by cheque** payer *ou* régler par chèque; **to pay in cash** payer en espèces; **to pay in advance** payer d'avance; **to pay in full** payer intégralement *ou* en totalité; **to pay on demand** *or* **on presentation** payer à vue *ou* à présentation; **pay to bearer** payez au porteur; **pay to bearer clause** clause *f* au porteur

◇ *Acct* **pay ledger** livre *m* de paie

◇ *pay (advice) slip* bulletin *m* de paie *ou* de salaire

▸ **pay back** *vt sep (loan, lender)* rembourser

▸ **pay in** *vt sep (money, cheque)* verser sur un compte

▸ **pay off** *vt sep (debt, loan, mortgage)* rembourser

payable 1 *adj* payable; **payable in 24 monthly instalments/in advance** payable en 24 mensualités/d'avance; **to make a cheque payable to sb** faire *ou* libeller un chèque à l'ordre de qn; **please make your cheque payable to Miss Johnston** veuillez libeller votre chèque à l'ordre de Miss Johnston; **payable at sight** payable à vue; **payable to order** payable à ordre; **payable to bearer** payable au porteur
  2 *n Am* **payables** factures *fpl* à payer

pay-as-you-earn, *Am* **pay-as-you-go** *n* prélèvement *m* de l'impôt à la source

payback *n* récupération *f (du capital investi)*

◇ *payback period* délai *m* de récupération, période *f* de remboursement

PAYE *n Br (abbr* **pay-as-you-earn)** prélèvement *m* de l'impôt à la source

“

There may be an obligation for the band members to deduct income tax (Pay As You Earn) from the salaries of any employees. In this case, it is necessary to set up a **PAYE** scheme with the Inland Revenue, to deduct tax and National Insurance, and to pay these over on a regular monthly basis.

”

payee *n (of postal order, cheque)* bénéficiaire *mf*; *(of bill)* porteur *m*, preneur *m*

paying bank *n* domiciliataire *m*, établissement *m* payeur, domiciliation *f* bancaire

paying-in *n*

◇ *paying-in book* carnet *m* de versements

◇ *paying-in slip* bordereau *m ou* feuille *f* de versement

payment *n* paiement *m*, versement *m*; **to make a payment**

effectuer un versement; **to stop payment on a cheque** faire opposition à un chèque; **on payment of £100** contre paiement de 100 livres; **payment by instalments** paiement échelonné *ou* par versements, paiement à tempérament; **in easy payments** avec facilités de paiement; **payment on account** paiement partiel; **payment in advance** paiement d'avance, paiement par anticipation; **payment in arrears** paiement arriéré; **payment in cash** paiement en espèces; **payment by cheque** paiement par chèque; **payment on delivery** livraison *f* contre remboursement; **payment in full** paiement intégral; **payment in kind** paiement *ou* avantages *mpl* en nature

◇ **payment advice** avis *m* de paiement

◇ **payment day** jour *m* de paiement, jour de règlement

◇ **payment facilities** facilités *fpl* de paiement

◇ **payment order** ordre *m* de paiement

◇ **payment schedule** échéancier *m* (de paiement)

payroll *n* (**a**) *(list of employees)* liste *f* du personnel, registre *m* des salaires (**b**) *(money paid)* masse *f* salariale

◇ *Acct* **payroll ledger** journal *m* *ou* livre *m* de paie

◇ **payroll tax** impôt *m* sur la masse salariale

peak price *n St Exch* prix *m* maximum

peg *vt St Exch (prices) (fix)* fixer; *(stabilize)* stabiliser; **to peg sth to the rate of inflation** indexer qch sur le taux de l'inflation; **oil**

was pegged at $20 a barrel le prix du pétrole était fixé à 20 dollars le baril; **export earnings are pegged to the exchange rate** le revenu des exportations varie en fonction du taux de change

penal *adj*

◇ **penal interest** intérêts *mpl* moratoires

◇ **penal rate** taux *m* d'usure

penalty interest *n* pénalité *f* de retard, intérêts *mpl* moratoires

penny *n Br (coin, unit of currency)* penny *m*; *Am (coin)* cent *m*

◇ *Br St Exch* **penny shares** actions *fpl* d'une valeur de moins d'une livre sterling

◇ *Am St Exch* **penny stocks** actions *fpl* d'une valeur de moins d'un dollar

pension *n* pension *f*; *(after retirement)* (pension de) retraite *f*

◇ **pension fund** caisse *f* de retraite, fonds *m* de pension

◇ **pension plan** plan *m* de retraite

◇ **pension scheme** régime *m* de retraite

> **"**
>
> These interlocking shareholders have an interest in each other's prosperity, partly because they do business with one another, partly because they have invested in each other. Unlike a **pension fund** in either Britain, America or even Japan, these interlocking shareholders have strong economic reasons to care about the performance of the firms in which they own shares.
>
> **"**

pensionable adj (person) qui a droit à une pension; (after retirement) qui a droit à sa retraite

◇ **pensionable age** âge m de la mise à la retraite

PEP n (abbr **personal equity plan**) ≃ PEA m

p/e ratio n Acct (abbr **price/earnings ratio**) ratio m cours-bénéfices, rapport m cours-bénéfices, PER m

perceived value n valeur f perçue

perform vi (of company) fonctionner; (of shares, investment, currency) se comporter; **the Edinburgh branch is performing very well** les résultats de la succursale d'Édimbourg sont très satisfaisants; **how did the company perform in the first quarter?** comment la société a-t-elle fonctionné au premier trimestre?; **shares performed well yesterday** les actions se sont bien comportées hier

performance n (a) (of contract, task) exécution f (b) (of company) résultats mpl, performance f; (of shares, investment, currency) performance; **the country's poor economic performance** les mauvais résultats économiques du pays; **sterling's performance on the Stock Exchange** le comportement en Bourse de la livre sterling

◇ **performance bond** garantie f de bonne fin ou de bonne exécution

◇ **performance ratio** coefficient m ou ratio m d'exploitation

period n période f

◇ **period bill** effet m à terme

◇ **period of grace** délai m de grâce

periodic adj

◇ **periodic inventory** inventaire m périodique

◇ **periodic payments** paiements mpl périodiques

permanent adj permanent(e)

◇ **permanent assets** actif m immobilisé

◇ **permanent credit** accréditif m permanent

permission n permission f, autorisation f

◇ St Exch **permission to deal** visa m (de la COB)

perpetual adj perpétuel(elle)

◇ **perpetual inventory** stock m stratégique

◇ **perpetual loan** emprunt m perpétuel (elle)

personal adj personnel(elle)

◇ **personal account** St Exch compte m de tiers; Acct compte propre

◇ **personal assets** patrimoine m

◇ Banking **personal assets profile** profil m patrimonial

◇ **personal credit** crédit m personnel

◇ **personal equity plan** ≃ plan m d'épargne en actions

◇ Banking **personal identification number** code m confidentiel (d'une carte bancaire)

◇ Br **Personal Investment Authority** = organisme chargé de surveiller les activités des conseillers financiers indépendants et de protéger les petits investisseurs

◇ *Banking* **personal loan** prêt *m* personnel, prêt personnalisé

◇ **personal property** biens *mpl* personnels

◇ **personal withdrawals** levées *fpl* de compte

peseta *n* peseta *f*

petition in bankruptcy *n* demande *f* de mise en liquidation judiciaire; **to file a petition in bankruptcy** déposer son bilan; **filing of a petition in bankruptcy** dépôt *m* de bilan

petrocurrency *n* pétromonnaies *fpl*

petrodollar *n* pétrodollar *m*

petty cash *n* petite caisse *f*; **they'll pay you back out of petty cash** ils vous rembourseront avec la petite caisse

◇ **petty cash book** livre *m* de petite caisse

◇ **petty cash box** petite caisse *f*

◇ **petty cash voucher** bon *m* de petite caisse

pfennig *n* pfennig *m*

physical *adj*

◇ **physical assets** immobilisations *fpl* non financières

◇ **physical capital** capital *m* existant

◇ **physical inventory** inventaire *m* effectif

PIA *n Br* (*abbr* **personal investment authority**) = organisme chargé de surveiller les activités des conseillers financiers indépendants et de protéger les petits investisseurs

PIBOR *n* (*abbr* **Paris Interbank Offer Rate**) TIOP *m*

piggybacking *n Banking* portage *m*

PIN *n* (*abbr* **personal identification number**) **PIN (number)** code *m* confidentiel (*d'une carte bancaire*)

pit *n St Exch* corbeille *f*

place 1 *n* lieu *m*
  2 *vt St Exch* (*shares*) placer, disposer

◇ **place of issue** lieu *m* d'émission

placement *n St Exch* (*of shares*) placement *m*

planning-programming-budgeting system *n Acct* système *m* de planification-programmation-budgétisation, rationalisation *f* des choix budgétaires

plastic *Fam* **1** *n* (*credit cards*) cartes *fpl* de crédit; **to put sth on the plastic** payer qch avec une carte de crédit; **do they take plastic?** est-ce qu'ils acceptent les cartes de crédit?
  2 *adj*

◇ **plastic money** cartes *fpl* de crédit

pledge 1 *n* gage *m*, garantie *f*
  2 *vt* donner en gage *ou* en garantie; **to pledge one's property** engager son bien; **to pledge se-**

curities déposer des titres en garantie; **pledged securities** valeurs *fpl* nanties

◇ *pledge holder* détenteur (trice) *m,f* de gage(s)

▸**plough back,** *Am* **plow back** *vt sep* réinvestir (**into** dans); **to plough the profits back into the company** réinvestir les bénéfices dans la société

▸**plough in,** *Am* **plow in** *vt sep* (*money*) investir

ploughback, *Am* **plowback** *n* bénéfices *mpl* réinvestis

▸**plow back, plow in** *Am* = plough back, plough in

plowback *Am* = ploughback

plunge *vi* (**a**) (*of price, rate, currency*) chuter, dégringoler; **sales have plunged by 30%** les ventes ont chuté de 30% (**b**) *St Exch* (*of investor, speculator*) risquer de grosses sommes

P/N *n* (*abbr* **promissory note**) billet *m* à ordre, effet *m* à ordre

PO *n* (**a**) (*abbr* **Post Office**) poste *f* (**b**) (*abbr* **postal order**) mandat *m* postal

◇ *PO Box* BP *f*, boîte *f* postale

point *n St Exch* point *m*; **the Dow Jones index is up/down two points** l'indice Dow Jones a augmenté/baissé de deux points

pool *vt* (*capital, profits, ideas, resources*) mettre en commun

pooling of interests *n Am* (aborption-)fusion *f*, unification *f*

portable *adj* (*pension, mortgage*) transférable

portfolio *n* (*of shares*) portefeuille *m*

◇ *portfolio analysis* analyse *f* de portefeuille

◇ *portfolio diversification* diversification *f* de portefeuille

◇ *portfolio insurance* assurance *f* de portefeuille

◇ *portfolio management* gestion *f* de portefeuille

◇ *portfolio manager* gestionnaire *mf* de portefeuille

◇ *portfolio securities* valeurs *fpl* de portefeuille

> **"**
>
> Mr Bergsten also believes that the euro will see a sharp rise in its exchange rate, although that has certainly not yet proved true. Nevertheless, many observers still believe that large **portfolio diversification** from dollars to euro could reach $500 billion or even $1 trillion over the next three years.
>
> **"**

position 1 *n* (**a**) (*circumstances*) état *m*, situation *f*; **the cash position is not good** la situation de la caisse laisse à désirer; **our financial position is improving** notre situation financière s'améliore (**b**) *St Exch* position *f*; **to take a long/short position** prendre une position longue/courte

◇ *position trader* spéculateur (trice) *m,f* sur plusieurs positions

positive prescription *n* prescription *f* acquisitive

post 1 *n Br* (*mail*) courrier *m* **2** *vt* (**a**) *Acct* (*entry*) passer; **to post an amount** passer un montant; **to post the books** passer les écritures

(**b**) *St Exch* **to post security** déposer des garanties

◇ ***post office*** (bureau *m* de) poste; **the Post Office** *(organization)* ≃ la Poste

◇ ***post office account*** compte *m* chèque postal

postal order *n Br* mandat *m* postal, mandat poste

postdate *vt (cheque)* postdater

pound *n (unit of currency)* livre *f*

◇ ***pound sign*** symbole *m* de la livre

◇ ***pound sterling*** livre *f* sterling

PPB *n (abbr* **planning-programming-budgeting system)** *Acct* système *m* de planification-programmation-budgétisation, rationalisation *f* des choix budgétaires

prebill *vt Acct* préfacturer

prebilling *n Acct* préfacturation *f*

predate *vt (cheque)* antidater

preemption right *n St Exch* droit *m* de préemption

preference *n St Exch* droit *m* de priorité

◇ *Br* **preference dividend** dividende *m* privilégié *ou* prioritaire

◇ *Br* **preference share** action *f* privilégiée *ou* de priorité

preferential *adj (treatment)* préférentiel(elle)

◇ ***preferential creditor*** créancier(ère) *m,f* privilégié(e)

◇ ***preferential rate*** tarif *m* préférentiel

preferred *adj* privilégié(e)

◇ ***preferred creditor*** créancier (ère) *m,f* privilégié(e)

◇ ***preferred debt*** dette *f ou* créance *f* privilégiée

◇ *Am St Exch* **preferred stock** actions *fpl* privilégiées *ou* de priorité

pre-inventory balance *n Acct* balance *f* avant inventaire

premium *n St Exch* **to pay a premium** verser *ou* acquitter un premium; **to issue shares at a premium** émettre des actions au-dessus du pair *ou* de leur valeur nominale

◇ ***premium bonds*** ≃ obligations *fpl* à lots

◇ ***premium discount*** ristourne *f* de prime

◇ ***premium on redemption*** prime *f* de remboursement

prepaid *adj* prépayé(e); *Acct* payé(e) d'avance, constaté(e) d'avance

◇ ***prepaid income*** produit *m* constaté d'avance

prepayment *n* paiement *m* à l'avance, paiement préalable; *Acct* charge *f* constatée d'avance

◇ ***prepayment clause*** clause *f* de remboursement par anticipation

◇ ***prepayment penalty*** indemnité *f* de remboursement par anticipation

present 1 *adj* actuel(elle); **the present year** l'année courante

2 *vt (invoice)* présenter; **to present a cheque for payment** présenter un chèque à l'encaissement; **to present a bill for acceptance** présenter une traite à l'acceptation

◇ *present capital* capital *m* appelé

◇ *Acct present value* valeur *f* actuelle *ou* actualisée

presentation *n (showing)* présentation *f*; **presentation for acceptance** présentation à l'acceptation; **presentation for payment** présentation au paiement; **payable on presentation of the coupon** payable contre remise du coupon; **on presentation of the invoice** au vu de *ou* sur présentation de la facture; **cheque payable on presentation** chèque *m* payable à vue

◇ *Banking presentation date* date *f* de présentation

presentment *n (of bill of exchange)* présentation *f*

pre-tax *adj* brut(e), avant impôts

◇ *pre-tax profit* bénéfice *m* brut *ou* avant impôts

price 1 *n* prix *m*; *(of shares)* cours *m*, cote *f*; **to rise** *or* **go up in price** augmenter

2 *vt* (**a**) *(decide cost of)* fixer le prix de

(**b**) *(ascertain cost of)* s'informer du prix de; *(estimate value of)* évaluer, estimer la valeur de

(**c**) *Econ (quantity)* valoriser

◇ *price bid* offre *f* de prix

◇ *Econ prices and incomes policy* politique *f* des prix et des salaires

◇ *price index* indice *m* des prix

◇ *price inflation* inflation *f* des prix

◇ *St Exch price maker* fixeur *m* de prix

◇ *Banking price of money* prix *m ou* loyer *m* de l'argent

◇ *St Exch price spreads* écarts *mpl* de cours

◇ *price structure* structure *f* des prix

> **❝**
>
> National Power and its partner in duopoly, PowerGen, are the only game in town. Buy from them or buy candles. They can name their price and they do. One recent Friday, for example, generators raised the **price bid** into the pool at noon by 440 per cent above the sale price at 7am.
>
> **❞**

price-earnings ratio *n St Exch* ratio *m* cours-bénéfices, rapport *m* cours-bénéfices

primary *adj Econ* primaire

◇ *primary dealer* = spécialiste en valeurs du Trésor

◇ *Am primary earnings per share* bénéfices *mpl* premiers par action

◇ *St Exch primary market* marché *m* primaire

◇ *Acct primary ratio* ratio *m* des bénéfices d'exploitation sur le capital employé

prime *adj*

◇ *prime bill* papier *m* commercial de premier ordre

◇ *prime bond* obligation *f* de premier ordre

◇ *Am prime cost* prix *m* de revient de base

◇ *prime lending rate* taux *m* de base bancaire

◇ *prime rate* taux *m* d'escompte bancaire préférentiel

principal *n (capital)* capital *m*; *(of debt)* principal *m*; **principal and interest** capital et intérêts

priority share n St Exch action f privilégiée, action de priorité

private adj (a) (not state-run) privé(e) (b) (personal) personnel(elle)
◇ **private bank** banque f privée
◇ **private income** rentes fpl
◇ **private investment** investissement m ou placement m privé
◇ **private investor** investisseur m privé
◇ **private limited company** société f à responsabilité limitée
◇ **private pension** retraite f complémentaire
◇ **private sector** secteur m privé

privileged debt n dette f privilégiée

prize bond npl obligation f à lots, valeur f à lots

production n production f
◇ **production budget** budget m de production
◇ **production costs** coûts mpl de production
◇ Acct **production overheads** frais mpl généraux de production

profit n bénéfice m, profit m; **profits were down/up this year** les bénéfices ont diminué/augmenté cette année; **to make a profit** faire un bénéfice ou des bénéfices; **to show a profit** rapporter un bénéfice ou des bénéfices; **to move into profit** (of business) devenir rentable; **to sell sth at a profit** faire un bénéfice sur la vente de qch; **profit and loss** pertes fpl et profits; **profit before tax** bénéfices avant impôts

◇ Acct **profit balance** solde m bénéficiaire
◇ Acct **profit centre** centre m de profit
◇ **profit equation** équation f de bénéfice
◇ **profit indicator** indice m de profit
◇ Acct **profit and loss account** compte m de résultat; (formerly) compte de pertes et profits
◇ Acct **profit and loss statement** compte m de résultat; (formerly) compte de pertes et profits
◇ **profit margin** marge f bénéficiaire
◇ **profit motive** motivation f par le profit
◇ **profit optimization** optimisation f du ou des profits
◇ **profit outlook** perspectives fpl de profit
◇ **profit tax** impôt m sur les bénéfices
◇ **profit warning** = annonce d'une baisse prochaine des bénéfices d'une entreprise

> **"**
>
> City professionals are naturally wary of a company which has issued three **profit warnings** in the space of two years – the most recent arriving in July. But other market players are more optimistic. They smell more corporate action and they are probably right.
>
> **"**

profitability n rentabilité f
◇ **profitability index** indice m de rentabilité
◇ **profitability value** (of a company) valeur f de rendement

profitable *adj (business, deal, investment)* rentable; **it would not be profitable for me to sell** cela ne me rapporterait pas grand-chose de vendre

profit-centre accounting *n Acct* = comptabilité par centres de profits

profit-sharing *n* participation *f* aux bénéfices, intéressement *m* aux bénéfices; **we have a profit-sharing scheme** nous avons un système de participation (aux bénéfices)

profit-taking *n* prise *f* de bénéfices

profit-volume ratio *n* rapport *m* profit sur ventes

pro forma 1 *n (invoice)* facture *f* pro forma
2 *adj*
◊ **pro forma bill** traite *f* pro forma
◊ **pro forma invoice** facture *f* pro forma

progressive tax *n* impôt *m* progressif

projected turnover *n* chiffre *m* d'affaires prévisionnel

promissory note *n* billet *m* à ordre, effet *m* à ordre

prompt note *n* rappel *m* d'échéance

property *n (real estate)* biens *mpl* immobiliers
◊ *Br* **property assets** patrimoine *m* immobilier
◊ *Br* **property loan** prêt *m* immobilier
◊ **property shares** valeurs *fpl* immobilières
◊ **property speculation** spéculations *fpl* immobilières

◊ **property tax** impôt *m* foncier

prospectus *n St Exch (about share issue)* appel *m* à la souscription publique

provident fund *n* caisse *f* de prévoyance

provision *n (allowance)* provision *f*; **to make provision for sth** prévoir qch; **provision for bad debts** provision pour créances douteuses; *Acct* **provision for depreciation** provision pour dépréciation *ou* amortissement; *Acct* **provision for liabilities** provision pour sommes exigibles

◊ **provision of capital** prestation *f* de capitaux

provisional budget *n* budget *m* prévisionnel

prudence concept *n Acct* principe *m* de prudence

> **"**
>
> The 1987 SORP stated that the **prudence concept** has to be modified because 'proper accounting practice within the legal framework' includes accounting that 'best commercial practice' would find imprudent. The instance cited was where debt charges continue to be included in revenue accounts for financing assets whose useful life is over.
>
> **"**

PSBR *n Br Econ (abbr* **public sector borrowing requirement)** = besoins d'emprunt du secteur public non couverts par les rentrées fiscales

public 1 *n* **the (general) public** le (grand) public; **to issue shares**

to the public placer des actions dans le public

2 *adj* public(ique); *St Exch* **to go public** être coté(e) en Bourse

◇ *public company* société *f* d'État

◇ *Econ public debt* dette *f* publique *ou* de l'État

◇ *Banking public deposits* = avoirs des différents services du gouvernement britannique à la Banque d'Angleterre

◇ *public enterprise* (company) entreprise *f* publique

◇ *public expenditure* dépenses *fpl* publiques

◇ *public finance* finances *fpl* publiques

◇ *public funds* fonds *mpl* publics

◇ *public limited company* ≃ société *f* anonyme

◇ *public loan* emprunt *m* public

◇ *public monies* deniers *mpl* de l'État

◇ *St Exch public offering* offre *f* publique

◇ *public sector* secteur *m* public

◇ *public sector borrowing requirement* = besoins d'emprunt du secteur public non couverts par les rentrées fiscales

◇ *public sector deficit* déficit *m* du secteur public

◇ *public sector earnings* revenus *mpl* du secteur public

◇ *St Exch public share offer* offre *f* publique de vente

◇ *public spending* dépenses *fpl* publiques

◇ *Br public utility* service *m* public

◇ *Br public utility company* société *f* d'utilité publique

punt *n* livre *f* irlandaise

punter *n Fam St Exch* (speculator) boursicoteur(euse) *m,f*, boursicotier(ère) *m,f*

purchase 1 *n* (a) (act of buying, thing bought) achat *m*; **to make a purchase** faire un achat (b) (of company) rachat *m*

2 *vt* acheter, acquérir; **to purchase sth from sb** acheter qch à qn; **to purchase sth on credit** acheter qch à crédit; *Acct* **to purchase a debt** racheter une créance

3 *vi* acheter; **now is the time to purchase** c'est maintenant qu'il faut acheter

◇ *Acct purchase account* compte *m* d'achats

◇ *Am Acct purchase accounting* = méthode de comptabilité utilisée lors de l'acquisition d'une entreprise, dans laquelle les résultats de la filiale n'apparaissent pas dans le bilan de la société mère

◇ *purchase budget* budget *m* des approvisionnements

◇ *Acct purchase of debts* rachat *m* des créances

◇ *Acct purchase entry* écriture *f* d'achats

◇ *Acct purchase invoice* facture *f* d'achat

◇ *Acct purchase invoice ledger* journal *m* factures-fournisseurs

◇ *Acct purchase ledger* (grand-)livre *m* d'achats

◇ *Acct purchase method* méthode *f* d'achat

◇ *purchase note* bordereau *m* d'achat

◇ *purchase order* (for goods, service) bon *m* de commande; *St Exch* (for shares) ordre *m* d'achat

◇ *purchase tax* taxe *f* à l'achat

◇ *purchase value* valeur *f* d'achat

purchasing power *n* capacité *f* d'achat

push *vt St Exch* **to push shares** placer des valeurs douteuses

put *n St Exch*

◇ *put band* période *f* de validité d'une option de vente

◇ *put bond* emprunt *m* à fenêtre

◇ *put and call* double option *f*, stellage *m*

◇ *put option* option *f* de vente

◇ *put warrant* warrant *m* à la vente

▶ **put up** *vt sep* **(a)** *(money)* fournir; **who's putting the money up for the new business** qui finance la nouvelle entreprise?

(b) *(increase) (price)* faire monter, augmenter

P/V *n* (*abbr* **profit-volume ratio**) rapport *m* profit sur ventes, ratio *m* de volume de bénéfices

qualified *adj (modified)* mitigé(e)
◇ *Banking* **qualified acceptance** acceptation *f* conditionnelle *ou* sous condition
◇ *Acct* **qualified report** rapport *m* réservé

quarter *n (three-month period)* trimestre *m*; **profits were up during the last quarter** les bénéfices ont augmenté au cours du dernier trimestre

quarterly 1 *adj* trimestriel(elle) **2** *adv* tous les trimestres

quasi-money *n* quasi-monnaie *f*

quick *adj* rapide
◇ *Acct* **quick assets** actif *m* liquide
◇ **quick ratio** ratio *m* de liquidité immédiate

quid *n Br Fam (pound sterling)* livre *f*

quittance *n* quittance *f*

quotable *adj St Exch* cotable

quotation *n St Exch* cotation *f*, cours *m*; **the latest quotations** les derniers cours; **to seek a share quotation** faire une demande d'admission *ou* d'inscription à la cote

quotation-driven *adj St Exch (market)* à prix affichés

quote *vt St Exch (shares)* coter; **gold prices were quoted at £500** l'or a été coté à 500 livres
◇ **quoted company** société *f* cotée en Bourse
◇ **quoted investment** valeurs *fpl* mobilières de placement
◇ **quoted price** cours *m* inscrit à la cote officielle
◇ **quoted securities** valeurs *fpl* de Bourse
◇ **quoted share** action *f* cotée, action inscrite à la cote officielle

quote-driven *adj St Exch (market)* à prix affichés

raid *St Exch* **1** *n* raid *m*
   2 *vt* **to raid the bears** chasser le découvert

raider *n St Exch* raider *m*

raise 1 *n Am (pay increase)* augmentation *f* (de salaire)
   2 *vt* **(a)** *(price, rate, salary)* augmenter; **to raise interest rates** augmenter les taux d'intérêt
   (b) *(cheque)* faire
   (c) *(capital)* mobiliser, procurer; *(funds)* collecter
   (d) *(taxes)* lever; *(loan)* émettre

▸ **rake in** *vt sep Fam (money)* amasser; **they must be raking it in** ils doivent s'en mettre plein les poches

rally 1 *n (of prices, shares, business)* reprise *f*
   2 *vi (of prices, shares, business)* se redresser, reprendre; **the market rallied** les cours ont repris; **the pound rallied in the afternoon** la livre est remontée dans l'après-midi

random walk *n St Exch* marche *f* aléatoire

range *n St Exch* fourchette *f*, écart *m*; **opening/closing range** fourchette de cours d'ouverture/de clôture

rank 1 *n (of debt, mortgage)* rang *m*

   2 *vi* **(a)** *(of creditor, claimant)* **to rank before/after sb** prendre rang *ou* passer avant/après qn; **to rank equally (with sb)** prendre *ou* avoir le même rang (que qn)
   (b) *Law (of share)* **to rank after sth** être primé(e) par qch; **to rank before sth** avoir la priorité sur qch

rate *n (of inflation, tax, interest)* taux *m*; **the rate is 20p in the pound** le taux est de 20 pence par livre
  ◇ **rate band** plage *f ou* fourchette *f* de taux
  ◇ **rate of exchange** cours *m ou* taux *m* du change
  ◇ **rate of increase** taux *m* d'accroissement
  ◇ **rate of inflation** taux *m* d'inflation
  ◇ **rate of return** *(on investment)* taux *m* de rendement
  ◇ **rate of return pricing** fixation *f* de prix au taux de rendement établi
  ◇ **rate of taxation** taux *m* d'imposition

rateable value *n* valeur *f* locative imposable

ratio *n* ratio *m*, rapport *m*

rationing *n (of funds)* rationnement *m*; **banks are warning of**

The pyramid of ratios

La pyramide des ratios

(a) ROCE(Return on capital employed)/Retour sur capitaux permanents
(b) ROS(Return on sales)/Retour sur ventes
(c) AUR(Asset Utilization Ratio)/Taux d'utilisation des actifs

(a) Operating profit/Bénéfice d'exploitation
Capital employed/Capitaux permanents

(b) Operating profit/Bénéfice d'exploitation
Sales/Ventes

(c) Sales/Ventes
Operating assets/Actif d'exploitation

Administration costs/Frais administratifs
Sales/Ventes

Marketing costs/Coûts de marketing
Sales/Ventes

Production costs/Coûts de production
Sales/Ventes

Financial costs/Frais financiers
Sales/Ventes

Sales/Ventes
Fixed assets/Actif immobilisé

Debtors/Débiteurs
Credit sales/Ventes à crédit

Creditors/Créditeurs
Purchases/Achats

Material costs/Coût des matériaux
Sales/Ventes

Direct labour/Main d'oeuvre directe
Sales/Ventes

Production overheads/Frais généraux de production
Sales/Ventes

Raw material stock/Stocks de matières premières
Usage ratio/Ratio d'utilisation

Finished goods stock/Stocks de produits finis
Cost of sales/Coût des ventes

mortgage rationing les banques annoncent qu'elles vont limiter le nombre de prêts immobiliers

ready *adj*

◇ *ready cash, ready money* argent *m* comptant *ou* liquide; **to pay in ready cash** *or* **money** payer (au) comptant

◇ *ready reckoner* barème *m*

real *adj (actual)* réel(elle)

◇ *real accounts* comptes *mpl* de valeur

◇ *real assets* biens *mpl* immobiliers

◇ *real cost* coût *m* réel

◇ Am *real estate* biens *mpl* immobiliers

◇ Am *real estate mortgage investment conduit* obligation *f* garantie par hypothèque

◇ *real income* revenu *m* réel

◇ *real profit* profit *m* réel

◇ *real salary* salaire *m* réel

◇ *real terms* termes *mpl* réels; **salaries have fallen in real terms** les salaires ont baissé en termes réels

◇ *real value* valeur *f* effective

realign *vt (currencies)* réaligner

realignment *n* réalignement *m*; **realignment of currencies** réalignement monétaire

realizable *adj* réalisable

◇ *realizable assets* actif *m* réalisable

◇ *realizable securities* valeurs *fpl* réalisables

realization *n* réalisation *f*

realize *vt (convert into cash)* réaliser; *(yield financially)* rapporter; **to realize a high price** *(of goods)* atteindre un prix élevé; *(of seller)* obtenir un prix élevé;

how much did they realize on the sale? combien est-ce qu'ils ont gagné sur la vente?; **these shares cannot be realized** il n'y a pas de marché pour ces titres

real-time trading *n St Exch* cotation *f* en temps réel

reassess *vt (damages)* réévaluer; *(taxation)* réviser; **you have been reassessed** votre situation fiscale a été réexaminée

reassessment *n (of damages)* réévaluation *f*; *(of taxation)* révision *f*

rebate *n* (a) *(refund)* remboursement *m*; *(of tax)* dégrèvement *m* (b) *(discount on purchase)* rabais *m*, ristourne *f*

recapitalization *n (of company)* recapitalisation *f*, changement *m* de la structure financière

recapitalize *vt (company)* recapitaliser, changer la structure financière de

> **"**
>
> China is still deflating, its banking system needs to be **recapitalized**, but [the] government's ability to raise enough taxes to do it is poor, while consumers save and do not spend to protect their own futures.
>
> **"**

receipt 1 *n* (a) *(proof of payment)* reçu *m* (**for** de); *(in supermarket, bar)* ticket *m* de caisse, reçu de caisse; *(for letter, parcel)* récépissé *m*, accusé *m* de réception; *(for rent, insurance)* quittance *f*

(b) **receipts** *(takings)* recettes *fpl*, rentrées *fpl*; **receipts and**

expenditure recettes et dépenses *fpl*

2 *vt* acquitter, quittancer; **to receipt a bill** acquitter une facture

◇ *receipt book* carnet *m* de quittances

receivable **1** *n* **receivables** *(debts)* comptes *mpl* clients, créances *fpl*; *(bills)* effets *mpl* à recevoir

2 *adj (account, bill)* à recevoir

receive *vt* recevoir; *(money, salary)* toucher; *St Exch* **to receive a premium** encaisser un premium

receiver *n (in bankruptcy)* administrateur(trice) *m,f* judiciaire; **to be in the hands of the receiver(s)** être en règlement *or* redressement judiciaire

◇ *Am receiver general* receveur *m* des impôts

receivership *n* **to go into receivership** être placé(e) en règlement *or* redressement judiciaire

receiving order *n* ordonnance *f* de mise sous séquestre

recipient *n (of cheque, bill)* bénéficiaire *mf*

recognised investment exchange *n* marché *m* d'investissement agréé

reconcile *vt (figures, bank statements)* rapprocher; *Acct (accounts, entries)* faire cadrer, faire accorder

reconciliation *n (of figures, bank statements)* rapprochement *m*; *Acct (of accounts, entries)* ajustement *m*

◇ *reconciliation account* compte *m* collectif

◇ *Acct reconciliation statement* état *m* de rapprochement

recourse *n* recours *m*; **endorsement without recourse** endossement *m* à forfait

recover **1** *vt (debt)* recouvrer; *(money, deposit)* récupérer; **to recover one's expenses** rentrer dans ses fonds

2 *vi (of economy, currency)* se redresser; *(of prices, shares)* se redresser, remonter

recovery *n* **(a)** *(of debt)* recouvrement *m*; *(of money, deposit)* récupération *f*

(b) *(of economy)* relance *f*, redressement *m*; *(of prices, shares)* redressement, remontée *f*; *(of currency)* redressement *m*

rectification *n Acct (of entry)* modification *f*, rectification *f*

rectify *vt Acct (entry)* modifier, rectifier

recurrent expenses *npl* dépenses *fpl* courantes

recycle *vt (funds)* remettre en circulation

red **1** *n* **to be in the red** *(of person)* avoir un découvert, être dans le rouge; *(of company)* être en déficit; *(of account)* avoir un solde déficitaire; **to be £5,000 in the red** *(of person)* avoir un découvert de 5 000 livres; *(of company)* avoir un déficit de 5 000 livres; *(of account)* avoir un solde déficitaire de 5 000 livres

2 *adj Am* **to go into red ink** *(of person)* être à découvert; *(of company)* être en déficit; *(of*

account) avoir un solde déficitaire

redeem *vt* (**a**) *(bond, share)* réaliser; *(coupon)* échanger
(**b**) *(annuity, mortgage)* rembourser; *(loan)* rembourser, amortir; *(bill)* honorer; *(debt)* amortir, se libérer de

redeemable *adj (bond, loan, mortgage)* remboursable; *(share)* rachetable

redemption *n* (**a**) *(of bond)* remboursement *m*; *(of share)* rachat *m* (**b**) *(of annuity, loan, mortgage)* remboursement *m*

◇ **redemption date** date *f* d'échéance

◇ **redemption fee** prime *f* de remboursement

◇ **redemption price** prix *m* de rachat

◇ **redemption premium** prime *f* de remboursement

◇ **redemption value** valeur *f* de remboursement *ou* de rachat

◇ **redemption yield** rendement *m* à l'échéance

―――
"

Income shares come in two forms. Those in the Schroder Split fund, Martin Currie Extra Return and Second St David's for instance, will be repaid at 100p at the end of the trust's life – so long as it has sufficient assets after paying all the zeros. In the meantime they get all the income. The current yield is over 7 per cent and should increase. This seems attractive, except that those who buy above **redemption price** and hold to **redemption** are bound to suffer a capital loss.

"
―――

reduce *vt (expenditure, investment)* réduire; *(price)* baisser; *(output)* ralentir

reduced rate *n* taux *m* réduit

reduction *n* (**a**) *(of expenditure, investment)* réduction *f*; *(of prices)* baisse *f*; *(of taxes)* allègement *m* (**b**) *(discount)* rabais *m*, remise *f*; **to make a reduction (on sth)** faire un rabais *ou* une remise (sur qch)

refer *vt Banking* **to refer a cheque to drawer** refuser d'honorer un chèque; **refer to drawer** *(on cheque)* voir le tireur

referee *n* **referee in case of need** *(on bill of exchange)* adresse *f* au besoin

reference *n (testimonial) (from bank)* référence *f*

◇ **reference rate** taux *m* de référence

refinance 1 *vt (loan)* refinancer **2** *vi (of company)* se refinancer

refinancing *n* refinancement *m*

refloat *vt (loan)* émettre de nouveau; *(company)* renflouer, remettre à flot

refund 1 *n* remboursement *m*; **to get a refund** se faire rembourser
2 *vt (person, money)* rembourser; **to refund sb sth, to refund sth to sb** rembourser qch à qn

refundable *adj* remboursable

refunding *n* remboursement *m*

◇ **refunding clause** clause *f* de remboursement

◇ **refunding loan** prêt *m* de remboursement

register 1 n (book) registre m; (list) liste f; **to enter sth in a register** inscrire qch dans un registre

2 vt (shares) immatriculer; (mortgage) inscrire

◇ St Exch **register of shareholders** registre m des actionnaires

registered adj

◇ **registered bond** obligation f nominative

◇ **registered capital** capital m déclaré

◇ **registered debenture** obligation f nominative

◇ Can **registered retirement savings plan** régime m enregistré d'épargne-retraite

◇ St Exch **registered securities** titres mpl nominatifs, valeurs fpl nominatives

◇ St Exch **registered share certificate** certificat m nominatif d'action(s)

◇ St Exch **registered stock** titres mpl nominatifs, valeurs fpl nominatives

registration n (of name, luggage) enregistrement m; (of shares, company) immatriculation f; (of mortgage) inscription f

◇ St Exch **registration body** chambre f d'enregistrement

◇ **registration fees** droits mpl d'inscription

◇ **registration and transfer fees** droits mpl d'inscription et de transfert

reimburse vt rembourser; **to reimburse sb for sth** rembourser qn de qch

reinvest vt réinvestir

reinvestment n réinvestissement m

reissue 1 n (of banknotes, shares) nouvelle émission f

2 vt (banknotes, shares) émettre de nouveau

release 1 n (a) (of debtor) libération f (b) (of credits, funds) déblocage m, dégagement m

2 vt (a) (debtor) libérer (b) (credits, funds) débloquer, dégager

relevant adj Acct

◇ **relevant costs** coûts mpl attribuables

◇ **relevant range** fourchette f pertinente d'activité

REMIC n Am (abbr **real estate mortgage investment conduit**) obligation f garantie par hypothèque

reminder n rappel m (de compte); **reminder of account due** rappel m d'échéance

◇ Acct **reminder entry** poste m de mémoire

remit 1 vt (a) (payment) remettre

(b) (cancel) (debt) remettre, faire remise de; **to remit sb's fees** dispenser qn de ses frais; **to remit sb's income tax** dispenser ou exempter qn d'impôt

3 vi (pay) régler, payer; **please remit by cheque** veuillez régler ou payer par chèque

remittance n (money) paiement m, règlement m; **return the form with your remittance** renvoyez le formulaire avec votre paiement ou règlement

◇ **remittance advice** avis m de remise

◇ **remittance date** date f de remise

◇ *remittance of funds* remise *f* de fonds

remortgage *vt (house, property)* hypothéquer de nouveau, prendre une nouvelle hypothèque sur

remote *adj* Banking *(payment)* à distance

◇ *remote banking* *n* banque *f* à distance

remuneration *n* rémunération *f* (**for** de); **to receive remuneration for sth** être rémunéré(e) pour qch

◇ *remuneration package* = salaire et avantages complémentaires

> **"**
>
> This had led to the development of top executives receiving not a salary but a 'total **remuneration package**' which includes a whole range of fringe benefits. For example, cheap mortgages supplied by employers are one important way in which higher income earners maintain real higher standards of living.
>
> **"**

render *vt (bill, account)* remettre; **as per account rendered** suivant compte remis

rent 1 *n* loyer *m*; **for rent** *(sign)* à louer

2 *vt* louer; **to rent sth from sb** louer qch à qn

rental *n*

◇ *rental charges* charges *fpl* locatives

◇ *rental income* revenus *mpl* locatifs

repatriate *vt (funds)* rapatrier

repatriation *n (of funds)* rapatriement *m*

repay *vt (person, money, debt)* rembourser

repayable *adj* remboursable; **the amount is repayable in five years** la somme est remboursable en cinq ans

repayment *n* remboursement *m*; **repayments can be spread over 12 months** les remboursements peuvent être échelonnés sur 12 mois

◇ *repayment mortgage* prêt-logement *m (qui n'est pas lié à une assurance-vie)*

◇ *repayment options* formules *fpl* de remboursement

replacement cost *n* coût *m* de remplacement

repo *n (abbr repurchase)* rachat *m*; Banking, St Exch réméré *m*

◇ Banking, St Exch *repo agreement, repo operation* opération *f* de réméré *ou* de prise en pension, opération repo

◇ *repo rate* taux *m* de réméré *ou* de prise en pension

report *n* Acct *(balance sheet)* bilan *m*

reporting limit *n* St Exch seuil *m* d'annonce obligatoire

repurchase 1 *n* rachat *m*; Banking, St Exch réméré *m*

2 *vt* racheter

◇ Banking, St Exch *repurchase agreement* pension *f* livrée, opération *f* de réméré *ou* de prise en pension

◇ Banking, St Exch *repurchase rate* taux *m* de réméré *ou* de prise en pension

resale *n* revente *f*

◇ *resale value* valeur *f* à la revente

reschedule *vt (debt)* rééchelonner

resell *vt* revendre

reserve *n (of money)* réserve *f*; **to draw on the reserves** puiser dans les réserves
◇ *reserve account* compte *m* de réserve
◇ *reserve capital* capital *m* de réserve
◇ *reserve currency* monnaie *f* de réserve
◇ *Acct reserve fund* fonds *m* de réserve
◇ *Banking reserve ratio* taux *m* de mise en réserve

“

But an increase in the supply of dollars implied a persistent US balance of payments deficit (e.g. exporters to the USA accept payments in dollars, or payments overseas by US residents are made in dollars), and this would undermine confidence in the dollar as a **reserve currency** because dollar claims were growing in relation to US gold reserves.

”

residual income *n* revenu *m* résiduel

responsibility accounting *n Acct* comptabilité *f* par centres de responsabilité

retail *n* (vente *f* au) détail *m*
◇ *retail bank* banque *f* de détail
◇ *retail price* prix *m* de détail
◇ *Br Econ Retail Price Index* indice *m* des prix de détail

retained *adj Acct*

◇ *retained earnings* revenu *m* non distribué
◇ *retained profit* bénéfices *mpl* non distribués

retainer *n* provision *f*; **to pay sb a retainer** verser une provision à qn

retire *vt (bill, bonds, shares)* retirer

retired *adj (bill, bonds, shares)* retiré(e)

retirement *n (of bill, bonds, shares)* retrait *m*
◇ *retirement savings plan* plan *m* d'épargne retraite

retrench 1 *vt (expenditure, costs)* restreindre
2 *vi* restreindre ses dépenses, faire des économies

retrenchment *n (of expenditure, costs)* réduction *f*

retroactive *adj* rétroactif(ive)

return 1 *n* (a) *(yield)* rapport *m* (**on** de); **how much return do you get on your investment?** combien est-ce que ton investissement te rapporte?; **to bring a good return** rapporter un bon bénéfice; *Acct* **return on capital** retour *m* sur capital; *Acct* **return on capital employed** retour sur capitaux permanents; **return on capital invested** retour sur capitaux investis; **return on equity** rendement *m* sur fonds propres; **return on investment** retour sur investissements; **return on net assets** rendement de l'actif net; **return on sales** retour sur ventes
(b) **returns** *(profit)* bénéfices *mpl*
(c) *(for declaring tax)* (formulaire *m* de) déclaration *f* d'impôts
2 *vt (profit, interest)* rapporter

◇ Acct **returns ledger, returns book** journal m des rendus

revaluation n (of currency, property) réévaluation f

revalue vt (currency, property) réévaluer

Revenue n Br Fam **the Revenue** ≃ le fisc

revenue n revenu m; (from land, property) revenu, rentes fpl; (from sales) recettes fpl

◇ **revenue account** (part of ledger) compte m de recettes; (profit and loss account) compte m d'exploitation

◇ Am **revenue bond** obligation f à intérêt conditionnel

◇ **revenue centre** centre m de revenus ou de profit

reverse vt Acct (entry) contre-passer

◇ Acct **reverse entry** écriture f inverse

◇ St Exch **reverse repo operation** opération f de mise en pension

◇ **reverse takeover** contre-OPA f

revolver credit n Am crédit m renouvelable, crédit revolving

revolving adj

◇ Br **revolving credit** crédit m renouvelable, crédit revolving

◇ **revolving fund** fonds m de roulement

"

And the whole point of credit cards and other forms of **revolving credit** is that they don't come to an end. This puts a new burden on the credit user: the need to decide not to use a form of credit, or stop using it, instead of the need to decide to use it.

"

RIE n (abbr **recognised investment exchange**) marché m d'investissement agréé

rig St Exch **1** n (rise) hausse f factice; (fall) baisse f factice

2 vt **to rig the market** manipuler la Bourse

rigging n St Exch spéculation f, agiotage m

right n St Exch droit m préférentiel de souscription

◇ **rights issue** émission f de nouvelles actions à taux préférentiel

ring n St Exch **the Ring** le Parquet

RIO n (abbr **return on investment**) retour m sur investissements

rise 1 n (in price, cost of living) hausse f; (in bank rates, interest) relèvement m, hausse; **the rise in the price of petrol** la hausse du prix de l'essence; St Exch **to speculate on a rise** jouer à la hausse

2 vi monter, augmenter; **the pound has risen against the dollar** la livre s'est appréciée vis-à-vis du dollar; **gold has risen in value by 10%** la valeur de l'or a augmenté de 10%

risk n (possibility) risque m

◇ **risk analysis** analyse f des risques

◇ Am St Exch **risk arbitrage** arbitrage m risque

◇ **risk assessment** évaluation f des risques

◇ **risk capital** capital m à risque

◇ *risk management* gestion *f* des risques

◇ *St Exch risk premium* prime *f* de risque de marché

◇ *risk spreading* répartition *f* des risques

◇ *St Exch risk warning* = avertissement donné aux personnes désirant investir dans les produits dérivés, les renseignant sur les risques inhérents à ce genre d'investissement

risk-reward ratio *n St Exch* ratio *m* risque-rentabilité

ROCE *n (abbr* **return on capital employed***)* retour *m* sur capitaux permanents

rogue trader *n St Exch* opérateur *m* peu scrupuleux

ROI *n (abbr* **return on investment***)* retour *m* sur investissements

▶ **roll over** *vt sep (interest rates)* renouveler

rolling *adj*

◇ *Acct rolling budget* budget *m* glissant

◇ *Acct rolling plan* plan m glissant

rollover *n (in taxation)* (disposition *f* de) roulement *m*; *(of loan)* reconduction *f*

◇ *rollover credit* crédit *m* renouvelable

◇ *rollover loan* prêt *m* renouvelable

ROS *n (abbr* **return on sales***)* retour *m* sur ventes

Royal Mint *n Br* ≃ (l'hôtel *m* de) la Monnaie

royalty *n (for invention)* redevance *f*; **royalties** *(for author, musician)* droits *mpl* d'auteur

RPI *Br Econ (abbr* **Retail Price Index***)* indice *m* des prix de détail

RTGS *n Banking (abbr* **Real-Time Gross Settlement***)* RTGS *m*

◇ *RTGS system* système *m* RTGS

rubber cheque *n Fam* chèque *m* en bois

RUF *n (abbr* **revolving underwriting facility***)* facilité *f* renouvelable de prise ferme

▶ **rule off** *vt sep (account)* clore, arrêter

run *n (on currency, Stock Exchange)* ruée *f* (**on** sur); *(on bank)* retrait *m* massif; **there was a run on the dollar** il y a eu une ruée sur le dollar

running account *n Banking* compte *m* courant

safe *n* coffre-fort *m*

safe-deposit box *n* coffre *m* *(dans une banque)*

safe-keeping *n* garde *f*; **to place securities in the bank for safe-keeping** mettre des valeurs en dépôt à la banque

salary *n* salaire *m*; **to draw one's salary** toucher son salaire

◇ *salary earner* salarié(e) *m,f*
◇ *salary scale* échelle *f* ou tarif *m* des salaires
◇ *salary structure* structure *f* des salaires

sale *n* vente *f*; **sales** *(turnover)* chiffre *m* d'affaires; *St Exch* **sale for the account** vente à terme

◇ *sales account* compte *m* des ventes
◇ *sales audit* audit *m* de vente
◇ *sales budget* budget *m* des ventes
◇ *St Exch* *sales fee* frais *mpl* d'achat *ou* d'acquisition
◇ *sales figures* chiffre *m* de vente
◇ *sales invoice* facture *f* de vente
◇ *Acct* *sales ledger* grand-livre *m* ou journal *m* des ventes
◇ *sale price* prix *m* de vente
◇ *sales ratio* ratio *m* des ventes
◇ *Am* *sales tax* taxe *f* à la valeur ajoutée, TVA *f*

Samurai bond *n Fam St Exch* obligation *f* Samouraï

sandbag *n (in takeover bid)* = tactique de temporisation utilisée par une entreprise faisant l'objet d'une OPA

save 1 *vt (money) (keep for future)* mettre de côté; *(not waste)* économiser; **how much money have you got saved?** combien d'argent avez-vous mis de côté?; **buying in bulk saves 10%** l'achat en gros fait économiser 10%

2 *vi* économiser, faire des économies; **to save on sth** économiser sur qch

save-as-you-earn *adj Br* = plan d'épargne à contributions mensuelles produisant des intérêts exonérés d'impôts

saver *n* épargnant(e) *m,f*

saving *n* (a) *(thrift, economy)* économie *f*, épargne *f*; **measures to encourage saving** des mesures pour encourager l'épargne

(b) *(money saved)* économie *f*; **we made a saving of £500 on the usual price** nous avons fait une économie de 500 livres sur le prix habituel; **savings** économies *fpl*; *Econ* dépôts *mpl* d'épargne

⋄ *savings account* compte *m* (de caisse) d'épargne

⋄ *savings bank* caisse *f* ou banque *f* d'épargne

⋄ *savings bond, savings certificate* ≃ bon *m* d'épargne

⋄ *Am savings and loan association* ≃ caisse *f* d'épargne-logement

⋄ *savings plan* plan *m* d'épargne

⋄ *savings rate* taux *m* d'épargne

⋄ *savings scheme* plan *m* d'épargne

SAYE *n Br* (*abbr* **save-as-you-earn**) = plan d'épargne à contributions mensuelles produisant des intérêts exonérés d'impôts

scalper *n Fam St Exch* spéculateur(trice) *m,f* à la journée

scarce currency *n* devise *f* forte

schilling *n* schilling *m*

scrap value *n* (*of asset, share*) valeur *f* à la casse, valeur liquidative

screen *n St Exch*

⋄ *screen trader* opérateur (trice) *m,f* sur écran

⋄ *screen trading* opérations *fpl* sur écran

⋄ *screen trading system* système *m* informatisé de transaction

scrip *n St Exch* titre *m*

⋄ *scrip certificate* certificat *m* d'actions provisoire

⋄ *Am scrip dividend* certificat *m* de dividende provisoire

⋄ *scrip issue* attribution *f* d'actions gratuites

scripholder *n St Exch* détenteur(trice) *m,f* de titres

SDR *n* (*abbr* **special drawing right**) DTS *m*

SEAQ *n* (*abbr* **Stock Exchange Automated Quotations System**) système *m* de cotation automatisé

> **"**
>
> Take the London Stock Exchange. It was dragged kicking and screaming into Big Bang in 1986, but since then it has seemed pretty effective, in the main. It gave up its trading floor before most other exchanges; its computerised **SEAQ** trading system has been highly successful at pulling business in European blue-chip shares from continental bourses.
>
> **"**

seasonal *adj* (*demand, fluctuations*) saisonnier(ère)

⋄ *seasonal adjustment* ajustement *m* saisonnier

SEC *n* (*abbr* **Securities and Exchange Commission**) = commission américaine des opérations de Bourse, ≃ COB *f*

second *adj* second(e), deuxième

⋄ *second debenture* obligation *f* de deuxième rang

⋄ *second mortgage* deuxième hypothèque *f*

⋄ *second quarter* (*of financial year*) deuxième trimestre *m*

secondary *adj* secondaire

⋄ *Acct secondary cost centre* centre *m* d'analyse auxiliaire

⋄ *St Exch secondary market* marché *m* secondaire

sector *n Econ* secteur *m*; **the**

banking sector le secteur bancaire; **whole sectors of society live below the poverty line** des catégories sociales entières vivent en dessous du seuil de pauvreté

secure vt (a) *(obtain) (loan)* obtenir (b) *(guarantee) (debt, loan)* garantir; **the loan is secured by mortgages on several properties** le prêt est garanti par plusieurs hypothèques

secured *adj*

◇ **secured bond** obligation f cautionnée

◇ **secured creditor** créancier (ère) m,f privilégié(e)

◇ **secured debenture** obligation f cautionnée

◇ **secured debt** créance f garantie

◇ **secured loan** prêt m garanti

◇ **secured note** billet m garanti

securitization n St Exch titrisation f

securitize vt St Exch titriser

security n (a) *(financial guarantee)* garantie f; *(for payment of debt)* caution f, cautionnement m; *(collateral)* nantissement m; *(person)* garant(e) m,f; **to give sth as security** donner qch en cautionnement; **to stand security for sb** se porter garant ou caution pour qn; **to lend money on security** prêter de l'argent sur nantissement ou sur garantie; **to lend money without security** prêter de l'argent à découvert; **what security do you have for the loan?** quelle garantie avez-vous pour couvrir ce prêt?

(b) St Exch **securities** titres mpl, valeurs fpl

◇ **Securities and Exchange Commission** = commission américaine des opérations de Bourse, ≃ COB f

◇ **securities department** service m des titres

◇ **securities firm** maison f de titres

◇ **securities house** société f de Bourse

◇ **security interest** privilège m

◇ **Securities and Investment Board** = commission britannique des opérations de Bourse, ≃ COB f

◇ **securities market** marché m des titres, marché des valeurs (mobilières)

◇ **securities portfolio** portefeuille m de titres

seed n

◇ **seed capital** capital m initial

◇ **seed money** capital m initial

seesaw effect n effet m balançoire

segment n Acct

◇ **segment margin** marge f sectorielle

◇ **segment reporting** analyse f par secteur d'activité

self-assessment n Br *(for tax purposes)* = système de déclaration des revenus selon lequel le contribuable évalue lui-même ce qu'il doit au fisc

◇ *self-assessment form* formulaire *m* de déclaration de revenus

self-financing 1 *n* autofinancement *m*

2 *adj* autofinancé(e)

self-liquidating *adj* auto-amortissable

❝

However, for a banker such loans are not directly **self-liquidating**, as little or no foreign exchange is directly generated from such projects to service external debt. Instead, the bank assumes that such schemes will boost overall economic growth and exports, thereby providing the necessary foreign currency receipts.

❞

self-regulatory organization *n Br St Exch* organisme *m* auto-réglementé *ou* autonome

self-tender *n* = proposition de rachat présentée par une entreprise à ses actionnaires

sell 1 *vt* vendre ; *St Exch (shares)* vendre, réaliser ; **to sell sth to sb, to sell sb sth** vendre qch à qn

2 *vi St Exch* **to sell short** vendre à découvert ; **to sell at best** vendre au mieux

◇ *sell order* injonction *f* à la vente

◇ *sell price* prix *m* (du) comptant

▸ **sell forward** *vt sep St Exch* vendre à terme

▸ **sell off** *vt sep St Exch* vendre

▸ **sell out** *vt sep St Exch* vendre, réaliser

seller *n (person)* vendeur(euse) *m,f*

◇ *St Exch seller's option* prime *f* vendeur

◇ *St Exch seller's market* marché *m* à la hausse

selling *n St Exch (of shares)* vente *f*, réalisation *f*

◇ *selling cost* frais *mpl* commerciaux

◇ *Acct selling price* prix *m* de vente

◇ *Acct selling price variance* variance *f* du prix de vente

semi-variable *adj (costs)* semi-variable

sensitive *adj (market)* sensible

serial bond *n St Exch* obligation *f* échéant en série

SERPS *n Br (abbr State Earnings-Related Pension Scheme)* = retraite versée par l'État, calculée sur le salaire

service *vt (loan, debt)* assurer le service de

SET *n (abbr secure electronic transaction)* SET *f*

❝

Each bank or financial institution has a unique key; a trusted third party holds and issues keys that merchants and acquirers need to decrypt each other's **SET** messages.

❞

set 1 *n (of bills of exchange)* jeu *m*

2 *adj (price)* fixe

3 *vt (fix) (price)* fixer, déterminer ; **to set a value on sth** évaluer qch, estimer la valeur de qch; **a deficit ceiling has been set** un plafonnement du déficit a été imposé *ou* fixé; **the price was set at $500** le prix a été fixé à 500 dollars; **how are exchange rates set?** comment les taux de change sont-ils déterminés?

setback *n St Exch* tassement *m*, repli *m*

settle *vt* (**a**) *(account)* régler; *(bill)* acquitter, régler; *(debt, fine)* payer

(**b**) *(money, allowance, estate)* constituer; **to settle an annuity on sb** constituer une rente à qn

settlement *n* (**a**) *(of account)* règlement *m*; *(of bill)* acquittement *m*, règlement; *(of debt, fine)* paiement *m*; **I enclose a cheque in settlement of your account** veuillez trouver ci-joint un chèque en règlement de votre compte

(**b**) *St Exch* liquidation *f*

◇ *settlement day* jour *m* de (la) liquidation

◇ *settlement discount* remise *f* pour règlement rapide

◇ *settlement note* feuille *f* de liquidation

◇ *settlement period* délai *m* de règlement, terme *m* de liquidation

◇ *settlement price* cours *m* de liquidation

◇ *settlement value* valeur *f* liquidative

set-up *n Acct*

◇ *set-up costs* frais *mpl* de lancement

◇ *set-up fee* *(for account)* frais *mpl* de constitution

share **1** *n* (**a**) *St Exch* action *f*,

titre *m*; **to allot shares** attribuer des actions; **to issue shares** émettre des actions; **to transfer shares** transférer des actions; **to hold** *or* **have shares (in)** détenir des actions (dans); **to own 51% of the shares** détenir 51% du capital

(**b**) *(portion)* part *f*; **to give sb a share of the profits** donner à qn une part des bénéfices

2 *vi* **to share in the profits** avoir part aux bénéfices

◇ *Banking, St Exch* **share account** compte-titres *m*

◇ *share capital* capital *m* social

◇ *St Exch* **share certificate** titre *m* d'action(s), certificat *m* d'actions

◇ *St Exch* **share dealing** opérations *fpl* de Bourse

◇ *St Exch* **share dividend** dividende *m* d'action

◇ *St Exch* **share fluctuation** mouvement *m* des valeurs

◇ *St Exch* **share index** indice *m* boursier *ou* des valeurs boursières

◇ *St Exch* **share issue** émission *f* d'actions, émission boursière

◇ *St Exch* **share ledger** registre *m* des actionnaires

◇ *St Exch* **share market** marché *m* des valeurs mobilières

◇ *St Exch* **share option** option *f* d'achat des actions

◇ *St Exch* **share portfolio** portefeuille *f* d'actions

◇ *St Exch* **share premium** prime *f* d'émission

◇ *St Exch* **share prices** cours *mpl* des actions

◇ *St Exch* **share price index** indice *m* des cours d'actions

◇ *St Exch* **share register** registre *m* des actions

◇ *St Exch* **share splitting** division *f ou* fractionnement *m* des actions

◇ *St Exch* **share swap** échange *m* d'actions

shareholder *n St Exch* actionnaire *mf*, détenteur *m* de titres

◇ *shareholders' equity* capitaux *mpl ou* fonds *mpl* propres, avoir *m* des actionnaires

◇ *Acct* *shareholders' funds* haut *m* de bilan

◇ *shareholders' meeting* réunion *f* d'actionnaires

◇ *shareholders' register* registre *m* des actionnaires

""

For small firms the cost of raising capital through public stock issues is prohibitively expensive, but in Japan this is not the main problem as firms are significantly less reliant on equity finance. Although firms are more dependent on external fundraising, the proportion of **shareholders' equity** in total assets is lower than in other advanced capitalist economies.

""

shareholding *n St Exch* actionnariat *m*; **he has a major shareholding in the company** il est un des principaux actionnaires de la société

shark *n Fam (in business)* raider *m*, requin *m*

◇ *shark watcher* détecteur *m* de requin

▸ **shore up** *vt sep (currency)* soutenir; **Brazil started selling off its foreign currency reserves in an attempt to shore up its currency** le Brésil a vendu une partie de ses réserves de change afin de

soutenir sa monnaie

short 1 *n St Exch* **shorts** titres *mpl* courts

2 *adv St Exch* **to go** *or* **sell short** vendre à découvert; **to buy short** acheter à court terme

◇ *short bill* traite *f* à courte échéance

◇ *St Exch* *short covering* couverture *f* de position

◇ *St Exch* *short hedge* couverture *f* courte *ou* de vente

◇ *short payment* moins-perçu *m*

◇ *St Exch* *short position* position *f* vendeur *ou* baissière; **to take a short position** acheter à la baisse

◇ *St Exch* *short rate* taux *m* à court terme

◇ *St Exch* *short selling* vente *f* à découvert

◇ *short squeeze* short squeeze *m*

short-dated *adj (bill)* à courte échéance; *(paper)* court(e)

short-term *adj* à court terme

◇ *short-term bond* obligation *f* à court terme

◇ *short-term borrowings* emprunts *mpl* à court terme

◇ *short-term capital* capital *m* à court terme

◇ *short-term credit* crédit *m* (à) court terme

◇ *short-term debt* dette *f* à court terme

◇ *short-term financing* financement *m* à court terme

◇ *short-term interest rate* taux *m* d'intérêt à court terme

◇ *short-term investment* investissement *m ou* placement *m* à court terme

◇ *short-term liabilities* passif *m* à court terme

◇ *short-term loan* emprunt *m* à court terme

◇ *short-term maturity* échéance *f* à court terme

> **"**
>
> The move came after the company had failed to find major investors to provide an emergency loan to repay more than $100,000,000 due on **short-term borrowings**. Neither the Securities and Exchange Commission nor the Federal Reserve Bank of New York were prepared to assist, and on Feb. 17 the company made 5,000 employees redundant.
>
> **"**

SIB *n* (*abbr* **Securities and Investment Board**) = commission britannique des opérations de Bourse, ≃ COB *f*

sickness benefit *n Br Admin* indemnité *f* de maladie

sight *n* **at sight** sur présentation, à vue

◇ *sight bill* effet *m* (payable) à vue

◇ *sight deposit* dépôt *f* à vue

◇ *sight draft* traite *f* à vue

◇ *sight letter of credit* crédit *m* utilisable à vue

◇ *sight paper* papier *m* à vue

◇ St Exch *sight quotation* cotation *f* à vue

sighting *n* (*of bill*) présentation *f*

silent partner *n Am* associé *m* commanditaire, bailleur *m* de fonds

silver *n* argent *m*

simple *adj*

◇ *simple interest* intérêt *m* simple

◇ St Exch *simple position* position *f* élémentaire

single *adj* **to be in single figures** être inférieur(e) à dix; **inflation is now in single figures** l'inflation est descendue à moins de dix pour cent

◇ EU *single currency* monnaie *f* unique

◇ EU *Single (European) Market* marché *m* unique (européen)

> **"**
>
> For a start, long-term interest rates are still falling … Falling oil and commodity prices have helped. So has the squeeze on government borrowing in the run-up to the launch of Europe's **single currency** next year.
>
> **"**

single-entry bookkeeping *n Acct* comptabilité *f* en partie simple

sink 1 *vt* (a) (*debt, loan*) amortir (b) (*invest*) investir

2 *vi* (*of prices, currency, rate, profits*) baisser, diminuer; **the dollar has sunk to half its normal value** le dollar a perdu la moitié de sa valeur; **profits have sunk to an all-time low** les bénéfices sont au plus bas

sinking fund *n* fonds *mpl* d'amortissement, caisse *f* d'amortissement

sister company *n* société *f* sœur

sleeping partner *n Br* associé

m commanditaire, bailleur *m* de fonds

sliding *adj*
◇ **sliding peg** parité *f* crémaillère
◇ **sliding scale** *(for tax)* barème *m*; *(for prices, salaries)* échelle *f* mobile

sliding-scale *adj*
◇ **sliding-scale depreciation** amortissement *m* dégressif
◇ **sliding-scale taxation** impôt *m* dégressif

sluggish *adj (market, business, economy)* calme, stagnant(e); **trading is always rather sluggish on Mondays** les affaires ne marchent jamais très fort le lundi

slush fund *n* caisse *f* noire

> One of the more controversial aspects of the budget was an increase in the so-called 'MPs' **slush fund**' (more correctly the National Development Fund) to K100,000 annually for each member. The fund was originally intended to fund small-scale enterprises and services in each constituency but MPs were virtually unaccountable for its distribution and use.

small *adj*
◇ **small investor** petit(e) porteur(euse) *m,f*
◇ **small saver** petit(e) épargnant(e) *m,f*
◇ **small shareholder** petit(e) porteur(euse) *m,f*

SmallCap *n St Exch* = indice boursier américain composé d'actions de sociétés à petite et moyenne capitalisation

smart *adj*
◇ *Banking* **smart card** carte *f* (bancaire) à puce, carte à mémoire
◇ **smart money** placement *m* astucieux

social *adj*
◇ **social assets** patrimoine *m* social
◇ **social security** *(system)* Sécurité *f* sociale; *(benefit)* prestations *fpl* sociales; **to be on social security** toucher une aide sociale
◇ **social security benefits** prestations *fpl* sociales
◇ **social security contribution** prélèvement *m* social
◇ **social security provisions** prévoyance *f* sociale
◇ **social security system** régime *m* de Securité sociale

SOFFEX *n St Exch* (*abbr* **Swiss Options and Financial Futures Exchange**) SOFFEX *f (bourse suisse pour le négoce des options et des contrats à terme)*

soft **1** *n* **softs** biens *mpl* non durables
2 *adj*
◇ **soft commodities** biens *mpl* non durables
◇ **soft currency** devise *f* ou monnaie *f* faible
◇ **soft loan** prêt *m* bonifié

sola of exchange *n* seule *f* de change

solvency *n* solvabilité *f*
◇ **solvency ratio** ratio *m* ou taux *m* de solvabilité

solvent *adj* solvable; **in such**

cases the directors must declare that the company is solvent dans de tels cas, l'entreprise doit déclarer être solvable

sort code *n Banking* code *m* guichet

sorting code *n Banking* code *m* guichet

source *n (of revenue)* source *f*; **income is taxed at source** les impôts sont prélevés à la source
◊ *Acct* **source and application of funds** état *m* de flux de trésorerie
◊ *Acct* **source and application of funds statement** tableau *m* de financement

special *adj*
◊ **special drawing rights** droits *mpl* de tirage spéciaux
◊ **special savings account** plan *m* d'épargne populaire

> ❝
> The system of **special drawing rights** (SDRs), agreed in 1968 and implemented in 1970, gave countries credits in the books of the IMF, fixed in value to gold and earning an interest rate of $1\frac{1}{2}$ per cent, which they could use to settle balance of payments deficits. This 'paper gold' was intended to take the heat off the dollar by increasing what was in effect the gold content of reserves.
> ❞

specie *n (coins)* espèces *fpl*; **to pay in specie** payer en espèces

speculate *vi St Exch* spéculer; **to speculate on the Stock Market** spéculer *ou* jouer en Bourse; **to speculate in oils** spéculer sur les valeurs pétrolières; **to speculate for a fall/rise** spéculer à la baisse/hausse

speculation *n St Exch* spéculation *f*; **speculation in oil** spéculation sur les valeurs pétrolières

speculative *adj St Exch* spéculatif(ive)
◊ **speculative buying** achats *mpl* spéculatifs
◊ **speculative securities** valeurs *fpl* spéculatives *ou* de spéculation
◊ **speculative selling** vente *f* spéculative
◊ **speculative shares** valeurs *fpl* spéculatives *ou* de spéculation

speculator *n St Exch* spéculateur(trice) *m,f*

spend 1 *n* dépenses *fpl*; **we must increase our marketing spend** nous devons augmenter le budget marketing
2 *vt (money)* dépenser; **to spend money on sth** dépenser de l'argent en qch

> ❝
> Devro will take a £10 million hit to pay for the cuts before the end of December, while a further £5 million will be felt next year. Mr Alexander said Devro would be investing in better equipment to improve its service to clients, by upping its capital expenditure **spend** to £20 million per year.
> ❞

spending *n* dépenses *fpl*
◊ **spending cuts** réductions *fpl* des dépenses
◊ *Econ* **spending power** pouvoir *m* d'achat

split *St Exch* **1** *n (of shares)* division *f*, fractionnement *m*

2 *vt* **to split shares** diviser *ou* fractionner des actions; **the shares were split 50%, one new share for each two shares held** les actions ont été fractionnées à raison d'une action nouvelle pour deux anciennes

◇ *split capital investment trust* SICAV *f* mixte

◇ *split coupon bond* obligation *f* à coupon partagé

spot *adj*

◇ *spot buying* achats *mpl* au comptant

◇ *spot cash* argent *m* comptant; **to pay spot cash** payer comptant

◇ *spot credit* crédit *m* ponctuel *ou* à court terme

◇ *St Exch* *spot deal* opération *f* *ou* transaction *f* (de change) au comptant

◇ *St Exch* *spot delivery* livraison *f* au comptant *ou* immédiate

◇ *St Exch* *spot exchange rate* cours *m* au comptant

◇ *spot goods* marchandises *fpl* livrables au comptant

◇ *St Exch* *spot market* marché *m* au comptant, marché du disponible

◇ *St Exch* *spot price* prix *m* au comptant, prix du disponible

◇ *St Exch* *spot quotation* cotation *f* à vue

◇ *St Exch* *spot rate* cours *m* du disponible, cours au comptant

◇ *St Exch* *spot trading* négociations *fpl* au comptant

◇ *St Exch* *spot transaction* opération *f* *ou* transaction *f* au comptant

spread *Banking, St Exch* **1** *n* *(between buying and selling prices)* différence *f*, écart *m*; *(range of investments)* diversification *f*

2 *vi* spéculer sur les différentiels de cours

Square Mile *n Fam* **the Square Mile** = la City de Londres, dont la superficie fait environ un mile carré

SRO *n Br St Exch (abbr self-regulatory organization)* organisme *m* auto-réglementé *ou* autonome

stabilization *n (of prices, currency, market)* stabilisation *f*

◇ *stabilization plan* plan *m* de stabilisation

stabilize **1** *vt (prices, currency, market)* stabiliser

2 *vi (of prices, currency, market)* se stabiliser

stag *n St Exch* loup *m*

stagger *vt (payments, instalments)* échelonner

◇ *staggered instalment* versement *m* échelonné

◇ *staggered payment* paiement *m* échelonné *ou* par versements échelonnés

stake *n (interest, share)* intérêt

m, part *f*; *(investment)* investissement *m*; *(shareholding)* participation *f*; **she has a 10% stake in the company** elle a une participation de 10% dans la société; **the company has a big stake in nuclear energy** la société a fait de gros investissements dans le nucléaire

stakeholder *n* partie *f* prenante

◇ *Br* **stakeholder pension** = plan de retraite à coût réduit conçu pour les travailleurs indépendants ou à temps partiel

> 〝
>
> Of course NatWest can argue that its own reputation (and selling power) can only be enhanced by L & G's brilliant track record – particularly for low-cost ISAs and as an enthusiastic advocate of cheap, no-frills **stakeholder pensions** … But from L & G's point of view, if customers get cannier about shopping around for individual financial products, then it will gain no marketing advantage from having its own products sold through a bank.
>
> 〞

stale *adj (cheque)* périmé(e), prescrit(e)

stamp duty *n* droit *m* de timbre

standard *adj* standard

◇ *standard allowance (in taxation)* déduction *f* forfaitaire

◇ *standard assessment system* régime *m* du forfait

◇ *standard cost* coût *m* standard

◇ *Acct* **standard cost accounting, standard costing** méthode *f* des coûts standards

◇ *standard rate (of tax)* taux *m* standard, taux *m* normal

standby *n* ligne *f* de crédit

◇ *standby credit* crédit *m* de réserve *ou* de soutien

◇ *standby letter of credit* caution *f* bancaire

standing *adj*

◇ *standing charges (on bill)* frais *mpl* d'abonnement

◇ *Br* **standing order** virement *m* automatique, ordre *m* permanent; **I get paid by standing order** je reçois mon salaire par virement bancaire

starting salary *n* salaire *m* de départ, rémunération *f* de départ

start-up *n (of business)* lancement *m*

◇ *start-up capital* capital *m* initial *ou* de départ

◇ *start-up costs* frais *mpl* de lancement *ou* d'établissement

◇ *start-up loan* prêt *m* initial *ou* de démarrage

state *n (country, administrative region)* État *m*

◇ *Am* **state bank** banque *f* de dépôts *(agréée par un État)*

◇ *state budget* budget *m* de l'État

◇ *state pension* pension *f* de l'État

statement *n (from bank)* relevé *m* de compte (bancaire)

◇ *Acct* **statement of account** état *m ou* bordereau *m ou* extrait *m* de compte

◇ *Acct* **statement of affairs** bilan *m* de liquidation

◇ *Acct* **statement of assets and liabilities** relevé *m* des dettes actives et passives

◇ *statement of expenditure,*

statement of expenses état *m* ou relevé *m* des dépenses

◇ *Am Acct* **statement of financial position** bilan *m*

◇ *statement of invoices* relevé *m* de factures

◇ *Acct* **statement of results** déclaration *f* de résultats

◇ *Acct* **statement of sources and applications of funds** tableau *m* de financement

state-owned *adj* nationalisé(e)

◇ *state-owned company* société *f* d'État, entreprise *f* publique

status enquiry *n* renseignements *mpl* de crédit, enquête *f* de solvabilité

statutory reserve *n* réserve *f* statutaire

steady 1 *adj (price, rate, Stock Market)* stable
  2 *vi (of price, rate, Stock Market)* se stabiliser

step costs *npl Acct* frais *mpl* progressifs

sterling *n* sterling *m*; **in sterling** en livres sterling; **five thousand pounds sterling** cinq mille livres sterling

◇ *sterling area* zone *f* sterling

◇ *sterling balances* soldes *mpl* en sterling

◇ *sterling bloc* bloc *m* sterling

stock *n* (a) *Br St Exch* valeurs *fpl*, actions *fpl*, titres *mpl*; *Am* actions *fpl* ordinaires; **stocks and shares** valeurs boursières ou mobilières, titres
  (b) *Acct (of goods)* stock *m*

◇ *Am St Exch* **stock average** indice *m* des titres

◇ *stock dividend* dividende *m* (en) action

◇ *stock exchange* bourse *f* des valeurs; **the Stock Exchange** la Bourse

◇ *Stock Exchange Daily Official List* cours *mpl* de clôture quotidiens

◇ *stock exchange dealer* opérateur(trice) *m,f* boursier(ère)

◇ *stock exchange order* ordre *m* de Bourse

◇ *stock exchange transaction* transaction *f* ou opération *f* boursière

◇ *Acct* **stock in hand** stock *m* en magasin ou existant

◇ *St Exch* **stock index** indice *m* de la Bourse

◇ *stock list* cours *mpl* de la Bourse

◇ *stock market* marché *m* boursier ou des valeurs; **the Stock Market** la Bourse

◇ *stock market boom* envolée *f* du marché boursier

◇ *stock market bubble* bulle *f* boursière

◇ *stock market fluctuation* mouvement *m* boursier

◇ *stock market forecast* prévision *f* boursière

◇ *stock market investment* placement *m* financier

◇ *stock market manipulation* manœuvre *f* boursière

◇ *stock market price* cours *m* de la Bourse

◇ *stock market report* bulletin *m* des cours de la Bourse

◇ *stock market value* valeur *f* en Bourse

◇ *stock option* stock-option *f*, option *f* de titres

◇ *stock option plan* plan *m* d'option sur titres

◇ *stock price level* niveau *m* de cours des actions

Stock Exchanges

Bourses

France

Bourse de Paris (**SBF**)
www.bourse-de-paris.fr

Switzerland/Suisse

Swiss Exchange (**SWX**)
recent amalgamation of three exchanges
www.swx.ch

Belgium/Belgique

Brussels Exchanges (**BXS**)
recent amalgamation of three exchanges
www.bxs.be

Canada

Toronto Stock Exchange (**TSE**)
www.telenium.ca/TSE

Montreal Stock Exchange (**MSE**)
www.telenium.ca/MSE

Alberta Stock Exchange (**ASE**)
www.telenium.ca/ASE

Vancouver Stock Exchange (**VSE**)
www.telenium.ca/VSE

Winnipeg Stock Exchange (**WSE**)
www.telenium.ca/WSE

Hong Kong

Stock Exchange of Hong Kong (**SEHK**)
www.sehk.com.hk

Singapore/Singapour

Stock Exchange of Singapore (**SES**)
www.ses.com.sg

GB/Grande-Bretagne

London Stock Exchange (**LSE**)
www.stockex.co.uk

London Metal Exchange (**LME**)
www.lme.co.uk

USA

American Stock Exchange (**Amex**)
www.amex.com

New York Stock Exchange (**NYSE**)
www.nyse.com

NASDAQ
www.nasdaq.com

Chicago Stock Exchange (**CHX**)
www.chicagostockex.com

Boston Stock Exchange (**BSE**)
www.bostonstock.com

Philadelphia Stock Exchange (**PHLX**)
www.phlx.com

Minneapolis Grain Exchange (**MGE**)
www.mgex.com

Arizona Stock Exchange (**AZX**)
www.azx.com

New York Cotton Exchange (**NYCE**)
www.nyce.com

Australia/Australie

Australian Stock Exchange (**ASX**)
www.asx.com.au

Japan/Japon

Tokyo Stock Exchange (**TSE**)
www.tse.or.jp

◊ **stock purchase plan** plan *m* d'option sur titres
◊ **stock transfer** cession *f* de parts
◊ **stock turnover** rotation *f* des stocks

"
... the maximum price which may be paid for a Share shall be not more than 5% above the average of the middle market quotations derived from the London **Stock Exchange Daily Official List** for the ten business days immediately preceding the date of purchase of the Share.
"

stockbroker *n St Exch* agent *m* de change, courtier(ère) *m,f* en Bourse

stockbroking *n St Exch* commerce *m* des valeurs en Bourse
◊ **stockbroking firm** société *f* de Bourse

stockholder *n St Exch* actionnaire *mf*
◊ **stockholder's equity** capitaux *mpl* ou fonds *mpl* propres, avoir *m* des actionnaires

stockjobber *n Br St Exch Formerly* = avant 1986, intermédiaire en Bourse qui traitait directement avec les agents de change et non avec le public

stockpicking *n St Exch* sélection *f* de titres

stop *vt Br (withhold)* **to stop payment** suspendre des paiements; **to stop a cheque** faire opposition à un chèque
◊ *St Exch* **stop loss** ordre *m* stop
◊ *St Exch* **stop order** ordre *m* stop

stop-loss *adj St Exch*
◊ **stop-loss order** ordre *m* stop
◊ **stop-loss selling** ordre *m* de vente stop

stored production *n Acct* production *f* stockée

straddle *n St Exch* ordre *m* lié, opération *f* à cheval; **to take a straddle position** = jumeler simultanément un achat sur une époque avec une vente sur une autre

"
There is a lower level of initial margin on straddle positions. A **straddle position** is a simultaneous long and short position in different months of the same futures contract, e.g. long one June ST3 contract and short one September ST3 contract. Because the daily price movements in a **straddle** are likely to be lower than in the individual contracts, the initial margin is lower.
"

straight-line *adj Acct*
◊ **straight-line depreciation** amortissement *m* linéaire
◊ **straight-line depreciation method** mode *m* ou méthode *f* d'amortissement linéaire
◊ **straight-line method** mode *m* ou méthode *f* linéaire
◊ **straight-line rate** taux *m* linéaire

street *n*
◊ *St Exch* **street dealing** transactions *fpl* hors Bourse
◊ *St Exch* **street market** marché *m* hors Bourse
◊ *St Exch* **street price** cours *m* hors Bourse

strengthen 1 vt *(financial position, currency, economy)* consolider

2 vi *(of financial position, currency, economy)* se consolider

strike price, striking price n St Exch prix m d'exercice

stripped bond n St Exch félin m, obligation f à coupon zéro

strong adj *(market)* ferme; *(currency, price)* solide; **the pound is getting stronger** la livre se raffermit

stub n *(of cheque)* souche f, talon m

subaccount n Acct sous-compte m

subledger n Acct grand livre m auxiliaire

subordinated debt n dette f subordonnée

subscribe 1 vt *(shares)* souscrire

2 vi *(to loan, share issue)* souscrire (**to** à)

◇ *subscribed capital* capital m souscrit

subscriber n *(to loan, share issue)* souscripteur(trice) m,f

subscription n *(to loan, share issue)* souscription f

◇ *subscription list* liste f de souscriptions

◇ *subscription right* droit m de souscription (d'actions)

subsidize vt subventionner; **the company was subsidized to the tune of £3 million** l'entreprise a reçu trois millions de livres de subventions

subsidy n subvention f

sum n *(amount of money)* somme f; *(total)* total m

◇ *sum payable* charge f à payer

summary balance sheet n Acct bilan m condensé

sundry 1 n **sundries** *(items)* articles mpl divers; *(costs)* frais mpl divers

2 adj divers(e)

◇ *sundry expenses* frais mpl divers, dépenses fpl diverses

◇ *sundry income* produits mpl accessoires

sunk costs npl coûts mpl irrécupérables

superannuation n *(pension)* pension f de retraite; *(contribution)* cotisation f pour la retraite

◇ *superannuation fund* caisse f de retraite

supermarket bank n = banque qui appartient à une chaîne de supermarchés

superstock n Am St Exch actions fpl à droit de vote double

supertax n impôt m sur les grandes fortunes

supplementary entry n Acct écriture f complémentaire

supplier n fournisseur(euse) m,f

◇ Acct **supplier credit** crédit-fournisseur m, avoir-fournisseur m

support 1 n *(funding)* soutien

m; **they depend on the government for financial support** ils sont subventionnés par le gouvernement; **what are your means of support?** quelles sont vos sources de revenus?

2 *vt* (**a**) *(financially)* subvenir aux besoins de

(**b**) *(price, currency)* maintenir

◊ EU **support price** prix *m* de soutien

surcharge 1 *n (on price)* supplément *m*; *(on tax)* majoration *f* (fiscale), majoration (d'impôt)

2 *vt* faire payer un supplément à

surplus *n Acct* plus-value *f*; **surplus of assets over liablilities** excédent *m* de l'actif sur le passif

surtax 1 *n* surtaxe *f*

2 *vt* surtaxer

suspense account *n* compte *m* d'ordre

swap 1 *n Banking, St Exch* échange *m* financier, swap *m*

2 *vt St Exch* swaper

◊ **swap agreements** accords *mpl* d'échanges

◊ **swap facilities** facilités *fpl* de crédits réciproques

◊ *St Exch* **swap option** option *f* sur swap de taux d'intérêt

swaption *n St Exch* option *f* sur swap de taux d'intérêt

❝

In addition to buying the gilts, Scottish Widows has been trying to peg its interest rate exposure by arranging deals to borrow from big companies or buy complex derivatives instruments known as **swaptions**.

❞

SWIFT *n* (*abbr* **Society for Worldwide Interbank Financial Telecommunication**) = société internationale de télécommunications financières interbanques

swingline *adj (loan, credit)* immédiatement disponible

Swiss franc *n* franc *m* suisse

switch 1 *n Br* Switch® = société de cartes de paiement britannique

2 *vt St Exch* **to switch a position** = reporter une position d'une échéance à une autre plus éloignée

◊ *Br* **Switch card**® = carte de paiement utilisée en Grande-Bretagne

◊ *St Exch* **switch trading** arbitrage *m*

switching *n St Exch* arbitrage *m* de portefeuille

syndicate *n* groupement *m*, syndicat *m*; **the loan was underwritten by a syndicate of banks** le prêt était garanti par un consortium bancaire; **a syndicate of British and French companies** un groupement de sociétés françaises et britanniques

syndicated *adj*

◊ **syndicated credit** crédit *m* consortial

◊ **syndicated loan** prêt *m* en participation

◊ *St Exch* **syndicated shares** actions *fpl* syndiquées

▸ **take over** *vt sep (buy out)* racheter; **they were taken over by a Japanese firm** ils ont été rachetés par une entreprise japonaise; *St Exch* **to take over an issue** absorber une émission

▸ **take up** *vt sep (bill)* honorer, retirer; *St Exch (option)* lever, consolider; *(shares)* souscrire à

takeover *n (of company)* rachat *m*, prise *f* de contrôle

◇ **takeover bid** offre *f* publique d'achat, OPA *f*; **to be the subject of a takeover bid** être l'objet d'une OPA; **to make** *or* **launch a takeover bid (for)** faire *ou* lancer une OPA (sur)

◇ *St Exch* **takeover stock** titres *mpl* ramassés

> **"**
>
> At the same time as building up the 15 per cent stake, GM would make a big cash injection into Jaguar – perhaps as much as £200m – to help the Coventry-based firm to fend off Ford, which has already announced it plans to take a 15 per cent holding as a prelude to a full **takeover bid**.
>
> **"**

takings *npl* recette *f*

tangible *Acct* **1** *n* **tangibles** actif *m* corporel, valeurs *fpl* matérielles

2 *adj*

◇ *tangible assets* actif *m* corporel, valeurs *fpl* matérielles

◇ *tangible fixed assets* immobilisations *fpl* corporelles

tap *n* valeur *f* du Trésor mise aux enchères; **long/medium/short tap** valeurs *fpl* émises à un prix déterminé par l'État à long/moyen/court terme

◇ *tap issue* émission *f* des valeurs du Trésor

◇ *tap stock* valeur *f* du Trésor mise aux enchères

tapering *adj (rate)* dégressif (ive)

taper relief *n Br* = réduction *f* progressive des impôts sur les plus-values en fonction du nombre d'années pendant lequel on détient un bien avant de le vendre

TARGET *n EU, Banking (abbr* **Trans-European Automated Real-Time Gross Settlement Transfer System)** TARGET *m*

target company *n* société *f* opéable

tax 1 *n (on income)* impôt *m*, contributions *fpl*; *(on goods, services, imports)* taxe *f*; **most of my**

income goes on tax la plus grande partie de mes revenus va aux impôts; **I paid over $5,000 in tax** j'ai payé plus de 5000 dollars d'impôts; **there is a high tax on whisky** le whisky est fortement taxé; **to levy a tax on sth** frapper qch d'une taxe; **to be liable to tax** être assujetti(e) à l'impôt; **before tax** hors taxe; *(income)* avant impôt; **after tax** après impôt; **exclusive of tax** hors taxe

2 *vt (person, company)* imposer, frapper d'un impôt; *(goods, services, imports)* taxer, frapper d'un taxe; **the rich will be more heavily taxed** les riches seront plus lourdement imposés; **luxury goods are taxed at 28%** les articles de luxe sont taxés à 28%

◇ *tax adjustment* redressement *m* d'impôt, redressement fiscal

◇ *tax allowance* abattement *m* fiscal, déduction *f* fiscale

◇ *tax assessment* avis *m* d'imposition, fixation *f* de l'impôt

◇ *tax audit* vérification *f* fiscale

◇ *tax avoidance* évasion *f* fiscale

◇ *tax band* tranche *f* d'imposition

◇ *tax base* assiette *f* fiscale

◇ *tax benefit* avantage *m* fiscal

◇ *tax bite* proportion *f* du revenu pris par l'impôt

◇ *tax bracket* tranche *f* ou fourchette *f* d'imposition

◇ *tax break* allègement *m* fiscal

◇ *tax burden* pression *f* fiscale, poids *m* de la fiscalité

◇ *tax ceiling* plafond *m* fiscal ou de l'impôt

◇ *tax centre* centre *m* des impôts

◇ *tax code* barème *m* fiscal

◇ *tax collector* percepteur *m* d'impôt, receveur *m* des contributions

◇ *tax consultant* conseiller (ère) *m,f* fiscal(e), conseil *m* fiscal

◇ *tax credit* aide *f* fiscale, avoir *m* fiscal

◇ *tax cut* baisse *f* ou réduction *f* des impôts

◇ *tax deduction* déduction *f* fiscale

◇ *Am* **tax dollars** impôts *mpl* *(payés par la population)*

◇ *tax evasion* fraude *f* fiscale

◇ *tax exemption* exemption *f* d'impôt

◇ *tax exile* = personne qui réside à l'étranger pour minimiser la responsabilité fiscale

◇ *tax form* déclaration *f* d'impôt

◇ *tax fraud* fraude *f* fiscale

◇ *EU* **tax harmonization** harmonisation *f* fiscale

◇ *tax haven* paradis *m* fiscal

◇ *tax holiday* période *f* de grâce *(accordée pour le paiement des impôts)*

◇ *tax incentive* incitation *f* fiscale, avantage *m* fiscal

◇ *tax inspection* contrôle *m* fiscal

◇ *tax inspector* inspecteur (trice) *m,f* des contributions directes ou des impôts

◇ *tax liability* *(of person)* assujettissement *m* à l'impôt; *(of goods, product)* exigibilité *f* de taxe

◇ *tax loophole* échappatoire *f* fiscale

◇ *tax loss* déficit *m* fiscal reportable

◇ *tax office* (bureau *m* de) perception *f*, centre *m* des impôts

⬦ **tax official** agent *m* du fisc

⬦ **tax privilege** privilège *m* fiscal

⬦ **tax rate** taux *m* d'imposition

⬦ **tax rebate** crédit *m* d'impôt

⬦ **tax reduction** abattement *m* fiscal

⬦ **tax refund** *(of income tax)* restitution *f* d'impôts; *(on goods)* détaxe *f*

⬦ **tax relief** dégrèvement *m* (fiscal)

⬦ **tax return** déclaration *f* de revenu, feuille *f* d'impôt

⬦ **tax revenue** recettes *fpl* ou rentrées *fpl* fiscales

⬦ **tax roll** rôle *m* d'impôt ou des contributions

⬦ **tax shelter** avantage *m* fiscal

⬦ **tax shield** protection *f* fiscale

⬦ **tax system** régime *m* fiscal ou d'imposition

⬦ **tax threshold** minimum *m* imposable, seuil *m* d'imposition; **the government has raised tax thresholds in line with inflation** le gouvernement a relevé les tranches de l'impôt pour tenir compte de l'inflation

⬦ **tax year** année *f* fiscale ou d'imposition

> ❝
>
> Business and the financial markets may have other cause to celebrate Mr Lafontaine's passing, not least London's lucrative eurobond market ... Mr Lafontaine was a keen advocate of **tax harmonisation** in the European union and was pushing for a flat rate withholding tax on offshore investments – a move which could have driven the trade in eurobonds out of the City of London.
>
> ❞

taxable *adj* imposable

⬦ **taxable base** base *f* d'imposition

⬦ **taxable income** revenu *m* imposable, assiette *f* fiscale ou de l'impôt

⬦ **taxable profit** bénéfice *m* fiscal ou imposable

⬦ **taxable transaction** opération *f* imposable

taxation *n* (a) *(of person, company)* imposition *f*, prélèvement *m* fiscal; *(of goods)* taxation *f*; **taxation at source** prélèvement de l'impôt à la source, imposition à la source (b) *(taxes)* impôts *mpl*, contributions *fpl*

tax-deductible *adj* déductible des impôts

tax-exempt, tax-free *adj* *(income)* exonéré(e) d'impôts; *(goods)* exonéré(e) de taxes

taxman *n Br Fam* **the taxman** le fisc

> ❝
>
> The company has never made profits to date. It always spent enough on developing new strands of business to ensure that there was nothing left over for the **taxman**. But it has now decided to show some profits. The **taxman** should be delighted.
>
> ❞

taxpayer *n* contribuable *mf*

technical correction *n St Exch* correction *f* d'un cours en Bourse

telebanking *n* banque *f* à domicile

telegraphic *adj* télégraphique

◊ *telegraphic transfer* transfert *m* télégraphique

telephone banking *n* banque *f* à domicile

telex 1 *n* télex *m*
2 *vt* envoyer par télex, télexer
◊ *telex transfer* virement *m* par télex

teller *n* caissier(ère) *m,f*, guichetier(ère) *m,f*

tenor *n* (of bill) (terme *m* d')échéance *f*

term *n* (**a**) terms (conditions) termes *mpl*; (rates, tariffs) conditions *fpl*, tarifs *mpl*; **on easy terms** avec facilités de paiement; **terms of credit** conditions de crédit; **terms of exchange** termes d'échange; **terms of payment** conditions *ou* termes de paiement
(**b**) (of bill of exchange) (terme *m* d')échéance *f*; **to set** *or* **put a term to sth** mettre fin *ou* un terme à qch
◊ *term bill* effet *m* à terme
◊ *term day* (jour *m* du) terme *m*
◊ *term deposit* dépôt *m* à terme
◊ *term draft* traite *f* à terme
◊ *term loan* (money lent) prêt *m* à terme (fixe); (money borrowed) emprunt *m* à terme (fixe)

terminable annuity *n* rente *f* à terme

terminal *adj*
◊ *terminal charges* charges *fpl* terminales
◊ *Acct* **terminal loss** perte *f* finale
◊ *St Exch* **terminal market** marché *m* à terme
◊ *terminal price* cours *m* du livrable

TESSA *n Br* (abbr **tax-exempt special savings account**) = plan d'épargne exonéré d'impôts

third quarter *n* (of financial year) troisième trimestre *m*

threshold *n* seuil *m*
◊ *EU* **threshold price** prix *m* du seuil

thrift *n Am* thrift (institution) (savings bank) caisse *f* d'épargne

ticket day *n St Exch* jour *m* de la déclaration des noms

▸**tie up** *vt sep* (money) immobiliser; **their money is all tied up in shares** leur argent est entièrement investi dans des actions

tied *adj*
◊ *tied agent* agent *m* lié
◊ *tied loan* prêt *m* conditionnel *ou* à condition

tied-up capital *n* capital *m* engagé

tie-up *n* (merger) (absorption-)fusion *f*, unification *f*

tiger economy *n* = pays à l'économie très performante; **the (Asian) tiger economies** les dragons *mpl ou* les tigres *mpl* asiatiques

time *n* (**a**) *(in general)* temps *m* (**b**) *(credit)* terme *m* ; *Am* **to buy sth on time** acheter qch à tempérament *ou* à terme

◇ *St Exch* **time bargain** marché *m* à terme

◇ **time bill** traite *f* à terme, traite à date fixe

◇ *Am* **time deposit** dépôt *m* à terme

◇ **time draft** traite *f* à terme

◇ **time loan** emprunt *m* à terme

◇ *St Exch* **time value** valeur *f* temporelle

Tobin tax *n Econ* = projet de taxation des transactions financières visant à réduire la spéculation

top 1 *n St Exch* **to buy at the top and sell at the bottom** acheter au plus haut et vendre au plus bas

2 *adj*

◇ **top rate** taux *m* maximum

top-heavy *adj* surcapitalisé(e)

total 1 *n* total *m* ; **the total comes to $389** cela fait au total 389 dollars; **the total payable** le total à payer

2 *adj (amount, cost, profit, loss)* total(e)

3 *vt* (**a**) *(add up)* additionner (**b**) *(amount to)* s'élever à

◇ **total annual expenses** consommations *fpl* de l'exercice

◇ **total assets** total *m* de l'actif

◇ **total asset value** valeur *f* de bilan

◇ **total fixed cost** coût *m* fixe total

◇ **total gross income** revenu *m* brut global

◇ **total liabilities** total *m* du passif

◇ **total loss** perte *f* totale

◇ **total net income** revenu *m* net global

◇ **total sales** chiffre *m* d'affaires global

tracker fund *n St Exch* fonds *m* indiciel *ou* à gestion indicielle

trade 1 *n (commerce)* commerce *m*, affaires *fpl*

2 *vt St Exch* négocier

3 *vi St Exch* *(of shares, commodity, currency)* se négocier, s'échanger (**at** à); **the shares were ⸱ ding at $2.20** les actions se négociaient à 2,20 dollars

◇ **trade agreement** accord *m* commercial

◇ **trade balance** balance *f* commerciale

◇ **trade bills** effets *mpl* de commerce

◇ *Acct* **trade credit** crédit *m* fournisseur *ou* commercial

◇ *Acct* **trade creditor** créancier (ère) *m,f* d'exploitation

◇ *Acct* **trade debt** dettes *fpl* d'exploitation

◇ *Acct* **trade debtor** compte *m* ou créance *f* client

◇ **trade deficit** déficit *m* commercial

◇ **trade discount** remise *f* professionelle

◇ **trade gap** déficit *m* commercial

◇ **trade policy** politique *f* commerciale

◇ *St Exch* **trade price** prix *m* de négociation

◇ *St Exch* **trade ticket** avis *m* d'opéré, avis d'opération sur titres

▸ **trade down** *vi St Exch* acheter des valeurs basses

▸ **trade up** *vi St Exch* acheter des valeurs hautes

traded option *n St Exch* option *f* négociable, option cotée

trader *n St Exch* opérateur (trice) *m,f*

trading *n* commerce *m*, négoce *m*; **trading on the Stock Exchange was heavy** le volume de transactions à la Bourse était important

◇ *Acct* **trading account** compte *m* d'exploitation

◇ **trading bank** banque *f* commerciale

◇ **trading capital** capital *m* engagé *ou* de roulement

◇ *St Exch* **trading day** jour *m* de Bourse

◇ *St Exch* **trading floor** parquet *m*, corbeille *f*

◇ **trading hours** heures *fpl* d'ouverture; *St Exch* horaires *mpl* des criées

◇ *St Exch* **trading member** intermédiaire *m* négociateur

◇ *St Exch* **trading month** mois *m* d'échéance

◇ *St Exch* **trading order** ordre *m* de négociation

◇ *Am St Exch* **trading post** parquet *m*, corbeille *f*

◇ *Acct* **trading profit** bénéfice *m* d'exploitation

◇ *Acct* **trading and profit and loss account** compte *m* de résultat

◇ *St Exch* **trading range** écart *m* de prix, fourchette *f* de cotation; **prices are stuck in a trading range** les prix ne varient pas beaucoup

◇ **trading results** résultats *mpl* de l'exercice

◇ *St Exch* **trading room** salle *f* des changes *ou* des marchés

◇ *St Exch* **trading session** séance *f* boursière

◇ **trading year** exercice *m* comptable

tranche *n (of loan, payment, shares)* tranche *f*

> ❝
>
> It is noticeable that the French **tranche**, covering 50 per cent of the issue, is being sold by a general offer for sale while the British **tranche**, half as large, is split between an offer and a placing with institutions.
>
> ❞

transaction *n* (a) *(deal)* opération *f* (commerciale), affaire *f*; *St Exch* transaction *f*; **cash transactions have increased** les mouvements d'espèces ont augmenté

(b) *(act of transacting)* conduite *f*, gestion *f*; **transaction of business will continue as normal** la conduite des affaires se poursuivra comme à l'accoutumé

⋄ St Exch **transaction costs** frais *mpl* de Bourse

⋄ St Exch **transaction tax** impôt *m* de Bourse

transfer 1 *n* (**a**) St Exch *(of shares, funds, capital)* transfert *m*; Banking *(of money from one account to another)* virement *m*
(**b**) Acct *(of debt)* transport *m*; *(of entry)* contre-passation *f*
2 *vt* (**a**) *(shares, funds, capital)* transférer; Banking *(money)* virer
(**b**) Acct *(debt)* transporter; *(entry)* contre-passer

⋄ **transfer advice** avis *m* de virement

⋄ Acct **transfer of charges** transfert *m* de charges

⋄ **transfer cheque** chèque *m* de virement

⋄ St Exch **transfer duty** droits *mpl* de transfert

⋄ St Exch **transfer by endorsement** transmission *f* par endossement

⋄ Acct **transfer entry** écriture *f* de virement, article *m* de contre-passation

⋄ **transfer fee** frais *mpl* de transfert

⋄ St Exch **transfer form** formule *f* de transfert

⋄ **transfer order** ordre *m* ou mandat *m* de virement

⋄ St Exch **transfer register** registre *m* des transferts

transferable *adj*

⋄ **transferable bond** obligation *f* transmissible ou transférable

⋄ **transferable credit** crédit *m* transférable

⋄ **transferable securities** valeurs *fpl* négociables ou mobilières

⋄ **transferable share** action *f* au porteur

transferee *n* St Exch *(of shares, funds, capital)* bénéficiaire *mf*

transferor *n* St Exch *(of shares, funds, capital)* vendeur(euse) *m,f*

traveller's cheque *n* Banking chèque *m* de voyage

treasury *n* *(funds)* trésor *m* (public); *(place)* trésorerie *f*; **the Treasury** *(government department)* ≃ le ministère des finances

⋄ **Treasury bill, Treasury bond** ≃ bon *m* du Trésor, certificat *m* de trésorerie

⋄ **Treasury note** billet *m* de trésorerie

⋄ **Treasury scrip** inscription *f* sur le grand-livre

⋄ Am **Treasury Secretary** ≃ ministre *m* des finances

⋄ **treasury swap** échange *m* cambiste

⋄ **Treasury warrant** mandat *m* du Tresor

"

Long-term **Treasury-bond** yields were as low as 7.75% towards the end of 1989. Bond prices have since fallen and yields risen, partly because of inflation worries, but more because of a worldwide liquidity squeeze which has caused bond yields to rise virtually everywhere. The 30-year **Treasury bond** yielded 8.45% on March 20th.

"

trial balance *n* Acct balance *f* d'inventaire

triple-A rating *n St Exch* notation *f* AAA

true *adj Acct*
◊ **true and fair view** *(of accounts)* image *f* fidèle
◊ **true discount** escompte *f* en dedans

trust *n (cartel)* trust *m*, cartel *m*
◊ **trust bank** banque *f* de gestion de patrimoine
◊ **trust company** société *f* fiduciaire

trusted third party *n Comptr (for Internet transactions)* tierce partie *f* de confiance

❝

At the moment a mere $200m worth of goods are sold across the Internet each year. All the estimates of this figure reaching $30 billion by the end of the decade will count for little unless somebody comes up with some kind of 'digital signature' that gives users the same assurance that face-to-face contact, a physical address or even a driving licence does in the real world. Ideally, a digital signature should be guaranteed by some **trusted third party** eg, a credit-card firm or a government body.

❞

TTP *n Comptr (abbr* **trusted third party***) (for Internet transactions)* TPC *f*

turnover *n (of company)* chiffre *m* d'affaires; *(of capital)* rotation *f*; **his turnover is £100,000 per annum** il fait 100 000 livres d'affaires par an
◊ **turnover tax** impôt *m ou* taxe *f* sur le chiffre d'affaires

UBR *n Br* (*abbr* **uniform business rate**) = taxe assise sur la valeur des locaux commerciaux, ≃ taxe *f* professionnelle

UCITS *n* (*abbr* **undertakings for collective investment in transferables**) OPCVM *m*

umbrella fund *n* fonds *m* de consolidation

unabsorbed cost *n* coût *m* non-absorbé

unaccounted for *adj* (*money*) qui manque; **these sixty pounds are unaccounted for in the balance sheet** ces soixante livres ne figurent pas au bilan; **there is still a lot of money unaccounted for** il manque toujours beaucoup d'argent

unallotted *adj St Exch* (*shares*) non réparti(e)

unappropriated *adj* (*money*) inutilisé(e), disponible
◇ *unappropriated profits* bénéfices *mpl* non distribués

unassigned revenue *n* recettes *fpl* non gagées

unaudited *adj* (*figures*) non certifié(e)

unavoidable costs *npl Acct* coûts *mpl* induits

unbalanced *adj* (**a**) *Acct* (*account*) non soldé(e) (**b**) (*economy*) déséquilibré(e)

unbankable *adj* (*bill*) non bancable
◇ *unbankable paper* papier *m* non bancable

uncallable *adj* (*bond*) non remboursable

uncalled *adj* (*capital*) non appelé(e)

uncashed *adj* (*cheque*) non encaissé

unclaimed *adj* (*dividend*) non réclamé(e)

unconditional order *n* ordre *m* (de payer) pur et simple

unconfirmed letter of credit *n* lettre *f* de crédit révocable

unconsolidated adj (debt) non consolidé(e)

uncovered adj (purchase, sale) à découvert; (cheque) sans provision
◇ **uncovered advance** avance f à découvert
◇ **uncovered balance** découvert m
◇ St Exch **uncovered position** position f non couverte

uncrossed adj (cheque) non barré(e)

underborrow vi (of company) ne pas emprunter assez

underborrowed adj (of company) sous-endetté(e)

underborrowing n (of company) sous-endettement m

undercapitalization n sous-capitalisation f

undercapitalized adj sous-capitalisé(e)

underfund vt sous-capitaliser

underfunded adj sous-capitalisé(e)

underfunding n sous-capitalisation f

underlying adj sous-jacent
◇ **underlying asset** actif m sous-jacent
◇ St Exch **underlying futures contract** contrat m à terme sous option
◇ **underlying mortgage** hypothèque f sous-jacente
◇ St Exch **underlying security** titre m sous-jacent

underperform vi (of shares) avoir un cours trop bas

undersubscribed adj St Exch (issue, share) non-souscrit(e)

underwater adj Am (share prices) décoté(e)
◇ **underwater option** option f à prix glissant à la baisse

underwrite vt St Exch (new issue) garantir, souscrire

underwriter n St Exch (of new issue) syndicataire mf
◇ **underwriter agent** agent m souscripteur

underwriting n St Exch (of new issue) garantie f, souscription f
◇ **underwriting agent** agent m souscripteur
◇ **underwriting syndicate** syndicat m de garantie ou de prise ferme

undischarged adj (debt) non liquidé(e); (bankrupt) non déchargé

undiscountable adj inescomptable

undistributed adj (money, earnings) non distribué(e)

◇ *undistributed profits* bénéfices *mpl* non distribués

unearned income *n* revenus *mpl* non professionnels, rentes *fpl*

unemployment *n* chômage *m*

◇ *Br unemployment benefit*, *Am unemployment compensation* allocation *f* chômage, indemnité *f* de chômage

◇ *unemployment fund* caisse *f* de chômage

unendorsed *adj (cheque)* non endossé(e)

unexchangeable *adj (securities)* impermutable, inéchangeable

unfavourable, *Am* **unfavorable** *adj (balance of trade, exchange rate)* défavorable

unforeseen expenses *npl* dépenses *fpl* non prévues au budget

unfunded *adj* sans capitaux suffisants

◇ *unfunded debt* dette *f* flottante *ou* non consolidée

ungeared *adj* sans endettement

◇ *ungeared balance sheet* bilan *m* sans emprunts *ou* à faible endettement

uniform *adj*

◇ *uniform accounting* comptabilité *f* uniforme

◇ *Br uniform business rate* = taxe assise sur la valeur des locaux commerciaux, ≃ taxe *f* professionnelle

unissued *adj (shares, share capital)* non encore émis(e)

unit *n* unité *f*

◇ *unit of account* unité *f* de compte

◇ *Br unit trust* SICAV *f*, fonds *m* commun de placement

unlimited *adj (funds)* inépuisable

◇ *unlimited company* société *f* à responsabilité illimitée *ou* infinie

◇ *unlimited liability* responsabilité *f* illimitée

unlisted *adj St Exch (share, security, company)* non coté(e), non inscrit(e) à la cote

◇ *unlisted market* Bourse *f* coulisse

◇ *unlisted securities market* marché *m* hors cote, second marché

> **"**
>
> Sherwood Group (steady at 760p and now capitalised at £140m) is looking too big for the **unlisted securities market** and a move up to the main market may well accompany Tuesday's year-end profits.
>
> **"**

unlock *vt (assets)* débloquer

unmortgaged *adj* libre d'hypothèques

unnegotiable *adj (cheque, bill)* non négociable

unpledged revenue *n* recettes *fpl* non gagées

unprofitable *adj (business)* peu rentable

unquoted *adj St Exch (share)* non coté(e)

◇ *unquoted company* société *f* non cotée

◊ *unquoted securities* valeurs *fpl* non cotées

unrealizable *adj (capital, assets)* non réalisable

unrealized *adj (capital, assets)* non réalisé(e); *(gain, loss)* latent(e)

unrecoverable *adj (debt)* inexigible

unredeemed *adj (loan)* non amorti(e), non remboursé(e); *(draft)* non honoré(e); *(mortgage)* non purgé(e)

unsecured *adj (loan, overdraft)* non garanti(e), à découvert
◊ *unsecured advance* avance *f* à découvert
◊ *unsecured creditor* créancier (ère) *m,f* ordinaire *ou* chirographaire
◊ *unsecured debenture* obligation *f* non garantie
◊ *unsecured debt* créance *f* chirographaire *ou* sans garantie
◊ *unsecured loan* prêt *m* non-garanti

> 66
>
> The position of a secured creditor is to be contrasted with that of an **unsecured creditor** who merely has a personal claim to sue for the payment of his debt and to invoke the available legal processes for the enforcement of any judgment that he may obtain.
>
> 99

unstable *adj (market, prices)* instable

unsteady *adj (prices)* variable; *(market)* agité(e)

unsubscribed *adj (capital)* non souscrit(e)

untaxed *adj (income)* exempt(e) d'impôt, exonéré(e) d'impôt; *(goods)* non imposé(e), non taxé(e)

untradable *adj St Exch* incotable

upside *adj St Exch*
◊ *upside potential* potentiel *m* de hausse
◊ *upside risk* risque *m* de hausse

upswing *n* mouvement *m* vers la hausse; **the Stock Market is on the upswing** la Bourse est en hausse

upward *adj*
◊ *upward movement* mouvement *m* de hausse
◊ *upward trend* tendance *f* à la hausse

usance *n Banking (time limit)* usance *f*; **at thirty days' usance** à usance de trente jours
◊ *usance bill* effet *m* à usance

USM *n St Exch (abbr unlisted securities market)* marché *m* hors cote, second marché

utility stocks *npl Am St Exch* valeurs *fpl* de services publics

valium picnic n Am Fam (quiet day on New York Stock Exchange) séance f morne

valorization n valorisation f

valorize vt valoriser

valuation n (a) (act) évaluation f, estimation f, expertise f; **to get a valuation of sth** faire évaluer ou estimer ou expertiser qch; **to make a valuation of sth** évaluer ou estimer ou expertiser qch

(b) (price) évaluation f; **the valuation put on the business is £100,000** l'affaire a été évaluée ou estimée ou expertisée à 100 000 livres

◇ **valuation charge** taxation f à la valeur

value 1 n valeur f; **to be of value** avoir de la valeur; **to be of no value** être sans valeur; **to be good/poor value (for money)** être d'un bon/mauvais rapport qualité-prix; **to go up/down in value** prendre/perdre de la valeur; **to set** or **put a value on sth** estimer la valeur de qch; **they put a value of £150,000 on the property** ils ont estimé ou expertisé la propriété à 150 000 livres; **of no commercial value** sans valeur commerciale; **to the value of** pour une valeur

de; **what will this do to the value of property?** quel effet est-ce que ça va avoir sur le prix de l'immobilier?

2 vt (goods, damage) évaluer, estimer, expertiser; **to have sth valued** faire évaluer ou estimer ou expertiser qch; **they valued the company at $10 billion** ils ont estimé la valeur de la société à 10 milliards de dollars

◇ Banking **value in account** valeur f en compte

◇ **value added** valeur f ajoutée

◇ **value analysis** analyse f de valeur

◇ **value for collection** valeur f à l'encaissement

◇ **value date** date f de valeur

◇ **value day** jour m de valeur

◇ **value engineering** analyse f de valeur

◇ **value in exchange** valeur f d'échange, contre-valeur f

◇ Banking **value in gold currency** valeur-or f

◇ **value at liquidation** valeur f liquidative ou de liquidation

◇ St Exch **value at maturity** valeur f à l'échéance

◇ **value for money audit** = estimation des performances d'une société à but non lucratif ou d'un service gouvernemental

◇ *value below rate* décote *f*

◇ *value in use* valeur *f* d'usage

value-added tax *n Br* taxe *f* sur la valeur ajoutée, *Can* taxe sur les ventes

variable 1 *n* variable *f*
2 *adj* variable

◇ *variable budget* budget *m* variable *ou* flexible

◇ *variable costs* coûts *mpl ou* frais *mpl* variables

◇ *Banking variable rate* taux *m* variable

variable-income *adj (bond, investment)* à revenu variable

variable-rate interest *n* intérêt *m* variable

variable-yield *adj (investments, securities)* à revenu variable

variance *n Acct* variance *f*, écart *m*

◇ *variance analysis* analyse *f* des écarts

VAT *n Br (abbr* **value-added tax)** TVA *f*; **exclusive of** *or* **excluding VAT** hors TVA; **subject to VAT** soumis(e) à la TVA; **to be VAT registered** être assujetti(e) à la TVA

◇ *VAT credit* crédit *m* de TVA

◇ *Fam VAT man* inspecteur *m* de la TVA

◇ *VAT rate* taux *m* de TVA

◇ *VAT registration number* code *m* assujetti TVA

◇ *VAT return* déclaration *f* de TVA

◇ *VAT statement* état *m* TVA

vault *n Banking* salle *f* des coffres

VCT *n (abbr* **venture capital trust)** FCPR *m*

vendor *n St Exch* vendeur (euse) *m,f*

◇ *vendor's lien* privilège *m* du vendeur

◇ *vendor's shares* actions *fpl* d'apport *ou* de fondation

venture *n* entreprise *f*

◇ *venture capital* capital-risque *m*

◇ *venture capital company* société *f* à capital-risque

◇ *venture capitalist* spécialiste *mf* de la prise de risques *(dans la finance)*

◇ *venture capital trust* fonds *m* commun de placement à risques

"

3i, the UK's largest **venture capital** provider, is pulling back from funding smaller companies that are not involved in technology or other growth areas. … The **venture capitalist** is setting up a special team to manage investments of less than £2m in non-technology companies to 'maximise value'. This could involve sales and mergers but not a flood of disposals.

"

vertical *adj*

◇ *vertical equity* équité *f* verticale

◇ *vertical spread* écart *m* vertical

vested interest *n* **to have a vested interest in a business** avoir des capitaux investis dans une entreprise, être intéressé(e) dans une entreprise; **vested interests** *(rights)* droits *mpl* acquis; *(investments)* capitaux *mpl* investis

Visa® *n* Visa *f*®; **to pay by Visa** ®
payer par Visa®
◊ **Visa® card** carte *f* Visa ®

volatile *adj St Exch* volatil(e)

volatility *n St Exch* volatilité *f*

voluntary liquidation *n* liquidation *f* volontaire

voting *n*
◊ *St Exch* **voting rights** *(of
shareholders)* droit *m* de vote
◊ **voting shares** actions *fpl* don-
nant droit au vote

voucher *n Acct* pièce *f* comp-
table

wage n wage(s) salaire m, paie f
◇ **wage(s) bill** masse f salariale, charges fpl salariales
◇ **wage bracket** fourchette f de salaire
◇ **wage ceiling** salaire m plafonné
◇ **wage differential** écart m salarial
◇ **wage freeze** gel m ou blocage m des salaires
◇ Acct **wages ledger** journal m de paie
◇ **wage pyramid** pyramide f des salaires

waiter n St Exch coursier m

Wall Street n Wall Street (quartier de la Bourse de New York); the Wall Street Crash le krach de Wall Street

war chest n caisse f spéciale; (of trade union) caisse de grève

warehousing n St Exch (of shares) parcage m

warrant n St Exch bon m de souscription d'actions

wasting asset n Acct actif m qui se déprécie

> 〝
> There is a series of complex rules for determining the true length of a lease … A lease will usually be a **wasting asset** for the purposes of capital gains tax when its duration does not exceed fifty years.
> 〞

watered stock n titres mpl dilués

weak adj (currency) faible; (market) en baisse, baissier (ère)

weaken 1 vt (currency) affaiblir, faire baisser; (market, prices) faire fléchir
2 vi (of currency) s'affaiblir, baisser; (of market, prices) fléchir

wealth n richesse(s) f(pl)
◇ **wealth tax** impôt m de solidarité sur la fortune

wealthy 1 npl the wealthy les riches mpl
2 adj riche

wear and tear n Acct dépréciation f fonctionnelle

weighted average n moyenne f pondérée
◇ Acct **weighted average cost** coût m moyen pondéré

weighting n indemnité f; London weighting indemnité de vie chère à Londres

white knight n St Exch chevalier m blanc

wholesale *adj* de gros
◇ *wholesale bank* banque *f* de gros
◇ Banking *wholesale market* marché *m* de gré à gré entre banques
◇ *wholesale price index* indice *m* des prix de gros

windbill *n* billet *m* de complaisance, effet *m* de complaisance

windfall *n* (*unexpected gain*) aubaine *f*
◇ *windfall profits, windfall revenues* profits *mpl* inattendus *ou* exceptionnels
◇ *windfall tax* impôt *m* sur les gains exceptionnels

> **"**
>
> Sir David Rowland, NatWest's chairman, said yesterday that this was just a stepping stone to other deals. The banking and insurance groups yesterday promised their investors £130m a year in savings, and analysts expect about £100m a year in **windfall revenues**, but this was not enough to quell the doubts of some big shareholders.
>
> **"**

window dressing *n* Acct habillage *m* de bilan

WIP *n* Acct (*abbr* **work in progress**) travail *m* en cours, encours *m* de production de biens

▸ **wipe off** *vt sep* (*debt*) annuler; **several millions of pounds were wiped off the value of shares** la valeur des actions a baissé de plusieurs millions de livres

withdraw *vt* (*money*) retirer; **I need to withdraw £500 from my account** il faut que je retire 500 livres de mon compte

withdrawal *n* (*of money*) retrait *m*; **to make a withdrawal** faire un retrait
◇ *withdrawal limit* plafond *m* (d'autorisation) de retrait
◇ *withdrawal notice* avis *m* de retrait
◇ *withdrawal slip* bordereau *m* de retrait

withholding tax *n* impôt *m* retenu à la source, retenue *f* fiscale

worker participation *n* participation *f* ouvrière

working *adj*
◇ *working account* compte *m* d'exploitation
◇ Acct *working assets* actif *m* circulant
◇ *working capital* fonds *mpl ou* capital *m* de roulement
◇ *working capital cycle* cycle *m* du besoin en fonds de roulement
◇ *working capital fund* compte *m* d'avances
◇ *working capital requirements* besoins *mpl* en fonds de roulement

work in progress *n* Acct travail *m* en cours, encours *m* de production de biens

world *adj* mondial(e)
◇ *World Bank* Banque *f* mondiale
◇ *world economy* conjoncture *f* économique mondiale
◇ *world markets* marché *m* mondial *ou* international
◇ *world reserves* réserves *fpl* mondiales

◇ *World Trade Organization* Organisation *f* mondiale du commerce

write *vt (cheque)* faire

▸ **write down** *vt sep (capital, stock)* réduire; *Acct (asset)* déprécier

▸ **write off** *vt sep (capital, stock)* amortir; *Acct (bad debt, asset)* passer par profits et pertes

▸ **write up** *vt sep (capital, stock)* augmenter; *Acct (asset)* revaloriser

write-down *n Acct* dépréciation *f*

> **❝**
>
> Coats Viyella … said yesterday it had grasped the nettle of under-performance, but was paying the price of reorganisation, with a half-year pre-tax loss of £13.7 million. The former FTSE 100 company said its restructuring had seen it take **write-downs** totalling £63.7 million, but the benefits would show through in the second half of the year.
>
> **❞**

write-off *n Acct* annulation *f* par écrit, passation *f* par pertes et profits

write-up *n Acct* augmentation *f*

written-down cost, written-down value *n Acct* valeur *f* amortie

X-Dax *n St Exch* the X-Dax
(index) le X-Dax, l'indice X-
Dax

Xetra-Dax *n St Exch* the Xetra-
Dax index l'indice *m* Xetra-Dax

Yankee bond *n Am* obligation *f*
Yankee

year *n (twelve-month period)* an
m; *(referring to duration)* année
f; **to earn £40,000 a year** gagner
40 000 livres par an; **the year
under review** l'exercice écoulé;
Acct **year ended 31 December
1999** exercice clos le 31 décembre 1999

◊ **year of assessment** année *f*
d'imposition

◊ *Acct* **year end** fin *f* d'exercice

◊ **year's purchase** taux *m* de capitalisation des bénéfices

year-end *adj Acct* de fin *f*
d'exercice

◊ **year-end accounts** compte *m*
de résultats

◊ **year-end audit** vérification *f*
comptable de fin d'exercice

◊ **year-end closing of accounts**
clôture *f* annuelle des livres

◊ **year-end loss** perte *f* de fin
d'exercice

◊ **year-end profits** bénéfices
mpl de fin d'exercice

yearly *adj* annuel(elle)

◊ **yearly payment** versement *m*
annuel

yen *n* yen *m*

yield 1 *n (from investments)* rapport *m*, rendement *m*; *(from
tax)* recette *f*, rapport

2 *vt (dividend, interest)* rapporter; *(income)* créer; **the investment bond will yield 5%** le bon
d'épargne rapportera 5%

◊ **yield capacity** productivité *f*

◊ **yield curve** courbe *f* des taux

◊ **yield gap** prime *f* de risque

ZBB *n Acct (abbr* **zero-base
budgeting** *)* BBZ *m*

zero-base budgeting *n Acct*
budget *m* base zéro, budgétisation *f* base zéro

zero coupon bond *n St Exch*
obligation *f* à coupon zéro

zero-rated *adj (for VAT)*
exempt(e) de TVA, exonéré(e)
de TVA; **in Britain, books are
zero-rated** en Grande-Bretagne, les livres sont exempts *ou*
exonérés de TVA

zero-rating *n* franchise *f* de
TVA, taux *m* zéro

As time goes by, national differences in the presentation and calculation of financial information are becoming less marked, but this must be seen against a historical context where accounting traditions are quite different:

- French accounting has been regulated by government since the seventeenth century and has its roots in taxation and management of the economy.

- British and American accounting are regulated in detail by the accounting profession, within a government framework, and have their roots in the industrial revolution, when it became necessary to monitor the financing of industrial projects.

- Historically, the balance sheet is the oldest financial statement. It originated when businesses established the practice of making an annual inventory of their property less their debts to estimate their wealth, with the difference between two annual inventories representing the gain or loss in the intervening year.

Modern financial reporting, however, does not typically carry out annual valuations, but maintains a database of financial transactions (the general or nominal ledger) from which the annual reports are derived. These reports are (a) the balance sheet, (b) the profit and loss account (or income statement), (c) the cash flow statement and (d) the notes to the accounts.

- The balance sheet shows, on the one hand, the sources of the company's finance (divided between that provided on a permanent basis by the owners – equity – and that which is borrowed and must be repaid – debt), and on the other hand, the production facilities and trading items – assets – which the finance is supporting. The assets are normally split between long-term productive capacity (fixed assets) and short-term trading items such as stocks of goods and invoiced amounts due from clients (current assets).

- The profit and loss account gives a detailed picture of revenues and expenses for the year.

- The cash flow statement analyses the changes in the financial structure of the company over the same year: how much cash has been generated from operations, how much has been invested in new capacity, and the consequences for these two flows on the company's debt position.

- The notes to the accounts have the same regulatory status as the prime statements and are generally used for the provision of supplementary analysis.

Financial reporting is done on what is called the "accruals" basis: it aims to record transactions when any contractual event takes place (e.g. when a product is delivered to the customer), not just cash flows (when clients pay their outstanding invoices). The profit and loss account is therefore an economic assessment, which is why there is a need for the cash flow statement which looks at the narrower cash aspect in isolation. All the economic transactions revert to cash in time, but accounting tries to track all economic events as they occur.

While the financial statements from different countries all give broadly the same information, presentation differs to some degree. The main building blocks of the balance sheet – equity, debt, fixed assets, current assets – are, however, preserved and easily recognised. The balance sheet works on the basis that the total of financing sources (debt and equity) will always equal the total of the uses of that finance (assets, fixed and current).

- The European Union has been a major force in harmonising the presentation of financial information, but recognises several formats. France and the UK generally use different formats within this constraint.

- France allows large companies to use international formats, and so not all French balance sheets necessarily look alike.

- There is a tradition in Europe that while recognised formats must be respected, companies are free to give additional information.

- In the US, there are no prescribed formats, although there are minimum categories of information. Formats for US companies will therefore vary, but majority practice is that shown in this book.

- Regulators generally accept a degree of fluidity between the financial statements and the notes. US and British companies have a tendency to keep their balance sheet presentation very simple, using highly aggregated figures, and put the detailed information in the notes.

Sample French Financial Statements

Compte de résultat
(en milliers de francs)

	Exercice 20X2	Exercice 20X1
Produits d'exploitation		
Ventes de production	232 488	211 788
Autres produits	1 723	1 634
Total	234 211	213 422
Charges d'exploitation		
Matières premières et charges externes	86 739	80 645
Frais de personnel	92 865	86 320
Dotations aux amortissements	18 543	18 023
Dotations aux provisions	2 678	—
Total	200 825	184 988
Résultat d'exploitation	33 386	28 434
Produits financiers		
Participations	2 178	2 106
Reprise sur provisions	200	—
Total	2 378	2 106
Charges financières		
Intérêts	5 653	5 832
Dotations aux provisions	486	—
Total	6 139	5 832
Résultat financier	(3 761)	(3 726)
Résultat courant avant impôts	29 625	24 708
Produits exceptionnels		
Cession d'immobilisations	5 887	678
Reprise d'amortissements dérogatoires	312	310
Total	6 199	988
Charges exceptionnelles		
Dotations aux amortissements dérogatoires	659	583
Cession d'immobilisations	6 677	—
Total	7 336	583
Résultat exceptionnel	(1 137)	405
Résultat avant impôts	28 488	25 113
Participation des salariés	1 267	1 188
Impôts sur les bénéfices	10 766	8 344
Résultat net de l'exercice	16 455	15 581

Annotations:

- Previous year's comparative figures are obligatory
- Vertical presentation now common, but may be presented as two columns with revenue to the right and expenses to the left
- EU requires split between trading operations and purely financial transactions
- Unusual or non-trading items shown separately
- Larger French companies must share profits with staff

Bilan

au 31 décembre
(en milliers de francs)

> Must show original cost as well as accounting value at balance sheet date

> The EU requires that fixed assets be split between intangible, tangible and financial

ACTIF	Montants bruts	Amortis- sements et provisions	20X2 Montants nets	20X1 Montant nets
Immobilisations incorporelles				
Marques	2 560	1 670	890	1 100
Immobilisations corporelles				
Terrains	4 890	—	4 890	4 890
Constructions	2 763	578	2 185	2 240
Installations techniques	1 326	652	674	805
Autres	1 547	662	885	968
Total	10 526	1 892	8 634	8 903
Immobilisations financières				
Participations	7 867	680	7 187	7 409
Créances rattachées	1 500	—	1 500	1 500
Total	9 367	680	8 687	8 909
Actif immobilisé	22 453	4 242	18 211	18 912
Actif circulant				
Stocks et en cours	13 266	1 215	12 051	12 897
Créances clients	51 683	2 528	49 155	47 488
Placements de trésorerie	3 400	—	3 400	
Banques et caisses	10 243	—	10 243	2 758
Total	78 592	3 743	74 849	63 143

> Classified within fixed or current assets in UK/US accounting

Charges constatées d'avance	1 324	—	1 324	1 415
Charges à répartir sur plusieurs exercices	2 240	896	1 344	1 792
Total de l'actif	104 609	8 881	95 728	85 262

PASSIF	Figures shown before and after allocation of the year's profit to dividend and reserves		20X2	20X1
		Avant répartition	Après répartition	Après répartition
Capitaux propres				
Capital social		5 657	5 657	5 657
Primes d'émission, de fusion et d'apport		17 244	17 244	17 244
Ecarts de réévaluation		218	218	218
Réserve légale		566	566	566
Réserves réglementées		357	387	357
Autres réserves		12 780	25 035	12 780
Report à nouveau		1 543	2 343	1 543
Résultat de l'exercice		16 455	—	—
Provisions réglementées		2 868	2 868	2 521
Total		57 688	54 318	40 886
Provisions	Provisions are potential liabilities and part of the "debt" block in the balance sheet			
Provisions pour risques		3 000	3 000	3 000
Provisions pour charges		5 362	5 362	2 398
Total		8 362	8 362	5 398
Emprunts obligataires		5 000	5 000	5 000
Emprunts et dettes auprès des établissements de crédit	Long-term debts shown separately from current operating items	4 331	4 331	9 876
Dettes d'exploitation				
Dettes fournisseurs		12 486	12 486	11 734
Dettes fiscales et sociales		7 438	7 438	6 854
Autres dettes		423	3 793	5 514
Total		29 678	33 048	38 978
Total du passif		95 728	95 728	85 262

Tableaux des Flux de Trésorerie

(en milliers de francs)

Format recommended by Ordre des Experts Comptables

	Exercice 20X2	Exercice 20X1
Opérations d'exploitation		
Résultat net	16 455	15 581
Elimination des charges et produits sans incidence sur la trésorerie ou non liés à l'exploitation		
amortissements et provisions	3 720	1 367
variations de stocks	846	(1 289)
transferts de charges du compte de charges à repartir	539	539
(plus) et moins values de cession	790	—
Incidence de la décalage de trésorerie sur opérations d'exploitation	(4 515)	(2 834)
Flux de trésorerie provenant de l'exploitation	<u>17 835</u>	<u>13 364</u>
Opérations d'investissement		
Décaissements provenant de l'acquisition d'immobilisations	(2 292)	(7 595)
Encaissements provenant de la cession d'immobilisations	5 887	—
Flux de trésorerie provenant des (affecté aux) opérations d'investissment	<u>3 595</u>	<u>(7 595)</u>
Opérations de financement		
Dividendes versés aux actionnaires	(4 900)	(3 943)
Remboursements d'emprunts	(5 545)	
Flux de trésorerie provenant des (affecté aux) opérations de financement	<u>(10 545)</u>	<u>(3 943)</u>
Variation de la trésorerie	10 885	1 826
Trésorerie à l'ouverture	2 758	932
Trésorerie à la clôture	13 643	2 758

Difference in balances over year explained by analysis

THE EUROPEAN UNION AND THE SINGLE CURRENCY

The drive towards Economic and Monetary Union (EMU) reached a crucial stage when eleven of the member states of the European Union launched a single currency – the euro – in January 1999. As from this date, when the member countries locked the exchange rate of their national currencies to the euro, the euro became the official currency of the EU and financial institutions began trading in euro on international markets. The eleven member countries share a single interest rate, set by the European Central Bank (ECB), and a single foreign exchange rate. However, consumers in EU countries will have time to gradually get used to the euro, as notes and coins in national currencies will continue to circulate until the year 2002, when they will be replaced by euro cash. During this transition period, dual pricing of goods (in both the traditional currency and in euro) will give people time to become accustomed to the new currency.

Britain did not join the first wave of countries to adopt the euro in 1999, but may commit itself to the single currency in the near future. Whatever happens, the advent of the euro zone means that the way in which financial transactions and business generally are conducted in Britain will be profoundly affected.

Euro reference rates

Permanently fixed euro rates against Euroland national currencies on the 31st December 1998:

Austria	= 13.7603 schillings
Belgium	= 40.3399 Belgian francs
Finland	= 5.94573 markka
France	= 6.55957 French francs
Germany	= 1.95583 marks
Holland	= 2.20371 guilders
Ireland	= 0.787564 Irish pounds
Italy	= 1936.27 lira
Luxembourg	= 40.33399 Luxembourg francs
Portugal	= 200.482 escudos
Spain	= 166.386 pesetas

History of the European Union and of the EMU project

Mar 1957	Treaty of Rome establishes the European Economic Community (EEC)
1971	The Werner Report sets out three-stage process for achieving EMU
Jan 1973	Britain, Ireland and Denmark join the EEC
Mar 1979	Creation of the EMS (European Monetary System): the ERM (Exchange Rate Mechanism) is established with 8 member currencies and the Ecu is introduced as the weighted average of all European currencies
1986–87	The Single European Act formalizes the programme for the European Single Market
1988	Publication of the Delors Report on economic and monetary union: this outlines concrete stages by which EMU is to be implemented
Jul 1990	Stage 1 of EMU: removal of exchange controls across Europe and abolition of capital controls
Feb 1992	Maastricht Treaty: enshrines principle of monetary union and prescribes convergence criteria for member states signing up to join the single currency
Jan 1993	The EEC becomes the European Union
Nov 1993	Maastricht Treaty enters into force when composition of the Ecu currency basket is frozen
Jan 1994	Stage 2 of EMU: European Monetary Institute (EMI) is founded as precursor to the European Central Bank
Dec 1995	New currency is officially christened the euro at European Council meeting in Madrid
Mar 1996	Start of the InterGovernmental Conference (IGC) in Turin: EU institutional reforms discussed and preparations made for EU enlargement
Dec 1996	Stability and Growth Pact ensures that economic discipline is maintained
1997	Draft Amsterdam Treaty signed: resolution on ERM II links currencies of non-participating member states to the euro
May 1998	EMU commences formally: EU heads of state decide which countries qualify for membership of the single currency, fix bilateral currency conversion rate and agree to keep their national economies in line with convergence criteria
Jun 1998	European Central Bank (ECB) inaugurated
Jan 1999	The euro becomes the official currency of the EMU participating states: conversion rates of the currencies of these states are locked to the euro
Jan 2002	Euro banknotes and coins scheduled to be introduced
Jul 2002	Stage 3 of EMU: National coins and notes to be withdrawn from circulation in EMU participating countries

The single currency and its implications for the UK

The issue of the single currency continues to be a controversial one in British politics. With the advent of Tony Blair's New Labour government in 1997, the political landscape in Britain changed and the government adopted a more pro-European tone and strategy than its Conservative predecessors, although refusing to commit the UK to the single currency just yet. The Chancellor has indicated that Britain is unlikely to join EMU before the next UK general election, and stipulated that UK membership will ultimately depend on the right economic conditions being met.

The changeover to the euro affects British businesses whether the UK joins the single currency or not. The new currency will have a major impact on the way in which financial transactions are conducted. In particular, for EMU countries - and therefore for European competitors of British firms - the advent of the euro will mean:

- cheaper transaction costs
- exchange rate stability
- price transparency

These factors will obviously pose immediate challenges and opportunities for countries within the euro zone. As they can now share one currency, they will no longer incur transaction costs when doing business with one another. Sharing one currency will also mean that the euro zone countries will no longer be vulnerable to exchange rate fluctuations when trading with each other. The euro will also result in price transparency across the euro zone, and this should make cross-border trade much more straightforward.

How will all this affect British firms? In today's era of globalisation, even British firms which have no direct trading links with continental Europe will not remain insulated from the effects of the euro for long. Some of the major areas in which they may be affected may be summarized as follows:

- Exchange rate risk: companies in the euro zone will benefit from the elimination of exchange rate risk, but if UK firms buy products priced in euro from these companies an exchange risk may be passed on to them. Similarly, UK export firms quoting in sterling while their competitors within the euro zone quote in euro will need to develop a strategy for managing exchange rate risk. But even a UK firm which doesn't deal directly with the euro zone may still be affected if, for example, it supplies businesses which do. It may find itself at a disadvantage if its European competitors find themselves in an improved position now that they no longer have to contend with fluctuating exchange rates.

- Accounting: obviously, firms who have direct trading links with countries in the euro zone will inevitably have to deal with the new currency and this may mean adapting their accounting system and introducing a multicurrency accountancy package that can handle the peculiarities of the euro environment. As many multi-nationals have indicated that from now on they would prefer to handle their finances and accounts in euro, thus simplifying accounting and reporting procedures, their subsidiaries in Britain will be required to follow suit (indeed UK firms in this category may find that they may soon have to use the new currency for trading within the UK itself).

- Organizational procedures: changes in a company's accounting systems will inevitably be linked to changes in the overall IT system that result from the introduction of the euro. This conversion process should ideally be phased in over a period of time. Equally, UK export firms may have to consider standardizing their prices across the euro zone, or establishing new price points in euro. On a more everyday level, they may suddenly be required to print invoices in euro, or may have to modify their cash management systems (eg. altering cash registers if they plan to accept euro cash).

- Banking: most banks now offer account facilities in euro, and therefore businesses can, if they so wish, lodge company accounts in euro or open euro bank accounts. Businesses which already have accounts in the currencies of participating countries may use this opportunity to consolidate them. Cheques denominated in euro have been processed by banks since January 4, 1999. As far as transferring money and processing transactions is concerned, banks provide a same-day payment system known as CHAPS euro; this system links up with TARGET (Trans-European Automated Real-Time Gross Settlement Express Transfer System) which is operated by the European Central Bank and connects the payment systems of other European countries. It will be possible to use this system to make both domestic and cross-border payments. BACS, which many companies use to pay their suppliers in sterling, oper-ates an automated system for handling amounts denominated in euro, allowing euro credits to be transferred electronically to UK bank accounts.

- Investment strategy: the emergence of a bigger and more liquid market should reduce the cost of borrowing. Individuals or companies wishing to borrow in euro (attracted perhaps by the prospect of lower interest rates in the euro zone) should remember that they will be exposed to the risk of exchange rate fluctuation between sterling and the euro unless they have an income stream in euro. Companies with a large income stream from the euro zone, however, may well want to explore the possibilities for borrowing in euro. Given that European financial markets are now trading in euro, larger firms may need to ask themselves how the conversion of bonds and equities will be affected. They may decide that equity markets are more lucrative in euro, and consequently to review their investment strategy. Likewise, companies with pension funds may need to liaise with fund managers to see if they have developed a fund management policy that takes account of the impact of the euro on the economy, especially as the elimination of exchange risk is likely to result in a diversification of portfolio investments throughout the euro zone. The euro will inevitably have a huge impact on financial institutions across Europe and may well ultimately give rise to new ways of financing corporate activity.

- Taxation: to facilitate use of the euro in UK firms, the Chancellor of the Exchequer announced in October 1997 that British businesses would be able to pay taxes in euro. As of January 1999, both the Inland Revenue and Customs and Excise accept payment of taxes in euro. Payments can be made by CHAPS, BACS direct credit or cheque: the interval between presentation of payment and conversion will be kept to a minimum to minimize exchange rate risk. However, while sterling continues to float against the euro it will not be possible for businesses to complete tax returns in euro (with the exception of certain customs declarations relating to imports from euro zone countries).

Useful information about the euro can be found at the following websites:

www.euro.gov.uk (The Treasury's euro preparations unit)
www.bankofengland.co.uk/euro.htm (Bank of England)
www.icaew.co.uk/euro.htm (Institute of Chartered
    Accountants in England and Wales)

Euro banknotes and coins
Like the pound and the dollar, the new currency has its own symbol: €

Euro banknotes are available in seven denominations: €5, €10, €20, €50, €100, €200 and €500. Each denomination has a specific dominant colour and a clearly different size to enable easy identification. Some of the draft designs of the notes are shown below. These designs, which were selected on the basis of an EU-wide competition, are inspired by the theme of the history of European architecture: the €5 note represents classical architecture, the €10 Romanesque, the €50 Renaissance, the €100 Baroque, the €200 note the age of iron and glass in architecture, and finally the €500 note illustrates the era of modern 20th century architecture. Windows and gateways will be the main motif for the front of the banknotes, symbolizing the spirit of openness and cooperation in the European Union. Bridges appear on the reverse side of the notes, serving as a metaphor for communication between the peoples of the Europe and between Europe and the rest of the world.

Distinctive features of the notes include:

- the 12 stars of the EU flag as logo on the front of the notes, and the EU flag in miniature on the back of the notes

- the initials of the European Central Bank in their five linguistic variants (BCE, ECB, EZB, EKT and EKP)

- the signature of the ECB's president, positioned close to these initials

- the name of the currency in Greek surmounted by its name in Latin (EURO)

- a holographic foil patch on the front of higher value notes (€50, €100, €200 and €500)

Front of a €20 banknote

Reverse side of a €20 banknote

- a foil stripe on the front of lower value notes (€5, €10 and €20)
- the value of the notes printed in bold figures on the top right hand side to aid the partially-sighted

Euro coins have one common European side and a national side. The European side (again, selected through an EU-wide competition) shows a map of Europe against a dynamic background of parallel lines on each of which appears the stars of the EU flag. The design for the national side of each coin was selected via a national competition in each participating country. The coins will be available in eight denominations ranging from one cent to 2 euro.

1 euro coin: front

Reverse side: Belgian

Reverse side: Spanish

50 euro cent coin: front

Reverse side: French

Reverse side: Irish

The euro and the dollar

The dollar is clearly the world's dominant currency (it is used for 50% of commercial transactions and over 80% of financial market transactions), but the advent of the euro means that its dominant position may be challenged in the long term.

A successful euro would be the first real competitor to the dollar since it outstripped sterling as the world's leading currency during the interwar period. If the single currency project is a success and the euro proves to be a strong currency, then the dollar-centred system that currently prevails in the global economy will be replaced by a system dominated by both the euro and the dollar. In particular, the euro is likely to provide a credible alternative to the dollar for trade with countries having close monetary, economic and geographical links with the European Union. According to this scenario, it is possible that the dollar and the euro will each end up controlling about 40% of world finance (with the remaining 20% divided up between the yen, Swiss franc and a few minor currencies).

An alternative, less optimistic, scenario however foresees a far less rosy future for the euro. Such a prognosis is based on a lacklustre assessment of Europe's economy (especially in contrast to the recent unprecedented growth of the US economy). Monetarists who support this view maintain that the euro will be seriously undermined by inherent weaknesses in the economic structure of the EMU participating countries and some even go so far as to suggest that sterling might become the hard currency alternative to the euro (assuming that Britain does not join EMU).

Advocates of the single currency hope however that the creation of the euro will eliminate the present gap in international monetary roles between the United States and Europe. They argue that the transformation of European financial markets under the euro will be a major factor in this process: the enhanced depth and liquidity of markets in Europe will serve to increase the new currency's attractiveness. This will have huge implications for the global money markets and indeed for the global economy. The switch from a world monetary system dominated by the dollar to a new system where the dollar is counterbalanced by the euro could produce a massive swing in global financial holdings. However, although some analysts believe that the euro could rival the dollar as a reserve currency as early as 2003, at this early stage in its history the future trajectory of the new currency cannot be predicted with any degree of certainty, and much will depend on the performance of the European economies in the next few years.

AA *nf Banque, Bourse* **(notation) AA** AA (rating), double-A rating

AAA *nf Banque, Bourse* **(notation) AAA** AAA (rating), triple-A rating

abaissement *nm (des prix, des taux, d'un impôt)* lowering, reduction; *(d'une monnaie)* weakening

abaisser *vt (prix, taux, impôt)* to lower, to reduce; *(monnaie)* to weaken

abandon *nm Bourse*
◊ *abandon de l'option, abandon de prime* relinquishment *or* abandonment of the option

abandonner *vt Bourse* **abandonner l'option** *ou* **la prime** to relinquish *or* abandon *or* surrender the option

abattement *nm (rabais)* reduction; *(d'impôts)* allowance
◊ *abattement à la base* basic personal allowance
◊ *abattement fiscal* tax allowance
◊ *abattement forfaitaire* fixed-rate rebate

abondement *n* = employer's contribution to company savings scheme

absorber *vt (entreprise)* to take over

absorption *nf (d'une entreprise)* takeover

absorption-fusion *nf* merger

abus de biens sociaux *nm Jur* misappropriation of funds

ac (a) *(abrév* **argent comptant**) cash (b) *(abrév* **année courante**) current year

acceptation n acceptance

◇ *acceptation bancaire* banker's acceptance

◇ *acceptation conditionnelle* qualified acceptance

◇ *acceptation partielle* partial acceptance

◇ *acceptation sous condition* conditional acceptance

accepter vt *(chèque, effet)* to accept, to sign, to honour

accepteur, -euse nm,f *(d'une facture, d'un effet)* acceptor, drawee

accord nm agreement

◇ *accord d'achat et de vente* buy-sell agreement

◇ *accord de clearing* clearing agreement

◇ Écon *accord commercial* trade agreement

◇ *accord de compensation* off-set agreement

◇ *accord de crédit* credit agreement

◇ Écon *Accord Général sur les Tarifs Douaniers et le Commerce* General Agreement on Tariffs and Trade

◇ UE *Accord monétaire européen* European monetary agreement

◇ Écon *Accord multilatéral sur l'investissement* multilateral agreement on investment

◇ Bourse *accord de taux futur* future rate agreement

◇ Bourse *accord de taux à terme* Forward Rate Agreement

accorder 1 vt *(découvert bancaire, remise)* to allow, to give; *(dommages-intérêts)* to award; *(prêt)* to authorize, to extend

2 s'accorder vpr *(se mettre d'accord)* to agree, to come to an agreement (**avec qn** with sb; **sur qch** on sth); **s'accorder sur le prix** to agree on the price

accrédité, -e nm,f (a) *(détenteur d'une lettre de crédit)* holder of a letter of credit (b) Compta beneficiary, payee

accréditer vt *(client)* to open an account for, to open credit facilities for; **être accrédité auprès d'une banque** to have credit facilities at a bank

accréditeur nm surety, guarantor

accréditif nm (a) *(lettre de crédit)* letter of credit; Compta credential
(b) *(crédit)* credit; **loger un accréditif sur une banque** to open credit facilities with a bank

◇ *accréditif permanent* permanent credit

accroissement nm increase; *(du capital)* accumulation

◇ *accroissement global net* aggregate net increment

accroître 1 vt to increase
2 s'accroître vpr to increase

accueil nm faire (bon) accueil à une traite to meet or honour a bill

accueillir vt *(traite)* to meet, to honour

accumulation nf accumulation

◇ *accumulation de capital* capital accumulation

◇ *accumulation des intérêts* accrual of interest

accumulé, -e adj *(intérêts)* accrued

accumuler 1 vt *(dettes)* to accumulate

2 s'accumuler *vpr (intérêts)* to accrue

accusé, -e 1 *adj (baisse, hausse)* sharp

  2 *nm*

◇ **accusé de réception** *(d'une lettre)* acknowledgement (of receipt); *(d'un colis)* receipt

achat *nm (action)* purchase, purchasing; *(chose achetée)* purchase; **faire un achat** to make a purchase; **faire l'achat de qch** to purchase sth; **la livre vaut neuf francs à l'achat** the buying rate for sterling is nine francs

◇ **achat au comptant** cash purchase

◇ **achat à crédit** credit purchase, purchase for the account

◇ **achat contre espèces, achat en espèces** cash purchase

◇ **achats institutionnels** institutional buying

◇ **achats spéculatifs** speculative buying

◇ *Bourse* **achat à terme** forward buying

acheter *vt* to buy, to purchase; **acheter qch à qn** *(faire une transaction)* to buy sth from sb; *(en cadeau)* to buy sth for sb; **acheter qch à crédit/(au) comptant** to buy sth on credit/for cash; *Bourse* **acheter à terme** to buy forward

acheteur, -euse *nm,f* buyer, purchaser; *Jur* vendee

acompte *nm (versement régulier)* instalment; *(avance, premier versement)* down payment, deposit; *(sur salaire)* advance; **payer par acomptes** to

pay by *or* in instalments; **payer ou verser un acompte de 4 000 francs** *ou* **4 000 francs en acompte (sur qch)** to make a down payment of 4,000 francs (on sth), to pay a deposit of 4,000 francs (on sth); **recevoir un acompte sur son salaire** to receive an advance on one's salary

◇ **acompte de dividende, acompte sur dividende** interim dividend

◇ **acompte provisionnel** interim *or* advance payment

acquéreur, -euse *nm,f* purchaser, buyer; *Jur* vendee

acquérir *vt* **(a)** *(acheter)* to buy, to purchase **(b)** *(obtenir)* to acquire, to gain

acquisition *nf (d'une entreprise)* acquisition; **faire l'acquisition d'une entreprise** to acquire a company

acquit *nm* receipt; **donner acquit de qch** to give a receipt for sth; **pour acquit** *(sur facture, quittance)* received (with thanks), paid

◇ **acquit de paiement** receipt

acquittement *nm (d'une dette)* payment, discharge; *(d'une facture, des droits)* payment

acquitter 1 *vt* **(a)** *(payer) (dette)* to pay off, to discharge; *(facture, droits)* to pay

  (b) *(comme preuve de paiement)* to receipt

  (c) *(chèque)* to endorse

  2 s'acquitter *vpr* **s'acquitter de qch** *(dette)* to pay sth off, to discharge sth; *(facture, droits)* to pay sth

acte *nm* act, deed

◇ *acte hypothécaire* mortgage deed

◇ *acte de vente* bill of sale

actif *nm Compta* assets; **excédent de l'actif sur le passif** excess of assets over liabilities

◇ *actif brut* gross assets

◇ *actif circulant* floating or current assets

◇ *actif circulant net* net current assets

◇ *actif corporel* tangible assets

◇ *actif corporel net* net tangible assets

◇ *actif différé* deferred asset

◇ *actif disponible liquide* available assets

◇ *actif d'exploitation* operating assets

◇ *actif fictif* fictitious assets

◇ *actif immobilisé* fixed or capital assets

◇ *actif incorporel* intangible assets

◇ *actif liquide* liquid assets

◇ *acif net* net assets or worth

◇ *actif net comptable* net accounting or book assets

◇ *actif net réévalué* net revalued assets

◇ *actif non-disponible immobilisé* illiquid assets

◇ *actif réalisable* realizable assets

◇ *actif réel* real assets

◇ *actif de roulement* current assets

◇ *actif sous-jacent* underlying asset

> **"**
>
> Les taux d'intérêt étant très bas, on devrait assister à une réallocation des **actifs** vers le long terme.
>
> **"**

action *nf Bourse* share; *(document)* share certificate; **actions** shares, equity, *Am* stock; **avoir des actions dans une société, détenir des actions d'une société** to have shares or a shareholding in a company; **émettre des actions sur un marché** to issue shares on a market; **les actions ont augmenté/baissé** shares rose/fell

◇ *action d'apport* (délivré au fondateur d'une société) founder's share; (émise par une société en contrepartie d'un apport en nature) vendor's share

◇ *action d'attribution* bonus share

◇ *action de capitalisation* capital share

◇ *action cotée (en Bourse)* quoted share

◇ *action de distribution* income share

◇ *action à dividende cumulatif* cumulative share

◇ *action gratuite* bonus share

◇ *action libérée* paid-up share

◇ *action nouvelle* new share

◇ *action ordinaire* Br ordinary share, Am common stock

◇ *action au porteur* bearer share

◇ *action de premier rang, action de priorité, action privilégiée* Br preference share, Am preferred stock

◇ *action privilégiée cumulative* cumulative preference share

◇ *action syndiquée* syndicated share

actionnaire *nmf Bourse Br* shareholder, *Am* stockholder

◇ *actionnaire majoritaire* majority *Br* shareholder or *Am* stockholder

◇ *actionnaire minoritaire* minority *Br* shareholder *or Am* stockholder

◇ *actionnaire de référence* major *Br* shareholder *or Am* stockholder

actionnariat *nm Bourse* shareholding

◇ *actionnariat intermédiaire* nominee shareholding

◇ *actionnariat ouvrier* employee shareholding

"

D'un autre côté se profile la possibilité d'une démocratisation de la propriété des entreprises avec la généralisation et la mutualisation de l'**actionnariat** (notamment par les fonds de pension) qui pourrait entraîner la véritable mort de Marx ... L'économie ouverte pourrait achever la mutation du capitalisme prédateur en un capitalisme redistributif en faisant des salariés les premiers actionnaires.

"

activité *nf Bourse (du marché)* activity; **sans activité** dull, slack; **en pleine activité** active, brisk

◇ *activité bancaire* banking

actuaire *nmf* actuary

actuariat *nm (profession)* actuarial profession

actuariel, -elle *adj* actuarial

adéquation des fonds propres *nf* capital adequacy

admettre *vt Bourse* **admettre une société à la cote** to list a company

administrateur, -trice *nm,f*

(d'une société, d'une banque) (non-executive) director

◇ *Jur administrateur judiciaire (de biens, d'une entreprise)* (official) receiver

administration *nf (gestion)* administration, management; *(ensemble des directeurs)* board of directors

◇ *administration fiscale* tax authorities

administrer *vt (société, biens)* to manage

admission *nf Bourse* **admission à la cote** admission to quotation, listing; **faire une demande d'admission à la cote** to seek admission to quotation

ad valorem *adj (droit, taxe)* ad valorem

affacturage *nm* factoring

affactureur *nm* factor

affaire *nf* (**a**) **affaires** *(activités commerciales)* business; **être dans les affaires** to be in business

(**b**) *(transaction)* deal, transaction; **faire affaire (avec qn)** to do a deal (with sb); **conclure une affaire (avec qn)** to clinch a deal (with sb)

(**c**) *(entreprise)* business, firm; **administrer** *ou* **gérer** *ou* **diriger une affaire** to run a business

◇ *affaire blanche* profitless *or* break-even deal

affectation *nf (d'une somme, de crédits)* assignment, allocation; **affectation aux dividendes** sum available for dividend

◇ *affectations budgétaires* budget appropriations

◇ *affectation de fonds* appropriation of funds

◇ *affectation hypothécaire* mortgage charge

affecter *vt (somme, crédits)* to assign, to allocate

afficher *vt (présenter)* to show; **afficher un déficit/un excédent** to show a deficit/a surplus

afflux *nm Compta* inflow

◇ *afflux de capitaux, afflux de fonds* capital inflow

> **"**
>
> Au Japon, le yen s'est une nouvelle fois renforcé par l'**afflux de capitaux** de la part des investisseurs, qui ne veulent pas rater la reprise de l'économie nippone. Celle-ci n'est pourtant pas encore assurée.
>
> **"**

AG *nf (abrév* **assemblée générale)** GM

agence *nf (d'une banque)* branch (office)

◇ *agence bancaire* bank branch

◇ *agence commerciale* mercantile agency

◇ *agence de notation* *Br* credit (rating) agency, *Am* credit bureau

◇ *agence de recouvrements* debt collection agency

agent *nm* agent

◇ *agent d'affacturage* factoring agent

◇ *Bourse* **agent de change** stockbroker, exchange dealer *or* broker

◇ *agent commercial* mercantile agent

◇ *agent comptable* accountant

◇ *agent du fisc* tax official

◇ *agent lié* tied agent

◇ *agent de recouvrement(s)* debt collector

◇ *agent souscripteur* underwriting *or* underwriter agent

◇ *agent du trésor* government broker

AGÉTAC, Agétac *nm Écon (abrév* **Accord Général sur les Tarifs Douaniers et le Commerce)** GATT

agio *nm* (a) *(dans un échange de devises)* agio (b) *Banque* **agios** *(quand on est à découvert)* bank charges; *(d'un emprunt)* interest payments

agiotage *nm Bourse* speculating, gambling

agioter *vi Bourse* to speculate, to gamble

agioteur, -euse *nm,f Bourse* speculator, gambler

agir *vi Bourse* **agir sur le marché** to manipulate the market

agitation *nf (sur le marché de la Bourse)* activity

agréé, -e *adj (organisme, agent)* recognized, authorized

agrément *nm (garantie financière)* bonding scheme

aide *nf (assistance)* assistance, help; *(sous forme d'argent)* aid

◇ *aide économique* economic aid

◇ *aide financière* financial aid *or* assistance

◇ *Compta* **aide fiscale** tax credit

ajustement *nm (des salaires, d'une monnaie, des prix)* adjustment

◇ *ajustement saisonnier* seasonal adjustment

ajuster vt (salaires, prix, monnaie) to adjust

alignement nm (a) Compta (d'un compte) making up, balancing

(b) (des prix) alignment (**sur** with); **l'alignement des salaires sur le coût de la vie** bringing salaries into line with the cost of living

(c) Écon (d'une monnaie, d'une économie) alignment

◊ **alignement monétaire** monetary alignment or adjustment

aligner vt (a) Compta (compte) to make up, to balance (b) (prix) to align, to bring into line (**sur** with) (c) Écon (monnaie, économie) to align

alimenter vt (compte bancaire) to pay money into

allègement nm (d'impôts, de charges, de dépenses) reduction

◊ **allègement fiscal** tax relief

alléger vt (impôts, charges, dépenses) to reduce

aller et retour n Bourse bed and breakfasting

allocation nf (a) (attribution) (d'argent) allocation; (de dommages-intérêts, d'une indemnité) awarding

(b) Bourse (de titres) allocation, allotment

(c) Admin (prestation financière) allowance, Br benefit, Am welfare

◊ **allocation chômage** unemployment benefit

◊ **allocation vieillesse** old-age pension

allouer vt (a) (attribuer) (argent) to allocate; (dommages-intérêts, indemnité) to award; (dépense, budget) to allow, to pass

(b) Bourse (titres) to allocate, to allot

(c) Admin (salaire, pension) to grant, to award

AME nm (abrév **Accord monétaire européen**) EMA

aménagement fiscal n tax adjustment

AMI nm Écon (abrév **Accord multilatéral sur l'investissement**) MAI

amorti, -e adj (bien) depreciated; (frais, investissement, capital) amortized

amortir 1 vt (a) (dette) to pay off, to amortize; (prêt) to repay; (obligation) to redeem

(b) Compta (équipement) to write off, to amortize, to depreciate

(c) (rentabiliser) **le matériel a été amorti dès la première année** the equipment had paid for itself by the end of the first year

2 s'amortir vpr (dépenses, investissement) to pay for itself

amortissable adj (dette) redeemable

amortissement nm (a) (d'une dette) repayment, amortization

(b) Compta (perte de valeur) depreciation

(c) (rentabilité) **l'amortissement d'un équipement est plus rapide si on emprunte à court terme** equipment pays for itself faster if it's paid for with a short-term loan

◊ **amortissement accéléré** accelerated depreciation

◇ *amortissement annuel* annual depreciation

◇ *amortissement anticipé* redemption before due date

◇ *amortissement dégressif* sliding scale depreciation

◇ *amortissement linéaire* diminishing balance (method)

an *nm* year; **par an** yearly, per year, per annum; **un prêt sur vingt ans** a loan over twenty years

analyse *nf* analysis

◇ *analyse des coûts* cost analysis

◇ *analyse coûts-bénéfices* cost-benefit analysis

◇ *analyse de coût et d'efficacité* cost-effectiveness analysis

◇ *analyse coût-profit* cost-benefit analysis

◇ *analyse des coûts et rendements* cost-benefit analysis

◇ *analyse des écarts* variance analysis

◇ *analyse du point mort* break-even analysis

◇ *anlayse de portefeuille* portfolio analysis

◇ *analyse du prix de revient* cost analysis

◇ *analyse des risques* risk analysis

◇ *analyse par secteur d'activité* segment reporting

◇ *analyse de valeur* value analysis *or* engineering

analyste *nmf* analyst

◇ *analyste financier* financial analyst

◇ *analyste du marché* market analyst

◇ *analyste en placements* investment analyst

animé, -e *adj (marché)* brisk, buoyant

année *nf* year

◇ *année budgétaire Br* financial year, *Am* fiscal year

◇ *Compta* **année civile** calendar year

◇ *année comptable* accounting year

◇ *année en cours* current year

◇ *année d'exercice Br* financial year, *Am* fiscal year

◇ *année fiscale* tax year

◇ *année d'imposition* year of assessment

◇ *année record* peak year

◇ *année de référence* base year

‘‘

Les créances douteuses ont augmenté au cours du premier semestre de l'**année fiscale** et les fonds propres ont fondu avec la chute du Nikkei.

’’

annexe 1 *adj (revenus)* supplementary

2 *nf Compta* **annexes** notes to the accounts

annuitaire *adj (dette)* redeemable by yearly payments

annuité *nf (dans le remboursement d'un emprunt)* annual instalment *or* repayment

◇ *Compta* **annuité d'amortissement** annual depreciation *or* writedown

◇ *Compta* **annuité constante** *(de remboursement)* fixed annual payment

◇ *annuité différée* deferred annuity

annulation *nf* (a) *(d'une réservation, d'une commande, d'un*

projet) cancellation; *(d'une dette)* cancellation, writing off
(b) Banque *(d'un chèque)* cancellation

annuler *vt* **(a)** *(dette)* to cancel, to write off
(b) Banque *(chèque)* to cancel

anticipation *nf* **payer par anticipation** to pay in advance
◊ **paiement par anticipation** advance payment, prepayment

anticipé, -e *adj (remboursement)* before due date; *(dividende, paiement)* advance

anticiper *vt* **anticiper un paiement** to pay in advance; **anticiper un paiement de dix jours** to pay ten days early

antidater *vt* to backdate, to antedate

appel *nm* call; **faire un appel de fonds** to call up capital
◊ Bourse **appel de couverture, appel de garantie, appel de marge** margin call

appelé, -e *adj (capital)* called-up

appoint *nm (revenu supplémentaire)* additional income

appointements *nmpl* salary; **toucher ses appointements** to draw one's salary

appointer *vt* **appointer qn** to pay sb a salary

apport *nm* **(a)** *(fait d'apporter)* contribution; Écon inflow, influx; **cette région bénéficie de l'apport (en devises) du tourisme** this area benefits from the financial contribution made by tourism; **sans apport extérieur nous étions perdus** without outside financial help we'd have

been ruined
(b) *(dans une entreprise)* initial share

◊ **apport d'argent frais** injection of new money

◊ Compta **apport en capital** capital contribution

◊ Compta **apport en espèces** *(dans un investissement)* cash contribution

◊ **apport de gestion** management buy-in

◊ Compta **apport en nature** contribution in kind

◊ Compta **apport en numéraire** cash contribution

> Il est vrai qu'au Cetelem, la fourchette de taux pour l'achat d'une voiture neuve, avec 25% d'**apport**, qui allait encore de 11,88% à 15% en avril, est passé en septembre de 9% à 13,92%.

apporter *vt (capitaux)* to contribute

appréciation *nf* appreciation
◊ **appréciation des investissements** investment appraisal
◊ **appréciation monétaire** currency appreciation
◊ **appréciation des risques** risk assessment

apprécier s'apprécier *vpr (augmenter)* to rise; **le franc s'est apprécié par rapport au dollar** the franc has risen against the dollar

appropriation *nf* appropriation
◊ **appropriation de fonds** em-

bezzlement, misappropria-
tion of funds

approvisionner *vt Banque*
(compte) to pay money into;
**son compte en banque n'est plus
approvisionné** his bank account
is no longer in credit

appui financier *nm* (financial)
backing; **la société ne bénéficie
pas d'un appui financier suffisant**
the company does not have sufficient financial backing

appuyer *vt* to back, to support;
appuyer qn financièrement to
back sb (financially), to give sb
financial backing

apurement *nm* (**a**) *(des
comptes)* auditing (**b**) *(d'une
dette, du passif)* discharge

apurer *vt* (**a**) *(comptes)* to audit
(**b**) *(dette, passif)* to discharge

AR *nm* *(abrév* **accusé de
réception**) acknowledgement
(of receipt)

arbitrage *nm Bourse* arbitrage

⋄ **arbitrage à la baisse** bear
closing

⋄ **arbitrage de change** arbitration of exchange

⋄ **arbitrage comptant-terme**
cash and carry arbitrage

⋄ **arbitrage sur indice** index arbitrage

⋄ **arbitrage risqué** risk arbitrage

arbitragiste *nmf Bourse* arbitrageur

argent *nm* *(richesse)* money;
payer en argent to pay (in)
cash; **placer son argent** to invest
one's money; **trouver de l'argent**
to raise money

⋄ **argent à bon marché** cheap
money

⋄ *Compta* **argent en caisse** cash
in hand; *(recettes)* takings

⋄ **argent comptant** cash

⋄ *Ordinat* **argent électronique**
e-cash, electronic money

⋄ **argent frais** new money

⋄ **argent au jour le jour** call
money, day-to-day money

⋄ **argent liquide** cash (in hand)

⋄ **argent mal acquis** dirty money

⋄ **argent mort** dead money

⋄ **argent sale** dirty money

⋄ *Ordinat* **argent virtuel**
e-cash, electronic money

⋄ **argent à vue** call money

> **❝**
>
> Les privatisations ont fait rentrer
> de l'**argent frais**, venu essen-
> tiellement de l'etranger.
>
> **❞**

arrérager 1 *vi* to be in arrears
2 s'arrérager *vpr* to fall into
arrears

arrérages *nmpl* arrears

arrêté de compte *nm Banque*
(fermeture) settlement of account; *(bilan)* statement of account

arrêter *vt Banque (compte)* to
close, to settle; *Compta
(comptes de l'exercice)* to close

arrhes *nfpl* deposit; **verser des
arrhes** to pay a deposit

arriéré *nm (dette)* arrears; **avoir
des arriérés** to be in arrears;
arriéré d'impôts tax arrears,
back taxes

arrivage *nm (de fonds)* accession

arrondir *vt (somme) (vers le
haut)* to round up; *(vers le bas)*
to round down; **arrondir au franc**

supérieur/inférieur to round up/down to the nearest franc

article *nm* *(d'une facture)* item; *(d'un compte)* entry
◊ *Compta* **article de contre-passation** transfer entry
◊ **articles de dépense** items of expenditure
◊ **articles divers** sundries

assainir *vt* *(budget, monnaie, économie)* to stabilize; *(bilan)* to balance; *(finances)* to reorganize

> **"**
>
> L'organisme chargé d'aider les banques japonaises à **assainir** leurs bilans a annoncé vendredi à Tokyo leur avoir racheté pour 1866 milliards de yens de créances douteuses.
>
> **"**

assainissement *nm* *(d'un budget, d'une monnaie, de l'économie)* stabilization; *(d'un bilan)* balancing; *(des finances)* reorganization
◊ **assainissement monétaire** stabilization of the currency

assemblée *nf* *(réunion)* meeting
◊ **assemblée extraordinaire** extraordinary meeting
◊ **assemblée générale** general meeting
◊ **assemblée générale d'actionnaires** general meeting of shareholders
◊ **assemblée générale annuelle** annual general meeting
◊ **assemblée générale extraordinaire** extraordinary general meeting

asseoir *vt* **asseoir un impôt** to calculate the basis for a tax;

asseoir l'impôt sur le revenu to base taxation on income

assiette *nf* *(d'un impôt, d'un taux)* base; *(d'une hypothèque)* = property or funds on which a mortgage is secured
◊ **assiette de l'amortissement** depreciation, depreciable base
◊ **assiette fiscale, assiette de l'impôt** taxable income

assignation *nf* *(de parts, de fonds)* allotment, allocation (**à** to)

assigner *vt* *(parts, fonds)* to allot, to allocate (**à** to)

association *nf* *(organisation)* organization *f*; *(collaboration)* partnership
◊ **association capital-travail** profit-sharing scheme
◊ **Association Française des Banques** French Bankers' Association

associé, -e *nm,f*
◊ **associé commanditaire** *Br* sleeping partner, *Am* silent partner
◊ **associé commandité** active partner
◊ **associé fictif** nominal partner
◊ **associé gérant** active partner

assujetti, -e 1 *adj* **être assujetti à l'impôt** to be liable for tax
2 *nm,f* = person liable for tax

assujettir *vt* **assujettir qn à qch** *(taxe, impôt, règlement)* to subject sb to sth

assujettissement *nm* *(à l'impôt)* liability

assurance *nf* insurance
◊ **assurance crédit** loan repayment insurance

◇ *assurance de portefeuille* portfolio insurance

assurance-vie *nf* life insurance

ATF *n Bourse* (*abrév* **accord de taux futur**) forward rate agreement, future rate agreement

attribuer *vt* (*salaire, prime*) to assign, to allocate (**à** to); *Bourse* (*actions, dividendes*) to allocate, to allot (**à** to)

attribution *nm* (*d'un salaire, d'une prime*) assigning, allocation; *Bourse* (*d'actions, de dividendes*) allocation, allotment

aubaine *nf* windfall

audit *nm* (**a**) (*service*) audit; **être chargé de l'audit d'une société** to audit a company
(**b**) (*personne*) auditor
◇ *audit externe* (*opération*) external audit; (*personne*) external auditor
◇ *audit interne* (*opération*) internal audit; (*personne*) internal auditor
◇ *audit opérationnel* operational audit

auditeur, -trice *nm,f* auditor
◇ *auditeur externe* external auditor
◇ *auditeur interne* internal auditor

augmentation *nf* (*des dépenses, du chômage, du capital, de l'inflation*) increase (**de** in)
◇ *augmentation des bénéfices* earnings growth
◇ *augmentation de prix* price increase

augmenter **1** *vt* (*impôts, taux d'intérêt, prix*) to increase, to put up, to raise; (*dépenses*) to increase

2 *vi* (*impôts, taux d'intérêt, prix*) to increase, to go up, to rise; (*dépenses*) to increase; **augmenter de valeur** to increase in value

autofinancé, -e *adj* self-financed; **8 milliards de francs autofinancés à un tiers seulement** 8 billion francs, only a third of which was self-financed

autofinancement *nm* self-financing

> **"**
>
> La chute de l'investissement en 1993, la baisse du coût de l'argent et la forte capacité d'**autofinancement** des entreprises atténuent fortement les tensions inflationnistes que pourrait exercer la reprise de l'activité.
>
> **"**

autofinancer s'autofinancer *vpr* to be self-financing

autorisation *nf*
◇ *autorisation de crédit* line of credit
◇ *autorisation de découvert* overdraft facility
◇ *autorisation d'émettre des billets de banque* note issuance facility
◇ *autorisation de prélèvement* direct debit mandate

AV *nm Banque* (*abrév* **avis de virement**) (bank) transfer advice

aval *nm* (*d'un effet de commerce*) endorsement, guarantee; **donner son aval à un billet** to endorse *or* guarantee a bill
◇ *aval bancaire* bank guarantee

avaliser *vt* (*effet de commerce*) to endorse, to guarantee

avaliseur, -euse *nm,f* endorser, guarantor, backer

avaliste *nmf* endorser, guarantor, backer

à-valoir *nm* advance (payment)

avance *nf* (*d'argent*) **avance (de fonds)** advance

◇ *avance bancaire* bank advance

◇ *avance à découvert* unsecured *or* uncovered advance

◇ *avances en devises* foreign currency loan

◇ *avance en numéraire* cash advance

◇ *avance de trésorerie* cash advance

avantage *nm* advantage

◇ *avantages accessoires* fringe benefits

◇ *avantages en espèces* cash benefits

◇ *avantage fiscal* tax benefit, tax incentive

◇ *avantages en nature* payments in kind

◇ *avantages sociaux* financial benefits

avis *nm*

◇ *avis d'appel de fonds* call letter

◇ *Bourse* **avis d'attribution** allotment letter

◇ *Banque* **avis de la banque** bank notification *or* advice

◇ *avis de crédit* credit advice

◇ *avis de débit* debit advice

◇ *avis de domiciliation* domiciliation advice

◇ *Bourse* **avis d'exécution** contract note

◇ *avis d'imposition* tax assessment

◇ *Bourse* **avis d'opération sur titres, avis d'opéré** trade ticket, contract note

◇ *avis de paiement* payment advice

◇ *avis de prélèvement* direct debit advice

◇ *avis de rejet* notice of returned cheque

◇ *avis de remise* remittance advice

◇ *avis de retrait (de fonds)* notice of withdrawal

◇ *Banque* **avis de virement** (bank) transfer advice

avoir *nm* (**a**) *(capital)* capital; *(sur compte)* credit; **doit et avoir** debit and credit; **obtenir un avoir** to be given credit, to obtain *or* to get credit

(**b**) **avoirs** assets

(**c**) *(attestation de crédit)* credit note

◇ *avoir en banque* bank credit

◇ *avoir en devises* foreign currency holding

◇ *avoirs disponibles* liquid assets

◇ *avoir fiscal* tax credit

"

Qu'est-ce que l'**avoir fiscal**? Comme son nom l'indique, l'**avoir fiscal** est un avoir qui revient à l'actionnaire, afin d'éviter à ce dernier de subir une double imposition. Pourquoi cela? ... Sans l'**avoir fiscal**, il y aurait bien une double imposition: au niveau de la société, puis au niveau de l'actionnaire.

"

avoir-client *nm Compta* customer credit

avoir-fournisseur *nm Compta* supplier credit

ayant-compte *nm Banque* account holder

back-office *nm Banque* back office

bailleur de fonds *nm (investisseur)* (financial) backer; *(associé passif) Br* sleeping partner, *Am* silent partner

baisse *nf* (a) *(des prix, du chômage, du taux de l'inflation)* fall, drop (**de** in); **la baisse du franc** the fall in the value of the franc; **revoir** *ou* **reviser les chiffres à la baisse** to revise figures downwards
(b) *Bourse (des cours, des valeurs)* fall; **spéculations à la baisse** bear speculations; **jouer** *ou* **spéculer à la baisse** to bear, to go a bear, to speculate for a fall; **acheter en baisse** to buy on a falling market; **les actions sont en baisse** shares are falling

baisser **1** *vt (prix, loyer)* to lower, to reduce, to bring down
2 *vi (prix, actions)* to fall; *(stocks)* to be running low; **le dollar a baissé** the dollar has weakened

baissier, -ère *Bourse* **1** *adj (marché)* bearish
2 *nm,f* bear

balance *nf Compta (d'un compte)* balance; **la balance est en excédent** there is a surplus; **faire la balance** to make up the balance sheet; **balance de l'actif et du passif** credit and debit balance, balance of assets and liabilities
◇ *Compta* **balance agée** aged debtors
◇ *Compta* **balance de caisse** cash balance
◇ *Écon* **balance du commerce, balance commerciale** balance of trade
◇ *Compta* **balance générale des comptes, balance des paiements** balance of payments

balancer *vt (compte)* to balance; **balancer les comptes** to balance *or* make up the books

bancable *adj* bankable

bancaire *adj (chèque, com-*

mission, crédit, dépôt, frais, prêt) bank; *(opération)* banking

bancarisation *nf* **la bancarisation de l'économie** the growing role of banks in the economy

bancarisé, -e *adj* **être bancarisé** to have an account with a bank, to use the banking system

bancassurance *nf* bancassurance

> **"**
>
> Le Lion de Trieste, comme l'appellent les Italiens, pouvait difficilement laisser passer sans réagir la création d'un groupe de **bancassurance** San Paolo IMI-INA, capable de talonner dans nombre de secteurs, notamment l'assurance-vie. Generali veut aussi échapper à l'appétit d'éventuels groupes étrangers.
>
> **"**

bancatique *nf Banque* electronic banking

bande de fluctuation *nf (d'une monnaie)* fluctuation band

banquable = bancable

banque *nf* (a) *(établissement, organisation)* bank (b) *(activité)* banking (c) *(secteur)* banking; **elle travaille dans la banque** she works in banking; **la haute banque** high finance

◇ *banque d'acceptation Br* accepting *or Am* acceptance house

◇ *banque d'affaires Br* merchant bank, *Am* investment bank

◇ *banque centrale* central bank

◇ *Banque centrale européenne* European central bank

◇ *banque de clearing* clearing bank

◇ *banque commerciale* commercial bank

◇ *banque compensatrice* clearing bank

◇ *banque confirmatrice* confirming bank

◇ *banque de crédit* credit bank

◇ *banque de dépôt* deposit bank

◇ *banque de détail* retail bank

◇ *banque à distance* remote banking

◇ *banque à domicile* telebanking, home banking

◇ *banque émettrice, banque d'émission* issuing bank *or* house

◇ *banque d'entreprise* corporate banking

◇ *banque d'épargne* savings bank

◇ *banque d'escompte* discount house *or* bank

◇ *Banque européenne d'investissement* European Investment Bank

◇ *Banque européenne de reconstruction et de développement* European Bank of Reconstruction and Development

◇ *la Banque de France* the Bank of France

◇ *banque de gestion de patrimoine* trust bank

◇ *banque de gros* wholesale bank

◇ *banque hypothécaire* mortgage bank

◇ *banque industrielle* industrial bank

◇ *Banque internationale pour*

Les grandes banques dans les pays francophones d'Europe

Major banks in continental French-speaking countries

France

Banque de France
www.banque-france.fr

Banque Nationale de Paris (BNP)
www.bnp.fr

Banque Populaire
www.banquepopulaire.fr

BRED - Banque Populaire
www.bred.fr

Caisse d'Épargne (Groupe)
www.caisse-epargne.fr

CIC – Crédit Industriel et

Commercial
www.cic-banques.fr

Crédit Agricole
www.credit-agricole.fr

Crédit Commerical de France (CCF)
www.ccf.fr

Crédit Lyonnais
www.creditlyonnais.com

Crédit Mutuel
www.creditmutuel.fr

Crédit du Nord
www.cdn.fr

Groupama
www.groupama-ge.fr

Groupe Cofinoga
www.cofinoga.com

Paribas
www.paribas.com

Société Générale
www.socgen.com

Suisse/Switzerland

Banque SCS Alliance
www.scsbank.ch

Banque Von Ernst
www.bank-von-ernst.com

BSI (Banca della Svizzera Italiana)
www.bsi.ch

Crédit Suisse
www.de.crédit.suisse.ch

UBS (Union de Banques Suisses)
www.ubs.com

Belgique/Belgium

BBL (Banque de Bruxelles Lambert)
www.bbl.be

CGER (Caisse Générale d'Épargne et de Retraite)
www.cger.be

Crédit Communal de Belgique
www.creditcommunal.be

La Générale de Banque
www.gbank.be

Kredietbank
www.kb.be

Luxembourg

BGL (Banque Générale du Luxembourg)
www.bgl.lu

la reconstruction et le développement International Bank for Reconstruction and Development

◇ *banque d'investissement* Br merchant bank, Am investment bank

◇ *banque en ligne* on-line bank

◇ *la Banque Mondiale* the World Bank

◇ *banque notificatrice* advising bank

◇ *banque de placement* issuing bank *or* house

◇ *banque privée* private bank

◇ *banque de recouvrement* collecting agency *or* bank

◇ *banque universelle* global banking

> **❝**
>
> Aux observateurs qui ont pu s'étonner, pendant le long feuilleton bancaire français, que le tabou d'une intervention étrangère soit demeuré si pesant et si efficace, les responsables gouvernementaux ou bancaires français avaient la réponse prête: 'Peut-être, mais avez-vous déjà essayé d'acheter une banque allemande?' Les pratiques européennes dans la **banque de dépôt** (la banque d'affaires, en général, est déjà internationalisée) demeurent nationales.
>
> **❞**

banqueroute *nf Jur* bankruptcy; **faire banqueroute** to go bankrupt

◇ *banqueroute frauduleuse* fraudulent bankruptcy

◇ *banqueroute simple* bankruptcy *(with irregularities*

amounting to a breach of the law)

banqueroutier, -ère *adj & nm,f* bankrupt

banquier, -ère *nm,f* banker

◇ *banquier d'affaires* Br merchant banker, Am investment banker

◇ *banquier escompteur* discounting banker

◇ *banquier prêteur* lending banker

barème *nm (tableau)* ready reckoner

◇ *barème fiscal, barème d'imposition* tax rate schedule *or* structure

barré, -e *adj (chèque)* crossed

barrer *vt (chèque)* to cross

bas, basse *adj (prix, taux de change, taux d'intérêt)* low

bas de laine *nm* nest egg; **le bas de laine des Français** the savings of small-time French investors

base *nf (fondement)* basis; **sur une base nette** on a net basis; **de base** *(prix, salaire)* basic

◇ *Compta* **base amortissable** basis for depreciation

◇ *Compta* **base de calcul** basis of calculations

◇ *base hors taxe* amount exclusive of VAT

◇ *base d'imposition* taxable base

BBZ *nm Compta (abrév* **budget base zéro***)* ZBB

BCE *nf (abrév* **Banque centrale européenne***)* European central bank

BEI *nf (abrév* **Banque européenne d'investissement***)* European Investment Bank

bénéfice nm (gain) profit; **bénéfice de** ou **pour l'exercice 1999** profits for the year 1999; **rapporter des bénéfices** to yield a profit; **donner** ou **dégager un bénéfice** to show a profit; **réaliser un bénéfice** to make a profit; **vendre qch à bénéfice** to sell sth at a profit

◇ **bénéfice par action** earnings per share
◇ **bénéfice après impôts** after-tax profit
◇ **bénéfice avant l'impôt** pre-tax profit
◇ **bénéfice brut** gross profit
◇ **bénéfice brut avant impôts** pre-tax profit
◇ **bénéfice cumulé** cumulative profit
◇ **bénéfices distribuables** distributable profits
◇ **bénéfice escompté** desired profit
◇ **bénéfices exceptionnels** excess profits
◇ **bénéfices de l'exercice** current earnings
◇ **bénéfice d'exploitation** operating or trading profit
◇ **bénéfices extraordinaires** excess profits
◇ **bénéfices financiers** interest received
◇ **bénéfice fiscal** taxable profit
◇ **bénéfice imposable** taxable profit
◇ **bénéfice marginal** marginal profit
◇ **bénéfice net** after-tax profit, net profit
◇ **bénéfice net dilué par action** fully diluted earnings per share
◇ **bénéfices non distribués** undistributed profits, retained profit
◇ **bénéfice transféré** profit transferred

> La compagnie la plus rentable du monde a vu son **bénéfice avant l'impôt** chuter de 15% dans les six premiers mois de l'année, passant ainsi à 260 millions de dollars.

bénéficiaire 1 adj (entreprise) profit-making; (compte) in credit; (bilan) showing a profit 2 nmf (a) Jur beneficiary (b) (d'un chèque) payee
◇ **bénéficiaire conjoint(e)** joint beneficiary

besoin nm need, requirement
◇ Compta **besoins de crédit** borrowing requirements
◇ Compta **besoins en fonds de roulement** working capital requirements
◇ Compta **besoins de trésorerie** cash requirements

BF nf (abrév **Banque de France**) Bank of France

bien nm possession; Jur assets; **biens** possessions, property
◇ **biens capitaux** capital goods or items
◇ **biens corporels** tangible assets
◇ **biens d'équipement** capital equipment or goods
◇ **biens immobiliers** real assets
◇ **biens meubles, biens mobiliers** personal property or estate, movables
◇ **biens personnels** personal property

◇ *biens de production* capital goods

◇ *Compta* *biens sociaux* corporate assets *or* funds

bilan *nm* (a) *Compta* statement; **bilan (comptable)** balance sheet; **dresser** *ou* **établir** *ou* **faire un bilan** to draw up a balance sheet
(b) *(de l'actif, des responsabilités)* schedule; **déposer son bilan** to file one's petition (in bankruptcy)
(c) *Banque (d'un compte)* balance

◇ *bilan annuel* annual accounts

◇ *bilan condensé* summary balance sheet

◇ *bilan consolidé* consolidated balance sheet

◇ *bilan de l'exercice* end-of-year balance sheet

◇ *bilan financier* financial statement

◇ *bilan de groupe* consolidated balance sheet

◇ *bilan intérimaire* interim statement

◇ *bilan de liquidation* statement of affairs

◇ *bilan d'ouverture* opening balance sheet

◇ *bilan prévisionnel* forecast balance sheet

billet *nm* (a) *(effet)* note, bill
(b) *(argent)* **billet (de banque)** *Br* (bank)note, *Am* bill; **un billet de cent francs** a hundred-franc *Br* note *or Am* bill

◇ *billet de complaisance* accommodation bill

◇ *billet à ordre* note of hand, promissory note

◇ *billet au porteur* bearer bill

◇ *billet de reconnaissance de dettes* IOU

◇ *billet du Trésor* Treasury bill

◇ *Banque* *billet de trésorerie* commercial paper

◇ *billet vert* dollar

billétique *nf Banque, Ordinat* cash dispenser technology

BIRD *nf (abrév* **Banque internationale pour la reconstruction et le développement)** IBRD

blanchiment *nm (d'argent)* laundering

blanchir *vt (argent)* to launder

bloc *nm* (a) *(ensemble) (d'actions, de titres)* block, parcel
(b) *(groupe d'actionnaires)* shareholding
(c) *(zone)* bloc

◇ *bloc de contrôle* controlling shareholding

◇ *bloc monétaire* currency bloc

◇ *bloc sterling* sterling bloc

> **❝**
> Débarrasser la SG d'un actionnaire minoritaire encombrant, en demandant à la BNP de rendre son **bloc de titres**, c'est pousser l'une des plus grandes banques françaises dans le giron d'un groupe étranger. Et les actionnaires qui ont apporté leurs titres SG à la BNP risqueraient d'être mécontents.
> **❞**

blocage *nm (du crédit)* freeze; *(de compte bancaire)* freezing

◇ *blocage des salaires* wage freeze

bloquer *vt (chèque)* to stop; *(compte bancaire)* to freeze, to stop; *(salaires, crédits)* to freeze

blue chip *nm* blue chip

BMTN *nm* (*abrév* **bon à moyen terme négociable**) MTN

bon *nm* (**a**) (*papier*) voucher, coupon (**b**) *Bourse* bond
- ⬦ **bon de caisse** (*justifiant sortie de fonds*) cash voucher; *Compta* interest-bearing note
- ⬦ **bon de commande** order form, purchase order
- ⬦ *Bourse* **bon d'épargne** savings bond *or* certificate
- ⬦ **bon pour francs** (*sur chèque*) = letters printed on cheque before amount to be written in figures
- ⬦ **bon à moyen terme négociable** medium term note
- ⬦ *Bourse* **bon nominatif** registered bond
- ⬦ *Bourse* **bon de participation** participation certificate
- ⬦ **bon de petite caisse** petty cash voucher
- ⬦ *Bourse* **bon au porteur** bearer bond
- ⬦ *Bourse* **bon de souscription d'actions** equity *or* subscription warrant
- ⬦ *Bourse* **bon de souscription de parts de créateurs d'entreprise** = stock option in start-up company with tax privileges
- ⬦ *Bourse* **bon du Trésor** Treasury bill; (*obligation à long terme*) Treasury bond

❝
A l'automne 1997, les **bons de souscription de parts de créateurs d'entreprise** (BSPCE) sont créés: il s'agit de stock-options à la fiscalité allégée pour les entreprises de moins de sept ans, non cotées et évo-

luant dans des secteurs innovants, à l'exclusion des activités bancaires, financières, d'assurances, de gestion ou de location d'immeuble ... Un an plus tard ... Didier Migaud, rapporteur général de la commission des finances de l'Assemblée nationale, fait adopter un amendement qui étend cette mesure aux entreprises de moins de quinze ans d'âge.
❞

bonification *nf* (**a**) (*rabais*) reduction (**b**) (*prime*) bonus

❝
Dans le financement automobile, il n'est pas rare de voir des offres à 7,5% environ. Dans de telles situations, ce sont les constructeurs qui assument une **bonification** d'environ 3 points.
❞

bonifié, -e *adj* (*prêt*) soft, at a reduced rate of interest

boom *Écon nm* boom

bordereau *nm* note, slip; (*formulaire*) form; **suivant bordereau ci-inclus** as per enclosed statement
- ⬦ **bordereau d'achat** (*dans le commerce*) purchase note
- ⬦ *Compta* **bordereau de caisse** cash statement
- ⬦ *Compta* **bordereau de compte** statement of account
- ⬦ **bordereau de débit** debit note
- ⬦ *Banque* **bordereau de dépôt** paying-in slip
- ⬦ *Banque* **bordereau d'encaissement** paying-in slip
- ⬦ *Banque* **bordereau de remise**

(d'espèces ou *de chèques)* paying-in slip

◇ *Banque* **bordereau de retrait** withdrawal slip

◇ *Compta* **bordereau de saisie** accounting entry sheet

◇ *Banque* **bordereau de versement** paying-in slip

bourse *nf* la Bourse (des valeurs) the stock exchange, the stock market; **la Bourse de Londres** the London Stock Exchange; **la Bourse monte/est calme** the market is rising/is quiet; **en** ou **à la Bourse** on the stock exchange *or* stock market; **jouer à la Bourse** to play the market, to speculate on the stock market; **coup de Bourse** deal on the stock exchange

◇ *Bourse* **de commerce** commodities exchange

◇ *Bourse* **coulisse** unlisted market

◇ *Bourse* **d'instruments financiers à terme** financial futures exchange

◇ *Bourse* **de(s) marchandises** commodities exchange

boursicotage *nm Bourse* dabbling *or* speculating on the stock market

boursicoter *vi Bourse* to dabble on the Stock Market

boursicoteur, -euse, boursicotier, -ère *nm,f Bourse* small-time speculator

BPA *nm (abrév* **bénéfice par action)** EPS

BPF *nm (abrév* **bon pour francs)** *(sur chèque)* = letters printed on cheque before amount to be written in figures

brouillard *nm* day book

◇ *Compta* **brouillard de caisse** cash book

brut, -e *adv* gross; **gagner 20 000 francs brut** to earn 20,000 francs gross, to gross 20,000 francs

BSPCE *nm Bourse (abrév* **bon de souscription de parts de créateurs d'entreprise)** = stock option in a start-up company with tax privileges

Buba *nf (abrév* **Bundesbank)** la **Buba** the Bundesbank

budget *nm* budget; **inscrire qch au budget** to budget for sth

◇ *Compta* **budget annuel** annual budget

◇ *Compta* **budget des approvisionnements** purchase budget

◇ *Compta* **budget base zéro** zero-base budgeting

◇ *Compta* **budget des charges** overhead *or* cost budget

◇ *Compta* **budget commercial** sales budget

◇ *Compta* **budget des dépenses** expense budget

◇ **budget équilibré** balanced budget

◇ *Écon* **budget de l'État** state budget

◇ *Compta* **budget d'exploitation** operating budget

◇ *Compta* **budget de fonctionnement** operating budget

◇ *Compta* **budget glissant** rolling budget

◇ **budget global** master *or* overall budget

◇ *Compta* **budget des investissements** capital budget

◇ *Compta* **budget prévisionnel** provisional budget

Bourses

Stock Exchanges

France

Bourse de Paris (**SBF**)
www.bourse-de-paris.fr

Suisse/Switzerland

Swiss Exchange (**SWX**)
fusion récente de trois Bourses
www.swx.ch

Belgique/Belgium

Brussels Exchanges (**BXS**)
fusion récente de trois Bourses
www.bxs.be

Canada

Toronto Stock Exchange (**TSE**)
www.telenium.ca/TSE

Montreal Stock Exchange (**MSE**)
www.telenium.ca/MSE

Alberta Stock Exchange (**ASE**)
www.telenium.ca/ASE

Vancouver Stock Exchange (**VSE**)
www.telenium.ca/VSE

Winnipeg Stock Exchange (**WSE**)
www.telenium.ca/WSE

Hong Kong

Stock Exchange of Hong Kong (**SEHK**)
www.sehk.com.hk

Singapour/Singapore

Stock Exchange of Singapore (**SES**)
www.ses.com.sg

GB/Grande-Bretagne

London Stock Exchange (**LSE**)
www.stockex.co.uk

London Metal Exchange (**LME**)
www.lme.co.uk

USA

American Stock Exchange (**Amex**)
www.amex.com

New York Stock Exchange (**NYSE**)
www.nyse.com

NASDAQ
www.nasdaq.com

Chicago Stock Exchange (**CHX**)
www.chicagostockex.com

Boston Stock Exchange (**BSE**)
www.bostonstock.com

Philadelphia Stock Exchange (**PHLX**)
www.phlx.com

Minneapolis Grain Exchange (**MGE**)
www.mgex.com

Arizona Stock Exchange (**AZX**)
www.azx.com

New York Cotton Exchange (**NYCE**)
www.nyce.com

Australia/Australie

Australian Stock Exchange (**ASX**)
www.asx.com.au

Japan/Japon

Tokyo Stock Exchange (**TSE**)
www.tse.or.jp

◇ *Compta* **budget de production** production budget

◇ *Compta* **budget des recettes** revenue budget

◇ *Compta* **budget renouvelable** continuous budget

◇ *Compta* **budget de trésorerie** cash budget

◇ *Compta* **budget des ventes** sales budget

budgétaire *adj (année) Br* financial, *Am* fiscal; *(contrainte, contrôle, gestion)* budgetary

budgétisation *nf* budgeting

◇ *Compta* **budgétisation base zéro** zero-base budgeting

bulle *nf Bourse*

◇ **bulle boursière** stock market bubble, surge on the Stock Market

◇ **bulle spéculative** speculative bubble

44

La crise asiatique est derrière nous ... La croissance européenne peut repartir. En revanche, nous sommes toujours confrontés au risque d'un krach à Wall Street, qui ne se produit pas. Or quand on baisse sur une **bulle spéculative**, les valeurs d'actifs tirent leur épingle du jeu.

🄸🄸

bulletin *nm (communiqué)* bulletin; *(d'entreprise)* newsletter; *(formulaire)* form

◇ *Bourse* **Bulletin de la Cote Of-** **ficielle** Stock Exchange Daily Official List

◇ *Bourse* **bulletin des cours** official (Stock Exchange) price list

◇ **bulletin de paie** pay (advice) slip, salary advice note

◇ **bulletin de salaire** pay (advice) slip, salary advice note

◇ **bulletin de souscription d'actions** share subscription or application form

◇ **bulletin de versement** paying-in or deposit slip

bureau *nm (agence)* office

◇ **bureau de change** bureau de change

◇ **bureau de cotation, bureau d'évaluation** credit *Br* agency or *Am* bureau

◇ **bureau de perception** tax office

◇ **bureau de poste** post office

business angel *nm (commanditaire)* angel

44

Ils ont été (ou sont encore) chef d'entreprise ou cadre dirigeant, et ils ont de l'argent. La création d'entreprise les titille et ils sont prêts à investir dans de jeunes sociétés en panne de capitaux. Ce sont les **business angels**: des investisseurs privés qui font aussi profiter l'entreprise de leurs conseils, de leur savoir-faire et de leurs relations.

🄸🄸

CA *nm* (**a**) *(abrév* **chiffre d'affaires)** turnover (**b**) *Can (abrév* **comptable agréé)** *Br* ≃ CA, *Am* ≃ CPA

CAC *nf Bourse (abrév* **Compagnie des agents de change)** = French stockbrokers' association; **l'indice CAC 40, le CAC 40** the CAC 40 (index) *(main Paris Stock Exchange Index)*

> 66
>
> Le **CAC 40** n'est pas l'indice de la production industrielle en France, mais l'indice qui traduit le tonus, la vitalité, les résultats des sociétés, choisies parmi les principales capitalisations, dont Paris est le principal marché de cotation.
>
> 99

cahier *nm (livre)* notebook
◇ *Compta* **cahier des achats** purchase ledger

CAHT *nm (abrév* **chiffre d'affaires hors taxes)** pre-tax turnover

caisse *nf* (**a**) *(coffre)* cash box; **les caisses de l'État** the coffers of the State

(**b**) *(argent)* cash (in hand); *(recette)* takings; **faire la** *ou* **sa caisse** to balance the cash, to do the till, *Br* to cash up; **avoir 4 000 francs en caisse** to have 4,000 francs in hand
(**c**) *(organisme)* fund
◇ *caisse d'amortissement* sinking fund
◇ *caisse de chômage* unemployment fund
◇ *caisse de compensation* = equalization fund for payments such as child benefit, sickness benefit, pensions
◇ *Banque* **Caisse des Dépôts et Consignations** = public financial institution which manages National Savings Bank funds and local community funds
◇ *caisse d'épargne* savings bank
◇ *caisse d'épargne-logement* *Br* ≃ building society, *Am* ≃ savings and loan association
◇ *caisse de garantie* credit guarantee institution
◇ **Caisse nationale d'Épargne** ≃ National Savings Bank
◇ *caisse noire* slush fund
◇ *Can* **caisse populaire** credit union
◇ *caisse de prévoyance* provident fund
◇ *caisse régionale* ≃ local (bank) branch
◇ *caisse de retraite* pension fund

calendrier *nm* schedule

◇ *Bourse* **calendrier des émissions** calendar of issues

◇ **calendrier de remboursement** repayment schedule

cambial, -e *adj* exchange

cambiste 1 *adj (marché)* foreign exchange
  2 *nmf* foreign exchange dealer *or* broker

camoufler *vt Compta* **camoufler un bilan** to window-dress the accounts

capacité *nf*

◇ **capacité d'achat** purchasing power

◇ **capacité de crédit, capacité d'emprunter** borrowing power *or* capacity

◇ **capacité d'endettement** borrowing *or* debt capacity

◇ **capacité de financement** financing capacity

◇ **capacité d'imposition** ability to pay tax

capital *nm* capital, assets; **une société au capital de cinq millions de francs** a company with a capital of *or* capitalized at five million francs; **avoir des capitaux dans une affaire** to have vested interests in a business; **fournir les capitaux pour un projet** to fund *or* finance a project; **investir** *ou* **mettre des capitaux dans une affaire** to invest in *or* put capital into a business; **posséder un capital** to have some capital; **les capitaux qui circulent** the capital in circulation; **capital et intérêt** capital and interest

◇ **capital actions** share capital, equity (capital)

◇ **capital appelé** called-up capital

◇ **capital d'apport** initial capital

◇ **capital autorisé** authorized (share) capital

◇ **capital circulant** circulating *or* floating capital

◇ **capital déclaré** registered capital

◇ **capital de départ** start-up capital

◇ **capital disponible** available capital

◇ **capital émis** issued (share) capital

◇ **capital d'emprunt** loan capital

◇ **capital engagé** tied-up capital, capital employed

◇ **capital d'établissement** invested capital

◇ **capital exigible** current liabilities

◇ **capital existant** physical capital

◇ **capital d'exploitation** *Br* working capital, *Am* operating capital

◇ **capitaux fébriles** hot money

◇ **capital fixe** fixed assets

◇ **capitaux flottants** hot money, floating capital

◇ **capitaux frais** new capital

◇ **capitaux gelés** frozen assets

◇ **capital humain** *(d'une entreprise)* manpower

◇ **capital improductif** idle *or* unproductive capital

◇ **capital initial** start-up capital

◇ **capitaux investis** capital invested

◇ **capital libéré** fully paid capital

◇ **capital nominal** nominal capital

◇ **capital d'origine** original capital

◇ *capitaux permanents* capital employed, long-term capital
◇ *capitaux propres* *Br* shareholders' *or* *Am* stockholders' equity
◇ *capital roulant* circulating capital
◇ *capital de roulement* *Br* working capital, *Am* operating capital
◇ *capital social* share capital
◇ *capital souscrit* subscribed capital
◇ *capital technique* (technical) equipment
◇ *capital versé* paid-up capital

> **❝**
>
> Près de 49% du **capital** de BMW est solidement placé entre les mains de la famille Quandt, le reste est placé entre les mains de quelques actionnaires …
>
> **❞**

capitalisable *adj* capitalizable

capitalisation *nf (des intérêts, des revenus)* capitalization
◇ *capitalisation boursière* market capitalization

> **❝**
>
> Le nouveau géant, dont la **capitalisation boursière** dépasse les 110 milliards de dollars, s'appellera au moins dans un premier temps BP-Amoco.
>
> **❞**

capitalistique *adj* capital-intensive

capital-risque *nm* venture capital, risk capital

capital-risqueur *nm* venture capitalist

> **❝**
>
> Directeur des pépinières du Nord-Pas-de-Calais et ancien banquier, Dominique Delzenne ne manque jamais de le rappeler: 'Les créateurs d'entreprise oublient trop souvent que les banquiers ne sont pas des **capital-risqueurs** et qu'ils n'assurent pas un service public. Ils doivent prendre un minimum de risques avec l'argent que leur confie leurs clients.'
>
> **❞**

carnet *nm*
◇ *carnet ATA* ATA carnet
◇ *Banque carnet de banque* pass book, bank book
◇ *Banque carnet de chèques* chequebook
◇ *carnet de dépenses* account book
◇ *carnet de dépôt* deposit book
◇ *carnet de quittances* receipt book
◇ *carnet à souche* counterfoil book
◇ *carnet de versements* paying-in book

carte *nf* card
◇ *carte accréditive* charge card
◇ *carte American Express®* American Express® card
◇ *carte Amex®* Amex® card
◇ *carte bancaire* bank card
◇ *carte bancaire à puce* smart card *(used as a bank card)*
◇ *carte Bleue®* = bank card with which purchases are debited directly from the customer's bank account
◇ *carte de crédit* credit card
◇ *carte de débit* debit card

◇ *carte d'identité bancaire* bank card

◇ *carte Mastercard*® Mastercard®

◇ *carte à mémoire* smart card

◇ *carte de paiement* debit *or* charge card

◇ *carte à puce* smart card

◇ *carte de réduction* discount card

◇ *carte de retrait* bank card

◇ *carte de Sécurité Sociale* ≃ National Insurance Card

◇ *carte Visa*® Visa® card

> **"**
>
> Malgré le développement de la monnaie scripturale (**cartes de paiement**, virements, etc) les Français restent attachés à leurs pièces et à leurs billets.
>
> **"**

cash-flow *nm* cash flow

◇ *cash-flow actualisé* discounted cash flow

◇ *cash-flow courant* current cash flow

◇ *cash-flow disponible* operating cash flow

◇ *cash-flow marginal* incremental cash flow

◇ *cash-flow net* net cash flow

> **"**
>
> L'activité de location simple, qui bénéficie d'un environnement particulièrement favorable, devrait contribuer à hauteur de 60% au **cash-flow courant** (résultat courant plus montant des amortissements) en 1999.
>
> **"**

caution *nf* (a) *(gage)* security, guarantee; **demander une caution** to ask for security; **fournir**

caution to give security

(b) *(garant)* surety, guarantor; **être caution de qn, se porter caution pour qn** to stand surety *or* security for sb

(c) *(pour appartement)* deposit; **verser une caution** to pay a deposit; **il faut verser 1000 francs de caution** a deposit of 1,000 francs must be paid

◇ *caution d'adjudication* bid bond

◇ *caution bancaire, caution de banque* bank guarantee

◇ *caution de soumission* bid bond

cautionnement *nm* (a) *(garantie)* surety, bond, guarantee (b) *(somme)* security, caution money

cautionner *vt (personne)* to stand surety for, to act as guarantor for

CB *nf (abrév* **Carte Bleue**®) = bank card with which purchases are debited directly from the customer's bank account

CBV *nm Bourse (abrév* **Conseil des Bourses de Valeurs**) = regulatory body of the Paris Stock Exchange

CC *nm Banque (abrév* **compte courant**) CA

CCP *nm (abrév* **compte chèque postal**) = post office account, *Br* ≃ Giro account, *Am* ≃ Post Office checking account

CCR *nm (abrév* **coefficient de capitalisation des résultats**) p/e ratio

Cecei *nm (abrév* **comité des établissements de crédit et des entreprises d'investissement**) = French public authority empowered to authorize suppliers of investment services

CEL nm (abrév **compte d'épargne logement**) = savings account (for purchasing a property)

cent[1] nm hundred; **pour cent** percent; **intérêt de sept pour cent** seven percent interest; **cent pour cent** one hundred percent

cent[2] nm (pièce de monnaie) cent

centime nm centime

centre nm centre

◇ Compta **centre d'analyse** cost centre

◇ Compta **centre d'analyse auxiliaire** secondary cost centre

◇ Compta **centre d'analyse opérationnel** operational cost centre

◇ Compta **centre d'analyse principal** main cost centre

◇ **centre de chèques postaux** PO cheque account centre

◇ **centre de coût** cost centre

◇ **centre des impôts** tax centre or office

◇ Compta **centre de profit** profit centre

◇ **centre de revenus** revenue centre

CERC nm (abrév **Centre d'études sur les revenus et les coûts**) = government body carrying out research into salaries and the cost of living

certain nm fixed or direct rate of exchange; **le certain de la livre est de 8,68 francs** the rate of exchange for the pound is 8.68 francs

certificat nm certificate

◇ Bourse **certificat de dividende provisoire** scrip dividend

◇ **certificat d'investissement** investment certificate

◇ **certificat d'investissement privilégié** preferential investment certificate

◇ Bourse **certificat nominatif d'action(s)** registered share certificate

◇ **certificat de non-paiement** (de chèque) notification of unpaid cheque; (de lettre de change) certificate of dishonour

◇ Bourse **certificat (d'actions) provisoire** share certificate, (provisional) scrip

◇ **certificat de trésorerie** treasury bond

◇ Bourse **cerificat de valeur garantie** contingent value right

cession nf Jur cession, transfer; (document) deed of transfer

◇ **cession d'actifs** sale of assets

◇ **cession de parts, cession de titres** sale or disposal of securities

> **"**
>
> Le titre De Dietrich chutait de 4,6%, à 60,10 euros, vendredi. Le groupe a annoncé un bénéfice net ... de 21,9 millions d'euros au premier semestre, contre 13,5 millions d'euros l'année précédente. Le groupe a réalisé une plus-value exceptionnelle de 10,21 millions d'euros à la faveur d'une **cession de titres**.
>
> **"**

cession-bail nf lease-back

cessionnaire *nm* (**a**) *Jur (d'un effet de commerce, d'une créance)* holder (**b**) *(d'un chèque)* endorser

chaebol *nm Écon* chaebol

chambre *nf*
◇ *Banque* **chambre de clearing** clearing house
◇ *Banque* **chambre de compensation** clearing house
◇ *Banque* **chambre de compensation automatisée** automated clearing house

change *nm* exchange; **le change est avantageux/défavorable** the exchange rate is good/bad; **au change du jour** at the current rate of exchange
◇ **change du dollar** dollar exchange

changer *vt (argent)* to change, to exchange; **changer un billet de banque** to change a banknote; **changer des dollars contre des francs** to change dollars into francs

charge *nf* (**a**) *(obligation financière)* charge, expense; *(impôt)* tax; **être à la charge de qn** *(transport, réparations)* to be chargeable to sb; **les frais de transport sont à notre charge** the cost of transport is chargeable to us (**b**) *(d'une dette) Br* servicing, *Am* service
◇ **charges courantes** current expenses
◇ **charge fictive** fictitious cost
◇ **charges financières** financial expenses
◇ **charges fiscales** tax
◇ **charges fixes** fixed costs
◇ **charges nettes** net costs

◇ **charge opérationnelle** operating cost
◇ **charge à payer** sum payable
◇ *Compta* **charges à payer** accrued expenses, accruals
◇ *Compta* **charges terminales** terminal charges

chargé *nm*
◇ **chargé de budget** account executive
◇ *Banque* **chargé de clientèle** account manager
◇ *Banque* **chargé de compte** account manager

charger *vt Banque (compte)* to overcharge (on)

chasser *vt Bourse* **chasser le découvert** to raid the bears

chef *nm (responsable)* head
◇ *Compta* **chef comptable, chef de la comptabilité** chief accountant
◇ *Banque, Bourse* **chef de file** lead manager

chèque *nm Br* cheque, *Am* check; **émettre** *ou* **faire un chèque** to write a cheque; **encaisser** *ou* **tirer** *ou* **toucher un chèque** to cash a cheque; **établir** *ou* **libeller un chèque à l'ordre de qn** to make a cheque out to sb; **faire opposition à un chèque** to stop a cheque; **payer** *ou* **régler par chèque** to pay by cheque; **refuser d'honorer un chèque** to refer a cheque to drawer; **remettre** *ou* **déposer un chèque à la banque** to pay a cheque into the bank; **un chèque de 600 francs** a cheque for 600 francs
◇ **chèque bancaire** cheque
◇ **chèque de banque** banker's cheque, banker's draft

◇ *chèque barré* crossed cheque
◇ *chèque en blanc* blank cheque
◇ *Fam chèque en bois* rubber cheque
◇ *chèque de caisse* credit voucher
◇ *chèque certifié* certified cheque
◇ *chèque en circulation* outstanding cheque
◇ *chèque non barré* uncrossed cheque
◇ *chèque à ordre* cheque to order
◇ *chèque ouvert* open cheque
◇ *chèque périmé* out-of-date cheque
◇ *chèque au porteur* cheque made payable to bearer, bearer cheque
◇ *chèque postal* post office cheque
◇ *chèque postdaté* post-dated cheque
◇ *chèque sans provision* bad cheque
◇ *chèque de voyage* traveller's cheque

<blockquote>
Les émetteurs de **chèques sans provision** pourraient en effet bénéficier d'un délai plus important pour régulariser leur situation.
</blockquote>

chèque-dividende *nm* dividend warrant

chéquier *nm Br* chequebook, *Am* checkbook

chevalier *nm Bourse*
◇ *chevalier blanc* white knight
◇ *chevalier gris* grey knight
◇ *chevalier noir* black knight

<blockquote>
Côté Elf, c'est un choc, et la riposte a du mal à s'organiser. Trois scénarios sont envisagés: contraindre l'agresseur à relever son offre, trouver un **chevalier blanc** pouvant venir à la rescousse – le nom de l'italien ENI est alors évoqué – ou lancer une offre publique d'échange sur l'assaillant. Cette dernière réplique sera préférée.
</blockquote>

chiffre *nm* (a) *(nombre)* figure, number; **en chiffres ronds** in round figures
(b) *(total)* amount, total; **les dépenses de la société atteignent un chiffre de quatre millions de francs** the company's spending has reached a figure of four million francs
◇ *chiffre d'affaires* turnover; **la société a** *ou* **fait un chiffre d'affaires d'un million de francs** the company has a turnover of a million francs
◇ *chiffre d'affaires annuel* annual turnover
◇ *chiffre d'affaires consolidé* group turnover
◇ *Compta chiffre d'affaires critique* breakeven point
◇ *Compta chiffre d'affaires global* total sales
◇ *Compta chiffre d'affaires prévisionnel* projected turnover, projected sales revenue
◇ *chiffre de vente* sales figures

<blockquote>
Valéo a limité à 4,6% la baisse de son **chiffre d'affaires consolidé** au premier semestre 1993.
</blockquote>

chiffrier *nm* counter cash book

chirographaire *adj (créance, créancier)* unsecured

choc boursier *nm* market crisis

chômer *vi* laisser chômer son argent to let one's money lie idle

chroniqueur boursier *nm* market commentator

chuter *vi (valeurs, monnaie)* to plunge

CI *nm (abrév* certificat d'investissement*)* investment certificate

ci-contre *adv* opposite; *Compta* porté ci-contre as per contra

circulant, -e *adj (billets, devises)* in circulation; *(capitaux)* circulating

circulation *nf (des billets, des capitaux, des devises)* circulation
◇ *circulation monétaire* circulation of money, money in circulation

circuler *vi (billets, devises)* to be in circulation; *(capitaux)* to be circulating; **faire circuler des effets** to keep bills afloat

classe *nf Compta* group of accounts
◇ *classe de revenu* income bracket

clause *nf* clause
◇ *Compta* **clause d'indexation** escalation *or* indexation clause
◇ *clause au porteur* pay to bearer clause
◇ *clause de remboursement* refunding clause
◇ *clause de remboursement*

par anticipation prepayment clause

clearing *nm Banque* clearing

clé RIB *nf Banque* = two-digit security number allocated to account-holders

client, -e *nm,f* client, customer
◇ *Compta* **client douteux** doubtful debt, possible bad debt

clos, -e *adj (achevé)* finished, concluded; *Compta* **exercice clos le 31 déc 1998** year ended 31 Dec 1998

clôture *nf (d'un compte)* closing
◇ *Compta* **clôture annuelle des livres** year-end closing of accounts
◇ *Compta* **clôture de l'exercice** end of the financial year

clôturer *vt Compta (comptes, livres)* to close

club d'investissement *nm* investment club

CMP *nm (abrév* coût moyen pondéré*)* weighted average cost

CNE *nm (abrév* Caisse nationale d'Épargne*)* ≃ National Savings Bank

COB *nf Bourse (abrév* Commission des opérations de Bourse*)* = French Stock Exchange watchdog

cocréancier, -ère *nm,f* joint creditor

code *nm (symboles)* code
◇ *code assujetti TVA* VAT registration number
◇ *code confidentiel (pour carte bancaire)* personal identification number, PIN number
◇ *code général des impôts* general tax code

◊ *Banque* **code guichet** bank branch or sort code

◊ *Banque* **code personnel** *(pour carte bancaire)* personal identification number, PIN number

◊ *Banque* **code porteur** personal identification number, PIN number

◊ **code SICOVAM** = 5-digit code allocated to French securities by the central securities depository

codébiteur, -trice *nm,f* joint debtor

CODEVI, codevi *nm* *(abrév* **Compte pour le développement industriel)** = type of instant-access government savings account

> **❝**
>
> Plafonnés à 30 000 francs de dépôts et rémunérés à 2,25 %, les **codevi** (comptes pour le développement industriel) doivent être considérés comme des outils de trésorerie complémentaires. Permettant tous les allers et retours possibles, ils tiennent office, dans la plupart des cas, de comptes rémunérés à des conditions de taux nettement plus avantageuses que celles couramment offertes sur le marché.
>
> **❞**

coefficient *nm* *(proportion)* ratio

◊ **coefficient d'activité** activity ratio

◊ **coefficient de capital** output ratio

◊ **coefficient de capitalisation des résultats** price-earnings ratio

◊ *Compta* **coefficient d'exploitation** performance *or* operating ratio

◊ **coefficient de liquidité** liquidity ratio

◊ **coefficient de solvabilité** risk asset ratio, solvency coefficient

◊ **coefficient de trésorerie** cash ratio

coffre *nm Banque* safe-deposit box; **les coffres de l'État** the coffers of the State

◊ **coffre de nuit** night safe

coffre-fort *nm* safe

cofinancer *vt* to finance jointly

collectif budgétaire *nm* interim budget

colonne *nf (de chiffres)* column

◊ *Compta* **colonne créditrice** credit column

◊ *Compta* **colonne débitrice** debit column

comité *nm* committee

◊ **comité des établissements de crédit et des entreprises d'investissement** = French public authority empowered to authorize suppliers of investment services

commandite *nf (fonds)* = capital invested by sleeping partner(s)

◊ **commandite par actions** partnership limited by shares

◊ **(société en) commandite simple** limited partnership, mixed liability company

commandité, -e *nmf* active partner

commanditer *vt (soutenir financièrement)* to finance *(as a limited partner)*

commercialiser *vt (effet)* to negotiate

commis *nm (dans une banque, une administration)* clerk; *Bourse* floor trader; **premier commis** chief clerk

◊ *commis aux comptes* government auditor

◊ *commis aux écritures* accounting clerk

◊ *commis principal* chief clerk

commissaire aux comptes *nm* government auditor

commissariat aux comptes *nm* auditorship

commission *nf (pourcentage)* commission, percentage; *(frais de courtage)* brokerage; **3% de commission** 3% commission; **il reçoit** *ou* **touche une commission de 5% sur chaque vente** he gets a commission of 5% on each sale; **être payé à la commission** to be paid on a commission basis

◊ *Banque* **commission d'acceptation** acceptance fee

◊ *commission d'affacturage* factoring charges

◊ *commission d'arrangement* over-riding commission

◊ *commission de change* agio

◊ *commission de chef de file* management fee

◊ *commission de compte* account fee

◊ *commission de désintéressement* drop dead fee

◊ *commission d'endos* endorsement fee

◊ *commission d'engagement* commitment fee

◊ *commission de garantie* underwriting fee

◊ *commission de gestion* agency fee

◊ *commission immédiate* flat fee

◊ *commission de montage* loan origination fee

◊ *Bourse* **Commission des opérations de Bourse** = French Stock Exchange watchdog

◊ *commission de placement* underwriting fee

◊ *Bourse* **commission de rachat** redemption fee

◊ *Bourse* **commission de souscription** front load

◊ *Banque* **commission de tenue de compte** account handling fee

commissionnaire *nm* (commission) agent, broker

◊ *commissionnaire en banque* outside broker

◊ *commissionnaire en gros* factor

compensable *adj (chèque)* clearable, payable; **être compensable à Paris** to be cleared at Paris, to be domiciled in Paris

compensateur, -trice *adj* compensatory

compensation *nf* compensation; *(de chèque)* clearing

compensatoire *adj* compensatory

compenser *vt (chèque)* to clear

complémentaire *adj Compta (écriture)* supplementary

comportement *nm Bourse (du marché, des cours, des actions)* performance

comporter **se comporter** *vpr (fonctionner)* to perform; **ses actions se sont bien comportées** his shares have performed well

composé, -e *adj (intérêts)* compound

compta *nf Fam (abrév* **comptabilité)** accounts, accounting

comptabilisation *nf Compta* posting, entering in the accounts; *(dénombrement)* counting; **faire la comptabilisation de qch** to enter sth in the accounts

comptabiliser *vt Compta* to post, to enter in the accounts; *(dénombrer)* to count

comptabilité *nf* (**a**) *(livres)* accounts; *(technique)* bookkeeping, accounting; **passer qch en comptabilité** to put sth through the books *or* accounts; **tenir la comptabilité** to keep the books *or* the accounts (**b**) *(service)* accounts department; **adressez-vous à la comptabilité** apply to the accounts department

◇ *comptabilité analytique* cost accounting

◇ *comptabilité analytique d'exploitation* operational cost accounting

◇ *comptabilité budgétaire* budgeting

◇ *comptabilité de caisse* cash basis accounting

◇ *comptabilité commerciale* business accounting

◇ *comptabilité en coûts actuels* current cost accounting

◇ *comptabilité par coûts historiques* historical cost accounting

◇ *comptabilité des coûts variables* direct cost accounting

◇ *comptabilité de la dépréciation* depreciation accounting

◇ *comptabilité d'engagements* accrual accounting

◇ *comptabilité d'exploitation* cost accounting

◇ *comptabilité financière* financial accounting

◇ *comptabilité générale* general accounts; *(système)* financial accounting

◇ *comptabilité de gestion* management accounting

◇ *comptabilité informatisée* computerized accounts

◇ *comptabilité en partie double* double-entry bookkeeping

◇ *comptabilité en partie simple* single-entry bookkeeping

◇ *comptabilité de prix de revient* cost accounting

◇ *comptabilité publique* public finance

◇ *comptabilité uniforme* uniform accounting

comptable **1** *adj (travail)* accounting, bookkeeping; *(machine, méthode, plan)* accounting

2 *nmf* accountant

◇ *Can* **comptable agréé** *Br* chartered accountant, *Am* certified public accountant

comptant **1** *adv* **payer comptant** to pay (in) cash; **payer cent francs comptant** to pay a hundred francs in cash; **acheter/vendre qch comptant** to buy/sell sth for cash

2 *nm* cash; **acheter/vendre qch au comptant** to buy/sell sth for cash; **payable au comptant** *(lors d'un achat)* *Br* cash *or* *Am* collect on delivery; *(sur présentation de titre, de connaissance)* payable on presentation; **comptant contre documents** cash against documents

compte nm (a) *Compta* account; **comptes** *(comptabilité)* accounts; **tenir les comptes** to keep the accounts *or* the books; **faire ses comptes** to make up *or* do one's accounts; **vérifier les comptes** to audit the books

(b) *Banque* account; **ouvrir un compte (en banque)** to open a bank account; **verser de l'argent à son compte, alimenter son compte** to pay money into one's account

◇ *compte accréditif* charge account

◇ *compte d'achats* purchase account

◇ *Compta compte d'affectation* appropriation account

◇ *Compta comptes analytiques d'exploitation* operational cost accounts

◇ *comptes annuels* annual accounts

◇ *comptes approuvés* certified accounts

◇ *Banque compte bancaire, compte en banque* Br bank account, Am banking account

◇ *Banque compte bloqué* frozen account, Am escrow account

◇ *compte de caisse* cash account

◇ *Banque compte de caisse d'épargne* savings account

◇ *compte de capital* capital account

◇ *compte centralisateur* central account

◇ *compte de charges* expense account

◇ *Banque compte chèques* Br current account, Am checking account

◇ *compte chèque postal* = account held at the Post Office, ≃ Br giro account

◇ *Compta comptes clients* accounts receivable, Am receivables

◇ *compte commercial* office or business account

◇ *compte de compensation* clearing account

◇ *Banque compte conjoint* joint account

◇ *Compta comptes consolidés* consolidated accounts

◇ *Compta compte de contrepartie* contra account

◇ *compte courant* Br current account, Am checking account

◇ *compte à crédit* credit account

◇ *Banque compte créditeur* account in credit, credit balance

◇ *Banque compte débiteur* account in debit, debit balance

◇ *Banque compte à découvert* overdrawn account

◇ *compte définitif* final accounts

◇ *Banque compte de dépôt* deposit account

◇ *Banque compte de dépôt à vue* drawing account

◇ *compte des dépenses et recettes* income and expenditure account

◇ *compte détaillé* itemized account

◇ *Banque compte en devises étrangères* foreign currency account

◇ *Banque compte d'épargne* savings account

◇ *Banque compte d'épargne logement* savings account *(for purchasing a property)*

◇ *Banque compte étranger*

non-resident *or* foreign account

◇ *Compta* **compte d'exploitation** *Br* trading account, *Am* operating account

◇ *Compta* **comptes fournisseurs** book debts

◇ *Compta* **comptes de gestion** management accounts

◇ *Banque* **compte inactif** dead account

◇ **compte individuel** personal account

◇ **comptes intégrés** consolidated accounts

◇ **compte d'intermédiaire** nominee account

◇ **compte d'investissement** investment account

◇ *Banque* **compte joint** joint account

◇ *Banque* **compte (sur) livret** savings account

◇ *Can* **compte de non-résident** non-resident *or* foreign account

◇ **compte numéroté** numbered account

◇ *Banque, Compta* **compte ouvert** open account

◇ *Compta* **compte de pertes et profits** *(anciennement)* profit and loss account

◇ *Compta* **compte de prêt** loan account

◇ **compte prête-nom** nominee account

◇ **compte de produits** income account

◇ **compte professionnel** business account

◇ *Bourse* **compte de profits et pertes** *(anciennement)* profit and loss account

◇ *Bourse* **compte propre** personal account

◇ **compte des recettes et des dépenses** revenue account

◇ **compte de régularisation** *(de l'actif)* prepayments and accrued income; *(du passif)* accruals and deferred income

◇ *Banque* **compte rémunéré** interest-bearing account

◇ **compte de réserve** reserve account

◇ *Compta* **compte de résultat** profit and loss account, *Am* income statement

◇ *Compta* **comptes de résultats courants** above-the-line accounts

◇ *Compta* **comptes de résultats exceptionnels** below-the-line accounts

◇ *Compta* **compte de résultat prévisionnel** interim profit and loss account, *Am* interim income statement

◇ **comptes semestriels** interim accounts

◇ **comptes sociaux** company accounts

◇ **compte de stock** inventory account

◇ *Bourse* **compte à terme** forward account

◇ **comptes trimestriels** interim accounts

◇ **comptes de valeur** real accounts

◇ **compte des ventes** sales account

> **"**
>
> La crise touche également les banquiers qui doivent eux aussi rétablir leurs **comptes d'exploitation** et leurs bilans à un moment où les contraintes du ratio Cooke se font plus rigoureuses.
>
> **"**

compte-titres *nm Bourse*
share account

━━ **"** ━━━━━━━━━━━

Avec le **compte-titres** ordinaire, vous disposez d'une totale liberté. Tant sur le choix des
placements (actions françaises
ou internationales, fonds pro-
filés ...), que sur les possibilités
de retrait. En contrepartie, vos
plus-values seront imposables
au taux de 26% si l'ensemble
de vos cessions de valeurs mobilières excède un seuil, théori-
quement fixé à 50 000 francs
pour 1999. Un niveau bien vite
atteint.

━━━━━━━━━━━ **"** ━━

comptoir *nm (établissement)*
bank; *(de banque)* branch
◊ **comptoir d'escompte** discount house

comptoir-caisse *nm* cash desk

concédant *nm* grantor

concordat *nm* bankrupt's certificate

concours bancaire *nm* bank
lending

conjoncture boursière *nf*
market trend

conseil *nm* (a) *(personne)* consultant
   (b) *(assemblée)* council, committee; *(d'une entreprise)*
board; *(réunion)* meeting
◊ **conseil d'administration**
board of directors
◊ **Conseil des Bourses de Valeurs** = regulatory body of
the Paris Stock Exchange
◊ **conseil Ecofin** ECOFIN
◊ **conseil financier** financial
consultant *or* adviser

◊ **conseil fiscal** tax consultant
◊ **Conseil national du crédit**
National Credit Council
◊ **conseil en placements** investment advice

conseiller, -ère *nm,f (spécialiste)* adviser, consultant
◊ **conseiller financier** financial
adviser *or* consultant
◊ **conseiller financier indépen-
dant** independent financial
adviser
◊ **conseiller fiscal** tax consultant
◊ **conseiller en placements** investment adviser

consentir *vt (prêt, avance)* to
grant

conservateur, -trice *nm,f*
◊ **conservateur des hypothèques** mortgage registrar
◊ *Bourse* **conservateur de titres**
custodian

conservation *nf Bourse* custody
◊ **conservation internationale**
(d'actions) global custody
◊ **conservation nationale** *(d'actions)* local custody, subcusto-
dy

consigner *vt (argent)* to deposit

consolidation *nf (d'une dette)*
funding, financing; *(des bénéfices, des fonds, d'un bilan)* consolidation

consolidé, -e 1 *adj (dette)* funded, financed; *(bénéfices, fonds,
bilan)* consolidated
   2 *nm* **consolidés** consols

consolider *vt (dette)* to fund, to
finance; *(bénéfices, fonds, bilan)*
to consolidate; **le franc a consolidé son avance à la Bourse** the

franc has strengthened its lead on the stock exchange

consommation *nf Écon* consumption

◊ *Compta* **consommations de l'exercice** total annual expenses

constant, -e *adj* constant; **en francs/dollars constants** in constant francs/dollars

constaté, -e *adj (valeur)* registered; **constaté d'avance** *(charge)* prepaid

continuité d'exploitation *nf* going-concern status

contrat *nm* contract

◊ *Bourse* **contrat de prêt** loan agreement

◊ *Bourse* **contrat à terme** forward *or* futures contract

◊ *Bourse* **contrat à terme d'instruments financiers** financial futures contract

◊ *Bourse* **contrat à terme sous option** underlying futures contract

◊ *contrat de vente* bill of sale

contre-écriture *nf Compta* contra-entry

contre-offre *nf* counter-offer

❝ ──────

Pour arriver à une solution rapide, le patron de TotalFina suggère même aux actionnaires d'Elf de refuser l'augmentation de capital nécessaire pour financer la **contre-offre**, qui sera proposée à l'assemblée générale le 3 septembre.

────── ❞

contrepartie *nf* **(a)** *(compensation)* compensation; **en**

contrepartie in return (**de** for) **(b)** *(dans une transaction)* other party **(c)** *Compta* contra; *(d'une inscription)* counterpart; *(d'un registre)* duplicate; **en contrepartie** per contra **(d)** *Bourse* hedging, market making; **faire (de) la contrepartie** to operate against one's client

◊ *contrepartie financière* financial compensation; **vous aurez la contrepartie financière de la perte subie** you will be financially compensated for the loss incurred

contre-passation *nf* **(a)** *Compta* journal entry, contra-entry; *(d'un article, d'une entrée)* reversing, transferring **(b)** *(d'un effet)* return, endorsement, backing

contre-passer *vt* **(a)** *Compta (article, entrée)* to reverse, to transfer **(b)** *(effet)* to return, to endorse, to back

contreseing *nm* countersignature

contresigner *vt* to countersign

contre-valeur *nf* exchange value; **pour la contre-valeur de 300 francs** in exchange for 300 francs

contribuable *nmf* taxpayer

❝ ──────

Nec plus ultra de la défiscalisation, la location en meublé professionnel permet d'alléger sensiblement l'impôt sur le revenu pour les **contribuables** les plus imposés.

────── ❞

contribution *nf Admin (impôt)*

tax; **contributions** *(à l'État)* taxes; *(à la collectivité locale) Br* ≃ council tax, *Am* ≃ local taxes; **(bureau des) contributions** tax office, *Br* ≃ Inland Revenue, *Am* ≃ Internal Revenue; **lever** *ou* **percevoir une contribution** to collect *or* levy a tax; **payer ses contributions** to pay one's taxes

◇ *contributions directes* direct taxation

◇ *contribution foncière* land tax

◇ *contributions indirectes* indirect taxation

◇ *contribution sociale généralisée* = income-based tax deducted at source as a contribution to paying off the French social security budget deficit

contrôle *nm Compta (des comptes)* checking, auditing

◇ *contrôle bancaire* banking controls

◇ *Compta* **contrôle du bilan** audit

◇ *contrôle budgétaire* budgetary control

◇ *contrôle des changes* (foreign) exchange control

◇ *contrôle de la comptabilité* accounting control

◇ *contrôle de comptes* audit

◇ *contrôle financier* financial control

◇ *contrôle fiscal* tax inspection

◇ *contrôle de gestion* management audit

◇ *contrôle monétaire* monetary control

″

Dans l'espoir d'enrayer la chute du rouble, la Banque centrale russe vient de mettre en place un **contrôle des changes**.

″

contrôler *vt Compta (comptes)* to check, to audit; **contrôler les livres** to check the books

contrôleur, -euse *nm,f (des comptes)* auditor

◇ *contrôleur du crédit* credit controller

◇ *contrôleur financier* financial controller

◇ *contrôleur de gestion* management accountant

◇ *contrôleur aux liquidations* controller in bankruptcy

convention *nf* agreement

◇ *convention de crédit* credit agreement

conversion *nf (d'argent, de devises étrangères, de titres, d'un emprunt)* conversion

convertibilité *nf* convertibility

convertible 1 *adj (obligation, monnaie)* convertible (**en** into) **2** *nf* convertible

″

Rappelons que les **convertibles** sont des obligations à taux fixe émises par des entreprises privées pour une durée de 5 à 8 ans et pouvant être échangées à tout moment contre des actions.

″

convertir *vt (argent, devises étrangères, titres, emprunt)* to convert (**en** into); **convertir des valeurs en espèces** to convert securities into cash; **convertir des rentes** to convert stock

convertissement *nm (de valeurs en espèces)* conversion (**en** into)

coporteur *nm* joint holder

corbeille *nf Bourse* trading floor
◊ *corbeille des obligations* bond-trading ring

correspondant en valeurs de Trésor *nm Bourse* reporting dealer

cotation *nf Bourse* quotation, listing
◊ *cotation en continu* continuous *or* all-day trading
◊ *cotation à la corbeille* floor trading
◊ *cotation au cours du marché* market quotation
◊ *cotation à la criée* open-outcry trading
◊ *cotation de l'or* gold fixing
◊ *cotation à vue* spot quotation

cote *nf Bourse (valeur)* quotation; *(liste)* share index; **inscrit** *ou* **admis à la cote** listed *or* quoted on the stock exchange; **retirer qch de la cote** *(société, actions)* to delist sth; **hors cote** *(actions)* unlisted; *(marché) Br* unofficial, *Am* over-the-counter
◊ *cote à la clôture, cote de clôture* closing price *or* quotation
◊ *cote officielle* official list
◊ *cote des prix* official list, official share list

coté, -e *adj Bourse* listed, quoted; **non coté** unlisted, unquoted; **être coté à 100 francs** to be trading at 100 francs

> **"**
> Tant qu'il n'est pas **coté** en Bourse, Amadeus reste discret sur ses bénéfices.
> **"**

coter *vt Bourse* to list, to quote; **des valeurs qui seront cotées en Bourse demain** shares which will go on the stock exchange tomorrow; **coter à l'ouverture/à la clôture** to open/close

cotisation *nf* (a) *(à une organisation)* subscription (b) *(à une caisse, à une mutuelle)* contribution
◊ *cotisations maladie* health insurance contributions
◊ *cotisation ouvrière* employee's contribution
◊ *cotisation patronale* employer's contribution
◊ *cotisations à la Sécurité sociale* ≃ National Insurance contributions
◊ *cotisations sociales* ≃ National Insurance and National Health contributions

cotiser *vi* (a) *(à une organisation)* to subscribe (**à** to) (b) *(à une caisse de retraite, à une mutuelle)* to contribute, to pay one's contributions (**à** to); **cotiser à la Sécurité sociale** ≃ to pay one's National Insurance (contributions)

coulisse *nf Bourse* outside market, kerb market

coulissier *nm Bourse* outside broker, kerb broker

coupe *nf* cut
◊ *coupes budgétaires* budget cuts

coupon *nm* coupon
◊ *Bourse* **coupon d'action** coupon
◊ *Bourse* **coupon attaché** cum dividend *or* coupon
◊ *Bourse* **coupon détaché, coupon échu** ex dividend *or* coupon

coupure *nf* denomination; **cou-**

pure de 50 francs 50-franc note; **50 000 francs en petites coupures** 50,000 francs in small notes *or* denominations; **en coupures usagées** in used notes

❝

Les banques, particulièrement concernées par la circulation des **coupures**, ne verraient pas d'un mauvais œil l'avènement d'une monnaie sans papier.

❞

Cour des Comptes *nf* ≃ Audit Office

courbe *nf* curve; *(graphe)* graph
◇ *Compta* **courbe des coûts** cost curve
◇ **courbe d'investissement** investment curve
◇ **courbe des prix** price curve
◇ **courbe des taux** yield curve

cours *nm* (a) *(d'argent)* currency; **avoir cours** to be legal tender
(b) *Bourse (de devises)* rate; **au cours (du jour)** at the current daily price; **quel est le cours du sucre?** what is the price *or* quotation for sugar?; **premier cours** opening price
◇ *Bourse* **cours acheteur** bid price
◇ *Bourse* **cours des actions** share prices
◇ *Bourse* **cours de la Bourse** market price
◇ *Banque, Bourse* **cours du change** rate of exchange, exchange rate
◇ *Bourse* **cours de clôture** closing prices
◇ **cours de compensation** settlement price

◇ *Banque, Bourse* **cours des devises** foreign exchange rate
◇ *Bourse* **cours du dont** call price
◇ **cours étranger** foreign exchange
◇ **cours forcé** forced currency
◇ **cours légal** legal tender; **avoir cours légal** to be legal tender
◇ **cours de liquidation** settlement price
◇ *Banque, Bourse* **cours officiel** official exchange rate
◇ *Bourse* **cours d'ouverture** opening price
◇ *Bourse* **cours vendeur** offer price

courtage *nm* *(profession)* brokerage, broking; *(commission)* brokerage, commission; **être vendu par courtage** to be sold on commission; **faire le courtage** to be a broker
◇ *Bourse* **courtage électronique** e-broking, on-line broking

courtier, -ère *nm,f* broker
◇ **courtier d'assurances** insurance broker
◇ *Bourse* **courtier de Bourse** stockbroker
◇ *Bourse* **courtier de change** exchange broker *or* dealer
◇ **courtier de commerce** general broker
◇ **courtier à la commission** commission agent
◇ *Bourse* **courtier électronique** e-broker, on-line broker
◇ *Bourse* **courtier intermédiaire** inter-dealer broker
◇ **courtier libre** outside broker
◇ **courtier de marchandises** commercial broker
◇ **courtier marron** outside broker

◇ *Bourse* **courtier en matières premières** commodity broker *or* dealer

◇ *Bourse* **courtier en valeurs mobilières** stockbroker

> **"**
>
> Si, d'ores et déjà, le marché mondial des changes est entièrement sous la coupe de réseaux privés électroniques, les marchés d'actions sont encore entre les mains des Bourses officielles classiques. Pour combien de temps encore? ... les banques d'affaires internationales demandent la constitution rapide d'un marché unifié et soutiennent les **courtiers électroniques** dans leur projet. Selon le quotidien allemand *Handelsblatt* ... des grands noms de la finance américaine comme Goldman Sachs, Morgan Stanley, J.P. Morgan et Merrill Lynch comptent fonder un marché électronique des actions en Europe.
>
> **"**

coût *nm* cost

◇ *Compta* **coût d'achat** *(sur bilan)* cost of goods purchased

◇ **coût d'acquisition** acquisition cost

◇ *Compta* **coûts attribuables** relevant costs

◇ **coûts cachés** hidden costs

◇ **coût du capital** capital cost

◇ **coûts de détention** holding costs

◇ **coûts discrétionnaires** discretionary costs

◇ *Compta* **coûts engagés** committed costs

◇ **coûts évitables** avoidable costs

◇ **coûts fixes communs** common fixed costs

◇ **coûts indirects** indirect costs

◇ **coûts induits** unavoidable costs

◇ **coûts irrécupérables** sunk costs

◇ *Compta* **coût moyen** average cost

◇ *Compta* **coût moyen pondéré** weighted average cost

◇ **coûts opérationnels** operational costs

◇ **coûts de production** production costs

◇ **coût réel** real cost

◇ **coût standard** standard cost

◇ **coût de la vie** cost of living

coûtant *adj* **au** *ou* **à prix coûtant** at cost price

coûter *vi* to cost

couvert, -e *adj* **être à couvert** *(pour un crédit)* to be covered; *Bourse* **vendre à couvert** to hedge, to sell for futures

couverture *nf* cover; *Bourse* margin, hedge; **une commande sans couverture** an order without security *or* cover; **exiger une couverture de 20% en espèces** to claim a margin of 20% in cash; **opérer avec couverture** to hedge

◇ *Bourse* **couverture courte** short hedge

◇ *Bourse* **couverture longue** long hedge

◇ *Bourse* **couverture (boursière) obligatoire** margin requirement

◇ **couverture du risque de crédit** loan risk cover

couvrir 1 *vt (emprunt)* to cover, to secure

2 se couvrir *vpr Bourse* to cover (oneself), to hedge

cpt (*abrév* **comptant**) cash

CRDS *nf* (*abrév* **contribution au remboursement de la dette sociale**) = income-based tax deducted at source as a contribution to paying off the French social security budget deficit

créance *nf* debt; *Jur* claim; **amortir une créance** to write off a debt; **mauvaise créance** bad debt
◇ **créance chirographaire** unsecured debt
◇ **créance douteuse** doubtful debt
◇ **créance exigible** debt due
◇ **créance garantie** secured debt
◇ **créance hypothécaire** debt secured by a mortgage
◇ **créance irrécouvrable** bad debt

> "
>
> Les **créances douteuses** ont augmenté au cours du premier semestre de l'année fiscale, et les fonds propres composés en partie des gains latents sur les portefeuilles de titres, ont fondu avec la chute du Nikkei.
>
> "

créancier, -ère *nm,f* creditor
◇ **créancier chirographaire** unsecured creditor
◇ **créancier d'exploitation** trade creditor
◇ **créancier hypothécaire** mortgagee
◇ **créancier nanti** secured creditor
◇ **créancier privilégié** preferential *or* preferred creditor

crédit *nm* (**a**) (*prêt*) credit; **acheter/vendre qch à crédit** to buy/to sell sth on credit; **faire crédit à qn** to give sb credit; **ouvrir un crédit à qn** to open a credit account in sb's favour *or* in sb's name; **ouvrir un crédit chez qn** to open a credit account with sb (**b**) (*en comptabilité*) credit side; **porter une somme au crédit de qn** to credit sb with a sum
◇ **crédit back to back** back-to-back credit
◇ **crédit bancaire, crédit en banque** bank credit
◇ **crédit bloqué** frozen credit
◇ **crédit commercial** trade credit
◇ **crédit à la consommation, crédit au consommateur** consumer credit
◇ **crédit consortial** syndicated credit
◇ **crédit (à) court terme** short-term credit
◇ **crédit croisé** cross-currency swap
◇ **crédit à découvert** open credit
◇ **crédits de développement** development loans
◇ **crédit différé** deferred credit
◇ **crédit documentaire** documentary credit, letter of credit
◇ **crédit dos à dos** back-to-back credit
◇ **crédit de droits** = delay in payment of indirect taxes
◇ **crédits d'équipement** equipment financing
◇ **crédits à l'exportation** export credit
◇ **crédit foncier** = government-controlled building society
◇ **crédit gratuit** interest-free credit

◇ **crédit immobilier** mortgage, home loan

◇ **crédits à l'importation** import credit

◇ **crédit d'impôt** *(abattement)* tax rebate ; *(report)* tax credit

◇ **crédit irrévocable** irrevocable letter of credit

◇ **crédit (à) long terme** long-term credit

◇ **crédit (à) moyen terme** medium-term credit

◇ **crédit permanent** *Br* revolving *or Am* revolver credit

◇ **crédit personnel** personal credit

◇ **crédit ponctuel (à court terme)** spot credit

◇ **crédit renouvelable** *Br* revolving *or Am* revolver credit

◇ **crédit de restructuration** new money

◇ **crédit renouvelable** *Br* revolving *or Am* revolver credit

◇ **crédit révocable** revocable letter of credit

◇ **crédit revolving** *Br* revolving *or Am* revolver credit

◇ **crédit de sécurité** swing line

◇ **crédit à taux réduit** low-interest loan

◇ **crédit à taux révisable** rollover credit

◇ **crédit à terme** term loan

◇ **crédit transférable** transferable credit

◇ **crédits de trésorerie** (short term) credit facilities

◇ **crédit de TVA** VAT credit

> **"**
>
> La Caixabank vient de procéder à une nouvelle baisse de l'ensemble des taux fixes de ses **crédits immobiliers**.
>
> **"**

crédit-acheteur *nm* buyer credit

crédit-bail *nm* leasing

> **"**
>
> Le secteur du **crédit-bail** se réduit comme peau de chagrin en Bourse. Cette semaine encore, la restructuration s'est accélérée avec l'annonce de l'OPA de PHRV sur Bail Saint-Honoré. La crise de l'immobilier et la fin du statut fiscal privilégié des Sicomi sont passées par là. De plus, la concurrence s'est intensifiée avec l'arrivée des banques sur le marché du **crédit-bail**.
>
> **"**

créditer *vt (compte)* to credit (**de** with) ; **créditer qn de 4000 francs** to credit sb *or* sb's account with 4,000 francs ; **faire créditer son compte d'une somme** to pay a sum into one's account

créditeur, -trice 1 *adj (compte, solde)* credit

2 *nm,f* = person whose account is in credit

crédit-fournisseur *nm* supplier credit

crédit-relais *nm Br* bridging loan, *Am* bridge loan

crédit-scoring *nm* credit scoring

Credoc *nm* *(abrév* **crédit documentaire)** documentary credit, letter of credit

criée *nf Bourse* open outcry

croissance *nf* growth ; **croissance du capital** capital growth

CSG *nf (abrév* **contribution sociale généralisée)** = income-based tax deducted at source as a contribution to paying off the French social security budget deficit

"

Le gouvernement pioche copieusement dans la poche des ménages avec l'augmentation de la **CSG** et la baisse de certains remboursements.

"

cumulatif, -ive *adj (actions, dividende)* cumulative

cumulé, -e *adj (intérêts)* accrued

cumuler *vt (intérêts)* to accrue

CVG *nm Bourse (abrév* **certificat de valeur garantie***)* CVR

DAB *nm* *Banque* (*abrév* **distributeur automatique de billets**) ATM

date *nf* date; **à trente jours de date** thirty days after date; **la facture n'a pas été payée à la date prévue** the bill wasn't paid on time
◇ *date butoir* cut-off date
◇ *date d'échéance* (*de dû*) maturity date, due date; (*de terme*) expiry date
◇ *date d'émission* date of issue
◇ *date d'exigibilité* due date
◇ *date de facturation* date of invoice
◇ *date de jouissance* date from which interest begins to run
◇ *date limite de paiement* deadline for payment
◇ *date d'ouverture de l'exercice* first day of the financial year
◇ *date de remise* remittance date
◇ *Banque* **date de valeur** value date

dater **1** *vt* (*lettre*) to date
2 *vi* to date (**de** from); **à dater de ce jour** (*d'aujourd'hui*) from today; (*de ce jour-là*) from that day

débâcle *nf* **débâcle (financière)** crash

débit *nm* *Compta* debit; (*sur un compte*) debit side; **inscrire** *ou* **porter un article au débit** to debit an entry; **porter une somme au débit de qn** to debit sb *or* sb's account with an amount
◇ *débit de caisse* cash debit
◇ *débit cumulé* cumulative debit
◇ *débit différé* deferred debit
◇ *débit immédiat* immediate debit

> Les cartes de paiement sont destinées au règlement chez un commerçant affilié, soit par **débit immédiat**, soit par **débit différé**.

débiter *vt* *Compta* (*compte*) to debit; **débiter une somme à qn, débiter qn d'une somme** to debit sb with an amount; **débiter une somme d'un compte** to debit an account with an amount, to debit an amount to an account; **débiter les frais de poste au client** to charge the postage to the customer

débiteur, -trice **1** *adj* (*compte, solde*) debit; **mon compte est débiteur de plusieurs milliers de**

francs my account is several thousand francs overdrawn **2** *nm,f* debtor

⋄ **débiteur hypothécaire** mortgagor

déblocage *nm (de crédits, de capitaux)* unfreezing; *(des prix, des salaires)* decontrolling; *(de fonds)* releasing, making available

débloquer *vt (crédits, capitaux)* to unfreeze; *(prix, salaires)* to decontrol; *(fonds)* to release, to make available

déboursement *nm* outlay, expenditure

débourser *vt (somme, argent)* to spend, to lay out

décaissement *nm* **(a)** *(retrait)* cash withdrawal; **faire un décaissement** to make a withdrawal **(b)** *(somme)* sum withdrawn; *Compta* **décaissements** outgoings

décaisser *vt (somme)* to withdraw

décharge *nf* (tax) rebate; **porter une somme en décharge** to mark a sum as paid

décharger *vt (compte)* to discharge; **décharger qn de qch** *(dette)* to discharge sb from sth; *(impôt)* to exempt sb from sth

déchéance *nf* **(a)** *(de droits, de titres, d'un brevet)* forfeiture; *(d'une police)* expiry **(b)** *Compta* **tomber en déchéance** to lapse

⋄ **déchéance du terme** event of default

déclaration *nf Compta* return

⋄ *Compta* **déclaration annuelle de résultats** annual statement of results

⋄ **déclaration de cessation de paiement** declaration of bankruptcy

⋄ **déclaration de dividende** dividend announcement, declaration of dividend

⋄ **déclaration de faillite** declaration of bankruptcy

⋄ **déclaration fiscale** income tax return

⋄ **déclaration d'impôts** tax return; **remplir sa déclaration d'impôts** to *Br* make *or Am* file one's tax return

⋄ **déclaration de résultats** statement of results, financial statement

⋄ **déclaration de revenu** income tax return

⋄ **déclaration de solvabilité** declaration of solvency

⋄ **déclaration de TVA** VAT return

⋄ *Bourse* **déclaration de valeur** declaration of value

déclarer **1** *vt Compta (dividende)* to declare; **déclarer ses revenus au fisc** to *Br* make *or Am* file one's tax return

2 se déclarer *vpr Bourse* **se déclarer acheteur/vendeur** to call/put the shares

déclassé, -e *adj Bourse (valeurs)* displaced

déclassement *nm Bourse (de valeurs)* displacement

décomposer *vt Compta (compte, résultats)* to analyse, to break down; *(dépenses)* to break down

décomposition *nf Compta (d'un compte, des résultats)* analysis, breakdown; *(des dépenses)* breakdown

décompte *nm* (**a**) *(solde)* balance; **payer le décompte** to pay the balance due *(on an account)* (**b**) *(relevé d'une opération)* detailed account, breakdown

décote *nf* (**a**) *(d'impôt)* tax relief (**b**) *(de devise, de société)* below par rating; **décote en Bourse** *(d'une action)* discount; **société qui souffre d'une décote** undervalued company
(**c**) *(baisse)* depreciation, loss in value

> **"**
>
> Du côté des hausses, c'est la SGE qui signe la plus forte ... Il y a une **décote** du cours de l'action et l'acquisition de Sogeparc qui survient après plusieurs autres opérations fait penser que le dividende devrait augmenter rapidement.
>
> **"**

décoté *adj (société, valeur)* undervalued

découvert *nm* (**a**) *Banque* **découvert (bancaire)** overdraft; **demander une autorisation de découvert** to apply for an overdraft; **accorder à qn un découvert** to allow sb an overdraft; **avoir un découvert** *ou* **être à découvert de 2 000 francs** *(autorisé)* to have a 2,000 franc overdraft; *(non autorisé)* to be overdrawn by 2,000 francs; **mettre un compte à découvert** to overdraw an account
(**b**) *Bourse* **acheter à découvert** to buy short; **vendre à découvert** to go a bear, to sell short

◇ **découvert de la balance commerciale** trade gap

◇ **découvert en blanc** unsecured overdraft

DECS *nm* (*abrév* **diplôme d'études comptables supérieures**) = postgraduate qualification in accounting

déductible *adj (dépense)* deductible; **déductible de l'impôt** tax-deductible

déduction *nf* deduction, allowance; **après déduction des impôts** after deduction of tax; **faire déduction de qch** to deduct *or* allow for sth; **sous déduction de 10%** less 10%, minus 10%; **entrer en déduction de qch** to be deductible from sth

◇ **déduction pour dons** deduction for donations

◇ **déduction fiscale** tax allowance

◇ **déduction forfaitaire** *(d'impôts)* standard allowance

déduire *vt* to deduct

défaillance d'entreprise *nf* business failure

défalcation *nf* deduction; *(d'une mauvaise créance)* writing off; **défalcation faite des frais** after deducting the expenses

défalquer *vt* to deduct (**de** from); *(mauvaise créance)* to write off

déficit *nm* deficit; **être en déficit** to be in deficit; **accuser/combler un déficit** to show/make up a deficit

◇ *Écon* **déficit de la balance commerciale** trade deficit

◇ *Écon* **déficit budgétaire** budget deficit

◇ **déficit de caisse** cash deficit

◊ *Écon* **déficit commercial** trade deficit *or* gap

◊ **déficit d'exploitation** operating deficit

◊ *Écon* **déficit extérieur** external deficit, balance of payments deficit

◊ **déficit fiscal remboursable** negative income tax

◊ **déficit fiscal reportable** tax loss

◊ *Compta* **déficit reportable** loss carry forward

◊ *Écon* **déficit du secteur public** public sector deficit

◊ **déficit de trésorerie** cash deficit

❝

Ces dépenses supplémentaires pourraient déséquilibrer le budget de l'état allemand, voire faire passer le **déficit budgétaire** au-dessus du maximum autorisé par les critères de convergence européens de Maastricht.

❞

déficitaire *adj (entreprise)* loss-making; *(compte)* in debit; *(budget)* in deficit, adverse; *(balance, solde)* adverse; *(bilan)* showing a loss; **être déficitaire** to show a deficit

défiscalisé, -e *adj* tax free

défiscaliser *vt* to exempt from tax

dégagement *nm (de fonds, de crédits)* release

dégager **1** *vt* (a) *(fonds, crédits)* to release (b) *(bénéfices, excédent)* to show

2 se dégager *vpr* **se dégager**

d'une dette to discharge *or* pay off a debt

dégeler *vt (avoir, crédits)* to unfreeze, to unblock

dégressif, -ive **1** *adj (impôt, amortissement)* graded, graduated; *(tarif, taux)* tapering **2** *nm* discount

dégrèvement *nm (remise)* reduction

◊ **dégrèvement (fiscal)** tax relief

❝

Il est possible d'obtenir des **dégrèvements** d'impôts locaux pouvant atteindre 100% l'année de l'inondation.

❞

dégrever *vt (produits)* to reduce tax on; *(contribuable)* to grant tax relief to; *(industrie)* to derate; *(propriété)* to reduce the assessment on

dégringoler *vi Bourse (valeurs)* to plunge

délai *nm* deadline

◊ **délai de crédit** credit period

◊ **délai de grâce** grace period, period of grace

◊ **délai de paiement** *(fixé par contrat)* term of payment; **demander un délai de paiement** to request a postponement of payment

◊ **délai de recouvrement des sommes** period for debt recovery

◊ **délai de récupération du capital investi** payback period

◊ **délai de règlement** settlement period

◊ **délai de remboursement** payback period

délaissé, -e *adj Bourse (valeurs)* neglected

délit d'initié *nm* insider dealing *or* trading

> **"**
>
> Que fait la police? La Commission des opérations de Bourse (COB), gendarme du marché, a bien du mal à débusquer les **délits d'initié.** Elle traque pourtant l'infraction, mais sans grand succès, puisque sur 1148 situations suspectes examinées en 1998, une petite dizaine à peine ont été répertoriées comme passibles de sanction!
>
> **"**

démantèlement d'entreprise *nm* asset stripping

démonétisation *nf* demonetization

démonétiser *vt* to demonetize

deniers *nmpl* money, funds
◇ **deniers de l'État** public funds

dépassement *nm* exceeding, excess; **il y a un dépassement de crédit de plusieurs millions** the budget has been exceeded by several million
◇ *dépassement budgétaire* overspending
◇ *Compta* **dépassement de coût** cost overrun

dépasser *vt (excéder)* to exceed; **les ventes ont dépassé le chiffre de l'an dernier** sales figures have overtaken last year's; **dépasser un crédit** to exceed a credit limit

dépeceur d'entreprise *nm* asset stripper

dépense *nf* expenditure, expense; **dépenses** expenses; **contrôler les dépenses** to check expenditure; **faire des dépenses** to incur expenses; **faire trop de dépenses** to overspend
◇ *Compta* **dépenses de caisse** cash expenditure
◇ *Compta* **dépenses en capital** capital expenditure *or* outlay
◇ *Écon* **dépenses de consommation** consumer expenditure
◇ *Compta* **dépenses courantes** current expenditure
◇ *Compta* **dépenses de création** above-the-line costs
◇ *Compta* **dépenses diverses** sundry expenses
◇ *Compta* **dépenses d'équipement** capital expenditure
◇ *Compta* **dépenses d'exploitation** operating costs
◇ **dépenses extraordinaires** extras
◇ *Compta* **dépenses de fonctionnement** operating costs
◇ *Compta* **dépenses d'investissement** capital expenditure
◇ *Compta* **dépenses nettes d'investissement** net capital expenditure
◇ **dépenses non prévues au budget** unforeseen expenses
◇ **dépenses prévues au budget** foreseen expenses
◇ *Écon* **dépenses publiques** public spending, government spending

dépenser *vt* to spend

déplacement *nm (de fonds)* movement

déplacer *vt (fonds)* to move

déplafonnement *nm (d'un*

prix) removal of the upper limit *or* the ceiling

déplafonner *vt (prix)* to remove the upper limit *or* the ceiling on; **déplafonner un crédit** to raise the ceiling on a credit, to raise a credit limit

déposant, -e *nm,f* depositor

déposer *vt (verser)* **déposer une caution** to leave a deposit; **déposer de l'argent (à la banque)** to deposit money (at the bank)

dépositaire *nmf (d'un fonds de placement)* custodian

dépôt *nm* (a) *Banque* deposit; **faire un dépôt** *(d'argent)* to make a deposit; **mettre qch en dépôt dans une banque** to deposit sth with a bank; **dépôt à sept jours de préavis** deposit at seven days' notice

(b) **en dépôt** *(argent, document, marchandises)* in trust; **avoir qch en dépôt** to hold sth in trust

◇ *Banque* **dépôt bancaire** bank deposit

◇ *Compta* **dépôt de bilan** *(d'une entreprise)* (filing of petition in) bankruptcy

◇ *Banque* **dépôt en coffre-fort** safe-deposit

◇ *Banque* **dépôt à court terme** short-term deposit

◇ *Banque* **dépôt à échéance fixe** fixed deposit

◇ *Banque* **dépôt d'espèces** cash deposit

◇ *Bourse* **dépôt de garantie** margin deposit

◇ **dépôt initial** initial margin

◇ *Banque* **dépôt interbancaire** interbank deposit

◇ **dépôt à terme** short-term investment

◇ *Banque* **dépôt à terme fixe** fixed deposit

◇ *Banque* **dépôt à vue** demand *or* sight deposit

"

Un mois après avoir subi un revers majeur avec le **dépôt de bilan** d'Iridium, le consortium de téléphonie par satellite, Motorola entend reprendre l'initiative. Selon l'édition du Wall Street Journal du lundi 13 septembre, le groupe américain d'électronique grand public s'apprêterait à acquérir General Instrument pour un montant proche de 10 milliards de dollars (9,52 milliards d'euros).

"

dépréciation *nf (dévaluation)* depreciation, fall in value

◇ *Compta* **dépréciation annuelle** annual depreciation

◇ *Compta* **dépréciation de créances** write-down of accounts receivable

◇ *Compta* **dépréciation fonctionnelle** *(du matériel)* wear and tear

déprécier 1 *vt (dévaluer)* to depreciate

2 se déprécier *vpr* to depreciate, to fall in value

déprédateur, -trice *nm,f (de fonds)* embezzler

déprédation *nf (de fonds)* embezzlement

DEPS *nm (abrév* **dernier entré, premier sorti)** LIFO

dernier, -ère 1 *adj (ultime)* last, final

2 nm **dernier entré, premier sorti** last in, first out

◇ Bourse **dernier cours** closing price

◇ **dernier prix** final offer

◇ Bourse **dernière proposition** final offer

◇ **dernier rappel** (de facture) final demand

descendre vi (prix) to come down, to fall; Bourse (actions) to drop, to fall; **descendre en flèche** to plummet

désencadrement nm (des crédits) unblocking

désencadrer vt (crédits) to unblock

désendettement nm degearing, clearing of debts

désendetter se désendetter vpr to clear one's debts

désescalade nf (de prix, des actions) downturn

déshypothéquer vt to free from mortgage

désindexation nf removal of index-linking

━━ 66 ━━

La **désindexation** des salaires sur les prix a limité les effets inflationnistes de la dépréciation de la lire.

━━ 99 ━━

désindexer vt to stop index-linking; **ces pensions ont été désindexées** these retirement schemes are no longer index-linked

désintéressement nm (de partenaire) buying out; (de créditeur) paying off

désintéresser vt (partenaire) to buy out; (créditeur) to pay off

désinvestir vt to disinvest in

désinvestissement nm disinvestment

◇ **désinvestissement marginal** marginal disinvestment

destination nf (usage) (de capitaux, de fonds) use

destiner vt (affecter) **destiner des fonds à qch** to allot or assign funds to sth; **cet argent est destiné à la recherche** this money is earmarked for or is going towards research

déstockage nm destocking

◇ Compta **déstockage de production** (poste de bilan) decrease in stocks

détail nm (a) (énumération) (d'un compte, d'un inventaire) items; (d'une facture) breakdown; **faire le détail de qch** to itemize sth, to break sth down

détaillé, -e adj (facture, relevé de compte) itemized

détailler vt (facture, relevé de compte) to itemize

détaxé, -e adj (produits, articles) duty-free

détente nf (des taux d'intérêt) lowering, easing

━━ 66 ━━

En réduisant l'écart de rendement avec les autres produits de placement, la **détente** des taux (d'intérêt) redonne un peu d'oxygène au livret A.

━━ 99 ━━

détenteur, -trice nm,f (d'argent, d'un compte) holder

◇ *détenteur d'actions, détenteur de titres* *Br* shareholder, *Am* stockholder

> **"**
>
> Les **détenteurs** de Sicav monétaires ou obligataires ont la possibilité de soustraire leurs plus-values à l'impôt en réinvestissant le produit de la vente dans l'immobilier d'habitation.
>
> **"**

détournement *nm*

◇ *détournement d'actif* embezzlement of assets

◇ *détournement de fonds* misappropriation of funds, embezzlement

détourner *vt (fonds)* to misappropriate, to embezzle

dette *nf* debt; **avoir des dettes** to be in debt (**envers** to); **faire des dettes** to run into debt; **avoir 10 000 francs de dettes** to be 10,000 francs in debt; **s'acquitter d'une dette** to pay off a debt; **assurer le service d'une dette** to service a debt

◇ *Compta* **dettes actives** accounts receivable

◇ *dettes bancaires* bank debts

◇ *dette caduque* debt barred by the Statute of Limitations

◇ *Compta* **dettes compte** book debts

◇ *Compta* **dette consolidée** consolidated *or* funded debt

◇ *dette courante* floating debt

◇ *Compta* **dette à court terme** short-term debt

◇ *Compta* **dettes à court terme** current liabilities

◇ *Écon* **la dette de l'État** the National Debt

◇ *dette exigible* debt due for (re)payment

◇ *dettes d'exploitation* trade debt

◇ *Écon* **dette extérieure** foreign debt, external debt

◇ *Compta* **dette flottante** floating debt

◇ *dette foncière* property charge

◇ *Compta* **dettes fournisseurs** accounts payable

◇ *dette d'honneur* debt of honour; *(hypothécaire)* mortgage debt

◇ *dette inexigible* unrecoverable debt

◇ *Compta* **dette inscrite** consolidated debt

◇ *Compta* **dette liquide** liquid debt

◇ *Compta* **dettes à long terme** long-term liabilities

◇ *Compta* **dettes à moyen terme** medium-term liabilities

◇ *Compta* **dette non consolidée** unfunded debt

◇ *Compta* **dettes passives** accounts payable, liabilities

◇ *dette privilégiée* preferred *or* privileged debt

◇ *Écon* **la dette publique** the National Debt

◇ *dette subordonnée* subordinated debt

◇ *dette véreuse* bad debt

Deutsche Mark *nm* Deutschmark

dévalorisation *nf* (a) *(action) (de la monnaie)* devaluation (b) *(résultat) (de la monnaie)* fall in value, depreciation

dévaloriser 1 *vt (monnaie)* to devalue; **dévaloriser une monnaie de 10%** to devalue a currency by 10%

  2 se dévaloriser *vpr (monnaie)* to depreciate

dévaluer 1 *vt (monnaie)* to devalue

  2 se dévaluer *vpr (monnaie)* to drop in value

devancement *nm (d'une échéance)* payment before the due date, prepayment

devancer *vt* **devancer une échéance** to settle an account early, to pay a bill before the due date

devis *nm* estimate, quotation; **établir un devis** to draw up an estimate *or* a quotation

devise *nf* currency

⋄ *devise contrôlée* managed currency

⋄ *devise convertible* convertible currency

⋄ *devise(s) étrangère(s)* foreign currency

⋄ *devise faible* soft *or* weak currency

⋄ *devise forte* hard *or* strong currency

⋄ *devise internationale* international currency

⋄ *devise non convertible* non-convertible currency

⋄ *devise soutenue* firm currency

devises-titres *nf* foreign security, exchange currency

devoir *vt* **devoir qch à qn** to owe sb sth; **reste à devoir** *(sur facture)* balance due

diagnostic financier *nm* financial healthcheck, diagnostic audit

différence *nf (entre deux prix)* difference; *Bourse (entre le cours offert et le cours demandé)* spread

différentiel *nm* differential

⋄ *différentiel de prix* price differential

⋄ *différentiel de taux* interest rate differential

digraphie *nf Compta* double-entry bookkeeping

diluer *vt (capital, actions)* to dilute; **diluer le bénéfice par action** to dilute equity; **diluer entièrement des actions** to fully dilute shares

dilution *nf (du capital, des actions)* dilution

⋄ *dilution du bénéfice par action* dilution of equity

diminution *nf* reduction, decrease (**de** in); **faire une diminution sur un compte** to allow a rebate on an account

directeur, -trice 1 *adj (équipe, instances)* management, executive; *(force)* directing, managing

  2 *nm,f (qui fait partie du conseil d'administration)* director; *(d'un magasin, d'un service)* manager

⋄ *directeur administratif et financier* administrative and financial manager

⋄ *directeur d'agence* branch manager

⋄ *directeur de banque* bank manager

⋄ *directeur du crédit* credit manager

⋄ *directeur financier* financial director *or* manager

⋄ *directeur de succursale* branch manager

direction *nf* (a) *(d'une entreprise, d'un magasin, d'un service)* management; **la direction** *(bureau)* the director's office; *(locaux)* head office; **avoir la direction d'une entreprise** to manage a company

  (b) *(service)* department

◇ *direction des crédits* credit management

◇ *direction par exceptions* management by exception

◇ *direction financière (gestion)* financial management; *(service)* finance department

◇ *Direction générale des Impôts* $Br \simeq$ Inland Revenue, $Am \simeq$ Internal Revenue

◇ *direction par objectifs* management by objectives

◇ *direction du trésor* finance department

dirigé, -e *adj (monnaie)* managed, controlled; *(économie)* controlled, planned

discount *nm* discount; **un discount de 20%** a 20% discount

discounter¹ *nm* discounter

discounter² *vt & vi* to sell at a discount

disponibilité *nf* disponibilités available funds, liquid assets

◇ *disponibilités en caisse* cash in hand

◇ *disponibilités monétaires* money supply

disponible 1 *adj (fonds, capital, solde)* available

  2 *nm* **le disponible** available assets, liquid assets

dissimulation d'actif *nf Jur* (fraudulent) concealment of assets

distribuer *vt (actions)* to allot, allocate; *(bénéfices)* to distribute; *(dividendes)* to pay

distributeur *nm*

◇ *distributeur automatique de billets* cash dispenser *or* point, automated teller machine

◇ *distributeur de monnaie* change machine

distribution *nf* distribution

◇ *Bourse distribution d'actions* share allotment *or* allocation

divers, -e 1 *adj* sundry, miscellaneous

  2 *nmpl* sundries

diversification *nf* diversification

◇ *Bourse diversification de portefeuille* portfolio diversification

dividende *nm* dividend; **toucher un dividende** to draw a dividend; **déclarer** *ou* **annoncer un dividende** to declare *or* announce a dividend; **avec dividende** cum div(idend), *Am* dividend on; **sans dividende** ex div(idend), *Am* dividend off

◇ *dividendes accrus* accrued dividends

◇ *dividende d'action, dividende en actions* share *or* stock dividend, dividend on shares

◇ *dividende par action* dividend per share

◇ *dividende anticipé* advance dividend

◇ *dividende brut* gross dividend

◇ *dividende cumulatif* cumulative dividend

◇ *dividende définitif* final dividend

◇ *dividende en espèces* cash dividend

◇ *dividende final* final dividend

◇ *dividende intérimaire, dividende par intérim* interim dividend

◇ *dividende majoré* grossed-up dividend

◇ *dividende net* net dividend

◇ *dividende prioritaire* preference dividend

◇ *dividende prioritaire cumulatif* preference cumulative dividend

◇ *dividende de priorité, dividende privilégié* preference dividend

diviser *vt Bourse (actions)* to split

division *nf Bourse (des actions)* splitting

document *nm* document; **rédiger un document** to draw up a document

◇ *documents contre acceptation* documents against acceptance

◇ *documents contre paiement* documents against payment

◇ *Compta document de synthèse* financial statement

doit *nm* debit, liability; *(d'un compte)* debit side; **doit et avoir** debits and credits; *(personnes)* debtors and creditors

dollar *nm* dollar; **un billet de cinq dollars** a five-dollar *Br* note *or Am* bill

◇ *dollar américain* US dollar, American dollar

domicile fiscal *nm* tax domicile

domiciliataire *nmf* paying agent

domiciliation *nf* domiciliation

◇ *domiciliation bancaire* payment *(by banker's order)*

domicilié, -e *adj (salaire)* paid directly into one's bank account

dommages-intérêts, dommages et intérêts *nmpl* damages; **obtenir des dommages-intérêts** *or* **dommages et intérêts** to be awarded damages

donation *nf Jur* donation

◇ *donation inter vivos* gift inter vivos

◇ *donations parents-enfants* donations from parents to children

donneur, -euse *nm,f*

◇ *donneur d'aval* guarantor *or* backer of bill

◇ *donneur de caution* guarantor

◇ *donneur d'ordre* principal

dormant, -e *adj (compte)* dormant; *(marché, capital)* unproductive, lying idle

dos *nm (d'un effet, d'un chèque)* back; **signer au dos d'un chèque** to endorse a cheque, to sign the back of a cheque; **voir au dos** see over *or* overleaf

dossier *nm* file, record

◇ *dossier crédit* credit file

◇ *Bourse dossier de demande d'introduction en Bourse* listing agreement

◇ *Banque dossier de demande de prêt* loan application form

dotation *nf Compta* provision

◇ *dotation aux amortissements* depreciation provision, allowance for depreciation

◇ *dotation en capital* capital contribution

◇ *dotation au compte de provisions* appropriation to the reserve

◇ *dotation aux provisions* charge to provisions

❝

En 1992, sur 65 milliards de **dotations aux provisions**, 20 étaient dus aux défaillances d'entreprises.

❞

doter *vt (hôpital, collège)* to endow

double *adj* double; **à double revenu** *(foyer, ménage)* two-income

◇ *double affichage (des prix)* dual pricing

◇ *Compta* **double circulation** *(de monnaies)* dual circulation

◇ *Compta* **double emploi** duplication (of entry)

◇ *double imposition* double taxation

◇ *Bourse* **double marché des changes** dual exchange market

◇ *Bourse* **double option** double option, put and call option

❝

Depuis le premier janvier, il est possible de payer en euros chez les commerçants qui l'acceptent. Le paiement peut s'effectuer avec une carte bancaire ou un chèque spécifique, en attendant l'arrivée des pièces et des billets en 2002. D'ici là, les commerçants ont tout intérêt à généraliser le **double affichage** des prix dans leur magasin, en francs et en euros, afin de familiariser leur clientèle avec la monnaie commune ... A la fin juin, 87% des hypermarchés et 70% des supermarchés présentaient leurs prix en francs et en euros.

❞

DPE *nf (abrév* **direction par exceptions**) management by exception

DPO *nf (abrév* **direction par objectifs**) MBO

drachme *nf* drachma

drainer *vt (capital, ressources)* to tap

dresser *vt (plan, contrat, bilan, liste)* to prepare, to draw up; *(facture)* to make out

droit *nm* (a) *(prérogative)* right (b) *(en argent)* fee; *(imposition)* duty; *(taxe)* tax

◇ *Bourse* **droit d'attribution** allotment right

◇ *droit de courtage* brokerage (fee)

◇ *Compta* **droit fixe** fixed rate of duty

◇ *Banque* **droits de garde** custody account charges

◇ *droits de mutation* capital transfer tax

◇ *Bourse* **droit de préemption** preemption right

◇ *Bourse* **droit de souscription** *(d'actions)* subscription right

◇ *droits de succession* inheritance tax, death duties

◇ *droit de timbre* stamp duty

◇ *droits de tirage* drawing rights

◇ *droits de tirage spéciaux* special drawing rights

◇ *Bourse* **droits de transfert** transfer duty

◇ *Bourse* **droits de vote** *(des actionnaires)* voting rights

❝

Les **droits de mutation** sur les immeubles d'habitation (parfois appelés frais de notaire) sont allégés de 20%.

❞

dû, due 1 *adj (somme)* due, owing

2 *nm* due; **payer son dû** to pay the amount owed

durée *nf (de crédit)* term; *(d'un prêt)* life

◇ *Compta* **durée d'amortissement** depreciation period

écart nm (entre deux chiffres) difference; *Compta* spread, variance; *Bourse* spread; **il y a un écart de cent francs entre les deux comptes** there is a discrepancy of a hundred francs between the two accounts; *Bourse* **l'écart entre le prix d'achat et le prix de vente** the spread between bid and asked prices

◇ *Bourse* **écart d'acquisition** goodwill

◇ **écart budgétaire** budgetary variance

◇ **écart de caisse** cash shortage

◇ **écarts de conversion** exchange adjustments

◇ *Bourse* **écarts de cours** price spreads

◇ **écart des coûts** cost variance

◇ **écart horizontal** horizontal spread;

◇ **écart net** net change *or* variance

◇ *Bourse* **écart de prime** option spread

◇ **écart de prix** price differential

◇ **écart salarial** wage differential

échange nm (a) *Banque, Bourse* swap

(b) *(commerce)* trade; **les échanges entre la France et l'Allemagne** trade between France and Germany

◇ *Bourse* **échange d'actions** share swap

◇ **échange cambiste** treasury swap

◇ **échanges commerciaux** trade

◇ **échange de créances** debt swap

◇ **échange de créances contre actifs** debt equity swap

◇ **échange de dette** debt swap

◇ **échange de devises** currency swap

◇ *Ordinat* **Échange Électronique de Données** Electronic Data Interchange

◇ **échange financier** swap

◇ **échanges industriels** industrial trade

◇ **échange d'intérêts et de monnaies** currency interest-rate swap

◇ **échanges internationaux** international trade

◇ **échange de taux d'intérêt** interest rate swap

◇ *Bourse* **échange à terme** forward swap

◇ **échanges en valeurs** turnover *(on a securities trading account)*

échanger 1 *vt* to exchange

2 s'échanger *vpr Bourse* to trade; **ces titres s'échangent à**

70 francs these securities are trading at 70 francs

échappatoire *nf* loophole
◊ *échappatoire comptabilité* accounting loophole
◊ *échappatoire fiscale* tax loophole

échauffement *nm (de l'économie)* overheating

échéance *nf (de dû)* maturity date, due date; *(de terme)* expiry date; **avant échéance** *(paiement, règlement)* before the due date; **à trois mois d'échéance** at three months' date; **emprunter à longue/à courte échéance** to borrow long/short; **prêter à longue/à courte échéance** to lend long/short; **venir à échéance** to fall due, to mature; **faire face à ses échéances** to meet one's financial commitments; **avoir de lourdes échéances** to have heavy financial commitments; **l'intérêt n'a pas été payé à l'échéance** the interest is overdue
◊ *échéance commune* equation of payment
◊ *Banque, Bourse échéance à court terme* short-term maturity
◊ *Banque échéance emprunt* loan maturity
◊ *Compta échéances de fin de mois* end-of-month payments
◊ *échéance fixe* fixed maturity
◊ *Banque, Bourse échéance à long terme* long-term maturity
◊ *échéance moyenne* average due date
◊ *Banque, Bourse échéance à moyen terme* medium-term maturity

◊ *Bourse échéance proche* near month
◊ *échéance à vue* sight bill or maturity

échéancier *nm* bill book; *Compta* due date file
◊ *échéancier de paiement* payment schedule

échelle *nf* scale
◊ *échelle mobile (des prix, des salaires)* sliding scale
◊ *échelle des salaires* salary scale
◊ *échelle des traitements* salary scale

échelonner *vt (paiements)* to spread (out); **les versements sont échelonnés sur dix ans** the instalments are spread (out) over ten years

échoir *vi (dette)* to fall due; *(investissement)* to mature; **le terme échoit le 20 de ce mois** the date for payment is the 20th of this month; **le délai est échu** the deadline has expired

échu, -e *adj (paiement)* due; *(intérêts)* outstanding

économie *nf* (a) *(système)* economy; **l'économie française** the French economy (b) **économies** *(épargne)* savings; **faire des économies** to save money
◊ *économie de marché* market economy

économiser 1 *vt (argent)* to economize, to save; **économiser de l'argent** to save money
2 *vi* to economize; **économiser sur qch** to economize on sth

écoulé, -e *adj* (a) *(du mois dernier)* of last month; **payable fin écoulé** due at the end of last month (**b**) *(passé)* **l'exercice écoulé** the last financial year

écrire *vt* to write; *Compta* **écrire la comptabilité** to write up the books

écriture *nf* *Compta* (**a**) *(opération)* entry, item; **passer une écriture** to make an entry (**b**) **écritures** *(comptes)* accounts; **tenir les écritures** to keep the accounts *or* the books; **arrêter les écritures** to close the accounts; **passer les écritures** to post (up) the books

◊ *écriture d'achats* purchase entry

◊ *écriture d'ajustement* corrected entry

◊ *écriture de clôture* closing entry

◊ *écriture complémentaire* supplementary entry

◊ *écriture comptable* accounting *or* journal entry

◊ *écriture conforme* corresponding entry

◊ *écriture d'inventaire* closing entry

◊ *écriture d'ouverture* opening entry

◊ *écritures en partie double* double-entry bookkeeping

◊ *écritures en partie simple* single-entry bookkeeping

◊ *écriture rectificative* corrected entry

◊ *écriture de régularisation* adjusting entry

◊ *écriture regroupement* consolidated entry

◊ *écriture de virement* transfer entry

ÉCU, écu *nm* *UE* *(abrév* **European currency unit)** ECU, ecu

EED *nm* *Ordinat* *(abrv* **Échange Électronique de Données)** EDI

effectif, -ive **1** *adj* *(coût, monnaie, taux)* effective; *(valeur, revenu)* real; *(circulation)* active; *(rendement)* actual
2 *nm*

◊ *effectif budgétaire* budgetary strength, *Am* authorized strength

effet *nm* (**a**) *(traite)* bill (**b**) *(résultat, conséquence)* effect

◊ *effet accepté* accepted bill

◊ *effet balançoire* see-saw effect

◊ *effet bancable* eligible list

◊ *effet bancaire* bill, draft

◊ *effet de cavalerie* kite

◊ *effet de commerce* bill of exchange

◊ *effet de complaisance* accommodation bill

◊ *effet à courte échéance* short, short-dated bill

◊ *effet à date fixe* fixed-term bill

◊ *effet en devise(s)* bill in foreign currency

◊ *effet de dilution* dilutive effect

◊ *effet domicilié* domiciled bill

◊ *effet à l'encaissement* bill for collection

◊ *Compta* *effets à encaisser* accounts receivable

◊ *effet endossé* endorsed bill

◊ *effet escomptable* eligible bill

◊ *effet escompté* discounted bill

◊ *effet de levier* gearing, leverage

◊ *effet de levier financier* financial gearing

◊ *effet libre* clean bill

⬦ *effet à longue échéance* long, long-dated bill

⬦ *Bourse* **effets nominatifs** registered stock

⬦ *effet à ordre* promissory note

⬦ *effet payable à vue* sight bill

⬦ *Compta* **effets à payer** bills payable

⬦ *effet au porteur* bearer bill, bill made out to bearer

⬦ *Bourse* **effets publics** government stock or securities

⬦ *Compta* **effets à recevoir** bills receivable

⬦ *effet en souffrance* overdue bill

⬦ *effet à taux flottant* floating rate note, FRN

⬦ *effet à terme* period or term bill

⬦ *effet à usance* usance bill

⬦ *effet à vue* sight bill or draft

effondrer s'effondrer *vpr (prix, marchés, cours, bénéfices)* to slump; *(monnaie)* to collapse; **le marché s'est effondré** the bottom has fallen out of the market

effort financier *nm* financial outlay

effritement *nm Bourse (des cours)* crumbling

effriter s'effriter *vpr Bourse (cours)* to crumble

électronique *adj (argent)* electronic

élément *nm Compta (d'un compte)* item

élevé, -e *adj (prix, taux)* high; **les dépenses sont élevées** expenditure is running high

élever 1 *vt (prix, taux)* to raise, to put up

2 s'élever *vpr* **s'élever à** to come to, to amount to; **la facture** s'élève à **mille francs** the bill comes to or amounts to a thousand francs

émetteur, -trice 1 *adj (banque, organisme)* issuing

2 *nm,f (de billets, d'actions, d'une carte)* issuer; *(d'un chèque)* drawer

émettre *vt (chèque, actions, billets de banque, timbres)* to issue; *(emprunt)* to float; *(lettre de crédit)* to open

❝

France Télécom va acquérir 2% du capital de Deutsche Telekom, qui achètera 2% des actions du groupe français. Pour financer cette opération, France Telecom **émettra** de nouvelles actions en Bourse, représentant 5% de son capital.

❞

émission *nf (d'un chèque, d'actions, de billets de banque)* issue; *(d'un emprunt)* flotation; *(d'une lettre de crédit)* opening

⬦ *Bourse* **émission d'actions** share issue

⬦ *Bourse* **émission d'actions gratuites** scrip issue

⬦ *Bourse* **émission boursière** share issue

⬦ *Bourse* **émission de conversion** conversion issue

⬦ *Banque* **émission fiduciaire** fiduciary or note issue

⬦ *Bourse* **émission obligataire, émission d'obligations** bond issue

⬦ *Bourse* **émission par séries** block issues

⬦ *Bourse* **émission des valeurs du Trésor** tap issue

émoluments *nmpl* *(d'un employé)* salary, pay; **percevoir des émoluments** to receive payment

employé, -e *nm,f* employee

◊ **employé de banque** bank clerk

◊ **employé aux écritures** accounts clerk

employer *vt* (**a**) *(faire travailler) (personne)* to employ (**b**) *Compta* to enter; **employer qch en recette** to enter sth in the receipts

emprunt *nm* (**a**) *(somme)* loan; **faire un emprunt** *(auprès d'une banque)* to take out a loan; **emprunt à 8%** loan at 8%; **procéder à un nouvel emprunt** to make a new loan issue; **amortir un emprunt** to redeem a loan; **contracter un emprunt** to raise a loan; **couvrir un emprunt** to cover a loan; **émettre un emprunt** to float a loan; **placer un emprunt** to place a loan; **rembourser un emprunt** to repay a loan; **souscrire un emprunt** to subscribe a loan

(**b**) *(action)* borrowing

◊ **emprunt consolidé** consolidated loan

◊ **emprunt de conversion** conversion loan

◊ **emprunt à court terme** short-term loan

◊ **emprunt à découvert** unsecured loan

◊ **emprunt en devises** currency loan

◊ **emprunt d'État** government loan

◊ *Bourse* **emprunt à fenêtre** put bond

◊ **emprunt forcé** forced loan

◊ **emprunt sur gage** loan against security

◊ **emprunt garanti** secured loan

◊ **emprunt indexé** indexed loan

◊ **emprunt à long terme** long-term loan

◊ **emprunt à lots** lottery loan

◊ *Bourse* **emprunt obligataire** bond issue, loan stock; *(titre)* debenture bond

◊ *Bourse* **emprunt obligataire convertible** convertible loan stock

◊ **emprunt or** gold loan

◊ **emprunt perpétuel** perpetual loan

◊ **emprunt personnel** personal loan

◊ **emprunt public** public loan

◊ **emprunt public d'État** government loan

◊ **emprunt remboursable sur demande** call loan, loan repayable on demand

◊ **emprunt de remboursement** refunding loan

◊ **emprunt à risques** nonaccruing loan

◊ **emprunts à taux fixe** fixed-rate borrowing

◊ **emprunt à terme (fixe)** term loan

◊ *Bourse* **emprunt sur titres** loan on securities *or* stock

emprunter *vt* to borrow; **emprunter qch à qn** to borrow sth from sb; **la société a dû emprunter pour s'acquitter de ses dettes** the company had to borrow to pay off its debts; **emprunter sur hypothèque** to borrow on mortgage; **emprunter sur titres** to borrow on securities; **emprunter à long/à court terme** to borrow long/short; **emprunter à intérêt** to borrow at interest

emprunteur, -euse 1 *adj*
borrowing
  2 *nm,f* borrower

encadrement *nm*
◇ *encadrement du crédit* credit
  control *or* restrictions
◇ *encadrement des prix* price
  control

encadrer *vt (prix, loyers, crédit)*
to control

encaissable *adj (chèque)* cashable; *(argent, traite)* collectable, receivable; **ce chèque est
encaissable à la banque** this
cheque can be cashed at the
bank

encaisse *nf* cash (in hand), cash
balance; *(d'un magasin)* money
in the till
◇ *encaisse disponible* cash in
  hand
◇ *encaisse métallique, encaisse or et argent* gold and
  silver reserves, bullion

encaissement *nm (d'un
chèque)* cashing; *(d'argent,
d'une traite)* collection, receipt
◇ *encaissements et décaissements* cash inflows and outflows

encaisser *vt (chèque)* to cash;
(argent, traite) to collect, to receive

encaisseur, -euse 1 *adj*
(banque, établissement) collecting
  2 *nm (d'un chèque)* payee; *(de
l'argent, d'une traite)* collector,
receiver

enchère *nf* bid; **les enchères**
bidding

enchérisseur, -euse *nm,f* bidder

encours, en-cours *nm Banque*
loans outstanding; **l'encours de
la dette** the outstanding debt
◇ *encours de crédit* outstanding credits
◇ *Banque encours débiteur
  autorisé* authorized overdraft
  facility
◇ *Compta encours de production de biens* work-in-
  progress

> **"**
>
> ... on peut retenir que la reprise
> économique est patente en
> Europe: ... et le problème d'un
> retour de l'inflation ne se pose
> qu'à la marge. Autrement dit, le
> placement en actions est natur-
> ellement intéressant par rapport
> aux autres produits alternatifs.
> En témoigne le dégonflement
> de l'**encours** des sicav moné-
> taires.
>
> **"**

endetté, -e *adj (pays, personne,
entreprise)* in debt

endettement *nm* (**a**) *(action)*
running *or* getting into debt;
(état) debt (**b**) *Compta* indebt-
edness, gearing
◇ *endettement des consommateurs* consumer debt
◇ *Écon endettement extérieur*
  foreign debt
◇ *Écon endettement intérieur*
  internal debt

endetter 1 *vt* **endetter qn** to get
sb into debt
  2 **s'endetter** *vpr* to get into debt

endiguement *nm Bourse*
hedging

endos *nm (sur effet, chèque)* endorsement

◇ **endos en blanc** blank endorsement

endossataire *nmf* endorsee

endossement *nm (sur effet, chèque)* endorsement

◇ **endossement en blanc** blank endorsement

endosseur, -euse *nm,f* endorser

engagement *nm* **(a)** *(de capital, d'investissements)* locking up, tying up; *(de dépenses, de frais)* incurring
(b) *(mise en gage) (au mont-de-piété)* pawning; *(auprès de créanciers)* pledging; *(d'une propriété)* mortgaging

◇ **engagement bancaire** (bank) commitment

◇ **engagement de dépenses** commitment of funds

◇ **engagement hors bilan** contingent liabilities

engager *vt* **(a)** *(capital, investissements)* to lock up, to tie up; *(dépenses, frais)* to incur
(b) *(mettre en gage) (au mont-de-piété)* to pawn; *(auprès de créanciers)* to pledge; *(propriété)* to mortgage

enregistrement comptable *nm Compta* accounting entry

enregistrer *vt (bénéfice)* to show; *Compta* **enregistrer une perte de...** to show a loss of...; *Bourse* **enregistrer une hausse/baisse** to rise/fall

entité *nf Compta* item

entrée *nf Compta (dans un livre de comptes)* entry

entreprise *nf (firme)* company, business; **les grandes entreprises** big business

◇ **entreprise d'investissement** investment company

◇ **entreprise marginale** = company with only a marginal profit

◇ **entreprise en participation** joint venture

◇ **entreprise publique** state-owned enterprise *or* company, public corporation

entretenir *vt Compta (comptes)* to keep in order

enveloppe *nf (somme)* sum; *(budget)* budget

◇ **enveloppe budgétaire** budget (allocation)

◇ **enveloppe fiscale** = tax-sheltered savings scheme

◇ **enveloppe salariale** wages bill

> **“**
>
> Paris négocie avec Ankara la vente de six navires chasseurs de mines pour une **enveloppe** de l'ordre de 4 milliards de francs.
>
> **”**

> **“**
>
> Première précaution à prendre: choisir l'**enveloppe fiscale** la plus adaptée à vos besoins (compte-titres ordinaire, Plan d'épargne en actions ou assurance vie).
>
> **”**

envoi *nm* sending

◇ **envoi de fonds** remittance (of funds); **faire un envoi de fonds à qn** to send *or* remit funds to sb

envolée *nf (hausse rapide)* rapid rise; **l'envolée du dollar** the rapid rise in the dollar

envoler s'envoler *vpr (cours, prix)* to soar

envoyer *vt* to send; *(fonds, mandat)* to send, to remit

EONIA *nm* *(abrév* **Euro OverNight Index Average)** EONIA

épargnant, -e *nm,f* saver, investor

épargne *nf (action)* saving; *(sommes)* savings; *(épargnants)* savers, investors
◊ *épargne complément de retraite* pension fund savings
◊ *épargne des entreprises* company reserves
◊ *épargne institutionnelle* institutional savings
◊ *épargne investie* investments
◊ *épargne liquide* on-hand savings
◊ *épargne mobilière* fixed savings
◊ *épargne négative* negative saving
◊ *l'épargne privée* private investors
◊ *l'épargne productive* reinvested savings

"
La nécessité de leur trouver des financements, bloque les taux d'intérêt à long terme à un niveau élevé et détourne l'**épargne privée** au détriment des investissements productifs.
"

épargne-logement *nm*
◊ *plan d'épargne-logement* home savings plan
◊ *prêt d'épargne-logement* home loan

épargner *vt* to save

épargne-retraite *nf* pension fund, retirement fund

éponger *vt (déficit)* to mop up, to absorb; **éponger le pouvoir d'achat excédentaire** to mop up excess purchasing power

équation *nf Compta* equation
◊ *équation de bénéfice* profit equation
◊ *équation de coût* cost equation

équilibration *nf (d'un budget)* balancing

équilibre *nm* en équilibre *(budget)* balanced
◊ *équilibre budgétaire* balanced budget

équilibrer *vt (budget)* to balance

érosion monétaire *nf* depreciation of money

escalade *nf (des prix, des taux d'intérêt)* escalation

escomptable *adj Compta* discountable

escompte *nm* **(a)** *(remise)* discount; **prendre à l'escompte un effet de commerce** to discount a bill of exchange; **présenter une traite à l'escompte** to have a bill discounted
(b) *Bourse (de valeurs)* call for delivery before settlement
◊ *escompte de banque* bank discount
◊ *escompte de caisse* cash discount
◊ *escompte de créances* invoice discounting
◊ *escompte en dedans* true discount
◊ *escompte en dehors* bank discount

◇ *escompte officiel* *Br* bank discount rate, *Am* prime rate
◇ *escompte de règlement* discount for early payment
◇ *escompte de traites* invoice discounting

escompter *vt* (a) *(traite)* to discount (b) *Bourse (valeurs)* to call for delivery of before settlement

escompteur *nm* discount broker

escudo *nm* escudo

espèces *nfpl (argent)* cash; **payer en espèces** to pay in cash
◇ *Compta* **espèces en caisse** cash in hand

estimatif, -ive *adj (valeur, état)* estimated

estimation *nf (d'un prix)* estimation
◇ *Compta* **estimation des frais** estimate of costs

établir *vt (budget)* to draw up, to establish; *(compte, contrat)* to draw up; *(prix)* to fix

établissement *nm* (a) *(d'un budget)* drawing up, establishing; *(d'un compte)* drawing up; *(des prix)* fixing
(b) *(institution)* establishment, institution
◇ *établissement bancaire* bank, banking institution
◇ *établissement de crédit* credit institution
◇ *Compta* **établissement déclarant** company making the return
◇ *établissement dépositaire* = financial institution holding securities on trust
◇ *établissement financier* financial institution

◇ *établissement payeur* paying bank

étalement *nm (de paiements)* spreading (out)

étaler *vt (paiements)* to spread (out)

étalon *nm (de poids et mesures)* standard
◇ *étalon de change-or* gold exchange standard
◇ *étalon devise* currency standard
◇ *étalon monétaire* monetary standard

étalonnage, étalonnement *nm* standardization

étalonner *vt* to standardize

étalon-or *nm* gold standard
◇ *étalon-or lingot* gold bullion standard

état *nm* (a) *(rapport)* form; *(des paiements)* schedule, list
(b) *(condition)* state, condition
◇ *état appréciatif* evaluation, estimation
◇ *Compta* **état de caisse** cash statement
◇ *Compta* **états comptables** accounting records
◇ *états comptables et commerciaux* internal company records
◇ *état de compte* bank statement, statement of account; *Compta* statement of account
◇ *état détaillé (d'un compte)* breakdown
◇ *état financier (rapport)* financial statement; *(situation)* financial standing *or* situation
◇ *Compta* **état de flux de trésorerie** cash flow statement, source and application of funds statement

◇ *état de fortune* financial standing *or* situation

◇ *état néant* nil return

◇ *état de rapprochement* reconciliation statement

◇ *état récapitulatif* final assessment, adjustment account

◇ *état TVA* VAT statement

étude de coût-efficacité *nf* cost-volume-profit analysis

EURIBOR *nm* (*abrév* **Euro Interbank Offered Rate**) EURIBOR

EURL *nf* (*abrév* **entreprise unipersonnelle à responsabilité limitée**) trader with limited liability

euro *nm* UE (*monnaie*) euro; **en euros** in euro

euro-certificat *nm* *Bourse* euro-certificate

eurochèque *nm* Eurocheque

eurodevise *nf* euro-currency

eurodollar *nm* eurodollar

Eurolande *nf* UE Euroland

euromarché *nm* euromarket

euromonnaie *nf* euro-currency

euro-obligation *nf* eurobond

Euro Stoxx *nm* *Bourse* Euro Stoxx; **l'Euro Stoxx 50** the Euro Stoxx 50 index

évaluation *nf* evaluation

◇ *évaluation du coût* cost assessment, costing

◇ *évaluation financière* financial appraisal

◇ *évaluation des risques* risk assessment

évaluer *vt* to evaluate; **évaluer les coûts de qch** to cost sth

évasion *nf* (*des capitaux*) flight

◇ *évasion fiscale* tax avoidance

> **❝**
> Le gouvernement a également décidé de créer, à titre provisoire, une taxe minimale, qui sous la forme d'un forfait imposé à tous les revenus non salariés, vise à contrer une **évasion fiscale** énorme.
> **❞**

examen financier *nm* financial review

examiner *vt* to examine; (*comptes*) to go through, to inspect

excédent *nm* (*d'un budget, d'une balance*) surplus; **dégager un excédent** to show a surplus

◇ *excédent budgétaire* budget surplus

◇ *Compta* **excédent de caisse** cash overs

◇ *excédents et déficits* overs and shorts

◇ *excédent de dépenses* deficit; **nous avons un excédent de dépenses** we are overspending

◇ *Compta* **excédent d'exploitation** operating profit

excédentaire *adj* (*budget*) surplus

excès *nm* excess; **excès des dépenses sur les recettes** excess of expenditure over revenue

ex-coupon *adv* *Bourse* ex coupon

ex-dividende *adv* *Bourse* ex dividend

ex-droit *adv Bourse* ex rights

exempt, -e *adj* **exempt d'impôts** tax- exempt

exemption *nf* exemption (**de** from)
◇ *exemption fiscale, exemption d'impôt* tax exemption

exercer *vt Bourse (option)* to exercise; **exercer par anticipation** to exercise in advance

exercice *nm Compta Br* financial year, *Am* fiscal year; **l'exercice de ce mois** this month's trading
◇ *exercice budgétaire* budgetary year
◇ *exercice comptable* accounting year
◇ *exercice en cours* current *Br* financial or *Am* fiscal year
◇ *exercice financier Br* financial or *Am* fiscal year
◇ *exercice fiscal* tax year

❝
Pour l'**exercice budgétaire** clos en mars dernier, la compagnie a enregistré un bénéfice net de 16,3 milliards de yens.
❞

❝
Sur les deux derniers **exercices fiscaux**, les pertes nettes cumulées du fabricant des Macintosh se sont élevées à 1,8 milliards de dollars.
❞

exigibilité *nf* **exigibilités** current liabilities; **exigibilité immédiate** immediately due
◇ *exigibilité de taxe* tax liability

exigible *adj (paiement)* due; *(dette, impôt)* due for payment, payable; **exigible à vue** payable at sight

existant *nm Compta* **existant en caisse** cash in hand; **l'existant en magasin, les existants** stock (in hand)

existence *nf Compta*
◇ *existences en caisse* cash in hand

exonération fiscale *nf* tax exemption

exonérer *vt (personne, entreprise)* to exempt (**de** from); **exonérer qn de l'impôt sur le revenu** to exempt sb from income tax

expansion monétaire *nf* currency expansion

expatriation *nf (d'argent, de capitaux)* movement abroad

expatrier *vt (argent, capitaux)* to invest abroad

expert-comptable *nm Br* ≃ chartered accountant, *Am* ≃ certified public accountant

exposition aux risques *nf* exposure

ex-répartition *adv* ex allotment

extinction *nf Compta (d'une dette)* discharge

extrabudgétaire *adj* extrabudgetary

extra-comptable *adj Compta (ajustement)* off-balance sheet

extrait *nm (d'un titre, d'un bilan)* abstract
◇ *extrait de compte Compta* statement of account; *Banque* bank statement

facilité *nf (possibilité)* facility
◊ *Banque* **facilités de caisse** overdraft facilities
◊ **facilités de crédit** credit facilities
◊ **facilité d'endettement** borrowing capacity
◊ **facilités de paiement** payment facilities, easy terms

factage *nm (livraison)* carriage and delivery, transport; **payer le factage** to pay the carriage

facteur *nm (élément)* factor
◊ **facteur coût** cost factor

facturation *nf Compta* invoicing, billing
◊ **facturation détaillée** itemized invoicing *or* billing

facture *nf* invoice, bill; **faire** *ou* **dresser** *ou* **établir une facture** to make out an invoice; **payer** *ou* **régler une facture** to settle an invoice, to pay a bill
◊ *Compta* **facture d'achat** purchase invoice
◊ **facture détaillée** itemized bill
◊ **facture originale** invoice of origin
◊ *Compta* **facture de vente** sales invoice

facturer *vt (personne)* to invoice, to bill; *(produit, service)* to charge for; **facturer qch à qn** to invoice sb for sth, to bill sb for sth

facturette *nf* credit card sales voucher

faculté *nf (droit)* option, right; **louer un immeuble avec faculté d'achat** to rent a building with the option of purchase
◊ *Bourse* **faculté du double** call of more
◊ *Bourse* **faculté de rachat** repo *or* repurchase agreement

failli, -e 1 *adj (commerçant)* bankrupt
2 *nm* (adjudicated) bankrupt
◊ **failli concordataire** certified bankrupt
◊ **failli déchargé** discharged bankrupt
◊ **failli non déchargé** undischarged bankrupt
◊ **failli réhabilité** discharged bankrupt

faillite *nf* bankruptcy, insolvency; **être en (état de) faillite** to be bankrupt *or* insolvent; **faire faillite** to go bankrupt, to fail; **déclarer** *ou* **mettre qn en faillite, prononcer la faillite de qn** to declare sb bankrupt; **se mettre en faillite** to file a petition in bankruptcy
◊ **faillite frauduleuse** fraudulent bankruptcy

◊ *faillite simple* bankruptcy

faux, fausse *adj (chèque)* forged; *(billet, pièce)* dud; *(argent)* counterfeit; *(bilan)* frauduleut

◊ *Compta* **faux bilan** fraudulent balance sheet

◊ *Compta* **fausse écriture** false entry

◊ *Compta* **faux en écritures** forgery

◊ *fausse facture* false bill

◊ *faux frais* incidental expenses

FCP *nm (abrév* **fonds commun de placement)** investment trust, mutual fund

FCPE *nm (abrév* **fonds commun de placement d'entreprise)** company investment fund

FCPR *nm (abrév* **fonds commun de placement à risques)** VCT

FDR *nm (abrév* **fonds de roulement)** working capital

FECOM *nm (abrév* **Fonds européen de coopération monétaire)** EMCF

félin *nm Bourse* stripped bond

fermer **1** *vt (compte)* to close
  2 *vi Bourse (actions)* to close; **les actions ont fermé à 55 francs** shares closed at 55 francs

fermeture *nf (d'un compte)* closing

feuille *nf (imprimé)* form

◊ *Compta* **feuille d'avancement** flow sheet

◊ *feuille d'impôt* tax return

◊ *Compta* **feuille de liquidation** settlement note

◊ *Banque* **feuille de versement** paying-in slip

FF *nm (abrév* **franc français)** French Franc

fiche *nf (formulaire)* form; *(papier)* sheet, slip; **remplir une fiche** to fill in *or* fill out a form

◊ *fiche de compte* accounts card

◊ *fiche de facture* account card

◊ *Compta* **fiche d'imputation** data entry form

fictif, -ive *adj (compte)* dead

fiduciaire 1 *adj (prêt, devise)* fiduciary; **en dépôt fiduciaire** in escrow, in trust; **avoirs en monnaie fiduciaire** *(d'une banque)* cash holdings; **une circulation fiduciaire excessive entraîne l'inflation** too much paper money in circulation leads to inflation
  2 *nm* fiduciary, trustee

fiduciairement *adv Jur* in trust

fiducie *nf Jur* trust

filière *nf Bourse* **établir la filière** to trace the succession of previous shareholders

◊ *filière électronique* electronic transfer

fin *nf* **(a)** *(de contrat)* expiry, expiration; **fin courant** at the end of the current month; **fin prochain** at the end of next month
  (b) *Banque* **sauf bonne fin** under reserve

◊ *fin d'année* year end

◊ *fin d'exercice* year end

final, -e *adj (règlement, solde)* final

finance *nf* **(a)** *(domaine)* finance; **le monde de la finance** the financial world; **la haute finance** *(milieu)* high finance; *(personnes)* the top bankers **(b)** **finances** *(argent)* finances; **les finances de la compagnie vont**

mal the company's finances are in a bad state

◇ *finance d'entreprise* corporate finance

◇ *finances publiques* public funds

financement *nm* financing, funding; **le financement du projet sera assuré par la compagnie** the company will finance *or* fund the project

◇ *financement par emprunt, financement par l'endettement* debt financing

◇ *financement initial* start-up capital

◇ *financement à long terme* long-term financing

◇ *financement à taux fixe* fixed-rate financing

financement-relais *nm* bridge financing

financer *vt (projet)* to finance, to fund; *(personne)* to back; **l'opération a été entièrement financée par emprunt** the transaction was 100% financed through borrowing; **BP financera le projet à 50%** BP will put up half of the funding for the project

financier, -ère 1 *adj* financial; **solide au point de vue financier** financially sound

2 *nm,f* financier

◇ *financier d'entreprise* corporate finance manager

financièrement *adv* financially

fisc *nm Br* ≃ Inland Revenue, *Am* ≃ Internal Revenue; **les employés du fisc** tax officials; **frauder le fisc** to evade tax

fiscal, -e *adj* fiscal, tax; **dans un but fiscal** for tax purposes

fiscaliser *vt* to tax

fiscaliste *nmf* tax consultant

fiscalité *nf* tax system

◇ *fiscalité écologique* green taxation

◇ *fiscalité excessive* excessive taxation

◇ *fiscalité indirecte* indirect taxation

> **"**
>
> Derrière la volonté affichée de protéger l'environnement à travers une **fiscalité écologique**, les mesures sont maigres … l'idée de taxer les activités polluantes, nuisibles au développement durable, pour alléger en revanche les charges sociales qui pèsent sur l'emploi, restera encore l'an prochain assez théorique.
>
> **"**

fixage *nm Bourse* fixing

fixation *nf (des impôts, des dommages-intérêts)* assessment

fixer *vt (prix)* to fix; **fixer le cours du change** to peg the exchange rate

fixeur de prix *nm Bourse* price maker

fléchir *vi (marché, devises)* to weaken; *(prix, cours, demande)* to fall, to drop; **les prix des actions fléchissent** share prices are down

fléchissement *nm (du marché, des devises)* weakening; *(des prix, des cours, de la demande)* fall, drop

flottant, -e 1 *adj (dette,*

capitaux, taux de change, police d'assurance) floating
   2 *nm Bourse* float

flottement *nm (d'une monnaie)* floating, fluctuation

flotter *vi (prix)* to fluctuate; *(monnaie)* to float; **faire flotter la livre** to float the pound

"

La banque centrale russe dépensait un milliard de dollars par semaine, dans la dernière période, pour soutenir le rouble. L'équipe au pouvoir a donc décidé d'élargir la bande de fluctuation de la monnaie, qui pourra désormais **flotter** entre 6 et 9,5 roubles pour un dollar.

"

flouze *nm Fam* cash

fluctuation *nf (du marché, des cours)* fluctuation (**de** in)

fluctuer *vi (marché, cours)* to fluctuate

flux *nm (de fonds)* flow
◊ *flux financier, flux monétaire* flow of money, monetary flow
◊ *flux de trésorerie* cash flow

FMI *nm (abrév* **Fonds monétaire international)** IMF

fondé, -e de pouvoir *nm,f (directeur de banque)* manager with signing authority

fonder *vt (dette)* to fund

fonds 1 *nm* **(a)** *(organisme)* fund **(b)** *(capital)* fund, funds **(c)** *Bourse* stocks, securities
   2 *nmpl (ressources)* funds; **réunir des fonds** to raise funds; **je n'ai pas les fonds suffisants pour ouvrir un magasin** I don't have the (necessary) funds *or* capital

to open a shop; **rentrer dans ses fonds** to get one's money back; **être en fonds** to be in funds; **faire** *ou* **fournir les fonds de qch** to put up the funds for sth; **mettre des fonds dans qch** to invest money in sth
◊ *fonds d'amortissement* sinking fund
◊ *fonds de caisse* cash in hand
◊ *fonds de capital-risque maison* captive fund
◊ *fonds de commerce* goodwill
◊ *fonds (de commerce) à vendre* business for sale *(as a going concern)*
◊ *fonds commun de placement* investment fund, mutual fund
◊ *fonds commun de placement d'entreprise* company investment fund
◊ *fonds commun de placement à risques* venture capital trust
◊ *fonds communs* pool
◊ *Bourse fonds consolidés* consolidated stock *or* annuities, *Br* consols
◊ *fonds dédié* captive fund
◊ *fonds disponibles* liquid assets, available funds
◊ *fonds de dotation* endowment fund
◊ *fonds d'État* Government stocks
◊ *Fonds européen de coopération monétaire* European Monetary Cooperation Fund
◊ *fonds à faible frais d'entrée* low-load fund
◊ *fonds fédéraux* Federal funds
◊ *fonds de garantie (d'un emprunt)* guarantee fund
◊ *fonds géré* managed fund
◊ *Bourse fonds à gestion indicielle, fonds indiciel* index *or* tracker fund

◇ *fonds d'investissement* investment fund

◇ *fonds liquides* available funds

◇ *fonds monétaire* money market fund

◇ *Fonds monétaire international* International Monetary Fund

◇ *Fonds national de l'emploi* = French national employment fund

◇ *Fonds national de garantie des salaires* national guarantee fund for the payment of salaries

◇ *fonds off-shore* offshore fund

◇ *Can fonds de parité* equalization fund

◇ *fonds de pension(s)* pension fund

◇ *fonds perdus* annuity; **placer son argent à fonds perdus** to purchase an annuity

◇ *fonds de placement sur le marché monétaire* money market fund

◇ *fonds de prévoyance* contingency fund

◇ *fonds propres* shareholders' equity, equity (capital)

◇ *fonds publics* Government stocks

◇ *fonds de réserve* reserve fund

◇ *fonds de retraite maison* ou *d'entreprise* ou *de groupe* occupational pension scheme

◇ *fonds pour risques bancaires généraux* fund for general banking risks

◇ *fonds de roulement* working capital

◇ *fonds de roulement net* net working capital

◇ *fonds social* company funds

◇ *Fonds social européen* European Social Fund

◇ *fonds de stabilisation des changes* exchange equalization account

"

Jamais les pressions n'auront été si fortes pour que la France favorise l'émergence de **fonds de pensions**. A écouter les hommes politiques, certains ministres, les chefs d'entreprise (unanimes), les économistes, l'absence de **fonds de pension** serait un frein terrible à l'économie française ... les **fonds de pension** et tout ce qui favorise la propriété capitalistique (épargne salariale, stock-options, etc.) permettent l'adhésion définitive des travailleurs/électeurs aux règles du jeu du marché, qu'ils comprennent et qu'ils intègrent.

"

"

La première banque française pour le montant des **fonds propres**, qui se dispute également la première place avec le Crédit Lyonnais pour le montant total des actifs (1647 millions de francs en 1992) ressent de plein fouet, comme l'ensemble de la profession bancaire, la chute brutale des crédits.

"

forfait *nm (contrat)* fixed-rate contract; *(somme)* lump sum; **être au forfait** to be taxed on estimated income

forfaitaire *adj (prix)* inclusive, fixed; *(indemnités)* basic

formule nf (a) *(méthode)* option; **nous avons aussi une formule à 1 000 francs** we also have a 1,000 franc option

(b) *Admin (formulaire)* form; **remplir une formule** to fill in *or* out a form

◇ *formule de chèque Br* cheque form, *Am* blank check

◇ *formules de crédit* credit options

◇ *formule de demande de crédit* credit application form

◇ *formule d'effet de commerce* form for bill of exchange

◇ *formules de paiement* methods of payment

◇ *formules de remboursement* repayment options

fort, -e adj (a) *(important)* *(perte)* heavy; *(somme)* large; **les prix sont en forte hausse** prices are soaring (b) *(devise)* strong

fourchette nf *(écart)* bracket, range; **une fourchette de 10 à 20%** a 10 to 20% band; **une fourchette comprise entre 1000 et 1500 francs** prices ranging from 1,000 to 1,500 francs

◇ *Bourse* **fourchette de cotation** trading range

◇ *Bourse* **fourchette de cours de clôture** closing range

◇ *Bourse* **fourchette de cours d'ouverture** opening range

◇ *fourchette d'imposition* tax bracket

◇ *fourchette de prix* price bracket *or* range

◇ *fourchette de salaire* wage bracket

◇ *fourchette de taux* rate band

fournir 1 vt *(lettre de crédit)* to issue (**sur** on); *(traite, chèque)* to draw (**sur** on); **fournir qch en nantissement** to lodge sth as collateral

2 vi **fournir aux dépenses** to contribute to the expenses

fournisseur en capitaux nm funder, supplier of capital

> Et les hostilités sont loin d'être terminées. Les deux PDG semblent tout à fait disposés à dépenser des sommes faramineuses pour séduire leurs **fournisseurs en capitaux**. Bien plus que pour leurs clients.

foyer fiscal nm household *(as a tax unit)*

fraction nf fraction; **par 10 francs ou fraction de 10 francs** for each 10 francs or fraction thereof

◇ *Compta* **fraction imposable** part subject to tax

◇ *fraction d'intérêt* interest accrued

fractionnement nm dividing up; *(des paiements)* spreading (out); *Bourse (des actions)* splitting

fractionner vt to divide up; *(paiements)* to spread (out); *Bourse (actions)* to split

frais nmpl expenses, costs; **tous frais payés** all expenses paid; **tous frais déduits** all expenses deducted; **sans frais** *(sur une lettre de change)* no expenses; **couvrir ses frais, rentrer dans ses frais** to get one's money back, to recover one's expenses, to break even; **menus frais** petty *or* incidental expenses

◇ *frais d'abonnement* standing charges

◇ *frais accessoires* incidental costs or expenses

◇ *frais accumulés* accrued expenses

◇ *frais d'administration* administration or administrative costs

◇ *frais d'administration générale* Br general overheads, Am general overhead

◇ *frais d'amortissement* amortization or depreciation charges

◇ *frais bancaires, frais de banque* bank charges

◇ *frais de Bourse* transaction costs

◇ *Banque frais de constitution (de compte)* set-up fee

◇ *frais consulaires* consular fees

◇ *Bourse frais de courtage* brokerage, commission

◇ *frais dégressifs* decreasing costs

◇ *frais différés* deferred charges

◇ *frais directs* direct costs

◇ *frais divers* sundry charges or expenses, sundries

◇ *frais de dossier* administration fee

◇ *frais d'encaissement* collection charges or fees

◇ *frais d'entrée (d'une sicav)* front-end or front-load fees; Bourse commission on purchase of shares

◇ *frais d'établissement* start-up costs

◇ *frais d'exploitation* operating costs

◇ *frais extraordinaires* extraordinary expenses

◇ *frais financiers* interest charges, financial costs

◇ *frais fixes* fixed charges

◇ *frais de fonctionnement* operating costs

◇ *frais généraux* Br overheads, Am overhead

◇ *frais généraux et frais de gestion* general and administrative expenses

◇ *frais de gestion* administration or administrative costs

◇ *frais d'installation* initial expenses

◇ *frais de lancement* set-up or start-up costs

◇ *frais de liquidation* closing-down costs

◇ *frais de main-d'œuvre* labour costs

◇ *frais de premier établissement* initial expenditure

◇ *frais professionnels* business charges or expenses

◇ *frais de recouvrement* collection charges

◇ *frais de représentation* expense account, entertainment allowance

◇ *frais de sortie* exit charges, back-end charges

◇ *frais de tenue de compte* account charges; *(de compte bancaire)* bank charges

◇ *frais de transfert* transfer fee

◇ *frais de trésorerie* finance costs

◇ *frais variables* variable costs

"

C'est dans les pays où la réglementation est le plus avancée, où la loi sanctionne les écarts par des pénalités de retard, des **frais de recouvrement** et des dommages et intérêts à payer par le débiteur indélicat, que le marché est mieux régulé et les délais plus courts.

"

franc¹ *nm* franc; **pièce de cinq francs** five-franc coin
◇ *franc belge* Belgian franc
◇ *franc français* French franc
◇ *franc lourd* new franc
◇ *franc luxembourgeois* Luxembourg franc
◇ *franc or* gold franc
◇ *franc suisse* Swiss franc
◇ *franc symbolique* *(lors d'un rachat d'entreprise)* nominal sum
◇ *franc vert* green franc

franc², franche *adj* free
◇ *franc d'impôts* tax-exempt

fraude *nf* fraud; **fraude fiscale** tax fraud, tax evasion

FRBG *nm* (*abrév* **fonds pour risques bancaires généraux**) FGBR

fric *nm Fam* cash

front-office *nm Banque* front office

fructifier *vi* *(capital)* to yield a profit; **faire fructifier son argent** to make one's money yield a profit

> **"**
> Dans l'intervalle, la marchandise aura tourné 3 ou 4 fois, et les distributeurs auront largement eu le temps de faire **fructifier** leur argent.
> **"**

FS *nm* (*abrév* **franc suisse**) Swiss Franc

fuite des capitaux *nf* flight of capital

fusion *nf* *(de sociétés)* merger, amalgamation; **opérer une fusion** to merge
◇ *fusions et acquisitions* mergers and acquisitions

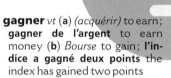

gagner *vt* (**a**) *(acquérir)* to earn; **gagner de l'argent** to earn money (**b**) *Bourse* to gain; **l'indice a gagné deux points** the index has gained two points

gain *nm* (**a**) *(profit)* gain, profit; **les gains et les pertes** the profits and the losses (**b**) *(rémunération)* gains, earnings
◊ *gains invisibles* invisible earnings
◊ *Compta gain latent* unrealized gain

garantie *nf* (**a**) *(d'une émission d'actions, d'un contrat)* underwriting; *(d'un emprunt)* backing, security
  (**b**) *(d'un paiement)* security, guarantee
◊ *garantie accessoire* collateral security
◊ *garantie bancaire* bank guarantee
◊ *garantie de bonne exécution, garantie de bonne fin* performance bond
◊ *garantie contractuelle* contractual guarantee
◊ *garantie conventionnelle* contractual cover
◊ *Bourse garantie de cours* hedging
◊ *garantie de crédit acheteur* buyer credit guarantee
◊ *garantie de crédit à l'expor-*

tation export credit guarantee
◊ *garantie d'exécution* contract bond
◊ *garantie hypothécaire* mortgage security
◊ *garantie offre* bid bond

garantir *vt* (**a**) *(dette)* to guarantee; **garantir le paiement d'une dette** to guarantee a debt (**b**) *(émission d'actions, contrat)* to underwrite; *(emprunt)* to back, to secure

GATT *nm Écon (abrév* **General Agreement on Tariffs and Trade**) GATT

gel *nm (blocage)* freeze
◊ *gel des crédits* credit freeze
◊ *gel des prix* price freeze
◊ *gel des salaires* wage freeze

gelé, -e *adj (bloqué) (compte, gelé)* frozen

geler *vt (bloquer)* to freeze

gérance *nf* management
◊ *gérance de portefeuille* portfolio management

gérant, -e *nm,f* manager
◊ *gérant de portefeuille* portfolio manager

gestion *nf (d'une entreprise, de travaux, des comptes)* management; *(d'affaires)* conduct;

mauvaise gestion bad management, mismanagement

◊ *gestion actif-passif* assets and liabilities management

◊ *gestion budgétaire* budgetary control

◊ *gestion de capital* asset management

◊ *gestion des coûts* cost management

◊ *gestion financière* financial management, financial administration

◊ *gestion de fonds* fund management

◊ *gestion indicielle* index fund management

◊ *gestion des investissements* investment management

◊ *gestion passive* passive management

◊ *gestion de portefeuille* portfolio management

◊ *gestion prévisionnelle* budgetary control

◊ *gestion des risques* risk management

◊ *gestion de trésorerie* cash management

"

Ces recrutements seront rendus possibles par un système de **gestion prévisionnelle** des effectifs.

"

gestionnaire *nmf (dirigeant)* administrator; *(d'un service)* manager

◊ *gestionnaire de fonds* fund manager

◊ *gestionnaire de portefeuille* portfolio manager

glissement *nm (d'une monnaie, des salaires)* slide

glisser *vi (monnaie, salaires)* to slip, to slide

grand-livre *nm Compta* ledger; **porter qch au grand-livre** to enter an item in the ledger

◊ *grand-livre d'achats* purchase ledger

◊ *grand-livre auxiliaire* subledger

◊ *grand-livre de la dette publique* National Debt register

◊ *grand-livre général* nominal ledger

◊ *grand-livre de ventes* sales ledger

gratuit, -e *adj (crédit)* interest-free

greffe *nm (de société par actions)* registry

greffier *nm* registrar

grille *nf* grid

◊ *Compta grille d'imputation* table of account codes

guelte *nf* commission, percentage *(on sales)*

guichet *nm Banque* position, window, *Am* wicket; **payer au guichet** to pay at the counter; **guichet fermé** *(sur panneau)* position closed

◊ *Banque guichet automatique (de banque)* cash dispenser *or* machine, automated teller machine

guichetier, -ère *nm,f (dans une banque)* counter clerk, teller

habiliter *vt Jur* to empower, to entitle; **être habilité (à faire qch)** to be empowered *or* entitled (to do sth); **habilité à signer** *(employé de banque)* authorized to sign

habillage *nm Compta (d'un bilan)* window-dressing

habiller *vt Compta (bilan)* to window-dress

hausse *nf* **(a)** *(des prix, du chômage, du coût de la vie)* increase, rise (**de** in); **une hausse de 4%** a 4% rise; **être à la hausse** to go up; **les prix ont subi une forte hausse** prices have increased sharply *or* shot up; **revoir** *ou* **réviser les chiffres à la hausse** to revise figures upwards

(b) *Bourse (des cours, des valeurs)* rise; **à la hausse** *(tendance, marché, position)* bullish; **en hausse** *(actions)* rising; **jouer** *ou* **spéculer à la hausse** to speculate on a rising market, to bull the market; **pousser les actions à la hausse** to bull the market; **les cours sont orientés à la hausse** there is an upward trend in share prices; **provoquer une hausse factice** to rig the market

◇ *hausse de prix déguisée* hidden price increase

hausser **1** *vt (prix, taux de l'escompte)* to raise, to put up; **le prix a été haussé de 10%** the price has gone up by 10%

2 *vi* to rise; **faire hausser les prix** to force up prices

haussier, -ère *Bourse* **1** *adj (marché)* bullish

2 *nm,f* bull

haut de bilan *nm Compta (fonds propres)* shareholders' funds

hauteur *nf* **participer à hauteur de 30%** to contribute up to 30%; **un actionnaire à hauteur de 5%** a shareholder with 5% of the shares

"

Pour l'instant, le français Aérospatiale et l'allemand Dasa (filiale de Daimler-Benz) sont les deux principaux partenaires du constructeur aéronautique, le britannique British Aerospace (Bae) n'étant présent qu'**à hauteur de** 20% et l'espagnol Casa, de 4,2%.

"

holding *nm* holding company

homologué, -e *adj (prix)* authorized

homologuer *vt (prix)* to authorize

honneur *nm* **faire honneur à qch** *(facture, chèque, traite)* to honour, to meet

hors *prép* **hors bilan** off-balance sheet; **hors Bourse** after hours; **hors budget** not included in the budget; **hors taxe** exclusive of tax; *(à la douane)* duty-free; **horsTVA** net of VAT

hors-cote *Bourse* **1** *adj* unlisted **2** *nm* unlisted securities market

hôtel de la Monnaie *nm* **l'hôtel de la Monnaie** the Mint *(in Paris)*

HT *adj (abrév* **hors taxe***)* exclusive of tax

hypothécable *adj* mortgageable

hypothécaire *adj* mortgage

hypothèque *nf* mortgage; **franc** *ou* **libre d'hypothèques** unmortgaged; **prendre une hypothèque** to take out a mortgage; **emprunter sur hypothèque** to borrow on mortgage; **avoir une hypothèque sur une maison** to have a mortgage on a house, to have one's house mortgaged; **purger une hypothèque** to pay off *or* clear *or* redeem a mortgage; **propriété grevée d'hypothèques** encumbered estate
◇ *hypothèque générale* blanket mortgage
◇ *hypothèque de premier rang* first legal mortgage

hypothéquer *vt* **(a)** *(propriété, titres)* to mortgage **(b)** *(dette)* to secure by mortgage

image fidèle *nf Compta* true and fair view

IME (*abrév* **Institut monétaire européen**) EMI

immatériel, -elle *adj (actif, valeurs)* intangible

immobilisation *nf* (**a**) *Compta* asset; **immobilisations** fixed *or* capital assets; **faire de grosses immobilisations** to carry heavy stocks
(**b**) *(de capital)* locking up, tying up, immobilization; *(d'actif, de valeurs)* freezing

◇ *immobilisations capitaux* capital *or* financial assets

◇ *immobilisations corporelles* tangible fixed assets

◇ *immobilisations financières* long-term investments

◇ *immobilisations incorporelles* intangible (fixed) assets

◇ *immobilisations non financières* physical fixed assets

immobilisé, -e *adj (capital)* locked-up, tied up, immobilized; *(actif, valeurs)* frozen

immobiliser *vt (capital)* to lock up, to tie up, to immobilize; *(actif, valeurs)* to freeze

immunité fiscale *nf* immunity from taxation

impasse budgétaire *nf* budget deficit

impayé, -e 1 *adj* (**a**) *(dette, facture)* unpaid, outstanding; *(comptes)* unsettled (**b**) *(effet)* dishonoured
2 *nm* outstanding payment

> **"**
>
> De même, des actions tendant à réduire les **impayés** de loyers et à renforcer les droits des petits propriétaires seront entreprises.
>
> **"**

imposé, -e 1 *adj (soumis à l'impôt)* taxed; **être lourdement imposé** to be heavily taxed
2 *nm,f* taxpayer

imposer *vt (personne, marchandises)* to tax; *(propriété)* to levy a rate on; **imposer des droits sur qch** to tax sth

imposition *nf* taxation

◇ *imposition en cascade* cascade taxation

◇ *imposition forfaitaire* basic-rate taxation

◇ *imposition progressive* progressive taxation

◇ *imposition à la source* taxation at source

impôt *nm* tax; **avant impôt** before tax; **après impôt** after tax; **frapper qch d'un impôt** to tax sth; **payer 5000 francs d'impôts** to pay 5,000 francs in tax(es)

◊ *impôt sur les bénéfices* profit tax

◊ *Bourse impôt de Bourse* transaction tax

◊ *impôt sur le capital* capital tax

◊ *impôt sur le chiffre d'affaires* turnover tax

◊ *impôt à la consommation* output tax

◊ *impôt dégressif* sliding scale or degressive taxation

◊ *impôt déguisé* hidden tax

◊ *impôt différé* deferred taxation

◊ *impôt direct* direct tax

◊ *impôt sur les dividendes* dividend tax

◊ *impôt sur les donations et les successions* gift and inheritance tax

◊ *impôt extraordinaire* emergency tax

◊ *impôt foncier* land or property tax

◊ *impôt sur les gains exceptionnels* windfall tax

◊ *impôt indiciaire* wealth tax

◊ *impôt indirect* indirect tax

◊ *impôts locaux* Br council tax, Am local taxes

◊ *impôt de luxe* tax on luxury goods

◊ *impôt sur la masse salariale* payroll tax

◊ *impôt négatif sur le revenu* negative income tax

◊ *impôt sur les plus-values* capital gains tax

◊ *impôt à la production* input tax

◊ *impôt progressif* progressive

tax; *(sur le revenu)* graduated income tax

◊ *impôt de quotité* coefficient tax

◊ *impôt retenu à la base, impôt retenu à la source* tax deducted at source, Br pay-as-you-earn tax, Am pay-as-you-go tax

◊ *impôt sur le revenu* income tax

◊ *impôt sur les sociétés* Br corporation tax, Am corporation income tax

◊ *impôt de solidarité sur la fortune* wealth tax

◊ *impôt sur le travail* payroll tax

> **"**
>
> Le taux maximal de l'**impôt sur le revenu** sera relevé de 31 à 36% dès l'an prochain, tandis que l'**impôt sur les sociétés** passera de 35 à 36%.
>
> **"**

improductif, -ive *adj (capitaux)* unproductive, idle

imputable *adj (dépenses)* chargeable (**sur** to)

imputation *nf (des dépenses)* charge, charging; **imputation d'un paiement** appropriation of money *(to the payment of a debt)*; **imputation à** charge to; **imputation d'une somme au crédit/débit d'un compte** crediting/debiting an amount to an account

◊ *imputations budgétaires* budget allocations

◊ *imputation des charges* cost allocation

imputer *vt* (**a**) *(déduire)* to deduct; **imputer qch sur qch** to deduct sth from sth

(**b**) *(attribuer)* to charge sth to sth; **imputer des frais à un compte** to charge expenses to an account; **imputer une somme à un budget** to allocate a sum to a budget

inacceptation *nf (d'un effet)* non-acceptance

inacquitté *adj (effet)* unreceipted

incertain *nm Bourse* variable exchange; **coter** *ou* **donner l'incertain** to quote on the exchange rate

incessibilité *nf* non-transferability

incessible *adj* non-transferable

incitation fiscale *nf* tax incentive

inconvertible *adj* inconvertible

incorporation *nf* incorporation **des réserves au capital** capitalization of reserves

incoté, -e *adj Bourse* unquoted

indemniser *vt* to compensate, to indemnify (**de** for); **indemniser totalement qn** to compensate sb in full; **indemniser qn de ses frais** to reimburse sb his/her expenses, to pay sb's expenses

indemnité *nf (allocation)* allowance, grant

◇ **indemnité de cherté de vie** cost-of-living allowance, *Br* weighting

◇ **indemnité de chômage** unemployment benefit

◇ **indemnité complémentaire** additional allowance

◇ **indemnité conventionnelle** contractual allowance

◇ **indemnité de déménagement** relocation grant *or* allowance

◇ **indemnité de logement** accommodation allowance

◇ **indemnité de maladie** sickness benefit

◇ **indemnité de résidence** housing allowance

◇ **indemnité de séjour** living expenses

◇ **indemnité de vie chère** cost-of-living allowance, *Br* weighting

indépensé, -e *adj* unspent

indexation *nf Écon* index-linking, indexation; **l'indexation des salaires sur les prix** the index-linking of salaries to prices

"

Les augmentations salariales ralentissent depuis que l'**indexation** des rémunérations sur le coût de la vie a été abandonnée.

"

indexé, -e *adj Écon* index-linked, indexed

indexer *vt Écon* to index-link, to index (**sur** to)

indicateur *nm* indicator

◇ **indicateur (d'activité) économique** economic indicator

◇ **indicateur de marché** market indicator

indice *nm* index

◇ *Bourse* **indice boursier** share index

◇ *Bourse* **l'indice CAC 40** the

Principaux indices boursiers

Main stock market indexes

Europe

Allemagne – DAX
  (= Deutscher Aktienindex)

France – CAC-40
  (= indice de la Compagnie des Agents de Change)

Italie – MIB 30
  (= indice boursier de Milan)

Royaume Uni – FT-SE 100
  (= indice boursier du Financial Times)

Suisse – SMI *(= indice boursier suisse)*

USA

DJIA *(= Dow-Jones Industrial Average)*

NASDAQ *(= National Association of Securities Dealers Automated Quotation Composite Index)*

Canada

TSE 300 index
  (= indice boursier de Toronto)

Australie/Australia

All Ordinaries index
  (= indice boursier de Sydney)

Extrême Orient/Far East

Hang Seng index
  (= indice boursier de Hong Kong)

Nikkei (Average)
  (= indice boursier de Tokyo)

* L'indice FT-SE ou Footsie 100 est le principal indice boursier européen. Il est composé des 100 valeurs les plus importantes de la Bourse de Londres et il est établi par le Financial Times en collaboration avec la Bourse de Londres. Il existe un autre indice, le FT 30, composé des 30 valeurs les plus importantes.

Le Dow Jones Industrial Average, ou DJIA, est le principal indice boursier américain; il est établi à la Bourse de New York.

Le Footsie 100 et le Dow Jones ainsi que l'indice boursier japonais Nikkei dominent la scène financière internationale.

* London's FT-SE, or "Footsie", index is the leading European stock exchange index. It is comprised of the top 100 listed companies on the London Stock Exchange, and is compiled jointly by the Financial Times and the London Stock Exchange Ltd. The FT-SE index is complemented by the FT 30 share index which focuses on the leading 30 listed companies.

The Dow Jones Industrial Average, or DJIA, is America's main stock exchange index and is based on the New York Stock Exchange.

The FT-SE and Dow Jones indices, as well as the Japanese Nikkei index, dominate the world of international finance.

CAC 40 index *(main Paris Stock Exchange Index)*

◊ *Bourse* **indice composé, indice composite** composite index

◊ *Bourse* **indice des cours d'actions** share price index

◊ **indice du coût de la vie** cost-of-living index

◊ *Bourse* **l'indice Dax** the Dax index

◊ *Bourse* **l'indice Dow Jones** the Dow Jones (Industrial) Average *or* Index

◊ *Bourse* **l'indice FTSE des 100 valeurs** the FTSE 100 share index

◊ *Bourse* **l'indice Hang Seng** the Hang Seng index

◊ *Bourse* **l'indice MidCAC** = Paris Stock Exchange index of 100 medium-range shares, ≃ MidCap index

◊ *Bourse* **l'indice Nikkei** the Nikkei index

◊ *Écon* **indice des prix de détail** Retail Price Index

◊ *Écon* **indice des prix de gros** wholesale price index

◊ **indice de profit** profit indicator

◊ **indice de rentabilité** profitability index

◊ *Bourse* **l'indice SBF** the SBF index *(broad based French Stock Exchange Index)*

◊ *Bourse* **indice des titres** stock average

◊ *Bourse* **indice des valeurs boursières** share index

◊ *Bourse* **l'indice Xetra-Dax** the Xetra-Dax index

indisponibilité *nf (de fonds)* unavailability, non-availability

indisponible *adj (fonds)* unavailable

indu *nm* **l'indu** money not owed

inescomptable *adj* undiscountable

inexigible *adj (remboursement, dette)* irrecoverable

inflation *nf Écon* inflation

◊ **inflation fiduciaire** inflation of the currency

◊ **inflation monétaire** monetary inflation

◊ **inflation des prix** price inflation

infléchir 1 *vt (faire diminuer)* to cut, to reduce
2 **s'infléchir** *vpr (diminuer) (cours)* to fall

ingénierie financière *nf* financial engineering

initié, -e *nm,f Bourse* insider

injecter *vt (argent, capitaux)* to inject (**dans** into); **injecter des millions dans une affaire** to inject *or* pump millions into a business

injection *nf (d'argent, de capitaux)* injection (**dans** into)

injonction à la vente *nf Bourse* sell order

inscription *nf Compta (dans un livre de comptes)* entry

◊ *Compta* **inscription comptable** accounting entry

◊ *Bourse* **inscription à la cote** quotation on the (official) list, listing; **faire une demande d'inscription à la cote** to apply for admission to the official list, to seek a share quotation

◊ *Compta* **inscription sur le grand-livre** journal entry

inscrire 1 *vt (dans un journal, un registre)* to enter, to record; **inscrire une dépense au budget** to include an item in the budget

2 s'inscrire *vpr Bourse* **s'inscrire en baisse/hausse** to fall/rise; **les valeurs industrielles s'inscrivent en baisse de 13 points à la clôture** industrial shares are closing 13 points down

inscrit, -e *adj Bourse* **inscrit à la cote officielle** listed; **non inscrite** unlisted

insolvabilité *nf* insolvency

insolvable *adj* insolvent

inspecteur, -trice *nm,f* inspector

◇ *inspecteur des contributions directes* tax inspector

◇ *Inspecteur des Finances* ≃ general auditor *(of the Treasury)*

◇ *inspecteur du fisc, inspecteur des impôts* tax inspector

◇ *inspecteur de la TVA* VAT inspector

instabilité *nf (du marché, du change, des prix)* instability

instable *adj (marché, change, prix)* instable

institut *nm* institute

◇ *institut monétaire* lender of last resort

◇ *Institut monétaire européen* European Monetary Institute

instrument *nm (document)* instrument; *Jur* (legal) instrument

◇ *instrument de commerce* instrument of commerce

◇ *instrument de couverture* hedging instrument

◇ *instrument de crédit* instrument of credit

◇ *instrument financier* financial instrument

◇ *instrument financier à terme* financial future

◇ *instrument négociable* negotiable instrument

◇ *instrument de négociation* trading instrument

◇ *instrument de placement* investment instrument

insuffisance *nf (de fonds, d'investissements)* insufficiency

◇ *insuffisance de capitaux* insufficient capital

◇ *insuffisance d'espèces* cash shortage

◇ *insuffisance de provision* insufficient funds *(to meet cheque)*

insuffisant, -e *adj (fonds, investissements)* insufficient

intégralement *adv* completely, in full; **rembourser intégralement une somme** to repay a sum in full; **intégralement libéré, intégralement versé** *(capital)* fully paid-up

interbancaire *adj* interbank

interdit bancaire *nm* ban on writing cheques; **être frappé d'interdit bancaire** to be banned from writing cheques

> **"**
>
> La loi sur le chèque frappe d'un **interdit bancaire** toute personne ayant émis un chèque sans provision.
>
> **"**

intéressement *nm* intéressement **(aux bénéfices)** profit-sharing scheme

intérêt *nm* interest; **emprunter**

à intérêt to borrow at interest; **laisser courir des intérêts** to allow interest to accumulate; **payer des intérêts** to pay interest; **rapporter des intérêts** to yield *or* bear interest; **placer son argent à 7% d'intérêt** to invest one's money at 7% interest; **sans intérêt** interest-free

◇ *intérêts arriérés* back interest

◇ *intérêt bancaire* bank interest

◇ *intérêt du capital* interest on capital

◇ *intérêts compensatoires* damages

◇ *intérêts composés* compound interest

◇ *intérêts courus* accrued interest

◇ *intérêts débiteurs* debit interest

◇ *intérêts pour défaut de paiement* default interest

◇ *intérêts à échoir* accruing interest

◇ *intérêts échus* accrued interest

◇ *intérêts exigibles* interest due and payable

◇ *intérêt fixe* fixed interest

◇ *intérêts moratoires* default interest, penalty *or* penal interest

◇ *intérêt négatif* negative interest

◇ *intérêts à payer* interest charges

◇ *intérêt sur prêt* interest on a loan

◇ *Bourse intérêt de report* contango

◇ *intérêt de retard* interest on arrears

◇ *intérêt simple* simple interest

◇ *intérêt à taux flottant* floating-rate interest

◇ *intérêt variable* variable-rate interest

intermédiaire *nmf* (a) *(personne)* intermediary; *(dans une transaction)* middleman
(b) *Bourse* market maker

◇ *intermédiaire financier* financial intermediary

◇ *intermédiaire négociateur* trading member

◇ *intermédiaire remisier (en Bourse)* intermediate broker

introduction *nf Bourse (de valeurs)* introduction

◇ *introduction en Bourse* flotation, listing on the Stock Market, *Am* initial public offering

introduire *vt Bourse (valeurs)* to introduce, to bring out

inventaire *nm* (a) *Compta* **inventaire (comptable)** book inventory
(b) *(d'un portefeuille de titres)* valuation

◇ *inventaire de fin d'année* accounts for the end of the *Br* financial *or Am* fiscal year

◇ *inventaire périodique* periodic inventory

investi, -e *adj (argent, capitaux)* invested

investir 1 *vt (argent, capitaux)* to invest (**dans** in); **investir des capitaux à l'étranger** to invest capital abroad
2 *vi* to invest (**dans** in); **investir à court/à long terme** to make a short-term/long-term investment

investissement *nm* investment; *(action)* investing, investment; **faire des investissements** to invest (money)

◇ *investissement de capitaux* capital investment

◇ *investissement à court terme* short-term investment

◇ *investissement direct* direct investment

◇ *investissement éthique* ethical investment

◇ *investissements à l'étranger, investissements étrangers* outward *or* foreign investment

◇ *investissement de l'étranger* inward investment

◇ *investissement immobilier* investment in real estate, property investment

◇ *investissement indirect* indirect investment

◇ *investissement industriel* investment in industry

◇ *investissements initiaux* initial investment

◇ *investissement institutionnel* institutional investment

◇ *investissement locatif* investment in rental property

◇ *investissement lourd* heavy investment

◇ *investissement privé* private investment

◇ *investissement de productivité* productivity investment

◇ *investissement à revenu fixe* fixed-rate investment

◇ *investissement à revenu variable* floating-rate investment

◇ *investissement en valeurs de redressement, investissement en valeurs de retournement* failure investment

investisseur *nm* investor

◇ *investisseur institutionnel* institutional investor

◇ *investisseur minoritaire* minority investor

◇ *investisseur privé* private investor

irréalisable *adj (valeurs)* unrealizable

irrécouvrable *adj (argent, créance)* irrecoverable

ISF *nm (abrév* **impôt de solidarité sur la fortune)** wealth tax

jeu *nm Bourse* speculating
◇ *jeu de Bourse* gambling on the stock exchange, stock exchange speculation
◇ *Compta jeu d'écritures* paper transaction
◇ *jeu sur les reports* speculating in contangos

joint-venture *nf* joint venture

jouer 1 *vt Bourse* **jouer la livre à la baisse/à la hausse** to speculate on a falling/rising pound
2 *vi Bourse* to speculate, to play the market; **jouer à la Bourse** to speculate *or* gamble on the stock exchange; **jouer à la hausse** to gamble on a rise in prices, to bull the market; **jouer à la baisse** to gamble on a fall in prices, to bear the market

joueur, -euse *nm,f Bourse* speculator
◇ *joueur à la baisse* bear
◇ *joueur à la hausse* bull

jouissance *nf (d'intérêts)* entitlement (**de** to)

jour *nm* (a) *(journée)* day
(b) *(date)* day; **à ce jour** up until now, to date; **intérêts à ce jour** interest to date
(c) **à jour** up to date; **tenir les livres à jour** to keep the books *or* the accounts up to date
(d) *Bourse* day

◇ *jour de Bourse* trading day
◇ *jour de la déclaration des noms* ticket day
◇ *jour férié* bank holiday
◇ *jour de grâce* day of grace
◇ *jours d'intérêt* interest days
◇ *jour de la liquidation* account *or* settlement day
◇ *jour d'option* option date
◇ *jour de paiement, jour de règlement* payment *or* settlement day
◇ *Bourse jour de la réponse des primes* option day
◇ *Bourse jour des reports* contango day
◇ *jour de valeur* value day
◇ *jour du terme* term day

journal *nm* (a) *(publication)* paper, newspaper (b) *Compta* ledger, account book
◇ *journal des achats* purchase *or* bought ledger
◇ *journal analytique* analysis ledger
◇ *journal de banque* bank book
◇ *journal de caisse* cash book
◇ *journal des effets à payer* bills payable ledger
◇ *journal des effets à recevoir* bills receivable ledger
◇ *journal factures-clients* sales invoice ledger
◇ *journal factures-fournisseurs* purchase invoice ledger

⋄ *journal de paie* wages or payroll ledger

⋄ *journal des rendus* returns ledger or book

⋄ *journal de trésorerie* cash book

⋄ *journal des ventes* sales ledger

journaliser *vt Compta* to enter, to write up in the books

journée *nf* day

⋄ *journée comptable* accounting day

jugement déclaratif de faillite *nm* adjudication in bankruptcy, declaration of bankruptcy

junk bond *nm* junk bond

krach *nm* (financial) crash

⋄ *krach boursier* stock market crash

⋄ *le krach de Wall Street* the Wall Street Crash

"

Lassés par les **krachs boursiers** et la chute du rendement des sicav monétaires, les épargnants rêvent d'un placement idéal, performant mais pas trop risqué.

"

lancement *nm* Bourse *(d'une société)* flotation; *(de titres boursiers, d'un emprunt)* issuing, issue; *(d'une souscription)* start

lancer *vt* Bourse *(société)* to float; *(titres boursiers, emprunt)* to issue; *(souscription)* to start; **lancer des titres sur le marché** to issue shares

l/c *nf (abrév* **lettre de crédit)** L/C

LCR *nf (abrév* **lettre de change relevé)** bills of exchange statement

leasing *nm* lease financing; **acheter qch en leasing** to lease sth, to buy sth on lease

LEP *nm (abrév* **livret d'épargne populaire)** = special tax-exempt savings account

lettre *nf (courrier)* letter
◇ *lettre accréditive* letter of credit
◇ *Bourse lettre d'allocation* letter of allotment
◇ *lettre d'aval* letter of guaranty
◇ *lettre d'avis* advice note, letter of advice
◇ *lettre de change* bill of exchange
◇ *lettre de change à l'extérieur* foreign bill
◇ *lettre de change relevé* bills of exchange statement

◇ *lettre de créance* letter of credit
◇ *Banque lettre de crédit* letter of credit; **émettre une lettre de crédit** to open a letter of credit
◇ *lettre de crédit circulaire* circular letter of credit
◇ *lettre de crédit documentaire* documentary letter of credit
◇ *lettre de crédit irrévocable* irrevocable letter of credit
◇ *lettre de gage* debenture bond; *(pour hypothèque)* mortgage bond
◇ *lettre de garantie* letter of guarantee
◇ *lettre de garantie bancaire* bank guarantee
◇ *lettre de garantie d'indemnité* letter of indemnity
◇ *lettre d'intention* letter of intent
◇ *lettre de nantissement* letter of hypothecation
◇ *lettre de relance des impayés* debt-chasing letter
◇ *Bourse lettre de souscription* letter of application

levée *nf* Bourse *(des actions, d'une option)* taking up
◇ *Banque levées de compte* personal withdrawals

lever *vt* Bourse *(actions, option)* to take up

liasse nf *(de billets de banque)* wad

libellé nm Compta *(d'une écriture)* particulars

libeller vt *(chèque, facture)* to make out; **chèque libellé à l'ordre de Y. Mourier** cheque made out or payable to Y. Mourier; **libellé en francs** *(chèque)* made out in francs; *(cours)* quoted or given in francs; **être libellé au porteur** to be made out to bearer, to be made payable to bearer

libération nf *(d'une dette)* payment in full, discharge; *(d'une action, du capital)* paying up; *(d'un débiteur)* discharge, release; *(d'un garant)* discharge
◇ **libération intégrale** *(d'une action)* payment in full

libératoire adj **avoir force libératoire** to be legal tender

libéré, -e adj *(action)* (fully) paid-up; **non (entièrement) libéré, partiellement libéré** partly paid-up; **un titre de 1000 francs libéré de 750 francs** ou **libéré à 75%** a 1,000-franc share of which 750 francs are paid up; **libéré d'impôt** tax paid

libre adj free; **libre d'hypothèque** free from mortgage; **libre d'impôt** tax-free
◇ **libre circulation** *(des capitaux)* free movement

lieu nm place
◇ **lieu d'émission** place of issue
◇ **lieu de paiement** place of payment

ligne nf Compta **au-dessus de la ligne** *(dépenses)* above-the-line
◇ Banque **ligne de crédit** line of credit, credit line

◇ Bourse **ligne de cotation** line of quotation
◇ Banque **ligne de découvert** line of credit, credit line
◇ Banque **ligne de substitution** backup line

limite nf limit
◇ **limite de la baisse** limit down
◇ **limite de crédit** credit limit
◇ **limite d'endettement** borrowing limit
◇ **limite de la hausse** limit up
◇ **limite inférieure** limit down
◇ **limite de position** position limit
◇ **limite supérieure** limit up

lingot nm ingot
◇ **lingot d'or** gold ingot or bar
◇ **lingots en or** gold bullion

liquidation nf (a) Jur liquidation; **être en liquidation** to have gone into liquidation; **entrer en liquidation** to go into liquidation; **mettre en liquidation** to put into liquidation, to liquidate (b) *(d'un compte, d'une dette)* settlement, clearing (c) Bourse settlement; *(d'une position)* liquidation
◇ **liquidation des biens** liquidation of assets
◇ **liquidation en espèces** cash settlement
◇ **liquidation de fin de mois** end-of-month settlement
◇ **liquidation forcée** compulsory liquidation
◇ **liquidation (par décision) judiciaire** official receivership
◇ **liquidation de quinzaine** Br fortnightly settlement or account, Am mid-month account
◇ **liquidation volontaire** voluntary liquidation

> Nombre d'entreprises affichent des pertes, ne respectent pas les normes de solvabilité ou ont arrêté leur activité de crédit. Deux, celles de Picardie et de Lorraine, sont en **liquidation**. La BZ est proche de la liquidation pour cause de pannes en série et de chute du prix de la cellulose.

liquide 1 *adj* liquid; **peu liquide** illiquid

   2 *nm (espèces)* (ready) cash; **je n'ai pas assez de liquide** I haven't enough cash; **vous payez par chèque ou en liquide?** are you paying by cheque or cash?

liquidité *nf* liquidity; **être à court de liquidité** to be short of funds; **liquidités** liquid assets

◇ *liquidités excédentaires* excess liquidities

◇ *liquidités obligatoires* mandatory liquid assets

◇ *liquidité du portefeuille* portfolio liquidity

> La Réserve fédérale ne remontera pas ses taux d'intérêt, bien qu'elle souhaite retirer de la circulation une partie des **liquidités** injectées depuis trois ans.

lire *nf (unité monétaire)* lira

liste *nf* list; **faire** *ou* **dresser** *ou* **établir une liste** to draw up *or* to make out a list

◇ *liste des actionnaires* list of shareholders

◇ *liste des souscripteurs* list of applications

livrable *adj Bourse* deliverable

livraison *nf Bourse (des titres)* delivery

◇ *livraison au comptant immédiate* spot delivery

◇ *livraison à terme* future *or* forward delivery

livre¹ *nf (unité monétaire)* pound; **un billet de cinq livres** a five-pound note

◇ *livre irlandaise* Irish pound, punt

◇ *livre sterling* pound (sterling)

◇ *livre verte* green pound

livre² *nm (registre)* book; *Compta* **tenir les livres** to keep the accounts *or* the books; **vérifier les livres** to check the books

◇ *Compta livre d'achats, livre des achats* bought ledger, purchase ledger

◇ *livre d'actionnaires* register of shareholders

◇ *livre de caisse* cash book

◇ *Compta livre de commerce, livre de comptabilité, livre de comptes* ledger, account book

◇ *Compta livre des créanciers* accounts payable ledger

◇ *Compta livre des débiteurs* accounts receivable ledger

◇ *livre de dépenses* cash book

◇ *livre d'échéance* bill book

◇ *Compta livre des effets à payer* bills payable ledger

◇ *Compta livre des effets à recevoir* bills receivable ledger

◇ *Compta livre des entrées* purchase ledger

◇ *Compta livre fractionnaire* day book, book of prime entry

◇ *livre d'inventaire* balance book

◇ *Compta* *livre journal* journal, day book

◇ *Compta* *livre de paie* pay ledger

◇ *Compta* *livre de petite caisse* petty cash book

◇ *Compta* *livre de trésorerie générale* general cash book

◇ *Compta* *livre des ventes* sales ledger

livrer *vt Bourse* to deliver; **livrer à terme fixe** to deliver at a fixed term; **prime pour livrer** seller's option; **vente à livrer** sale for delivery

livret *nm* book

◇ *Banque* *livret A* = tax-exempt savings account issued by the French National Savings Bank and the Post Office

◇ *Banque* *livret de caisse d'épargne* bank book, passbook

◇ *Banque* *livret de compte* bank book

◇ *Banque* *livret de dépôt* deposit book, passbook

◇ *Banque* *livret d'épargne logement* *Br* ≃ building society passbook, *Am* ≃ savings and loan association passbook

◇ *Banque* *livret d'épargne populaire (compte)* = special tax-exempt savings account; *(carnet)* savings book, passbook

"

Dans la panoplie des produits d'épargne liquide, le **Livret d'épargne populaire (LEP)** fait figure d'exception depuis sa création en 1982. Connu aussi sous le nom de Livret rose, il offre en effet une sur-rémuneration (4,75% aujourd'hui). L'explication? Avec son plafond de dépôts fixé à 40 000 francs, il symbolise pleinement l'épargne dite populaire.

"

livreur, -euse *nm,f Bourse* deliverer

LOA *nf* (*abrév* **location avec option d'achat**) lease financing

location avec option d'achat *nf* lease financing

location-gérance *nf* = agreement with a liquidator to manage a company in liquidation

loi *nf* law

◇ *loi antitrust* antitrust law

◇ *loi de Finances* Finance Act

◇ *loi des rendements décroissants* law of diminishing returns

longévité *nf (des capitaux)* life

lot *nm Bourse (d'actions)* parcel

loyer 1 *nm (de locaux)* rent **2** *nmpl* **loyers** lease revenue

◇ *le loyer de l'argent* the price of money

"

Bien que la croissance de l'économie américaine ne soit pas inflationniste et que les pays de la zone euro aient baissé leurs taux d'intérêt à court terme (de même que d'autres pays), le **loyer de l'argent** sur les écheances longues n'a cessé de se tendre.

"

main *nf Compta*
◇ *main courante* cash book
◇ *main courante de caisse* counter cash book
◇ *main courante de dépenses* paid cash book
◇ *main courante de recettes* received cash book

main-d'œuvre directe *nf* direct labour

maintenir 1 *vt* to maintain; **dividende maintenu à 5%** dividend maintained at 5%; **maintenir le change au-dessus du gold-point** to maintain the exchange above the gold-point

2 se maintenir *vpr* to hold up; **la livre se maintient par rapport au dollar** the pound is holding its own against the dollar; *Bourse* **ces actions se maintiennent à 57,5 francs** these shares remain firm at 57.5 francs

maison *nf (entreprise)* **maison (de commerce)** firm, company, business
◇ *Banque* **maison d'acceptation** *Br* accepting house, *Am* acceptance house
◇ *maison de banque* banking house
◇ *maison de courtage* brokerage house
◇ *maison d'escompte* discount house
◇ *maison de prêt* loan office *or* company
◇ *maison de titres* securities firm

majoration *nf* **(a)** *(de prix)* increase, mark-up
(b) *(sur une facture)* additional charge, surcharge; **frapper un immeuble d'une majoration de cinq pour cent** to put five percent on the valuation of a building
(c) *(d'actif)* overestimation, overvaluation
◇ *majoration fiscale, majoration d'impôt* surcharge on taxes

❝

Le pouvoir d'achat en Allemagne sera amputé par les **majorations fiscales,** tandis que les pertes d'emploi et le freinage des salaires se poursuivront.

❞

majorer *vt* **(a)** *(facture)* to make an additional charge on; **majorer une facture de 10%** *(faire payer en plus)* to put 10% on an invoice; *(faire payer en trop)* to overcharge by 10% on an invoice; **tous les impôts impayés**

avant la fin du mois seront majo-rés de 5% there will be a 5% additional charge on all taxes not paid by the end of the month

(b) *(actif)* to overestimate, to overvalue

majoritaire *Bourse* **1** *adj* majority; **se rendre majoritaire** to acquire a majority interest *or* shareholding; **il a une participation majoritaire dans la société** he has a majority interest *or* shareholding in the company

2 *nmf* majority shareholder

malversation *nf* embezzlement, corrupt administration (of funds)

mandat *nm (mode de paiement)* order; **toucher un mandat** to draw on *or* to cash a money order; **mandat sur la Banque de France** order on the Bank of France

◇ *Jur* **mandat d'action** receiving order (in bankruptcy)

◇ **mandat international** international money order

◇ **mandat de paiement** order to pay

◇ **mandat postal, mandat poste** *Br* postal order, *Am* money order

◇ **mandat du Trésor** Treasury warrant

◇ **mandat de virement** transfer order

mandataire liquidateur *nm* official receiver

mandat-carte *nm Br* postal order, *Am* money order *(in post-card form)*

mandat-contributions *nm Br*

postal order, *Am* money order *(for paying income tax)*

mandatement *nm* = payment by means of a money order

mandater *vt* (a) *(représentant)* to appoint, to commission (b) *(somme)* to pay by *Br* postal order *or Am* money order

manipulation *nf Bourse* manipulation, rigging

◇ **manipulation monétaire** currency manipulation

manœuvre boursière *nf Bourse* stock market manipulation

manquant *nm* shortfall, shortage

◇ **manquant en caisse** cash shortage

manque *nm Compta* shortfall

◇ **manque de caisse** cash unders

◇ **manque de capitaux** capital shortfall

manquer 1 manquer de *vt ind (argent)* to be short of, to lack

2 *v impersonnel* **il nous manque les capitaux nécessaires** we are short of the necessary capital

maquillage *nm (d'un chèque, d'un bilan)* falsification

maquiller *vt (chèque, bilan)* to falsify

marché *nm Bourse, Écon* market

◇ **marché d'acheteurs** buyer's market

◇ *Bourse* **marché des actions** share market, stock market

◇ *Bourse* **marché à la baisse, marché baissier** bear *or* buyer's market

◇ *marché **boursier*** stock market

◇ *marché **cambiste*** foreign exchange market

◇ *marché **de capitaux*** capital market

◇ *Bourse* **marché des changes** currency (exchange) market, foreign exchange market

◇ *Bourse* **marché des changes à terme** forward exchange market

◇ *Bourse* **marché au comptant** spot market

◇ *Bourse* **marché continu** continuous *or* all-day trading

◇ *Bourse* **marché des contrats à terme** futures market

◇ *Bourse* **marché de cotation** securities market

◇ *Bourse* **marché en coulisse** outside market

◇ *marché **demandeur*** buyer's market

◇ *Bourse* **marché des denrées et matières premières** commodity market

◇ *marché des devises (étrangères)* foreign exchange market

◇ *Bourse* **marché dirigé par les cotations** quotation-driven market

◇ *Bourse* **marché dirigé par les ordres** order-driven market

◇ *Bourse* **marché du disponible** spot market

◇ *marché **effectif*** available market

◇ *Bourse* **marché électronique privé** ECN, electronic communications network

◇ *marché d'équipement* capital goods market

◇ *marché de l'escompte* discount market

◇ *marché de l'eurodevise* euromarket, euro-currency market

◇ *Écon* **marché extérieur** foreign market

◇ *Bourse* **marché financier** money *or* financial market

◇ *Banque* **marché de gré à gré entre banques** interbank wholesale market

◇ *marché **gris*** grey market

◇ *Bourse* **marché à la hausse, marché haussier** bull *or* seller's market

◇ *Bourse* **marché hors cote** unlisted securities market, *Am* over-the-counter market

◇ *marché **hypothécaire*** mortgage market

◇ *Banque* **marché interbancaire** interbank market

◇ *marché **libre*** *Bourse* open market; *Écon* free market

◇ *marché **libre des capitaux*** open money market

◇ *Bourse* **marché des matières premières** commodity market

◇ *marché **mondial*** world *or* global market

◇ *Bourse* **marché mondial des actions** global equities market

◇ *marché **monétaire*** money market

◇ *marché **monétaire international*** international money market

◇ *Bourse* **marché mort** dead market

◇ *Bourse* **marché du neuf** primary market

◇ *marché **noir*** black market; **faire du marché noir** to buy and sell on the black market

◇ *Bourse* **marché des nouvelles émissions** new issue market

◇ *Bourse* **marché obligataire,**

marché des obligations bond market

◇ *Écon* **marché officiel** official market

◇ *Bourse* **marché à** ou **des options** options market

◇ *Bourse* **marché des options négociables de Paris** Paris traded options exchange, *Br* ≃ London International Financial Futures Exchange, *Am* ≃ Chicago Board Options Exchange

◇ **marché de l'or** gold market

◇ *Écon* **marché parallèle** parallel *or* black market

◇ **marché des prêts** loan market

◇ *Bourse* **marché primaire** primary market

◇ *Bourse* **marché à primes** options market

◇ **marché principal** core market

◇ *Bourse* **marché à prix affichés** quotation-driven market

◇ *Bourse* **marché RM** forward market

◇ *Bourse* **marché secondaire** secondary market

◇ *Bourse* **marché à terme** futures *or* forward market

◇ *Bourse* **marché à terme de devises** forward exchange market

◇ *Bourse* **marché à terme d'instruments financiers** financial futures *or* derivatives market, *Br* ≃ London International Financial Futures Exchange

◇ *Bourse* **marché des titres** securities market

◇ *Bourse* **marché des transactions hors séance** *Br* unlisted securities market, *Am* over-the-counter market

◇ *UE* **le Marché unique (européen)** the Single (European) Market

◇ *Bourse* **marché des valeurs mobilières** securities market

◇ *Bourse* **marché des valeurs de premier ordre** gilt-edged market, gilts market

◇ *Bourse* **marché vendeur** seller's market

"

Désormais, dans les milieux financiers, on ne parle plus, commme il y a un an, de la guerre entre Francfort, Londres et Paris, mais de la concurrence des nouveaux **marchés électroniques privés**, désignés sous le nom d'*electronic communications networks* (ou *ECN*). Concrètement, leur fonction est simple: au lieu de transmettre l'ordre d'un investissement aux marchés officiels, l'ECN amène lui-même les acheteurs et les vendeurs à se rencontrer sur son propre système électronique. Avec deux atouts majeurs: des frais de transaction nettement réduits et une garantie d'anonymat pour l'investisseur.

"

marche aléatoire *nf Bourse* random walk

marge *nf* margin

◇ *Compta* **marge d'autofinancement** cash flow

◇ **marge d'autofinancement disponible** free cash flow

◇ **marge bénéficiaire** profit margin

◇ **marge brute** gross margin

◇ *marge brute d'autofinancement* cash flow

◇ *marge commerciale* trading profit, gross margin

◇ *marge commerciale brute* gross profit margin

◇ *marge sur les coûts variables* contribution margin

◇ *marge de crédit* credit margin

◇ *marge étroite* fine price

◇ *marge de flottement, marge de fluctuation* (*d'une monnaie*) margin of fluctuation, fluctuation band

◇ *marge initiale* initial margin

◇ *marge d'intérêt* margin of interest

◇ *marge nette* net margin

◇ *marge nette d'exploitation* operating margin

◇ *marge de profit* profit margin

◇ *marge sectorielle* segment margin

> **"**
>
> Du coup, le courtier américain Montgomery Securities utilise une batterie d'indicateurs financiers et stratégiques pour évaluer les sociétés d'Internet, comme la **marge d'autofinancement disponible** (free cash flow), les parts de marché, le chiffre d'affaires par client ou par employé.
>
> **"**

margoulin *nm Fam* (*à la Bourse*) petty speculator

mark *nm* (*monnaie allemande*) (German) mark, Deutschmark

masse *nf* fund, stock; (*de personnes*) body

◇ *masse active* assets

◇ *masse des créanciers* (general) body of creditors

◇ *masse monétaire* money supply

◇ *masse des obligataires* body of debenture holders *or* bond-holders

◇ *masse passive* liabilities

◇ *masse salariale* wage(s) bill, payroll

matière *nf*

◇ *matière imposable* taxable income

◇ *Bourse* *matières premières et denrées* commodities

MATIF *nm Bourse* (*abrév* **marché à terme d'instruments financiers**) financial futures *ou* derivatives market, *Br* $\simeq$ LIFFE

matinée de Bourse *nf* morning session

maturité *nf* maturity; **mon compte d'épargne n'est pas encore arrivé à maturité** my savings account hasn't matured yet

MBA *nf Compta* (*abrév* **marge brute d'autofinancement**) cash flow

mécanisme *nm*

◇ *Écon, UE* *mécanisme de change* Exchange Rate Mechanism

◇ *Écon, UE* *mécanisme de change européen* European Exchange Rate Mechanism

◇ *mécanisme de l'escompte* discount mechanism

mécompte *nm* miscalculation, error in reckoning

MÉDAF *nm* (*abrév* **modèle d'évaluation des actifs**) CAPM

membre de compensation *nm Bourse* clearing member

mémoire *nm Compta* report

mensualisation *nf* payment on a monthly basis

mensualiser *vt* to pay monthly; **il est payé au trimestre mais il a demandé à être mensualisé** he is paid quarterly but has asked to be paid monthly

mensualité *nf* (a) *(paiement)* monthly payment; **payer par mensualités** to pay by monthly instalments; **il a payé son ordinateur en 36 mensualités** he paid for his computer in 36 monthly instalments (b) *(salaire)* monthly salary

◇ **mensualité de remboursement** monthly repayment

> **"**
> Pour les 50 000 francs sur 36 mois, les **mensualités de remboursement** ne varient que de 117 francs entre un taux de 15% et un taux de 10%.
> **"**

mercuriale *nf Bourse* commodity price list, market price list

métal *nm* metal
◇ **métal en barres** bullion
◇ **métal en lingots** ingots

métallique *adj (monnaie)* metallic

méthode *nf* method
◇ *Compta* **méthode d'achat** purchase method
◇ *Compta* **méthode d'amortissement dégressif** declining balance method
◇ *Compta* **méthode d'amortissement linéaire** straight-line depreciation method
◇ *Compta* **méthode de capitali-**

sation du coût entier full cost accounting (method)
◇ **méthode des coûts marginaux** marginal cost pricing
◇ *Compta* **méthode du coût de revient complet** full costing, full cost accounting (method)
◇ *Compta* **méthode des coûts standards** standard cost accounting, standard costing
◇ **méthode des coûts variables** direct costing
◇ *Compta* **méthode par** ou **à échelles** daily balance interest calculation
◇ **méthode linéaire** straight-line method

mettre *vt* (a) *(placer)* to put, to place; **mettre son argent à la banque** to put or deposit one's money in the bank
(b) *(investir)* to put, to invest; **mettre son argent en immeubles** to put or to invest one's money in property

MidCAC *nm Bourse* **le MidCAC, l'indice MidCAC** = Paris Stock Exchange index comprised of 100 medium-range shares, ≃ MidCap

mieux *adv Bourse* **acheter/ vendre au mieux** to buy/sell at best

millésime *nm (sur une monnaie)* date

milliard *nm* billion; **10 milliards de dollars** 10 billion dollars

million *nm* million; **un million de francs** a million francs; **un chiffre d'affaires de deux millions** a turnover of two million

minimum *nm* minimum
◇ **minimum imposable** tax threshold

◇ *minimum vieillesse* = basic old-age pension

ministère *nm* department, *Br* ministry

◇ *le ministère de l'Économie et des Finances* *Br* ≃ the Treasury, *Am* ≃ the Treasury Department

ministre *nm* minister, *Am* secretary

◇ *ministre de l'Économie et des Finances* Finance Minister, *Br* ≃ Chancellor of the Exchequer, *Am* ≃ Secretary of the Treasury

mise *nf (placement)* putting

◇ *mise en circulation (de l'argent)* circulation

◇ *mise en commun de fonds* pooling of capital

◇ *mise en demeure* formal demand

◇ *mise en demeure de payer* final demand

◇ *mise de fonds* investment, capital expenditure; **faire une mise de fonds** to put up capital; **ma première mise de fonds a été de 1000 livres** my initial outlay was £1,000

◇ *mise en gage* pawning, pledging

◇ *mise hors (action)* disbursement; *(somme)* sum advanced

◇ *mise en paiement (d'un dividende)* payment

◇ *mise en pension* borrowing against securities, pledging

◇ *mise sociale* = capital brought into a business by a partner

◇ *mise en valeur (d'un investissement)* turning to account

mobilisable *adj (capital)* realizable; *(actif, biens immobiliers)* mobilizable

mobilisation *nf (de capital)* realization; *(d'actif, de biens immobiliers)* mobilization; *(de fonds)* raising

mobiliser *vt (capital)* to realize; *(actif, biens immobilier)* to mobilize; *(fonds)* to raise

modalité *nf* method; **modalités** *(d'une émission)* terms and conditions

◇ *modalités de financement* financing terms *or* conditions

◇ *modalités de paiement, modalités de règlement* methods *or* terms of payment

mode *nm (manière)* method

◇ *Compta* **mode d'amortissement linéaire** straight-line depreciation method

◇ *Compta* **mode linéaire** straight-line method

◇ *mode de paiement, mode de règlement* method *or* means of payment

modèle d'évaluation des actifs *nm* capital asset pricing model

moins-perçu *nm* amount due, outstanding amount

moins-value *nf* depreciation, drop in value; *(après une vente)* capital loss

> **"**
> Les sicav monétaires offrent l'avantage de ne supporter que des frais très faibles et, surtout, de mettre les montants investis à l'abri de tout risque de **moins-value**.
> **"**

mois *nm* (a) *(période)* month; **un mois de crédit** a month's credit;

être payé au mois to be paid by the month

(**b**) *(salaire mensuel)* monthly salary; **toucher son mois** to receive one's (month's) salary

◊ *mois double* = extra month's salary paid as an annual bonus

◊ *Bourse mois d'échéance* trading month

Monep *nm Bourse* (*abrév* **marché des options négociables de Paris**) Paris traded options exchange, *Br* ≃ LIFFE, *Am* ≃ CBOE

monétaire *adj (circulation, politique, système, zone)* monetary; *(marché, masse)* money

monétarisme *nm Écon* monetarism

monétariste *adj & nmf Écon* monetarist

Monétique® *nf* electronic money, e-money

monnaie *nf (argent)* money; *(d'un pays)* currency

◊ *monnaie d'appoint* fractional money

◊ *monnaie de banque* bank money, deposit money

◊ *monnaie bloquée* blocked currency

◊ *monnaie circulante* active money

◊ *UE monnaie commune* common currency

◊ *monnaie de compte* money of account

◊ *monnaie de compte convertible* convertible money of account

◊ *monnaie courante* legal currency

◊ *monnaie dirigée* managed or controlled currency

◊ *monnaie divisionnaire* divisional *or* fractional money

◊ *monnaie électronique* electronic money, e-money

◊ *monnaie étrangère* foreign currency

◊ *monnaie faible* soft currency

◊ *monnaie fiduciaire* paper money, *Am* fiat money

◊ *monnaie flottante* floating currency

◊ *monnaie forte* hard currency

◊ *monnaie légale* legal tender

◊ *monnaie de marchandise* commodity money

◊ *monnaie non convertible* blocked currency

◊ *monnaie d'or* gold money

◊ *monnaie de papier* paper money

◊ *monnaie de réserve* reserve currency

◊ *monnaie scripturale* bank *or* deposit money

◊ *Fam monnaie de singe* Monopoly money

◊ *UE monnaie unique* single currency

◊ *UE monnaie verte* green currency

❝

Faute de pouvoir utiliser l'arme des taux de change, depuis la mise en place de la **monnaie unique**, les pays de la zone euro n'auraient plus d'autre recours que d'user de la flexibilité salariale pour maintenir leur compétitivité et favoriser l'emploi: c'est une idée aujourd'hui fréquemment avancée. Ce faisant, la création de l'Euroland n'a pas eu, pour l'heure, d'effets majeurs sur les salaires.

❞

monnayable *adj* convertible into cash

monnayer *vt (terrains, biens, actif)* to convert into cash

montage financier *nm* financial deal, financial operation

montant *nm (somme)* amount, sum; **quel est le montant du chèque/de la facture?** how much is the cheque/invoice for?; **cinq versements d'un montant de 500 francs** five payments of 500 francs (each); **j'ignore le montant de mes dettes** I don't know what my debts amount to

◊ *montant brut* gross amount

◊ *UE montants compensatoires (monétaires)* (monetary) compensatory amounts

◊ *montant exonéré de TVA* VAT exempt amount

◊ *montant forfaitaire* lump sum

◊ *montant net* net total

◊ *Compta montant à reporter* amount brought forward

◊ *montant du retour net* net return

◊ *montant total* total (amount)

monter 1 *vi (cours, prix)* to rise, to go up, to increase (**de** by)

2 se monter *vpr* se monter à to amount to; **les frais se montent à des milliers de francs** the expenses amount to thousands of francs; **la facture se monte à mille francs** the bill amounts *or* comes to a thousand francs

moratoire 1 *adj (paiement)* delayed by agreement

2 *nm* moratorium; **décréter un**

moratoire to declare a moratorium; **le moratoire des loyers** the moratorium on rents

mort, -e *adj (argent)* lying idle

motivation *nf* motivation, incentive

◊ *motivation par le profit* profit motive

mouvement *nm* (a) *(fluctuation)* fluctuation (b) *(déplacement)* movement; *(tendance)* trend

◊ *Bourse mouvement boursier* stock market fluctuation

◊ *Compta mouvement de caisse* cash transaction

◊ *mouvement de capitaux* movement *or* flow of capital

◊ *Bourse mouvement des cours* price fluctuation

◊ *mouvement des devises* currency fluctuation

◊ *Compta mouvement d'espèces* cash transaction

◊ *mouvement de fonds* movement *or* flow of capital

◊ *Bourse mouvement du marché* market fluctuation

◊ *mouvement des prix* change *or* fluctuation in prices

◊ *Bourse mouvement des valeurs* share fluctuation

moyennant *prép* (in return) for; **moyennant paiement de 500 francs** on payment of 500 francs; **moyennant finance** for a fee

moyenne pondérée *nf Compta* weighted average

multidevise *nf* multicurrency

nantir *vt (créancier)* to give security to, to secure; *(valeurs)* to pledge; **entièrement/partiellement nanti** *(créancier)* fully/partly secured

nantissement *nm* (**a**) *(action)* pledging
  (**b**) *(gage)* pledge, collateral (security); **déposer des titres en nantissement** to lodge stock as security; **emprunter sur nantissement** to borrow on security

◇ *Bourse* **nantissement d'actions** lien on shares

◇ *Banque* **nantissement flottant, nantissement général** floating charge

négoce *nm Bourse (de titres, d'actions)* dealing

négociabilité *nf* negotiability

négociable *adj (bon, traite)* negotiable, transferable, trad(e)able; **négociable en banque** bankable; **négociable en Bourse** negotiable on the stock exchange

négociant, -e *nm,f Bourse* trader

◇ **négociant courtier** broker-dealer

négociation *nf Bourse (transaction)* negotiation, transaction; *(d'un effet)* negotiation

◇ **négociations de bloc** block trading

◇ **négociations de Bourse** stock exchange transactions

◇ **négociations de change** exchange transactions

◇ **négociation au comptant** cash transaction

◇ **négociation à la criée** open-outcry trading

◇ **négociations à prime** options trading

◇ **négociations à terme** futures trading

négocier *Bourse* **1** *vt (titres, valeurs)* to trade (in)
  2 se négocier *vpr* **se négocier à** *(titres, valeurs)* to be trading at, to trade at

net, nette 1 *adj* (**a**) *(bénéfice, valeur, poids)* net; *Compta* **net après cessions** net of disposals; **net d'impôt** tax-free
  2 *adv* **cent francs net** a hundred francs net; **cela m'a rapporté 100 francs net** I cleared *or* netted 100 francs, I made a net profit of 100 francs
  3 *nm* net; **net à payer** *(sur bulletin de paie)* net pay, net payable

◇ *Compta* **net commercial** net profit

◇ **net financier** net interest income; *(à payer)* net interest charges

niveau *nm* level
◇ Bourse **niveau de cours des actions** stock price level
◇ Bourse **niveau de dépôt requis** margin requirement

nom d'emprunt *nm* Bourse nominee name

nominal, -e *Bourse* **1** *adj* nominal, par
2 *nm (d'une action)* nominal value; *(d'une obligation)* par value

nominatif, -ive **1** *adj* Bourse *(liste)* nominal; *(titres, actions)* registered
2 *nm* Bourse **dividende au nominatif** dividend on registered securities

non-acceptation *nf* Banque *(d'une lettre de change)* non-acceptance

non-compensé, -e *adj* Banque *(chèque)* uncleared

non-coté, -e *adj* Bourse unquoted

non-encaissé, -e *adj (chèque)* uncashed

non-souscrit, -e *adj (action, émission)* undersubscribed

non-valeur *nf (créance)* bad debt; *Bourse* worthless security

non-vérifié, -e *adj* Compta unaudited

notation *nf* Bourse rating
◇ **notation AA** double-A rating
◇ **notation AAA** triple-A rating

note *nf* **(a)** *(facture)* bill; *(dans un hôtel) Br* bill, *Am* check; **régler** *ou* **payer une note** to pay a bill **(b)** *(communication écrite)* note, memo
◇ **note d'avoir** credit note
◇ **note de commission** commission *or* fee note
◇ **note de crédit** credit note
◇ **note de débit** debit note
◇ **note de frais** expense account; *(présentée après coup)* expenses; *(facture)* expenses claim form; **mettre qch sur sa note de frais** to put sth on one's expense account
◇ **note d'information** offering circular

noté, -e *adj* Bourse rated; **noté AAA** triple-A rated

nouveau, -elle *adj* new; **jusqu'à nouvel ordre** until further notice; *Bourse* until cancelled;
◇ Bourse **nouvelle émission** new issue
◇ Banque **nouveaux emprunts** new borrowings

noyau dur *nm* Bourse = group of stable shareholders chosen for a company by the government on its flotation

numéraire **1** *adj* **espèces numéraires** legal tender
2 *nm* cash; **payer en numéraire** to pay in cash
◇ **numéraire fictif** paper currency

numéro *nm* number
◇ **numéro de chèque** cheque number
◇ Banque **numéro de compte** account number

OAT *nf* (*abrév* **obligation assimilable du Trésor**) = French Treasury bond

obligataire 1 *adj* (*créancier, émission, intérêts, marché*) bond; (*dette, emprunt*) debenture
  2 *nmf* bondholder, debenture holder

obligation *nf* (*titre*) bond, debenture
- ◇ *obligation amortissable* redeemable bond
- ◇ *obligation assimilable du Trésor* = French Treasury bond
- ◇ *obligation à bon de souscription d'actions* bond with share warrant attached
- ◇ *obligation cautionnée* secured *or* guaranteed bond
- ◇ *obligations convertibles* convertible bonds, convertibles
- ◇ *obligation à coupon partagé* split coupon bond
- ◇ *obligation à coupon zéro* zero coupon bond
- ◇ *obligation émise au pair* par bond
- ◇ *obligation d'État* government *or* Treasury bond
- ◇ *obligation garantie* guaranteed bond
- ◇ *obligation hypothécaire* mortgage bond
- ◇ *obligation indemnitaire* indemnity bond
- ◇ *obligation indexée* indexed *or* index-linked bond
- ◇ *obligation à intérêt variable* floating-rate bond
- ◇ *obligations longues* long-dated securities, longs
- ◇ *obligation à lots* prize *or* lottery bond
- ◇ *obligation multimarchés* global bond
- ◇ *obligation nominative* registered bond
- ◇ *obligation non amortissable* irredeemable bond
- ◇ *obligation non garantie* unsecured bond
- ◇ *obligation or* gold bond
- ◇ *obligation au porteur* bearer bond

◊ *obligation de premier ordre* prime bond

◊ *obligation à prime* premium bond

◊ *obligation à prime d'émission* OID bond, original issue discount bond

◊ *obligation remboursable* redeemable bond

◊ *obligations remboursables en actions* redeemable bonds

◊ *obligation à revenu fixe* fixed-rate bond

◊ *obligation à revenu variable* variable-income or floating-rate bond

◊ *Fam obligation Samouraï* Samurai bond

◊ *obligation de société* corporate bond

◊ *obligation à taux fixe* fixed-rate bond

◊ *obligation à taux variable* variable-income or floating-rate bond

◊ *obligation transférable, obligation transmissible* transferable bond

> **"**
>
> Non seulement les **obligations convertibles** permettent de profiter de la hausse de la Bourse mais elles offrent en outre la sécurité d'une obligation classique.
>
> **"**

obligé *nm* obliger *(guaranteeing a bill)*

OBSA *nf (abrév* **obligation à bon de souscription d'actions)** bond with share warrant attached

octroi *nm (de crédits, de subventions, d'un prêt)* granting

octroyer *vt (crédits, subventions, prêt)* to grant (**à** to)

offert *adj Bourse (cours)* offered

offrant, -e *nm,f (à une vente aux enchères)* **le plus offrant (et dernier enchérisseur)** the highest bidder; **vendre au plus offrant** to sell to the highest bidder

offre *nf (proposition)* offer, proposal; **recevoir/accepter une offre** to receive/accept an offer

◊ *offre publique d'achat* takeover bid; **faire** *ou* **lancer une offre publique d'achat (sur)** to make *or* launch a takeover bid (for)

◊ *offre publique d'échange* exchange offer, takeover bid for shares

◊ *offre publique de vente* public offering, public share offer

off-shore, offshore *adj (fonds, investissements, société)* offshore

oisif, -ive *adj (capital)* uninvested, idle

on-shore, onshore *adj (fonds, investissements, société)* onshore

OPA *nf (abrév* **offre publique d'achat)** takeover bid; **lancer une OPA (sur)** to make *or* launch a takeover bid (for)

◊ *OPA amicale* friendly takeover bid

◊ *OPA hostile, OPA inamicale, OPA sauvage* hostile takeover bid

OPCVM *nm Bourse (abrév* **organisme de placement collectif en valeurs mobilières)** collective investment fund, *Br* ≃ unit trust, *Am* ≃ mutual fund

◊ *OPCVM actions* ≃ equity-based *Br* unit trust *or Am* mutual fund

OPE *nf* (*abrév* **offre publique d'échange**) exchange offer, takeover bid for shares

opéable *adj* vulnerable to takeover bids

"
Naturellement, la valeur est **opéable** et d'aucuns commencent à envisager cette hypothèse. En pareil cas, le président a fait savoir que la société valait au moins deux fois plus cher que sa capitalisation boursière (de l'époque), ce qui donnerait une valeur de plus de 150 euros à chaque action.
"

opérateur, -trice *nm,f* trader; *Bourse* operator, dealer

◇ *Bourse* **opérateur à la baisse** operator for a fall, bear

◇ *Bourse* **opérateur boursier** stock exchange dealer

◇ *Bourse* **opérateur en couverture** hedger

◇ *Bourse* **opérateur sur écran** screen trader

◇ *Bourse* **opérateur à la hausse** operator for a rise, bull

◇ *Bourse* **opérateur d'un jour** day trader

opération *nf* (**a**) *Banque* (*transaction*) transaction, deal, operation
(**b**) *Bourse* transaction, deal

◇ *Bourse* **opération à la baisse** bear transaction

◇ **opération blanche** break-even transaction

◇ *Bourse* **opération boursière** stock exchange transaction

◇ *Compta* **opération de caisse** counter transaction

◇ *Compta* **opération en capital** capital transaction

◇ **opération de change** exchange transaction, swap

◇ *Bourse* **opération de change à terme** forward exchange transaction

◇ **opération de clearing** clearing transaction

◇ *Bourse* **opérations de clôture** late trading, trading at the finish

◇ **opération en commun** joint venture

◇ *Compta* **opération comptable** accounting operation

◇ **opération au comptant** *Bourse* spot deal *or* transaction; *Compta* cash transaction

◇ *Compta* **opérations courantes** normal business transactions

◇ *Bourse* **opérations de couverture** hedging

◇ *Bourse* **opération à découvert** short position

◇ *Bourse* **opérations sur écran** screen trading

◇ **opération d'escompte** discount operation

◇ **opération de face à face** back-to-back loan

◇ **opération financière** financial transaction

◇ *Bourse* **opération à la hausse** bull transaction

◇ **opération imposable** taxable transaction

◇ *Bourse* **opération de journée** day trade

◇ *Bourse* **opérations à option** option dealing *or* trading

◇ **opération de prêt** loan transaction

◇ *Bourse* **opération à prime** option deal

◇ *Bourse* **opération à terme** futures *or* forward transaction

◇ *Bourse* **opérations à terme** futures trading

◇ *Bourse* **opérations à terme sur matières premières** commodity futures

> **"**
>
> Il résoud leur problème de capital par des architectures et des **opérations financières** audacieuses qui ne se soucient guère de transparence, ni des actionnaires minoritaires.
>
> **"**

opérer 1 *vt (virement, paiement)* to make, to effect

2 *vi Bourse* **opérer à découvert** to take a short position, to go short

optimalisation *nf* optimization

◇ **optimalisation du profit, optimalisation des profits** profit optimization

optimaliser *vt* to optimize

optimisation *nf* optimization

◇ **optimisation du profit, optimisation des profits** profit optimization

optimiser *vt* to optimize

option *nf Bourse* option; **lever une option** to take up an option

◇ **option d'achat** call option, option to buy

◇ **option d'achat vendue à découvert** naked option

◇ **option sur actions** option on shares, share option

◇ **option américaine** American-style option

◇ **option à l'argent** at-the-money option

◇ **option de change** foreign currency option

◇ **option sur contrats à terme** futures option

◇ **option cotée** traded option

◇ **option au cours** at-the-money option

◇ **option en dedans** in-the-money option

◇ **option en dehors** out-of-the-money option

◇ **option du double** call of more

◇ **option d'échange** swap option

◇ **option européenne** European-style option

◇ **option sur indice** index option

◇ **option à la monnaie** at-the-money option

◇ **option négociable** traded option

◇ **option de titres** stock option

◇ **option de vente** put option, option to sell

OPV *nf (abrév* **offre publique de vente)** offer by prospectus

or *nm* gold

◇ **or en barre** gold bars, gold bullion; *Fam* **ces actions, c'est de l'or en barre** these shares are a rock-solid investment

◇ **or monnayé** gold coins

ORA *nfpl (abrév* **obligations remboursables en actions)** redeemable bonds

ordonnance *nf Jur* order, ruling

◇ **ordonnance de paiement** order *or* warrant for payment, order to pay

ordonnancement *nm* order to pay

ordonnancer *vt (paiement)* to authorize, to order; *(compte)* to initial, to pass for payment; *(dépense)* to sanction

ordonnateur, -trice *nm,f Admin* = official in charge of public expenditure and authorization of payment

ordre nm Banque, Bourse order; **exécuter un ordre** to fill an order; **payez à l'ordre de J. Martin** pay to the order of J. Martin; **libeller** ou **faire un chèque à l'ordre de qn** to make a cheque payable to sb, to make out a cheque to sb; **c'est à quel ordre?** who should I make it out to?, who should I make it payable to?; **non à ordre** (sur chèque) not negotiable

◊ **ordre d'achat** purchase order; Bourse buy order

◊ **ordre à appréciation** discretionary order

◊ Bourse **ordre de Bourse** stock exchange order

◊ **ordre au comptant** cash order

◊ Bourse **ordre conditionnel** contingent order

◊ Bourse **ordre environ** discretionary order

◊ Bourse **ordre lié** straddle

◊ **ordre limite, ordre limité** limit order

◊ **ordre au mieux** market order

◊ Bourse **ordre de négociation** trading order

◊ **ordre de paiement** payment order

◊ Banque **ordre permanent** standing order

◊ Banque **ordre de prélèvement (permanent)** direct debit

◊ Bourse **ordre à révocation** good-till-cancelled order

◊ Bourse **ordre stop** stop order, stop-loss order

◊ Bourse **ordre à terme** futures order

◊ Bourse **ordre tout ou rien** all-or-none order

◊ Banque **ordre de transfert permanent** banker's order, standing order

◊ Bourse **ordre de vente** order to sell

◊ Bourse **ordre de vente stop** stop-loss selling

◊ Banque **ordre de virement** transfer order

◊ Banque **ordre de virement automatique, ordre de virement bancaire** banker's order, Br standing order

Organisation mondiale du commerce nf World Trade Organization

organisme nm organization

◊ **organisme de crédit** credit institution

◊ **organisme de placement collectif** collective investment scheme

◊ **organisme de placement collectif en valeurs mobilières** collective investment fund, Br ≃ unit trust, Am ≃ mutual fund

oscillant, -e adj fluctuating

oscillation nf fluctuation, variation; **les oscillations du marché** the fluctuations of the market, the ups and downs of the market

◊ **oscillations saisonnières** seasonal fluctuations

osciller vi to fluctuate

oseille nf Fam (argent) cash, Br dosh, Am bucks

ouverture nf Bourse start of trading; **à l'ouverture, le dollar était à 5,98 francs** at the start of trading, the dollar was at 5.98 francs

ouvrir vi Bourse to open; **ouvrir en baisse/en hausse** to open down/up; **les valeurs pétrolières ont ouvert ferme** oils opened firm

pacson *nm Fam* **toucher le pacson** *(dans une affaire)* to make a bundle

paiement *nm* payment; *(d'un compte)* payment, settlement; **effectuer** *ou* **faire un paiement** to make a payment; **recevoir un paiement** to receive a payment; **contre paiement de 100 francs** on payment of 100 francs

◊ *paiement par anticipation* payment in advance, advance payment

◊ *paiement arriéré* payment in arrears

◊ *paiement d'avance* payment in advance, advance payment

◊ *Banque* *paiement par carte* card payment, payment by card

◊ *paiement par chèque* payment by cheque

◊ *paiement (au) comptant* cash payment, payment in cash

◊ *paiement différé* deferred payment

◊ *paiement contre documents* payment against documents

◊ *paiement échelonné* staggered payment

◊ *paiement électronique* electronic payment, payment by electronic transfer

◊ *paiement en espèces* payment in cash, cash payment

◊ *paiement intégral* payment in full

◊ *paiement par intervention* payment on behalf of a third party

◊ *paiement libératoire* payment in full discharge from debt

◊ *paiement en liquide* payment in cash, cash payment

◊ *paiement à la livraison* cash on delivery, COD

◊ *paiement en nature* payment in kind

◊ *paiement partiel* partial *or* part payment

◊ *paiements périodiques* periodic payments

◊ *paiement préalable* prepayment

◊ *paiements progressifs* graduated *or* increasing payments

◊ *paiement au prorata* payment pro rata

◊ *paiement reçu* inward payment

◊ *paiement en souffrance* overdue *or* outstanding payment

◊ *paiement à tempérament, paiement à terme* payment by *or* in instalments

◊ *paiement par versements échelonnés* staggered payment

pair *nm* par; **au-dessous/au-dessus du pair** below/above par; **au pair** at par

◊ *pair du change* par of exchange

◊ *pair commercial* par

◊ *pair intrinsèque* mint par

panier *nm Bourse (d'actions)* basket

◊ *Écon panier de devises, panier de monnaies* basket of currencies

papier *nm* bill; **papiers à trois mois (d'échéance)** bills at three months

◊ *papier bancable* bankable paper

◊ *papier non bancable* unbankable paper

◊ *papier de commerce, papier commercial* commercial *or* trade paper

◊ *papier commercial de premier ordre* prime bill

◊ *papier sur l'étranger* foreign bill

◊ *papier fait* guaranteed paper, backed bill

◊ *papier négociable* negotiable paper

◊ *papier à ordre* instrument to order

◊ *papier au porteur* bearer paper

◊ *papiers valeurs* paper securities

◊ *papier à vue* sight paper

papier-monnaie *nm* paper money, paper currency

paquet *nm Bourse (d'actions, de valeurs)* parcel, block

paradis fiscal *nm* tax haven

parafiscal, -e *adj* parafiscal

parafiscalité *nf* = taxes paid to the state and used for administrative purposes

parité *nf Bourse* parity; **à parité** at parity, at the money; **change à (la) parité** exchange at par *or* parity

◊ *parité du change* exchange rate parity, parity of exchange

◊ *parité à crémaillère* crawling *or* sliding peg

◊ *parité fixe* fixed parity

◊ *parité franc-mark* franc-mark parity

◊ *parité des monnaies* monetary parity

◊ *parité du pouvoir d'achat* purchasing power parity

◊ *parité rampante* crawling peg

parquet *nm Bourse* **le parquet** *(lieu)* the trading floor; *(personnes)* the stock exchange

part *nf (du marché, des bénéfices)* share; **avoir part aux bénéfices** to have a share in the profits, to share in the profits; **mettre qn de part (dans une affaire)** to give sb a share in the profits

◊ *part d'association* partnership share

◊ *part bénéficiaire* founder's share

◊ *part de fondateur* founder's share

◊ *part de marché* share of the market, market share

◊ *part patronale* employer's contribution

◊ *part salariale* employee's contribution

◊ *part sociale* share of capital, capital share

partager *vt* (a) *(diviser)* to divide; **partager proportionnellement** to divide pro rata (b) *(uti-*

liser en commun) to share; **il partage les bénéfices avec ses employés** he shares the profits with his employees

partenaire nm partner
◇ **partenaire financier** financial partner

participant, -e 1 adj (action, obligation) participating
2 nm,f participant (**à** in)

participation nf holding, share, interest (**à** in); **notre groupe a une participation de 25% dans cette société** our group has a 25% holding or share or interest in the company
◇ **participation aux bénéfices** profit sharing
◇ **participation majoritaire** majority holding or interest
◇ **participation minoritaire** minority holding or interest
◇ **participation ouvrière** worker participation
◇ **participation des salariés aux bénéfices** profit-sharing scheme

participer participer à vt ind (**a**) (financièrement) to contribute to; **participer aux frais** to pay one's share of the costs, to contribute towards the costs
(**b**) (partager) **participer aux bénéfices** to share in the profits

partie nf Compta **en partie double** double-entry; **en partie simple** single-entry
◇ **partie prenante** payee

pas-de-porte nm Jur (somme d'argent) key money

passation nf (**a**) Compta (d'une écriture) entering
(**b**) (d'un dividende) payment
◇ Compta **passation d'écriture** journal entry
◇ Compta **passation par pertes et profits** write-off

passe de caisse nf allowance to cashier for errors

passer vt Compta to enter, to post; **passer un article au grand-livre** to post an entry in the ledger; **passer écriture d'un article** to post an entry; **passer une somme au débit/au crédit** to debit/credit an account with a sum; **passer une somme en perte** to charge an amount to an account; **passer une somme en profit** to credit an amount to an account; **passer par pertes et profits** to transfer to profit and loss, to write off

passible adj (d'une amende) liable (**de** to); (d'un impôt, d'une taxe) liable, subject (**de** to)

passif nm Compta liabilities, debts; **l'actif et le passif** assets and liabilities; **inscrire** ou **passer une dette au passif** to enter a debt on the liabilities side
◇ **passif circulant** current liabilities
◇ **passif éventuel** contingent liabilities
◇ **passif exigible** current liabilities
◇ **passif à long terme** long-term liabilities
◇ **passif reporté** deferred liabilities

patrimoine nm (d'un individu) property, wealth, personal assets; (actif net) net assets
◇ **patrimoine immobilier** Br property assets, Am real-estate assets

◇ Banque **patrimoine social** social assets

payable adj payable; **effet
payable au 1 juillet** bill due on 1
July; **payable à 30 jours** payable
at 30 days' date; **payable en 12
mensualités** payable in 12
monthly instalments; **payable à
l'arrivée** payable on arrival;
payable à la banque payable at
the bank; **payable comptant**
payable in cash; **payable sur demande** payable on demand;
payable à l'échéance payable at
maturity; **payable à la livraison**
payable on delivery; **payable au
porteur** payable to bearer;
payable   sur   présentation
payable on demand or on presentation; **payable   à   vue**
payable on sight

payant, -e adj (a) (non gratuit)
(agence) charging a fee; (service) with a charge (b) (qui rapporte) profitable

payer vt (facture, impôts,
intérêts, personne) to pay;
(dette) to pay (off), to settle;
(effet) to honour; **payer qch à
qn** to buy sth for sb; **payer
d'avance** to pay in advance;
payer par carte de crédit to pay
by credit card; **payer par chèque**
to pay by cheque; **payer
comptant** ou **en liquide** to pay
cash; **payer à l'échéance** to pay
at maturity or due date; **payer
en espèces** to pay (in) cash;
payer intégralement ou **en totalité** to pay in full; **payer à l'ordre
de** (sur chèque) pay to the order
of; **payez au porteur** pay to
bearer; **payer à présentation** to
pay on presentation; **payer à
vue** to pay at sight

payeur, -euse 1 nm,f payer;
c'est un bon/mauvais payeur he
is a good/bad payer
2 nm Admin pay clerk

PC nf (abrév **pièce de caisse**) cash
voucher

PCG nm Compta (abrév **plan
comptable général**) chart of accounts

PEA nm (abrév **plan d'épargne en
actions**) investment trust, Br ≃
PEP

pécuniaire adj (situation) financial

PEE nm (abrév **plan d'épargne
d'entreprise**) company savings
scheme

> **"**
>
> L'argent versé sur un **PEE** est
> placé dans des fonds com-
> muns de placement d'entre-
> prise (FCPE). La plupart des
> sociétés offrent le choix entre
> un fonds monétaire sans risque,
> un fonds obligataire et un fonds
> dynamique placé en actions.
> Ces fonds peuvent miser sur
> tous les marchés et sur tous les
> pays alors qu'un PEA ne peut
> être constitué que d'actions
> françaises.
>
> **"**

PEL nm (abrév **plan épargne-
logement**) Br ≃ building society
account, Am ≃ savings and
loan association account

pénalité nf penalty
◇ **pénalité libératoire** full and
final penalty payment
◇ **pénalité de retard** late payment penalty; (pour livraison
tardive) late delivery penalty

pension nf (allocation) pension
◇ **pension de retraite** (retirement or old-age) pension
◇ **pension viagère** life annuity

PEP nm (abrév **plan d'épargne populaire**) special savings account

PEPS nm (abrév **premier entré, premier sorti**) FIFO

PER nm (a) (abrév **plan d'épargne retraite**) retirement savings scheme (b) (abrév **price/earnings ratio**) p/e ratio

percepteur nm Admin **percepteur (d'impôt)** collector of taxes, tax collector

perception nf Admin (d'impôts) collection, receipt
◇ **perception de dividende** receipt of a dividend
◇ **perception à la source** tax deduction at source

percevable adj Admin (impôt) collectable

percevoir vt Admin (impôts, droits, loyers) to collect; (revenus, indemnités, intérêts, commission) to receive, to be paid; **cotisations à percevoir** contributions still due; **percevoir les impôts à la source** to collect tax at source

perdre vt (argent) to lose; **perdre de sa valeur** to lose value; **le franc a encore perdu par rapport à la livre** the franc has slipped further against the dollar

performance nf Bourse (des actions, des titres) performance; **performance des cours de la Bourse** share price performance

performant, -e adj (investissement) profitable, high-yield

période nf period
◇ **période d'amortissement** depreciation period
◇ **période comptable** financial or accounting period, Am fiscal period
◇ Bourse **période de cotation obligatoire** mandatory quote period
◇ UE **période de double circulation** (de la monnaie nationale et de l'euro) double circulation period
◇ **période d'essor** boom
◇ **période de grâce** tax holiday
◇ **période de recouvrement** collection period
◇ **période de remboursement** payback period

personne nf
◇ **personne fictive** fictitious person
◇ **personne morale** corporate body, legal entity

personnel nm (d'une entreprise) personnel, staff, employees; **faire partie du personnel** to be a member of staff, to be on the payroll
◇ Banque **personnel de back-office** back office staff

perspective nf prospect, outlook
◇ **perspectives de profit** profit outlook

perte nf (d'argent) loss; **travailler** ou **fonctionner à perte** to operate at a loss; **vendre qch à perte** to sell sth at a loss; **passer une perte par profits et pertes** to write off a loss; **subir de lourdes pertes** to suffer heavy losses
◇ **perte de bénéfice** loss of profit
◇ **perte brute** gross loss

⋄ *perte en capitaux* capital loss
⋄ *perte de change* (foreign) exchange loss
⋄ *perte d'exploitation* operating loss
⋄ *perte finale* terminal loss
⋄ *perte d'intérêts* loss of interest
⋄ *perte latente* unrealized loss
⋄ *perte nette* net loss
⋄ *perte partielle* partial loss
⋄ *perte présumée* presumptive loss
⋄ *Compta* **pertes et profits exceptionnels** extraordinary items
⋄ *perte sèche* clear *or* dead loss
⋄ *Compta* **perte supportée** loss attributable
⋄ *perte totale* total loss
⋄ *Compta* **perte transférée** loss transferred

peseta *nf* peseta

petit, -e *adj* small
⋄ *petite caisse* petty cash
⋄ *petits épargnants, la petite épargne* small savers
⋄ *petit porteur* small investor *or* shareholder

pétrodollar *nm* petrodollar

pétromonnaie *nf* petrocurrency

pèze *nm Fam* cash, *Br* dosh, *Am* bucks

pfennig *nm* pfennig

pièce *nf* (a) *(monnaie)* **pièce (de monnaie)** coin; **pièce de deux francs** two-franc coin
(b) *(document)* document, paper
⋄ *Compta* **pièce de caisse** cash voucher
⋄ *pièce d'or* gold coin

pignoratif, -ive *adj* with a repurchase option

place *nf* (a) *(endroit)* place, location; **avoir du crédit sur la place** to have credit (facilities) locally; **chèque encaissable sur la place** cheque cashable locally
(b) *Bourse* market
⋄ *place boursière* stock market
⋄ *place financière* financial centre *or* market; **le dollar est à la hausse sur la place financière de New York** the dollar has risen on the New York exchange

> **"**
>
> La baisse de 5,4% de Francfort est la plus forte subie par cette **place financière** depuis le début de l'année.
>
> **"**

placement *nm* *(action)* investment, investing; *(argent)* investment; **faire des placements** to invest (money), to make investments; **faire un bon placement** to make a good investment
⋄ *placement en actions* equity investment
⋄ *placement à court terme* short-term investment
⋄ *placement éthique* ethical investment
⋄ *placement financier* stock market investment
⋄ *placement à long terme* long-term investment
⋄ *placement obligataire* bond investment
⋄ *placement offshore* offshore investment
⋄ *placement de père de famille*

gilt-edged investment, blue chip

◇ *placement privé* private investment

◇ *placement à revenus fixes* fixed-income or fixed-yield investment

◇ *placement à revenu variable* variable-income investment

> **"**
>
> Le Crédit Lyonnais, fort de son expérience avec le fonds Hymnos, contrôlé par un comité de congrégations religieuses, réfléchit au lancement de nouveaux **placements éthiques**. Tandis que Friends Ivory & Sime, le no 1 du secteur en Grande Bretagne, cherche des partenaires financiers en France pour développer des fonds socialement responsables, comme l'indique l'une de ses responsables.
>
> **"**

placer vt *(argent)* to invest; *(actions)* to place; **placer de l'argent dans les pétroles** to invest in oils; **placer à court terme/à long terme** to invest short-term/long-term; **placer à intérêts** to invest at interest; **placer de l'argent sur un compte** to put or deposit money in an account

plafond nm *(limite)* ceiling; **le franc a atteint son plafond** the franc has reached its ceiling or upper limit; **crever le plafond** to exceed the limit, to break the ceiling; **fixer un plafond à un budget** to put a ceiling on a budget, to cap a budget

◇ *Banque* **plafond d'autorisa-** *tion de retrait* withdrawal limit

◇ *plafond des charges budgétaires* budgetary limit

◇ *plafond du crédit* credit ceiling or limit

◇ *Banque* **plafond de découvert** overdraft limit

◇ *plafond de l'impôt* tax ceiling

◇ *Banque* **plafond de retrait** withdrawal limit

plage nf *(éventail)* range, band

◇ *plage de prix* price range

◇ *plage de taux* rate band

plan nm *(projet)* plan, project

◇ *Compta* **plan d'amortissement** depreciation schedule

◇ *plan d'assainissement* stabilization plan

◇ *Compta* **plan comptable** accounting plan

◇ *Compta* **plan comptable général, plan de comptes** chart of accounts

◇ *plan d'échéances* instalment plan

◇ *plan économique* economic plan

◇ *plan d'épargne* savings scheme or plan

◇ *plan d'épargne en actions* investment trust, *Br* ≃ personal equity plan

◇ *plan d'épargne entreprise* employee *Br* share or *Am* stock ownership plan

◇ *plan épargne-logement Br* ≃ building society account, *Am* ≃ savings and loan association account

◇ *plan d'épargne populaire* special savings account

◇ *plan d'épargne retraite* retirement savings plan or scheme

◇ *Compta* **plan de financement** funding *or* financial plan

◇ **plan d'investissement** investment plan

◇ *Bourse* **plan d'options sur titres** stock option plan

◇ **plan prévisionnel** forecast plan

◇ **plan de retraite** pension plan *or* scheme

◇ **plan de trésorerie** cash flow forecast

planche à billets *nf* **faire fonctionner la planche à billets** to print money

planification *nf Écon* planning

◇ **planification budgétaire** budget planning

◇ **planification financière** financial planning

planning *nm* plan, schedule; *(programme d'activités, de travail)* schedule

◇ *Compta* **planning des charges** expenditure planning

plus-value *nf (bénéfice)* capital gain, profit; *(augmentation de la valeur)* appreciation, increase in value; *(excédent) (d'impôts)* surplus; **réaliser une plus-value sur la vente d'un produit** to make a profit on the sale of a product; **les recettes présentent une plus-value de** the receipts show an increase of; **nos actions ont enregistré une plus-value** our shares have increased in value

◇ **plus-value sur titres** paper profit

> **❝**
>
> Le premier semestre s'est en effet terminé sur une perte de 140 millions de francs malgré une **plus-value** liée à la cession de 49% de Cofinoga.
>
> **❞**

PME *nm* (*abrév* **porte-monnaie électronique**) electronic wallet, electronic purse

point *nm* (**a**) *(endroit)* point, place
(**b**) *(dans un pourcentage, dans une échelle)* point; **l'indice CAC 40 a perdu un point hier** the CAC 40 index fell by a point yesterday
(**c**) *(stade)* point

◇ **point critique** break-even point

◇ **point mort** break-even point

◇ *Banque* **point retrait** cashpoint

◇ **point de retraite** pension point

◇ **points de retraite** accrued benefits

politique *nf* policy

◇ **politique budgétaire** budgetary *or* fiscal policy

◇ **politique conjoncturelle** economic policy *(responding to changes in the business cycle)*

◇ **politique de crédit** credit policy

◇ **politique de déflation, politique déflationniste** deflationary policy

◇ **politique de dividendes** dividend policy

◇ **politique économique** economic policy

◇ **politique fiscale** fiscal policy

◇ **politique d'inflation, politique inflationniste** inflationary policy

◇ **politique d'investissement** investment policy

◇ *Écon* **politique de libre-échange** free-trade policy

◇ **politique en matière de change** exchange policy

◇ *politique monétaire* monetary policy

ponction *nf (retrait)* withdrawal; **faire une grosse ponction sur un compte** to withdraw a large sum from an account; **c'est une ponction importante sur mes revenus** it makes a big hole *or* dent in my income
◇ Admin *ponction fiscale* taxation
◇ *ponction sociale* = contributions to the social security scheme, *Br* ≃ National Insurance contributions

ponctionner *vt (économies, pouvoir d'achat)* to make a hole *or* dent in; **on nous ponctionne un tiers de notre salaire en impôts** a third of our salary goes in tax

portage *nm Banque* piggybacking

portefeuille *nm* portfolio
◇ *portefeuille d'actions* share portfolio
◇ *portefeuille d'assurances* insurance portfolio
◇ *portefeuille effets* bills in hand, holdings
◇ *portefeuille indexé* indexed portfolio
◇ *portefeuille d'investissements* investment portfolio
◇ *portefeuille avec mandat* discretionary portfolio
◇ *portefeuille de marques* brand portfolio
◇ *portefeuille de titres* securities portfolio

"

Les créances douteuses ont augmenté au cours du premier semestre de l'année fiscale, et les fonds propres, composés en partie des gains latents sur les **portefeuilles de titres**, ont fondu avec la chute du Nikkei.

"

porte-monnaie électronique *nm* electronic wallet, electronic purse

"

Le **porte-monnaie électronique** arrive en France. ... Au total, quelque 200 000 **porte-monnaie électroniques**, ou PME, destinés à régler les achats de moins de 100 francs, devraient en effet équiper les Français d'ici à quelques mois, grâce à trois expériences. ... Il s'agit d'une carte à puce chargée avec une réserve d'argent, comparable à une carte téléphonique prépayée. Elle est destinée à régler les achats de petit montant, exclusivement en euros, précise-t-on au Crédit Mutuel de Strasbourg, qui mène le projet 'Mondex'.

"

porter *vt* (**a**) *(intérêts)* to bear (**b**) *(inscrire)* to enter, to inscribe; **porter un achat sur un compte** to enter a purchase on an account; **portez cela sur** *ou* **à mon compte** put that on my account, charge it to my account; **portez-le sur la note** put it on the bill; **porter une somme au crédit de qn** to credit sb's account with a sum

porteur, -euse *nm,f* (**a**) *(d'un chèque)* bearer, payee; *(d'un effet)* bearer, holder, payee;

payer au porteur *(sur chèque)* pay bearer **(b)** *Bourse (actionnaire) Br* shareholder, *Am* stockholder; **petit/gros porteur** small/big investor

◇ **porteur d'actions** *Br* shareholder, *Am* stockholder

◇ **porteur d'actions nominatives** registered *Br* shareholder *or Am* stockholder

◇ **porteur d'obligations** debenture holder, bondholder

◇ **porteur de parts** *Br* shareholder, *Am* stockholder

◇ **porteur de titres** *Br* shareholder, *Am* stockholder

> **"**
>
> Satisfaisants pour les **porteurs d'actions**, ces bénéfices fastueux irritent fortement les consommateurs britanniques, qui y voient la preuve que les prix pratiqués par BT sont abusifs.
>
> **"**

position *nf* **(a)** *(d'un compte)* balance; **demander sa position** to ask for one's balance

(b) *Bourse* position; **liquider une position** to close (out) a position; **prendre une position inverse sur le marché** to offset

◇ *Bourse* **position acheteur** long *or* bull position

◇ *Bourse* **position baissière** short *or* bear position

◇ **position de compte** balance

◇ **position courte couverte** covered (short) position

◇ **position couverte** covered position

◇ **position créditrice** credit balance

◇ **position débitrice** debit balance

◇ **position financière** financial position

◇ **position longue** long position

◇ **position non couverte** uncovered position

◇ **position ouverte** open position

◇ **position de place** open interest

◇ **position de trésorerie** cash (flow) situation

◇ **position vendeur** short *or* bear position

positionnement *nm (d'un compte)* calculation of the balance

positionner *vt (compte)* to calculate the balance of

possesseur *nm* owner; *(de valeurs, de titres)* holder

possession *nf* **la possession** *(d'une société)* the assets

postdater *vt* to postdate

poste *nm Compta* entry, item

◇ **poste de bilan** balance sheet item

◇ **poste créditeur** credit item

◇ **poste débiteur** debit item

◇ **poste extraordinaire** extraordinary item

◇ **poste de mémoire** reminder entry

pot-de-vin *nm* bribe; **verser des pots-de-vin à qn** to bribe sb

pourcentage *nm* percentage; **travailler au pourcentage** to work on a commission basis

poussée *nf (des prix, d'une monnaie, de l'inflation)* rise (**de** in)

◇ **poussée inflationniste** inflationary surge

pouvoir d'achat *nm* purchasing power, buying power

préavis *nm (notification)* (advance *or* prior) notice; *Banque* **dépôt à sept jours de préavis** deposit at seven days' notice

précompte *nm* **(a)** *(d'un compte)* advance deduction **(b)** *(de cotisations, d'impôts)* deduction at source

précompter *vt* **(a)** *(argent d'un compte)* to deduct in advance **(b)** *(cotisations, impôts)* to deduct at source; **précompter la Sécurité Sociale sur le salaire de qn** to deduct social security payments from sb's salary

préfinancement *nm* advance funding, pre-financing

préfinancer *vt* to fund in advance, to pre-finance

prélèvement *nm (action)* deduction (**sur** from); *(somme prélevée)* amount deducted; **faire un prélèvement sur un compte** to debit an account; **le prélèvement sera effectué le dernier jour de chaque mois** the deduction will be made on the last day of each month

◇ *UE* **prélèvements agricoles** agricultural levies

◇ *Banque* **prélèvement bancaire (automatique)** direct debit

◇ **prélèvement sur le capital** capital levy

◇ **prélèvement fiscal** taxation

◇ **prélèvement de l'impôt à la source** taxation at source

◇ **prélèvement libératoire** deduction (of tax) at source

◇ **prélèvements obligatoires** =

tax and social security contributions

◇ **prélèvement salarial, prélèvement sur salaire** deduction from wages

◇ **prélèvement social** social security contribution

> “
>
> Le Japon rechute dans la récession et l'Allemagne risque de suivre la même voie après l'alourdissement des **prélèvements fiscaux**, début 1994.
>
> ”

prélever *vt* to deduct in advance; *(compte)* to draw on; **prélever 10% sur qch** to make an advance deduction of 10% from sth; **prélever une commission de 2% sur une opération** to charge a 2% commission on a transaction; **dividende prélevé sur le capital** dividend paid out of capital; **prélever une somme sur un salaire** to deduct a sum from a salary; **prélever une somme sur un compte** to withdraw a sum from an account; **prélever qch à la source** to deduct sth at source

premier *nm* **premier entré, premier sorti** first in, first out

preneur, -euse *nm,f* buyer, purchaser; *(d'un chèque, d'une lettre de change)* payee

prépayer *vt* to prepay

préposé, -e *nm,f* employee

◇ **préposé à la caisse** cashier

prescription *nf*

◇ **prescription acquisitive** positive prescription

◇ **prescription extinctive** negative prescription

présentateur, -trice *nm,f* *(d'une traite, d'un chèque)* presenter

présentation *nf (d'une traite, d'un chèque)* presentation; **sur présentation de** on presentation of; **présentation à l'encaissement** *Banque* paying in, *Br* encashment; *Admin* presentation for collection; **présentation au paiement** presentation for payment

présenter *vt* **présenter une traite à l'acceptation** to present a bill for acceptance; **présenter un chèque à l'encaissement** to present a cheque for payment

prestation *nf* (a) *(allocation)* benefit, allowance; **verser les prestations** to pay out benefits; **recevoir des prestations** to receive benefits
(b) *(service)* service
◊ **prestation de capitaux** provision of capital
◊ **prestation indemnitaire** allowance, benefit
◊ **prestations maladie** sickness benefit
◊ **prestations sociales** social security benefits

prêt *nm* loan; **accorder/consentir un prêt** to allow/to grant a loan; **demander** *ou* **solliciter un prêt** to apply for a loan
◊ **prêt pour l'accession à la propriété** home loan
◊ **prêts d'aide à l'investissement** *ou* **au développement des entreprises** loan guarantee scheme
◊ **prêt bail** leasing
◊ **prêt bancaire** bank loan
◊ **prêt de banque à banque** interbank loan
◊ **prêt bonifié** loan at reduced rate of interest, soft loan
◊ **prêt conditionnel, prêt à condition** tied loan
◊ **prêt aux conditions du marché** hard loan
◊ **prêt à la consommation** consumer loan
◊ **prêt à court terme** short(-term) loan
◊ **prêt à découvert** overdraft loan
◊ **prêt de démarrage** start-up loan
◊ **prêt douteux** doubtful loan
◊ **prêt d'épargne-logement** home loan
◊ **prêt escompté** discounted loan
◊ **prêt à fonds perdus** loan without security
◊ **prêt sur gage** loan against security
◊ **prêt garanti, prêt avec garantie** guaranteed *or* secured loan, collateral loan
◊ **prêt d'honneur** loan on trust
◊ **prêt hypothécaire, prêt sur hypothèque** mortgage loan
◊ **prêt immobilier** *Br* property *or* *Am* real-estate loan
◊ **prêt initial** start-up loan
◊ **prêt à intérêts** loan at interest, interest-bearing loan
◊ **prêt sans intérêt** interest-free loan
◊ **prêts au jour le jour** loan at call
◊ **prêt à long terme** long(-term) loan
◊ **prêt sur nantissement** loan on collateral
◊ **prêt non-garanti** unsecured loan
◊ **prêt participatif** equity loan

◇ *prêt en participation* syndicated loan

◇ *prêts aux particuliers* personal loans

◇ *prêt personnalisé, prêt personnel* personal loan

◇ *prêt à la petite semaine* = short-term loan at high rate of interest

◇ *prêt remboursable sur demande* loan at call, loan repayable on demand

◇ *prêt de remboursement* refunding loan

◇ *prêt en souffrance* non-performing loan

◇ *prêt à tempérament* instalment loan

◇ *prêt à terme (fixe)* term loan

◇ *prêt sur titres* loan against securities

◇ *prêt à vue* loan at call, loan repayable on demand

prête-nom *nm (société)* nominee company

prétention *nf (financière)* expected salary; **envoyer curriculum vitae et prétentions (de salaire)** send CV and state salary requirements

prêter *vt* to lend, to loan; **prêter de l'argent à intérêt** to lend money at interest; **prêter à 8%** to lend at 8%; **prêter sur garantie** *ou* **gage(s)** to lend against security; **prêter à la petite semaine** to make a short-term loan at a high rate of interest

prêteur, -euse *nm,f* lender

◇ *prêteur en dernier ressort* lender of last resort

◇ *prêteur sur titre* money broker

prêt-relais *nm Br* bridging loan, *Am* bridge loan

prévision *nf* forecast

◇ *Bourse* **prévision boursière** stock market forecast

◇ *prévisions budgétaires* budget estimates *or* forecasts

◇ *prévision de trésorerie* cash flow forecast

◇ *prévision des ventes et profits* sales and profit forecast

prévisionnel, -elle *adj (coût)* estimated; *(budget)* predicted

prévoyance *nf* contingency, provision for the future

◇ *prévoyance sociale* social security provisions

prime *nf* (**a**) *Bourse* premium, option; **acheter à prime** to give for the call; **donner la réponse à une prime, répondre à une prime** to declare an option; **faire prime** to stand at a premium; **lever la prime** to exercise *or* take up an option

(**b**) *(subvention)* subsidy, grant
(**c**) *(sur salaire)* bonus

◇ *Bourse* **prime acheteur** buyer's option

◇ *prime du change* agio

◇ *Bourse* **prime de conversion** conversion premium

◇ *prime de développement* (government) development subsidy *or* grant

◇ *prime sur le dollar* dollar premium

◇ *Bourse* **prime d'émission** issue *or* share premium

◇ *prime en espèces* cash bonus

◇ *prime à l'exportation* export subsidy

◇ *prime de fusion* merger premium

◇ *prime d'illiquidité* illiquidity premium

◇ *prime à l'investissement* investment subsidy

◇ *prime de l'or* premium on gold

◇ *Bourse* **prime de remboursement** premium on redemption, redemption fee

◇ *Bourse* **prime de risque de marché** risk premium

◇ *Bourse* **prime vendeur** seller's option

principal *nm* principal, capital sum; *(de l'impôt)* = original amount of tax payable before surcharges

◇ *principal et intérêts* principal and interest

principe *nm* principle

◇ *principe de la continuité de l'exploitation* going-concern concept

◇ *Compta* **principe d'indépendance des exercices** accruals concept

◇ *Compta* **principe de la partie double** double-entry method

◇ *Compta* **principe de la partie simple** single-entry method

◇ *Compta* **principe de permanence, principe de la permanence des méthodes** consistency concept *or* principle

◇ *Compta* **principe de prudence** conservatism concept *or* principle

◇ *Compta* **principe de rattachement à l'exercice** accruals concept

◇ *Compta* **principe du rattachement des produits et des charges** matching principle

prise *nf*

◇ *prise de bénéfices* profit-taking

◇ *prise en charge (de frais)* payment, covering

◇ *prise de contrôle* takeover

◇ *prise à domicile* receipt at domicile

◇ *prise de participation (dans une entreprise)* acquisition of an interest in a company

◇ *Bourse* **prise de position** position taking

privé, -e *adj (banque, entreprise, secteur, investisseur)* private

privilège *nm* preferential right; **avoir un privilège sur qch** to have a lien *or* charge on sth

◇ *privilège du créancier* creditor's preferential claim

◇ *Banque* **privilège d'émission** exclusive right to issue banknotes

◇ *privilège fiscal* tax privilege

◇ *privilège général* general lien

◇ *privilège de souscription* preferential subscription right

◇ *privilège spécial* particular lien

privilégier *vt (banque)* to grant a charter to; *(créancier)* to give preference to

prix *nm* (a) *(coût)* price
(b) *Bourse* price; **actions cotées au prix de ...** shares quoted at the rate of …

◇ *Bourse* **prix acheteur, prix d'achat** bid price

◇ *prix de l'argent* price of money

◇ *prix du change* (exchange) premium

◇ *Bourse* **prix (au) comptant** spot price

◇ *Bourse* **prix de conversion** conversion price

◇ *prix coûtant* cost price

◇ *prix de détail* retail price

◇ *Bourse* **prix du disponible** spot price

◇ *Bourse* **prix d'émission** issue price

◇ **prix d'exercice** exercise price; *(d'option d'achat)* striking *or* exercise price

◇ **prix de facture, prix facturé** invoice *or Am* billing price

◇ **prix hors taxe** price net of tax, price before tax

◇ **prix de la main-d'œuvre directe** direct labour cost

◇ *Bourse* **prix du marché** market price; **acheter/vendre au prix du marché** to buy/sell at market price

◇ **prix maximum** peak price

◇ **prix de négociation** trade price

◇ **prix nominal** nominal price

◇ *Bourse* **prix offert** bid price

◇ *Bourse* **prix de l'option** option price

◇ *Écon* **prix plafond** ceiling price

◇ **prix de rabais** reduced *or* discount price

◇ **prix de rachat** redemption price

◇ *Bourse* **prix du report** contango rate

◇ **prix de revient** cost price

◇ *Écon* **prix seuil** floor price

◇ *UE* **prix du seuil** threshold price

◇ **prix taxe comprise** price inclusive of tax

◇ *Bourse* **prix à terme** forward price

◇ **prix tout compris, prix tous frais compris, prix toutes taxes comprises** all-inclusive price

◇ *Bourse* **prix vendeur** offer price

◇ **prix de vente** sale price, selling price

❝

Thomson a calculé que les salaires n'entraient qu'à hauteur de 15% dans le **prix de revient** final d'un tube cathodique produit à l'usine Polkolor de Piaseczno.

❞

procédure *nf Jur* proceedings

◇ **procédure de faillite** bankruptcy proceedings

producteur, -trice *adj* productive; **producteur d'intérêt** interest-bearing

production *nf* (a) *(fait de produire)* production; *(quantités produites)* production, output (b) *(produit)* product

◇ **production immobilisée** = fixed assets produced for use by the company

◇ **production intérieure brute** gross domestic product

◇ *Compta* **production stockée** *(poste de bilan)* stored production, production left in stock

◇ *Compta* **production vendue** sales

produire *vt (intérêt)* to bear, to yield

produit *nm (profit)* yield; *(recette)* proceeds; **le produit de la journée** the day's takings *or* proceeds

◇ **produits accessoires** sundry income

◇ *Compta* **produits annexes** incidental income

◇ *Banque* **produit bancaire** banking product

◇ *Compta* **produit brut** gross proceeds *or* income

◇ *Compta* **produit constaté**

d'avance prepaid *or* deferred income

◊ *Compta* **produits courants** current income

◊ *Compta* **produits exceptionnels** extraordinary income

◊ *Compta* **produits d'exploitation** operating income, income from operations

◊ **produit financier** *(dispositif d'investissement)* financial product; *Compta (recette)* interest received

◊ *Compta* **produits de gestion courante** income from operations

◊ **produit intérieur net** net domestic product

◊ **produit moyen** average revenue

◊ *Écon* **produit national** national product

◊ **produit national brut** gross national product

◊ **produit national net** net national product

◊ **produit net** net earnings *or* proceeds

◊ *Compta* **produits à recevoir** accrued income, accruals

◊ **produit de taux** interest-bearing financial product

"

Dominique Strauss-Kahn réserve dans son budget 2000 une petite surprise à ceux qui croyaient la réforme des stock-options enterrée. On chercherait en vain dans sa copie une allusion à ces **produits financiers** qui permettent aux cadres dirigeants d'acheter au rabais des actions de leur entreprise.

"

profil *nm* profile

◊ *Banque* **profil patrimonial** personal assets profile

profit *nm* profit; **vendre à profit** to sell at a profit; **profit de 12%** 12% profit

◊ *Compta* **profit brut** gross profit

◊ **profit espéré** anticipated profit

◊ **profits exceptionnels** windfall profits

◊ *Compta* **profits de l'exercice** year's profits

◊ *Compta* **profit d'exploitation** operating profit

◊ **profits fictifs** paper profits

◊ **profits non matérialisés** paper profits

◊ **profits mis en réserve** capital reserves

◊ **profit net** clear profit

◊ *Compta* **profits et pertes** profit and loss

◊ **profit réel** real profit

◊ **profit tout clair** clear profit

programme d'investissement *nm* investment programme

progressivité *nf* progressivity

◊ **progressivité de l'impôt** progressive increase in taxation

projet *nm* plan, project

◊ **projet de budget** budget estimates

proportionnalité *nf (rapport)* balance; *(répartition)* equal distribution

◊ **proportionnalité de l'impôt** fixed rate system of taxation

proportionnel, -elle *adj (impôt)* ad valorem, proportional

prorata *nm* proportion; **au pro-**

rata proportionately, pro rata; **au prorata de qch** proportionately to sth

proroger *vt* to extend; **proroger l'échéance d'un billet** to extend the maturity of a bill

prospectus *nm Bourse* **prospectus (d'émission)** prospectus

protection fiscale *nf* tax shield

protéger *vt Bourse (position)* to hedge

protestable *adj (effet)* protestable

protester *vt (effet)* to protest

protocole d'achat et de vente *nm* buy-sell agreement

provision *nf* (**a**) *Banque* funds; **verser une provision** *ou* **des provisions** to deposit funds; **manque de provision** *(sur chèque)* no funds; **provision d'une lettre de change** consideration for a bill of exchange; **faire provision pour une lettre de change** to provide for *or* protect a bill of exchange
(**b**) *Compta* provision, reserve

◊ *Compta* **provision pour amortissement** provision for depreciation, depreciation allowance

◊ *Compta* **provision pour créances douteuses** provision for bad debts

◊ *Compta* **provision pour dépréciation** provision for depreciation, depreciation allowance

◊ *Compta* **provision pour risques et charges** contingency and loss provision

> **"**
>
> Contrairement à la plupart de ses concurrents, le montant de ses **provisions** n'a jamais été obéré par des ventes exubérantes d'actifs mobiliers ou immobiliers.
>
> **"**

provisionnement *nm* funding

provisionner *vt Banque (compte)* to pay money into, to deposit funds into; *(lettre de change)* to provide for, to protect

publication des comptes *nf* disclosure (of accounts)

purger *vt (hypothèque)* to pay off

put *nm Bourse* put (option)

pyramide des salaires *nf* wage pyramid

qualification *nf Bourse* qualification *(by acquisition of shares)*

quasi-espèces *nfpl Compta* cash equivalents

quasi-trésorerie *nf Compta* cash equivalents

quittance *nf* receipt
◇ *quittance comptable* accountable receipt
◇ *quittance finale, quittance libératoire* receipt in full
◇ *Banque **quittance pour solde de tout compte*** closing account balance

quittancer *vt* to receipt

quitus *nm Compta* (final) discharge

quote-part *nf* share, quota; **apporter** *ou* **payer sa quote-part** to contribute one's share; **quote-part des bénéfices** share in the profits

> Les ressources du FMI sont limitées et ne dépasseraient pas aujourd'hui quinze milliards de dollars. Ces ressources proviennent des **quote-parts** versées par les 182 états qui en sont membres et qui disposent de droits de vote directement proportionnels à leurs apports.

quotité *nf Bourse (d'actions)* minimum number

rabais *nm* reduction, discount; **faire** *ou* **accorder un rabais sur qch** to give a discount on sth

◇ *rabais différé* deferred rebate

rachat *nm* (**a**) *(de valeur, de dette, d'obligation)* redemption (**b**) *(d'une entreprise)* buy-out (**c**) *Bourse (d'actions)* buy-back, repurchase

◇ *rachat d'entreprise par la direction* management buy-out

◇ *rachat d'entreprise financé par l'endettement* leveraged buy-out

◇ *rachat d'entreprise par les salariés* staff *or* employee buy-out

◇ *Compta rachat forfaitaire des créances* lump-sum purchase of accounts receivable

◇ *Bourse rachat gagnant* repurchase at a profit

racheter *vt* (**a**) *(valeur, dette, obligation)* to redeem (**b**) *(entreprise)* to buy out; **racheter les parts de qn** to buy sb out (**c**) *Bourse (actions)* to repurchase, to buy back; **se couvrir en rachetant** to cover a short position by buying back

radiation *nf (d'une dette)* cancellation

◇ *Bourse radiation de la cote* delisting

radier *vt* (**a**) *(dette)* to cancel (**b**) *Bourse* **radier qch de la cote** *(société, actions)* to delist sth

raffermir se raffermir *vpr (prix, marché)* to steady

> "
> Le mark s'est sensiblement **raffermi** au cours des dernières séances, profitant de l'affaiblissement du dollar.
> "

raffermissement *nm (des prix, du marché)* steadying

raid *nm Bourse* raid; **lancer/financer un raid** to mount/to finance a raid

raider *nm* (corporate) raider

rajuster *vt (taux d'intérêt)* to adjust, to revise

rallonge *nf Fam* extra money; **une rallonge de 1000 francs** an extra 1,000 francs

ramassage *nm Bourse (d'actions)* buying up

ramasser *vt Bourse (actions)* to buy up

rang *nm (d'une créance, d'une hypothèque)* rank

rappel nm (a) *(de paiement)* reminder (b) *(d'une somme déjà avancée)* calling in
◇ **rappel (de compte)** reminder
◇ **rappel d'échéance** prompt note
◇ **rappel de salaire** back pay

rapport nm (a) *(compte-rendu)* report

(b) *(profit)* yield, return; **en rapport** *(capital)* interest-bearing, productive; **d'un bon rapport** profitable; **d'un mauvais rapport** unprofitable

(c) *(proportion)* ratio, proportion
◇ **rapport d'activité** progress report
◇ **rapport annuel de gestion** annual report
◇ **rapport du commissaire aux comptes** auditor's report
◇ **rapport cours-bénéfices** price-earnings ratio
◇ **rapport coût-profit** cost-benefit ratio
◇ *Compta* **rapport d'exploitation** operating statement
◇ **rapport financier** financial report
◇ **rapport de parité** parity ratio
◇ **rapport profit sur ventes** profit-volume ratio
◇ **rapport réservé** qualified report
◇ **rapport de situation journalière** daily trading report

rapporter 1 vt (a) *(bénéfices, intérêts)* to yield; **rapporter de l'argent** to be profitable; **le compte d'épargne vous rapporte 7,5%** the savings account carries 7.5% interest

(b) *Compta (écriture)* to post
2 vi *(être rentable)* to be profitable, to yield a profit; **l'affaire a beaucoup rapporté à l'entre-**prise the deal brought in a lot of money for the company; **ça ne rapporte pas** it doesn't pay, there's no money in it; **ça peut rapporter gros** it can be very profitable

rapprochement bancaire nm *Compta* bank reconciliation

rapprocher vt *Compta* to reconcile

raquer vi *Fam* to pay up, to fork out

rareté nf *(de ressources, d'argent)* scarcity

ratio nm *Compta* ratio
◇ **ratio d'activité** activity ratio
◇ **ratio des bénéfices d'exploitation sur le capital employé** primary ratio
◇ **ratio de capitalisation** capitalization ratio
◇ **ratio capital-travail** capital-labour ratio
◇ **ratio capitaux empruntés-fonds propres** debt-to-equity ratio
◇ **ratio comptable** accounting ratio
◇ **ratio Cooke** capital adequacy ratio
◇ **ratio cours-bénéfices** price-earnings ratio
◇ **ratio de couverture de l'intérêt** interest coverage
◇ **ratio de distribution** distribution ratio
◇ **ratio d'endettement** debt or gearing ratio
◇ **ratio d'endettement global** overall gearing ratio
◇ **ratio d'endettement à terme** long-term gearing ratio
◇ **ratio d'exploitation** performance or operating ratio

La pyramide des ratios
The pyramid of ratios

(a) Retour sur capitaux permanents/ROCE (Return on capital employed)
(b) Retour sur ventes/ROS (Return on sales)
(c) Taux d'utilisation des actifs/AUR (Asset Utilization Ratio)

(a) Bénéfice d'exploitation/Operating profit
Capitaux permanents/Capital employed

(b) Bénéfice d'exploitation/Operating profit
Ventes/Sales

(c) Ventes/Sales
Actif d'exploitation/Operating assets

Frais financiers/Financial costs
Ventes/Sales

Coûts de production/Production costs
Ventes/Sales

Coûts de marketing/Marketing costs
Ventes/Sales

Frais administratif/Administration costs
Ventes/Sales

Main d'œuvre directe/Direct labour
Ventes/Sales

Frais généraux de production/Production overheads
Ventes/Sales

Coût des matériaux/Material costs
Ventes/Sales

Ventes/Sales
Actif immobilisé/Fixed assets

Stocks de matière première/Raw material stock
Ratio d'utilisation/Usage ratio

Débiteurs/Debtors
Ventes à crédit/Credit sales

Stocks de produits finis/Finished goods stock
Coût des ventes/Cost of sales

Créditeurs/Creditors
Achats/Purchases

◇ *ratio de gestion* financial or activity ratio

◇ *ratio d'intensité de capital* capital-output ratio

◇ *ratio de levier* leverage

◇ *ratio de liquidité (générale)* liquidity ratio

◇ *ratio de liquidité immédiate, ratio de liquidité restreinte* quick ratio, acid test ratio

◇ *ratio de rentabilité (nette)* (net) profit ratio

◇ *ratio de solvabilité* solvency ratio

◇ *ratio de trésorerie* cash ratio

◇ *ratio des ventes* sales ratio

◇ *ratio de volume de bénéfices* profit/volume ratio, P/V

rationalisation des choix budgétaires *nf Compta* planning-programming-budgeting system

rattachement *nm Compta* matching

réaction *nf* reaction; *Bourse* il y a eu une vive réaction de la livre sterling sur le marché des changes sterling has reacted sharply on the exchange market

réaffecter *vt (subventions)* to reassign, to reallocate

réalisable *adj (avoirs)* realizable

réalisation *nf (d'avoirs)* realization; *(d'actions)* selling out; *(d'un bénéfice)* making

réaliser *vt (avoirs)* to realize; *(actions)* to sell out; *(bénéfice)* to make; **réaliser un capital** to realize an asset, to convert an asset into cash; **réaliser un chiffre d'affaires de 10 millions de francs** to have a turnover of 10 million francs; **réaliser des économies** to economize

rebond *nm (d'actions, de marché, de monnaie)* recovery

rebondir *vi (actions, marché, monnaie)* to pick up again, to recover

recapitalisation *nf* recapitalization

recapitaliser *vt* to recapitalize

> **"**
>
> Tradepoint: créée en 1992 par des transfuges du London Stock Exchange, cette Bourse électronique a été **recapitalisée** en mai 1999. A cette occasion, les ECN Instinet et Archipelago ainsi que les banques d'affaires Morgan Stanley, J.P. Morgan et Warburg et l'investisseur American Century ont fait leur entrée au capital.
>
> **"**

récépissé *nm* receipt

◇ *récépissé de dépôt* deposit receipt

recette *nf* (a) *(somme)* takings; **recettes et dépenses** receipts and expenditure, incomings and outgoings (b) *(d'argent dû)* collection; *(bureau)* tax office; **faire la recette de l'argent/des contributions** to collect the money/contributions

◇ *recette annuelle* annual income or revenue

◇ *recette brute* gross income or earnings

◇ *recettes de caisse* cash receipts

◇ *recettes fiscales* tax revenue

◇ *recette journalière* daily takings

◇ *recette nette* net income or receipts

◊ *recettes non gagées* unassigned *or* unpledged revenue

◊ *recettes publiques* government revenue

> **"**
>
> Des déficits budgétaires structurels se sont ainsi installés dans tous les grands pays (c'est à dire des déficits suffisamment importants pour qu'une forte croissance de l'économie, donc des **recettes fiscales,** ne puisse pas les annuler).
>
> **"**

receveur, -euse *nm,f Admin*

◊ *receveur des contributions* tax collector

◊ *receveur des Finances* district tax collector

recevoir *vt* **à recevoir** *(effets, intérêts)* receivable

rechange *nm Banque (d'un effet)* redraft

reconnaissance de dette *nf (document)* IOU

recouponnement *nm Bourse* renewal of coupons

recouponner *vt Bourse* to renew the coupons of

recouvrable *adj (argent, dette)* recoverable; *(impôt)* collectable

recouvrement *nm* **(a)** *(d'argent, d'une dette)* recovery; *(de l'impôt)* collection; **faire un recouvrement** to recover a debt; **l'impôt est mis en recouvrement après le 31 octobre** payment of tax is due from 31 October **(b) recouvrements** *(dettes)* outstanding debts

recouvrer *vt (argent, dette)* to recover; *(impôt)* to collect;

créances à recouvrer outstanding debts

rectification *nf* rectification, correction; *Compta (d'un compte)* adjustment

rectifier *vt* to rectify, to correct; *Compta (compte)* to adjust

reçu *nm* receipt

◊ *Can* **reçu de caisse** (till) receipt

◊ *reçu certifié* accountable receipt

◊ *reçu en duplicata* receipt in duplicate

◊ *reçu d'espèces* cash receipt

◊ *reçu libératoire* receipt in full discharge

recul *nm* decline, drop; **le recul du yen par rapport au dollar** the fall of the yen against the dollar

reculer *vi (titres, valeurs)* to fall

récupérable *adj (dette)* recoverable; *(TVA)* reclaimable

récupération *nf* **(a)** *(d'une dette)* recovery; *(de TVA)* reclaiming **(b)** *(des débours)* recoupment

récupérer *vt* **(a)** *(dette)* to recover; *(TVA)* to reclaim **(b) récupérer ses débours** to recoup one's expenditure

reddition *nf (de comptes)* rendering

redevable *adj* **être redevable de l'impôt** to be liable for tax

redevance *nf (pour un service)* fees

◊ *redevance pétrolière* oil royalty

redressement *nm* **(a)** *Compta (d'un compte)* adjustment **(b)** *(d'une monnaie, de l'économie)* recovery

◇ *redressement économique* economic recovery

◇ *redressement financier* gearing adjustment

◇ *Admin redressement fiscal, redressement d'impôt* tax adjustment

◇ *redressement judiciaire* receivership; **être mis en redressement judiciaire** to go into receivership

> ❝
>
> Le **redressement** financier qui s'opère est cependant dû également pour une large part aux restructurations engagées par le prédécesseur de M. Jobs.
>
> ❞

redresser **1** *vt (erreur)* to rectify; *Compta (compte)* to adjust **2 se redresser** *vpr (monnaie, économie)* to recover, to rally

redû *nm* balance due, amount owed

réduction *nf (des prix, des taux d'intérêt, des impôts)* reduction (**de** in), lowering (**de** of); *(des dépenses, des frais)* reduction (**de** in), cutting (**de** of); *(du capital)* writing down

réduire *vt (prix, taux d'intérêt, impôts)* to reduce, to lower; *(dépenses, frais)* to reduce, to cut; *(capital)* to write down

rééchelonnement *nm (d'une dette)* rescheduling

rééchelonner *vt (dette)* to reschedule

rééquilibrer *vt (budget)* to rebalance

réescompte *nm* rediscount

réescompter *vt* to rediscount

réévaluation *nf (d'une monnaie, de l'actif)* revaluation; *(des prix, d'un budget)* reassessment

réévaluer *vt (monnaie, actif)* to revalue; *(prix, budget)* to reassess

référence *nf Compta* **référence au meilleur** benchmarking

refinancement *nm* refinancing

refinancer *vt* to refinance

refluer *vi* **faire refluer le dollar/yen** to keep down the value of the dollar/yen

> ❝
>
> Les interventions massives, sur le marché des changes, de la Banque du Japon se sont révélées totalement inefficaces. De surcroît, la banque centrale nippone, soucieuse d'empêcher l'apparition de tensions inflationnistes dans l'archipel, a résisté aux pressions gouvernementales qui lui demandaient, pour faire **refluer** le yen, d'assouplir sa politique monétaire.
>
> ❞

réforme *nf* reform

◇ *réforme monétaire* monetary reform

refus *nm* refusal

◇ *refus d'acceptation* non-acceptance

◇ *refus de paiement* non-payment

regagner *vt (après perte)* to win back; **le dollar a regagné quelques cents sur le marché des changes** the dollar has regained a few cents on the foreign exchange market

régime *nm (système)* scheme, system

⬦ *régime d'assurance vieillesse* old age pension fund or scheme

⬦ *régime fiscal* tax system

⬦ *régime du forfait* standard or fixed-rate assessment system

⬦ *régime d'imposition* tax system

⬦ *régime du réel* full assessment system

⬦ *régime de retraite* pension scheme or plan

⬦ *régime de retraite par capitalisation* funded pension scheme

⬦ *régime de retraites complémentaires* = graduated pension scheme

⬦ *régime de Sécurité sociale* social security system

> **"**
>
> Les cotisations aux **régimes de retraite** représentent un "placement obligatoire" important, près de 20% du salaire d'un cadre.
>
> **"**

registre nm (de comptes) account book

⬦ Bourse **registre des actionnaires** register of shareholders, shareholders' register

⬦ Bourse **registre des actions** share register

⬦ Compta **registre de comptabilité** account book, ledger

⬦ **registre des obligataires** debenture register

⬦ **registre des salaires** payroll

⬦ **registre des transferts** transfer register

règle nf (mesure) rule

⬦ Compta **règles comptables** accounting rules

règlement nm (a) (d'un compte) settlement; (d'une facture, d'une dette) payment; **en règlement de** in settlement of; **faire un règlement par chèque** to pay by cheque; **pour règlement de tout compte** in full settlement (b) Bourse settlement

⬦ **règlement en espèces** cash payment or settlement

⬦ Jur **règlement judiciaire** liquidation; **se mettre en règlement judiciaire** to go into liquidation or receivership

⬦ **(marché du) règlement mensuel** forward market

réglementation nf control, regulation

⬦ **réglementation des changes** exchange control

régler 1 vt (compte) to settle; (facture, dette, personne) to pay; **régler qch en espèces** to pay cash for sth; **régler qch par chèque** to pay for sth by cheque 2 vi to pay

regrèvement nm tax increase

regroupement nm (a) (de sociétés) amalgamation, merger (b) (de comptes) consolidation

regrouper 1 vt (a) (sociétés) to amalgamate, to merge (b) (comptes) to consolidate
2 se regrouper vpr (sociétés) to amalgamate, to merge

régularisation nf (de dividende) equalization; (d'un compte, des charges) adjustment

régulariser vt (dividende) to equalize; (compte, charges) to adjust

régularité nf **régularité et sincérité des charges** true and fair nature of expense

régulation nf (de la Bourse) regulation; **la régulation du marché des changes** foreign exchange control

réhabilitation nf Jur (de failli) discharge

réhabilité, -e nm,f discharged bankrupt

réimposer vt (produit) to reintroduce tax on, to retax

réimposition nf retaxation

réinscription nf Compta re-entry, re-registering

réinscrire vt Compta to re-enter, to re-register

réinvestir vt to reinvest; (bénéfices) to plough back

relevé nm statement
◊ **relevé de caisse** cash statement
◊ Banque **relevé de compte** bank statement
◊ **relevé des dépenses** statement of expenditure
◊ **relevé des dettes actives et passives** statement of assets and liabilities
◊ **relevé de factures** statement of invoices
◊ **relevé de fin de mois** monthly or end-of-month statement
◊ **relevé d'identité bancaire** = document giving details of one's bank account
◊ Banque **relevé d'identité postal** = document giving details of one's post office account
◊ **relevé remis** account tendered

relèvement nm (des salaires, d'un tarif, d'un impôt, des taux d'intérêt) raising, increasing

relever vt (a) (salaires, tarif, impôt, taux d'intérêt) to raise, to

increase; **relever le cours du franc** to raise the value of the franc (**b**) **relever un compte** to make out a statement of account

reliquat nm remainder; (d'un compte) balance

relutif, -ive adj **avoir un effet relutif** to strengthen the equity capital of a company

> ❝
> Le paiement cash évite toute création de titres supplémentaires. La rentabilité de Red Roof étant supérieure à celle d'Accor (9% de marge nette, contre 5,3% pour le français), l'opération aura un effet **relutif** (hausse du bénéfice net par action) pour Accor, dès cette année.
> ❞

relution nf strengthening of equity capital

remboursable adj (prêt) repayable; (caution, versement) refundable; (obligation, coupon) redeemable; **remboursable sur une période de 25 ans** repayable over (a period of) 25 years; **remboursable au pair** repayable at par

remboursement nm (des dépenses) repayment, reimbursement; (d'un prêt) repayment; (d'une caution, d'un versement, d'un achat, des frais) refund; (d'une obligation, d'un coupon) redemption; (d'un effet) retirement
◊ **remboursement anticipé** redemption before due date
◊ **remboursement in fine** bullet repayment

rembourser vt (**a**) (dépenses)

to repay, to reimburse; *(prêt)* to repay; *(caution, versement, achat, frais)* to refund; *(obligation, coupon)* to redeem; *(effet)* to retire (**b**) *(personne)* to repay, to reimburse

rémére *nm Banque, Bourse* repo

remettant *nm Banque* = person who pays money or a cheque into a current account

remetteur, -euse 1 *adj* *(banque)* remitting
2 *nm,f* remitter

remettre *vt* (**a**) *(donner)* to remit; **remettre un chèque à l'encaissement** to cash a cheque (**b**) *(dette)* to cancel

remise *nf* (**a**) *(fait de remettre)* remittance; **payable contre remise du coupon** payable on presentation of the coupon; **faire une remise (de fonds) à qn** to send sb a remittance (**b**) *(d'une dette)* cancellation; **faire remise d'une dette** to cancel a debt
◇ **remise de fonds** remittance of funds
◇ **remise à vue** demand deposit

remisier *nm Bourse* half-commission man, intermediate broker

remontée *nf (d'une monnaie, des valeurs, des prix)* recovery; **faire une belle remontée** to make a good recovery

remonter *vi (monnaie, valeurs, prix)* to go back up

remplir *vt (formulaire, questionnaire)* to fill in, to fill out, to complete; *(chèque)* to write, to make out

remployer *vt (argent, fonds)* to reinvest

rémunérateur, -trice *adj* *(activité)* remunerative, profitable; *(placement)* interest-bearing

rémunération *nf* (**a**) *(somme versée)* remuneration, payment (**de** for); **en rémunération de vos services** as payment for your services (**b**) *(salaire)* salary
◇ **rémunération du capital** return on capital
◇ **rémunération de départ** starting salary

rémunérer *vt* (**a**) *(travail, services)* to pay for (**b**) *(salaires)* to pay

renchérir 1 *vt (prix)* to raise
2 *vi* (**a**) *(prix)* to go up, to increase (**b**) **renchérir sur qn** *(aux enchères)* to outbid sb

> 66
>
> Des jours difficiles se préparent: la dévaluation du rouble va certes aider les exportateurs, mais elle va aussi **renchérir** le prix des produits importés.
>
> 99

renchérissement *nm (d'un prix)* increase

rendement *nm (d'un investissement, d'une obligation)* yield, return, profit; *(des actions)* earnings; **à gros rendement** *(investissement, obligation)* high-yield; *(actions)* high-earning
◇ **rendement actuariel brut** gross redemption yield, gross actuarial return
◇ **rendement annuel** annual return

◊ *rendement brut* gross yield or return

◊ *rendement constant* fixed yield

◊ *rendement coupon* coupon yield

◊ *rendements décroissants* diminishing returns

◊ *rendement à l'échéance* yield to maturity, redemption yield

◊ *rendement sur fonds propres* return on equity

◊ *rendement marginal du capital* marginal return on capital

◊ *rendement moyen* average yield

◊ *rendement net* net return

◊ *rendement réel* inflation-adjusted yield

rendre *vt (sujet: investissement)* to yield

renouveler *vt (crédit)* to extend

renouvellement *nm (d'un crédit)* extension

renseignement *nm (information)* piece of information; **renseignements** information

◊ *renseignements de crédit* status or credit enquiry

rentabiliser *vt* to make profitable

rentabilité *nf* profitability, cost-effectiveness (**de** of); *(d'un investissement, des ventes)* return (**de** on)

◊ *rentabilité nette d'exploitation* net operating profit

rentable *adj* profitable

rente *nf* (a) rentes *(revenu)* private income; **avoir cent mille francs de rentes** to have a private income of a hundred thousand francs

(b) *(pension)* annuity, pension

(c) *(emprunt d'État)* government loan or bond

◊ *rentes amortissables* redeemable stock or loans

◊ *rente annuelle* annuity

◊ *rentes sur l'État* government stock or funds

◊ *rente à paiement différé* deferred annuity

◊ *rentes perpétuelles* irredeemable securities

◊ *rente de situation* guaranteed income

◊ *rente à terme* terminable annuity

◊ *rente viagère* life annuity or interest

> ❝
>
> On connaît l'attachement viscéral des Français à la disponibilité de leur épargne. Comment leur fera-t-on admettre qu'ils devront mettre de côté pendant toute la durée de leur vie active des sommes dont ils n'auront, finalement, jamais l'entière disponibilité, la société gestionnaire se chargeant de la leur redistribuer au compte-gouttes jusqu'au terme de leur existence, selon la technique de la **rente viagère**?
>
> ❞

rentrée *nf (d'argent)* receipt; **rentrées** income, money coming in; **avoir des rentrées d'argent** to have a regular income or money coming in regularly

◊ *Compta rentrées de caisse* cash receipts

◊ *rentrées de devises* foreign exchange inflows

◊ *rentrées fiscales* tax revenue

◊ *rentrées journalières* daily takings

◇ *Compta* **rentrées et sorties de caisse** cash receipts and payments

rentrer *vi* **rentrer dans ses frais** to recover one's expenses, to get one's money back, to break even

répartir *vt* (a) *(dividende)* to distribute; *(coûts)* to break down; *Bourse (actions)* to allot, to allocate (b) *(étaler) (versements, dépenses)* to spread (out) (c) *(impôts)* to assess

répartiteur, -trice *nm,f Admin* (**commissaire**) **répartiteur** tax assessor

répartition *nf* (a) *(de tâches, d'argent)* division, distribution; *(d'une dividende)* distribution; *(de coûts)* breakdown; *Bourse (d'actions)* allotment, allocation; **première et unique répartition** first and final dividend; **nouvelle répartition** second dividend; **dernière répartition** final dividend (b) *(des versements, des dépenses)* spreading (out) (c) *(des impôts)* assessment

◇ **répartition des actifs** asset allocation

◇ **répartition des risques** risk spreading

repli *nm Bourse* fall, drop

replier se replier *vpr Bourse* to fall back, to drop

répondre répondre à *vt ind Bourse (prime)* to declare

réponse des primes *nf Bourse* declaration of options

report *nm* (a) *Compta (en bas de page)* (balance) carried forward; *(en haut du page)* (balance) brought forward

(b) *Compta (d'une écriture)* entering up, posting

(c) *Bourse* contango, continuation; **en report** *(actions, titres)* taken in, carried over; **prendre des actions en report** to take in or carry over shares

◇ *Compta* **report déficitaire sur les exercices précédents** loss carry back

◇ *Compta* **report déficitaire sur les exercices ultérieurs** loss carry forward

◇ *Compta* **report d'échéance** extension of due date

◇ *Compta* **report de l'exercice précédent** carried forward from the previous financial year

◇ *Compta* **report à l'exercice suivant** carried forward to the next financial year

◇ *Compta* **report à nouveau** carried forward

reporté, -e *nm,f Bourse (d'actions)* giver

reporter *vt* (a) *Compta (balance, total) (en bas de page)* to carry forward; *(en haut de page)* to bring forward; **solde à reporter** balance carried forward

(b) *Compta (écriture)* to enter up, to post

(c) *Bourse* to continue, to contango; **(faire) reporter des titres** to carry stock; **(faire) reporter un emprunteur** to take in stock for a borrower; **se faire reporter** to be carried over

reporteur *nm Bourse (d'actions)* taker

reprendre *vi Bourse* to rally; **les cours ont repris** the market rallied

représentant, -e *nm,f* representative
◇ *représentant fiscal* fiscal agent

reprise *nf Bourse (des cours)* recovery
◇ *Compta* **reprises sur provisions** recovery *or* write-back of provisions

requin *nm* **requin (de la finance)** shark, raider

RES *nf (abrév* **rachat de l'entreprise par ses salariés)** staff *or* employee buy-out

réserve *nf (stock)* reserve; **en réserve** in reserve, set aside
◇ *réserve d'achat* credit limit
◇ *réserves bancaires* bank reserves
◇ *réserves de change* monetary reserves
◇ *réserve pour créances douteuses* bad debts reserve
◇ *réserves en devises (étrangères)* foreign exchange reserves
◇ *réserves en espèces* cash reserves
◇ *réserves excédentaires* excess reserves
◇ *réserve liquide* liquid assets, cash reserve
◇ *réserve métallique* bullion reserve
◇ *réserves mondiales (de matières premières)* world reserves
◇ *réserves monétaires internationales* international monetary reserves
◇ *réserves non distribuées* capital reserves
◇ *réserves obligatoires* federal fund
◇ *réserve d'or* gold reserves
◇ *réserve de prévoyance* contingency reserve

◇ *réserve statutaire* statutory reserve

❝

La devise allemande a terminé la semaine à plus de 3,51 francs. Une mauvaise affaire pour la Banque de France qui continue de reconstituer ses **réserves de change**.

❞

résorber *vt (surplus, déficit)* to absorb; *(dettes)* to clear

responsabilité *nf (morale)* responsibility (**de** for); *Jur (légale)* liability (**de** for)
◇ *responsabilité illimitée* unlimited liability
◇ *responsabilité limitée* limited liability

resserrement du crédit *nm Écon* credit squeeze

ressources *nfpl* resources
◇ *ressources d'appoint* additional sources of income
◇ *ressources du budget* budgetary resources
◇ *ressources financières* financial resources
◇ *ressources fiscales* tax resources

restant *nm* rest, remainder; *(d'un compte)* balance
◇ *restant en caisse* cash surplus

restituable *adj* repayable

restitution *nf* repayment, refund
◇ *restitution d'impôts* tax refund
◇ *Jur restitution d'indu* return of payment made in error

restreindre *vt (crédit, dépenses)* to restrict, to limit

restriction *nf* restriction

◇ *restrictions budgétaires* budget restrictions

◇ *restriction du crédit* credit squeeze *or* restrictions

◇ *restrictions de transfert* transfer restrictions

restructuration *nf (de dette)* rescheduling

restructurer *vt (dette)* to reschedule

résultat *nm Compta* profit

◇ *résultat brut* gross return

◇ *résultat courant* profit before tax and extraordinary items

◇ *résultat économique* economic profit

◇ *résultat exceptionnel* extraordinary profit or loss

◇ *résultat de l'exercice* profit or loss for the financial year, statement of income

◇ *résultat d'exploitation* operating profit or loss

◇ *résultat final* final statement

◇ *résultat financier* financial profit or loss

◇ *résultat net* net return

◇ *résultat net consolidé* consolidated statement of net income

◇ *résultat de la période* profit or loss for the financial period

◇ *résultats prévisionnels* earnings forecast

retard *nm* delay; **en retard** *(compte, paiement)* outstanding, overdue; **ils sont en retard dans leurs paiements** they're behind *or* in arrears with their payments

◇ *retard de paiement* delay in payment, late payment

retarder *vt* to delay; *(paiement)* to defer, to delay

retenir *vt (somme)* to keep back, to deduct (**sur** from)

retenue *nf (d'une somme)* deduction; **faire une retenue de 5% sur les salaires** to deduct *or* withhold 5% from salaries

◇ *retenue fiscale* withholding tax

◇ *retenue à la source* payment (of income tax) at source, *Br* ≃ PAYE, *Am* ≃ pay as you go

retirer 1 *vt* (**a**) *(argent)* to withdraw, to take out; **retirer des marchandises de la douane** to take goods out of bond

(**b**) *(effet)* to retire, to withdraw; *(monnaies)* to withdraw from circulation, to call in

2 **se retirer** *vpr* **se retirer des affaires** to retire from business

retour *nm* (**a**) *(amortissement)* return

(**b**) *(effet)* dishonoured bill, bill returned dishonoured

◇ *retour sur achat* purchase return

◇ *retour sur investissement* return on investment, ROI

◇ *retour sur ventes* return on sales

retrait *nm* (**a**) *(d'argent)* withdrawal; **faire un retrait** to make a withdrawal; **faire un retrait de 5 000 francs** to withdraw 5,000 francs (**b**) *(d'un effet)* withdrawal; *(de monnaies)* withdrawal from circulation, calling in

◇ *retrait automatique* automated withdrawal

◇ *retrait d'espèces* cash withdrawal

retraite *nf (pension)* pension

◇ *retraite par capitalisation* loanback pension

◇ *retraite complémentaire* private pension

◇ *retraite indexée sur le revenu* earnings-related pension

◇ *retraite minimum* guaranteed minimum pension

◇ *retraite vieillesse* retirement pension

retrancher *vt* to deduct, to take off

rétribution *nf* payment

rétroactif, -ive *adj* retrospective, retroactive; **augmentation avec effet rétroactif au 1 septembre** increase backdated to 1 September

rétrospective *nf* review

réunion *nf* meeting

◇ *réunion d'actionnaires* shareholders' meeting

◇ *réunion des créanciers* creditors' meeting

revalorisation *nf* (**a**) *(d'une monnaie)* revalorization, revaluation (**b**) *(des salaires, des retraites)* upgrading

revaloriser *vt* (**a**) *(monnaie)* to revalorize, to revalue (**b**) *(salaires, retraites)* to upgrade

revendre *vt* Bourse *(titres)* to sell out

revente *nf* Bourse *(de titres)* selling out

revenu *nm* (**a**) *(d'une personne, d'une entreprise)* income; *(de l'État)* revenue; **avoir de gros/petits revenus** to have a large/small income; **revenu imposable après déduction des abattements fiscaux** taxable income after deduction of tax allowances

(**b**) *(d'un investissement)* yield, return

◇ *revenus accessoires* incidental income

◇ *revenus actuels* current earnings *or* income

◇ *revenu annuel* annual income

◇ *revenu brut* gross income

◇ *revenu brut global* total gross income

◇ *revenu cumulé* cumulative revenue

◇ *revenu disponible* disposable income

◇ Admin *revenu familial* family income

◇ *revenu fictif* notional income

◇ *revenu fixe* fixed income

◇ *revenu imposable* taxable income

◇ *revenu des intérêts* earned interest, interest income

◇ *revenu locatif* rental income

◇ *revenu marginal* marginal revenue *or* income

◇ *revenu minimum d'insertion* $Br \simeq$ income support, $Am \simeq$ welfare

◇ Écon *revenu national* national income

◇ Écon *revenu national brut* gross national income

◇ Écon *revenu national net* net national income

◇ *revenu net* net income

◇ *revenu net global* total net income

◇ Bourse *revenu(s) obligataire(s), revenu(s) des obligations* income from bonds

◇ *revenu personnel disponible* disposable personal income

◇ *revenu réel* real income

◇ *revenu résiduel* residual income

◇ *revenus salariaux* earned income

◇ *Écon* **revenus du secteur public** public sector earnings

◇ **revenu de société** corporate income

◇ **revenu du travail** earned income

◇ **revenu variable** income from variable-yield investments

> **"**
>
> L'objectif est de réduire l'écart entre le **revenu** net perçu par les salariés et son coût global pour l'entreprise.
>
> **"**

reversement *nm* transfer *(of funds from one account to another)*

reverser *vt (somme)* to transfer (**à** *ou* **sur** to); *(impôt)* to pay

réviser *vt (compte)* to check

réviseur *nm Compta* auditor

◇ **réviseur comptable** auditor

◇ **réviseur externe** external auditor

◇ **réviseur interne** internal auditor

RIB *nm (abrév* **relevé d'identité bancaire)** = document giving details of one's bank account

RIP *nm (abrév* **relevé d'identité postale)** = document giving details of one's post office account

risque *nm* risk

◇ **risque de change** exchange *or* currency risk

◇ **risque de contrepartie** credit risk

◇ *Bourse* **risque de marché** market risk

ristourne *nf (rabais)* discount; **une ristourne de 15%** a 15% discount; **faire une ristourne à qn** to give sb a discount

◇ **ristourne de fidélité** customer loyalty discount

◇ **ristourne de prime** premium discount

ristourner *vt (réduire)* to give a discount of; **il nous a ristourné 15% du prix** he gave us a 15% discount

rôle *nm (liste)* roll, register

◇ *Admin* **rôle des contributions** tax roll

◇ **rôle d'impôt** tax roll

rompu *nm Bourse (d'actions, de titres)* odd lot

rotation *nf*

◇ **rotation des capitaux** turnover of capital

◇ **rotation des clients** debtors' turnover

◇ **rotation des fournisseurs** creditors' turnover

◇ *Bourse* **rotation de portefeuille** churning

◇ *Bourse* **rotation de portefeuille-action** equity switching

◇ *Bourse* **rotation de portefeuille-obligation** gilt switching

rouge *nm* **être dans le rouge** to be in the red; **sortir du rouge** to get out of the red

roulant, -e *adj (fonds, capital)* working

roulement *nm (de fonds)* circulation; *(de capitaux)* turnover

rouler *vi (argent)* to circulate freely

rouvrir *vt (compte)* to reopen

RTGS *nm Banque, UE (abrév* **Real-Time Gross Settlement)** RTGS; **système RTGS** RTGS system

salaire *nm (mensuel)* salary; *(hebdomadaire, journalier)* wage
◊ *salaire après impôts* after-tax salary
◊ *salaire brut* gross salary *or* pay
◊ *salaire de départ* starting salary
◊ *salaire fixe* fixed wage
◊ *salaire indirect* fringe benefits
◊ *salaire minimum* minimum wage
◊ *salaire net* net salary *or* pay
◊ *salaire nominal* nominal wages
◊ *salaire plafonné* wage ceiling
◊ *salaire réel* real wage

salarié, -e 1 *adj* (**a**) *(travailleur) (payé au mois)* salaried; *(payé à la semaine)* wage-earning (**b**) *(travail)* paid
2 *nm,f (payé au mois)* salaried employee; *(payé à la semaine)* wage-earner

salle *nf* room
◊ *Bourse* **salle des changes** trading *or* dealing room
◊ *Banque* **salle des coffres** vault
◊ *Bourse* **salle des marchés** trading *or* dealing room

SARL *nf (abrév* **société à responsabilité limitée)** limited (liability) company

sauf *prép Compta* **sauf erreur ou omission** errors and omissions excepted

SBF *nf (abrév* **Société des bourses françaises)** = company which runs the Paris Stock Exchange, $\simeq$ *Br* LSE, $\simeq$ *Am* NYSE; **le SBF 120** = broad-based French stock exchange index

scission *nf (d'une société)* demerger; *(d'actif)* divestment

script *nm Bourse* scrip

scriptural, -e *adj* cashless

séance *nf (réunion)* session, meeting; *Bourse* (trading) session
◊ *Bourse* **séance boursière** trading session
◊ *séance de clôture* closing session
◊ *séance d'ouverture* opening session

second marché *nm Bourse* secondary market, unlisted securities market

secteur *nm* sector
◊ *secteur privé* private sector
◊ *secteur publique* public sector

sécuriser *vt (paiement)* to securitize; **sécuriser un financement** to guarantee a loan

sélection *nf Bourse* selection

◇ *sélection de titres* stockpicking

◇ *sélection de portefeuille* portfolio selection

SEO *Compta* (*abrév* **sauf erreur ou omission**) E & OE

serpent *nm UE* (currency) snake

◇ *serpent monétaire européen* European currency snake

service *nm* (**a**) *(département)* department

(**b**) *(d'un emprunt, d'une dette)* servicing; **assurer le service d'un emprunt/d'une dette** to service a loan/debt

(**c**) *(prestation)* service

◇ *services de caisse* counter services

◇ *service de (la) comptabilité* accounts department

◇ *service des émissions* issue department

◇ *service de facturation* invoice department

◇ *services financiers* financial services

◇ *services d'investissement* investment services

seuil *nm* threshold

◇ *Bourse seuil d'annonce obligatoire* disclosure threshold

◇ *seuil d'imposition* tax threshold

◇ *seuil de prix* price threshold

◇ *seuil de rentabilité* break-even point

SICAF, sicaf *nf* (*abrév* **société d'investissement à capital fixe**) closed-end investment company

SICAV, sicav *nf* (*abrév* **société d'investissement à capital variable**) (**a**) *(organisme) Br* ≃

unit trust, *Am* ≃ mutual fund (**b**) *(action)* ≃ share in a *Br* unit trust *or Am* mutual fund

◇ *SICAV actions* equity-based unit trust

◇ *SICAV éthique* ethical investment fund

◇ *SICAV mixte* split capital investment trust

◇ *SICAV monétaire* money-based unit trust, ≃ money market fund

◇ *SICAV obligataire* bond-based unit trust

❝

La contrainte financière reste très forte: restreintes par les banques, les entreprises se désendettent (l'encours des crédits est encore en baisse à la rentrée) et préfèrent acheter des **sicav monétaires** plutôt qu'investir.

❞

SICOVAM, Sicovam *nf Bourse* (*abrév* **société interprofessionnelle pour la compensation des valeurs mobilières**) = French central securities depository

❝

Connue du grand public pour les codes qu'elle diffuse, la **Sicovam** est le dépositaire national français de titres. Après la réorganisation de ses structures et le lancement d'un nouveau système de règlement-livraison, la société est devenue un acteur essentiel pour le passage à l'euro.

❞

signature électronique *nf* digital signature

SIT *nm* (*abrév* **système interbancaire de compensation**) = interbank automated clearing system, ≃ CHAPS

situation *nf* (**a**) (*état*) state, condition; (*d'un compte*) balance
(**b**) (*document*) statement of finances
◇ **situation en banque** financial position *or* situation
◇ **situation de caisse** cash statement
◇ **situation financière** financial situation *or* position
◇ **situation hebdomadaire** (*de la Banque de France*) weekly report
◇ **situation nette** (*d'une société*) net assets *or* worth
◇ **situation de trésorerie** cash flow situation

SME *nm* (**a**) (*abrév* **système monétaire européen**) EMS (**b**) (*abrév* **serpent monétaire européen**) European currency snake

sociétaire *nmf* (*d'une société anonyme*) *Br* shareholder, *Am* stockholder

société *nf* (*entreprise*) company, firm; **se monter en société** to set up in business
◇ **société par actions** *Br* joint-stock *or Am* incorporated company
◇ **société d'affacturage** factoring company
◇ **société affiliée** *Br* affiliated company, *Am* affiliate
◇ **société anonyme** *Br* ≃ public limited company, *Am* ≃ corporation
◇ **société d'assurance** insurance company

◇ **société de Bourse** stockbroking *or* brokerage firm, securities house
◇ **société de capital-risque** venture capital company
◇ **société en commandite** limited partnership
◇ **société en commandite par actions** partnership limited by shares
◇ **société en commandite simple** limited partnership
◇ **société commune** joint venture
◇ **société de conseil en investissement** investment consultancy
◇ **société coopérative** cooperative
◇ **société cotée en Bourse** listed company
◇ **société cotée à la Cote officielle** quoted company
◇ **société de crédit** loan company
◇ **société de crédit immobilier** *Br* ≃ building society, *Am* ≃ savings and loan association
◇ **société de crédit mutuel** mutual insurance company, *Br* ≃ friendly society
◇ **société émettrice** issuing company
◇ **société d'État** state-owned *or* public company
◇ **société d'exploitation en commun** joint venture
◇ **société de factoring** factoring company
◇ **société fictive** dummy company
◇ **société fiduciaire** trust company
◇ **société financière** finance company *or Br* house

◇ *société de gestion* holding company

◇ *société de gestion de portefeuille* $Br \simeq$ unit trust, $Am \simeq$ mutual fund

◇ *société (en) holding* holding company

◇ *société d'investissement* investment company

◇ *société d'investissement à capital fixe* closed-end investment fund

◇ *société d'investissement à capital variable* $Br \simeq$ unit trust, $Am \simeq$ mutual fund

◇ *société de leasing* leasing company

◇ *société mère* parent company

◇ *société de mutualité* mutual insurance company, $Br \simeq$ friendly society

◇ *société en nom collectif* partnership

◇ *société non cotée* unquoted company

◇ *société offshore* offshore company

◇ *société opéable* target company

◇ *société en participation* joint venture

◇ *société de placement* investment trust

◇ *société à portefeuille* holding company

◇ *société de prévoyance* provident society

◇ *société à responsabilité illimitée, société à responsabilité infinie* unlimited company

◇ *société à responsabilité limitée* limited (liability) company

◇ *société de secours mutuel* mutual insurance company, $Br \simeq$ friendly society

◇ *société sœur* sister company

◇ *société d'utilité publique* Br public utility company, Am utility

44

Il existe deux grandes familles de **sociétés de capital-risque**: les nationales et les régionales. Ces dernières investissent des montants plus faibles que les structures nationales. Elles sont plus généralistes et elles ont vocation à participer au développement économique de leur région.

77

44

Les **sociétés d'investissement** américaines redistribuent toutes à leurs clients, à grand renfort de publicité, entre 12% et 14% d'intérêts annuels en moyenne ces cinq dernières années.

77

solde *nm (de compte)* balance; **pour solde** in settlement; **pour solde de tout compte** in full settlement; **régler le solde** to pay the balance

◇ *solde actif* credit balance

◇ *solde bancaire, solde en banque* bank balance

◇ *solde bénéficiaire* credit balance

◇ *solde en caisse* cash balance

◇ *solde créditeur* credit balance

◇ *solde cumulé* cumulative balance

◇ *solde débiteur* debit balance

◇ *solde à découvert* outstanding balance

◇ *solde déficitaire* debit balance

◇ *solde disponible* available balance

◇ *solde de dividende* final dividend

◇ *solde dû* balance due

◇ *solde de fin de mois* end-of-month balance

◇ *Compta* *solde à nouveau* balance brought forward

◇ *Compta* *solde nul* nil balance

◇ *solde d'ouverture* opening balance

◇ *solde passif* debit balance

◇ *Compta* *solde reporté* balance brought forward

◇ *Compta* *solde à reporter* balance carried forward

◇ *Compta* *solde de trésorerie* cash balance

solder 1 *vt (compte)* to balance, to close; *(dette)* to settle, to pay (off); **solder l'arriéré** to make up back payments

  2 **se solder** *vpr* **se solder par qch** to show sth; **les comptes se soldent un bénéfice/un déficit de 10 000 francs** the accounts show a profit/a deficit of 10,000 francs

solvabilité *nf* solvency, creditworthiness

solvable *adj* solvent, creditworthy

somme *nf* (a) *(d'une addition)* sum, total amount; **la somme s'élève à 100 francs** the total amounts to 100 francs

  (b) *(argent)* **somme (d'argent)** sum (of money); **payer une grosse** *ou* **forte somme** to pay a large sum *or* amount of money; **dépenser une somme de 500 francs** to spend (a sum of) 500 francs

◇ *somme due* amount *or* total due

◇ *somme* *forfaitaire* lump sum

◇ *somme nette* net amount

◇ *Compta* *sommes payables* sums payable

◇ *somme totale* total amount, sum total

sommier *nm Compta* cash book, ledger

sortie *nf* (a) *(de devises)* export; *(de capital)* outflow

  (b) **sorties** outgoings; **ce mois-ci il y a eu plus de sorties que de rentrées** outgoings have exceeded incomings this month

◇ *sorties de fonds* expenses, outgoings

◇ *sorties de trésorerie* cash outgoings *or* outflow

souche *nf (de chèque, de ticket)* counterfoil, stub

souffrance *nf* **en souffrance** *(coupon, dette)* outstanding, unpaid; *(effet)* overdue, outstanding

soulte *nf Bourse* equalization payment

"

Les conditions de l'offre d'échange des certificats en actions risquent de réserver une autre mauvaise surprise. Les détenteurs de CI se verraient, en effet, offrir une action contre un certificat à condition de s'acquitter d'une **soulte** dont le montant pourrait atteindre 2 à 7% de la valeur de l'action! Cette **soulte** se justifierait à double titre: elle serait la contrepartie du droit de vote dont sont assorties les actions et le prix à payer pour bénéficier de la plus grande liquidité du marché des actions par rapport à celui du CI.

"

soumis, -e adj (à un impôt) liable, subject (**à** to); **soumis à l'impôt sur le revenu** liable to income tax

source nf source; **imposé à la source** taxed at source
◇ **source de revenus** source of revenue

sous-compte nm subaccount

souscoté, -e adj (action, marché, monnaie) undervalued

souscripteur, -trice nm,f (**a**) (d'un emprunt) subscriber (**de** to) (**b**) Bourse (des actions) applicant

souscription nf (**a**) (à un emprunt) subscription (**à** to) (**b**) Bourse (à des actions) application (**à** for)

souscrire 1 vt Bourse (actions) to apply for
  2 souscrire à vt ind (**a**) Bourse

(actions) to apply for (**b**) (emprunt) to subscribe to

sous-jacent adj (fonds, titre) underlying

soutenir vt (monnaie, économie) to support, to bolster up; **soutenir des cours par des achats** to support prices by buying

"

La banque centrale russe dépensait un milliard de dollars par semaine, dans la dernière période, pour **soutenir** le rouble. L'équipe au pouvoir a donc décidé d'élargir la bande de fluctuation de la monnaie, qui pourra désormais flotter entre 6 et 9,5 roubles pour un dollar.

"

spécialiste nmf specialist
◇ **spécialiste en valeurs du Trésor** primary dealer

spécialité nf Br speciality, Am specialty
◇ **spécialité budgétaire** budgetary speciality

spécifier vt to specify; Bourse **spécifier un cours** to make a price

spéculateur, -trice nm,f Bourse speculator
◇ **spéculateur à la baisse** bear
◇ **spéculateur sur devises** currency speculator
◇ **spéculateur à la hausse** bull
◇ **spéculateur à la journée** day trader, scalper
◇ **spéculateur sur plusieurs positions** position trader

spéculatif, -ive adj Bourse speculative

spéculation *nf Bourse* speculation
◊ **spéculation à la baisse** bear trading
◊ **spéculation à la hausse** bull trading
◊ **spéculations immobilières** property speculation
◊ **spéculation à la journée** day trading

spéculer *vi Bourse* to speculate; **spéculer en Bourse** to speculate on the Stock Market; **spéculer à la baisse** to speculate for a fall *or* on a falling market, to go a bear; **spéculer à la hausse** to speculate for a rise *or* on a rising market, to go a bull; **spéculer sur les valeurs pétrolières** to speculate in oils

spread *nm Bourse* spread
◊ **spread horizontal** horizontal spread
◊ **spread vertical** vertical spread

stabilisation *nf (d'une monnaie, des prix, du marché)* stabilization

stabiliser 1 *vt (monnaie, prix, marché)* to stabilize
2 se stabiliser *vpr (monnaie, prix, marché)* to stabilize

stabilité *nf (d'une monnaie, des prix, du marché)* stability, steadiness

stable *adj (monnaie, prix, marché)* stable, steady

stand by *nm* standby agreement

stellage *nm Bourse* put and call (option), double option

sterling *adj* sterling

stimulation financière *nf* cash incentive

stock *nm (des marchandises)* stock; *Compta* **stocks** *Br* stock, *Am* inventory
◊ **stock existant** stock in hand
◊ **stock final** closing stock
◊ **stock initial** opening stock
◊ **stock en magasin** stock in hand
◊ **stock d'or** *(d'une Banque d'État)* gold reserve
◊ **stock d'ouverture** opening stock
◊ **stock stratégique** perpetual inventory

stock-option *nf Bourse* stock option

> **"**
>
> Une **stock-option** est le droit attribué à un cadre d'acheter une action de son entreprise, à un prix et dans un délai donnés. Il peut lever l'option, c'est-à-dire décider d'acheter l'action au prix d'exercice fixé au moment de l'attribution. A condition de respecter le délai. La plus-value potentielle est égale à la différence entre le prix auquel il peut acheter l'action et le vrai prix en Bourse.
>
> **"**

stop-vente *nf Bourse* stop-loss selling

structure *nf* structure
◊ **structure des coûts** cost structure
◊ **structure de(s) prix** price structure
◊ **structure des salaires** wage *or* salary structure

subvention *nf* subsidy, grant

◇ *subventions en capital* capital grants

◇ *subvention d'investissement* investment grant

subventionné, -e *adj* subsidized; **subventionné par l'État** State-aided

subventionner *vt* to subsidize, to grant financial aid to

superdividende *nm* surplus dividend

surcapitalisation *nf* overcapitalization

surcapitalisé, -e *adj* overcapitalized

surcharger *vt (chèque, écriture)* to alter

surcoté, -e *adj (action, marché, monnaie)* overvalued

surémission *nf* overissue

surenchère *nf (enchère plus élevée)* higher bid; *(lors d'une tentative d'acquisition d'entreprise)* counterbid

> 〞
>
> En cas d'accord, M. Desmarest a confirmé son intention de relever son offre. Cependant la **surenchère** ne sera pas considérable, car la proposition initiale comporte déjà une prime de 20% pour les actionnaires d'Elf.
>
> 〞

surenchérir *vi* to bid higher; **surenchérir qn** to outbid sb, to bid higher than sb

surendetté, -e *adj Écon* overindebted

surendettement *nm Écon* excessive debt; **courir un risque de surendettement** to run a risk of getting into excessive debt

surface financière *nf* financial standing

surimposer *vt* (a) *(augmenter l'impôt sur)* to increase the tax on (b) *(frapper d'un impôt trop lourd)* to overtax

surimposition *nf* (a) *(augmentation de l'impôt)* increase of taxation (b) *(excessif)* over-taxation

surinvestissement *nm* overinvestment

suroffre *nf* counterbid

surpayer *vt (personne)* to overpay; *(produit)* to pay too much for

surplus *nm* surplus

◇ *surplus exceptionnels, surplus extraordinaires* excess profits

◇ *surplus monétaire* monetary surplus

sursalaire *nm* bonus, extra pay

sursouscription *nf Bourse* oversubscription

sursouscrire *vt Bourse* to oversubscribe

sursouscrit, -e *adj Bourse* oversubscribed

surtaxe *nf* (a) *(en sus)* surtax, surcharge (b) *(taxe excessive)* excessive tax

surtaxer *vt* (a) *(frapper d'une taxe supplémentaire)* to surtax, to surcharge (b) *(frapper d'une taxe excessive)* to overtax

survaleur *nf* goodwill; **amortissement de la survaleur** *ou* **des survaleurs** goodwill amortization

> **"**
> Vivendi suit une ligne claire de développement qui passe par deux métiers bien définis: l'environnement et la communication. D'autre part, il a répondu aux inquiétudes de certains concernant le poids de l'endettement sur les résultats à venir, de même que sur l'amortissement des **survaleurs**.
> **"**

suspendre *vt (paiement, travail)* to suspend, to stop; **suspendre le paiement d'un chèque** to stop a cheque

swap *nm Bourse* swap
◊ *swap d'actifs* asset swap
◊ *swap de change* exchange rate swap

syndicat *nm (de financiers)* syndicate
◊ *syndicat financier* (financial) syndicate
◊ *syndicat de garantie* underwriting syndicate
◊ *syndicat de prise ferme* underwriting syndicate

système *nm* system
◊ *système bancaire* banking system
◊ *Banque système de compensation* clearing system
◊ *système comptable* accounting system
◊ *système fiscal* tax system
◊ *Bourse système informatique de cotation* computerized trading system
◊ *Bourse système informatisé de transaction* screen-trading system
◊ *Écon système monétaire* monetary system
◊ *Écon système monétaire européen* European monetary system
◊ *système de participation aux bénéfices* profit-sharing scheme
◊ *système de primes* bonus scheme
◊ *système de retraite* pension scheme
◊ *système de retraite par répartition* contributory pension plan

table *nf (liste, recueil)* table
- *table des intérêts* interest table
- *table des parités* parity table, table of par values

tableau *nm (liste)* list, table
- *Compta* *tableau d'amortissement* depreciation schedule
- *tableau comptable* (financial) statement
- *Compta* *tableau des emplois et ressources* funds flow statement, cash flow statement
- *Compta* *tableau de financement* funds flow statement, cash flow statement
- *Compta* *tableau des flux de trésorerie* cash flow statement

talon *nm* (a) *(de chèque)* counterfoil, stub (b) *(de coupon)* talon

tantième *nm (de bénéfices)* percentage, quota; **le tantième des administrateurs** the directors' percentage of the profits

TARGET *nm Banque, UE (abrév* **Transferts Express Automatisés Transeuropéens à Réglement Brut en Temps Réel)** TARGET

tarif *nm* (a) *(prix)* rate

(b) *(tableau des prix)* price list, *Br* tariff
- *tarif de base* basic rate
- *tarif dégressif* sliding-scale tariff, tapering charge
- *tarif d'encaissement* collection rate
- *tarif forfaitaire* fixed rate
- *tarif minimum* minimum charge
- *tarif préférentiel* preferential rate
- *tarif réduit* cheap rate
- *tarif des salaires* salary scale

taux *nm (montant, pourcentage)* rate; **à taux fixe** fixed-rate; **taux de 8%** rate of 8%; **emprunter à un taux de 7%** to borrow at 7%
- *taux d'accroissement* rate of increase *or* of growth
- *Écon* *taux d'activité* participation rate
- *Compta* *taux d'actualisation* net present value rate, rate of discount
- *taux actuariel* yield to maturity
- *Compta* *taux d'amortissement* rate of depreciation, depreciation rate
- *taux annualisé* annual percentage rate, APR
- *taux de l'argent* money rate

◇ *taux de l'argent au jour le jour* overnight (money) rate

◇ *taux d'autofinancement* cash flow rate

◇ *taux bancaire* bank rate

◇ *taux de base (bancaire)* base rate

◇ *Compta* *taux de capitalisation* price-earnings ratio

◇ *taux de change* exchange rate, rate of exchange

◇ *taux de change à l'achat* bank buying rate

◇ *taux de change en cours* current rate of exchange

◇ *taux de change fixe* fixed exchange rate

◇ *taux de change flottant* floating exchange rate

◇ *taux de change multiple* multiple exchange rate

◇ *taux de change à la vente* bank selling rate

◇ *taux de conversion* conversion rate

◇ *taux de couverture du dividende* dividend cover

◇ *taux de crédit export* export credit rate

◇ *taux de croissance* growth rate

◇ *taux de déport* backwardation rate

◇ *taux de désintéressement* drop-dead rate

◇ *taux directeur* intervention rate

◇ *taux d'échange* rate of exchange, exchange rate

◇ *taux effectif global* annual percentage rate

◇ *Banque* *taux d'emprunt* borrowing rate

◇ *taux d'épargne* savings rate

◇ *taux d'escompte* discount rate

◇ *taux flottant* floating rate

◇ *taux d'imposition* tax rate, rate of taxation

◇ *taux d'imposition effectif* *Br* effective *or Am* average tax rate

◇ *Écon* *taux d'inflation* rate of inflation, inflation rate

◇ *Banque* *taux interbancaire offert* interbank offered rate

◇ *Banque, Écon* *taux d'intérêt* interest rate, rate of interest

◇ *Banque, Écon* *taux d'intérêt à court terme* short-term interest rate

◇ *Banque, Écon* *taux d'intérêt légal* official rate of interest

◇ *Banque, Écon* *taux d'intérêt à long terme* long-term interest rate

◇ *Banque, Écon* *taux d'intérêt nominal* nominal (interest) rate

◇ *taux d'intervention* intervention rate

◇ *le taux du jour* today's rate

◇ *Compta* *taux linéaire* straight-line rate

◇ *Banque* *taux de liquidité* liquidity ratio

◇ *Banque* *taux Lombard* Lombard rate

◇ *Bourse* *taux long obligataire* long-term bond rate

◇ *taux marginal d'imposition* marginal tax rate

◇ *taux maximum* top rate

◇ *taux minimum* minimum rate

◇ *taux de mise en réserve* reserve ratio

◇ *taux moyen du marché monétaire* money-market rate

◇ *taux nominal* nominal yield

◇ *taux normal* standard rate

◇ *taux officiel* official rate

◇ *Banque* *taux officiel d'es-*

compte minimum lending rate

◇ *taux plafonné* cap

◇ *Can Banque* **taux préférentiel** prime rate

◇ *Banque* **taux de prêt** lending rate

◇ *taux de profit net* net profit ratio

◇ *taux proportionnel (d'un crédit)* annual percentage rate

◇ *Bourse* **taux de rachat** repo rate

◇ *taux réduit* reduced rate

◇ *Banque* **taux de référence** reference rate

◇ *Banque* **taux de référence interbancaire** interbank reference rate

◇ *taux de rendement* rate of return

◇ *taux de rendement actuariel brut* gross annual interest return

◇ *taux de rendement courant* current yield

◇ *taux de rendement à l'échéance* yield to maturity

◇ *taux de rentabilité* rate of return

◇ *taux de rentabilité interne* internal rate of return

◇ *Bourse* **taux de report** contango rate

◇ *taux standard* standard rate

◇ *taux de TVA* VAT rate

◇ *taux uniforme* uniform rate

◇ *taux d'usure* penal rate

◇ *Compta* **taux d'utilisation des actifs** asset utilisation ratio

◇ *taux variable* floating or variable rate

◇ *taux zéro* zero rating; **taxer à taux zéro** to zero rate

“

Tous les chiffres qui révèlent l'intensité de la croissance, donc les risques d'inflation, et donc une éventuelle remontée des taux américains, font peur à la Bourse. Ainsi, pendant des semaines, les opérateurs français ont attendu avec anxiété le verdict de la Réserve fédérale américaine (Fed) du mardi 24 août. L'annonce du relèvement des **taux directeurs** d'un quart de point a finalement soulagé les boursiers.

”

“

Même en pariant sur une légère baisse du **taux d'épargne,** il est peu probable que les Français augmentent significativement leurs dépenses.

”

taxable *adj* dutiable, taxable

taxation *nf (par l'impôt)* taxation; *(contrôle)* assessment

◇ *taxation à la valeur* valuation charge

taxe *nf (prélèvement)* tax; **hors taxes** exclusive of tax; **toutes taxes comprises** inclusive of tax

◇ *taxe à l'achat* purchase tax

◇ *taxe d'aéroport* airport tax

◇ *taxe d'apprentissage* = tax paid by businesses to fund training programmes

◇ *taxe sur le chiffre d'affaires* turnover tax

◇ *taxe exceptionnelle* exceptional tax, special levy

◇ *taxe de luxe* tax on luxury goods

⋄ *Admin* **taxe parafiscale** exceptional tax, special levy

⋄ **taux plafond** cap, ceiling rate

⋄ **taxe professionnelle** = tax paid by businesses and self-employed people

⋄ **taxe à la valeur ajoutée,** *Can* **taxe sur les ventes** *Br* value-added tax, *Am* sales tax

taxer *vt* (a) *(personne, alcool, cigarettes)* to tax; **taxer qch à 10%** to put a 10% tax on sth (b) *(prix)* to regulate, to fix; *(salaire)* to regulate the rate of

TEG *nm* (*abrév* **taux effectif global**) APR

TEMPÉ *nm* (*abrév* **Taux Moyen Pondéré en Euros**) EONIA

tendance *nf* tendency, trend

⋄ **tendance à la baisse** *(dans l'économie)* downward trend or tendency, downtrend; *(à la bourse)* bearish tendency

⋄ *Écon* **tendances conjoncturelles** economic trends

⋄ **tendance de croissance** growth trend

⋄ **tendance à la hausse** *Écon* upward trend or tendency; *Bourse* bullish tendency

⋄ *Bourse* **tendance du marché** market trend

teneur, -euse *nm,f*

⋄ *Compta* **teneur de livres** bookkeeper

⋄ *Bourse* **teneur de marché** market maker

tenir *vt* (a) **tenir qch à bail** to hold a lease on sth (b) *(s'occuper de)* to keep; **tenir la caisse** to be in charge of the cash; **tenir la comptabilité** *ou* **les livres** to keep the accounts *or* the books

tenu, -e *adj Bourse (cours)* steady, firm

tenue *nf Bourse (des cours)* steadiness, firmness; *(du marché)* state; **le franc n'est pas la seule monnaie à souffrir de la bonne tenue du mark** the franc is not the only currency to suffer from the steadiness *or* firmness of the mark

⋄ *Compta* **tenue de caisse** petty cash management

⋄ *Compta* **tenue des comptes, tenue des livres** bookkeeping

terme *nm* (a) **à court terme** *(effet)* short-dated; *(emprunt, placement, crédit)* short-term; *(argent)* at short notice, at call; **à long terme** *(effet)* long-dated; *(emprunt, placement, crédit)* long-term; **à terme fixe** fixed-term; **arriver à terme** *(plan d'épargne)* to reach fruition

(b) *Bourse* settlement; **à terme** *(compte, cours, livraison, marché)* forward; **livrable à terme** for forward delivery; **acheter/vendre à terme** to buy/sell forward; **placer de l'argent à terme** to invest in futures

(c) *(versement)* instalment; **acheter à terme** to buy on credit; **payable en deux termes** payable in two instalments

(d) **termes** *(d'un accord, d'un contrat)* terms

⋄ **termes d'échange** terms of exchange

⋄ **terme d'échéance** tenor

⋄ **termes de paiement** terms of payment

terminal *nm Ordinat* terminal, VDU

⋄ **terminal électronique de**

paiement electronic payment terminal

théorique *adj (profits)* paper

TIBEUR *nm (abrév* **Taux Interbancaire Européen)** EURIBOR

tiers, tierce **1** *adj* third
2 *nm (impôt)* interim tax payment *(equal to one third of tax paid in the previous year)*
◊ *tiers bénéficiaire (d'un chèque, d'un effet)* beneficiary
◊ *tierce caution* contingent liability
◊ *tierce porteur* second endorser

TIOP *nm Banque (abrév* **taux interbancaire offert à Paris)** PIBOR

TIP *nm Banque (abrév* **titre interbancaire de paiement)** bank giro transfer

tirage *nm* **(a)** *(d'un chèque, d'une lettre de change)* drawing, emission; *(d'un prêt)* drawdown
(b) *(de loterie)* draw **(de** for); **les obligations sont rachetées par voie de tirage** debentures are redeemed by lot
◊ *tirage en l'air, tirage en blanc* kite flying, kiting
◊ *tirage au sort* drawing lots

tiré, -e *nm,f (d'un chèque, d'une lettre de change)* drawee

tirer **1** *vt (chèque, lettre de change)* to draw **(sur** on); **avez-vous tiré des chèques depuis cette date?** have you written any cheques since then?; **ce chèque a-t-il déjà été tiré?** has this cheque cleared yet?
2 *vi* **tirer à découvert** to overdraw; **tirer à vue** to draw at sight

tireur, -euse *nm,f (d'un chèque, d'une lettre de change)* drawer

titre *nm Bourse (valeur)* security; *(certificat)* certificate; **titres** stocks and shares, securities, *Am* stock; **prendre livraison de titres** to take delivery of stock; **vendre des titres** to sell stock; **titres déposés en nantissement** securities lodged as collateral; **titres détenus en garantie** stocks held as security
◊ *Bourse* **titre d'action** share certificate
◊ *titre commercial* commercial bill
◊ *titre de créance* loan note, debt instrument
◊ *titre de crédit* proof of credit
◊ *Bourse* **titres dilués** watered stock
◊ *Bourse* **titres émis** issued securities
◊ *Bourse* **titres fiduciaires** paper securities
◊ *Bourse* **titres flottants** shares available on the market
◊ *Bourse* **titres libérés** fully paid-up securities
◊ *Bourse* **titres longs** long-dated securities, longs
◊ *titre à lots* lottery loan bond
◊ *Bourse* **titres négociables** negotiable stock
◊ *Bourse* **titre nominatif** registered security
◊ *titre d'obligation* loan *or* bond note
◊ *titre de paiement* document of payment; **le titre de paiement doit être envoyé à ...** remittance by cheque or money order to be sent to ...
◊ *titre participatif, titre de participation* equity investment *or* loan

◇ *Bourse* **titres de placement** marketable securities

◇ *Bourse* **titres en portefeuille** securities (in portfolio)

◇ **titre au porteur** bearer bond, negotiable instrument

◇ **titre de prêt** loan certificate

◇ *Bourse* **titre provisoire** scrip certificate

◇ *Bourse* **titres ramassés** take-over stock

◇ **titre de rente** government bond

◇ *Bourse* **titres à revenu fixe** fixed-rate securities

◇ *Bourse* **titres à revenu variable** floating-rate securities

◇ *Bourse* **titre sous-jacent** underlying security

◇ *Bourse* **titres à terme** futures

◇ **titre universel de paiement** *(joint à la facture)* payment form, universal payment order

> **"**
>
> Les détenteurs de **titres au porteur** disposent d'une période de six mois pour faire inscrire leurs **titres** sous forme nominative.
>
> **"**

titrisation *nf Bourse* securitization

titulaire *nmf (d'un titre, d'un certificat, d'un compte)* holder

◇ **titulaire d'action** shareholder

TJJ *nm (abrév* **taux d'argent au jour le jour)** overnight rate

TMM *nm (abrév* **taux moyen du marché monétaire)** money-market rate

total, -e 1 *adj* total

    2 *nm* total; **le total des recettes**

et des dépenses total revenue and expenditure; **faire le total des bénéfices** to add up the profits, to calculate the total profit

◇ **total de l'actif** total assets

◇ **total global** grand total

◇ **total du passif** total liabilities

◇ **total à payer** total payable

touchable *adj (chèque)* that can be cashed; *(effet)* collectable

toucher *vt (salaire)* to get, to draw; *(chèque)* to cash; *(intérêts)* to receive, to get; *(traite)* to collect

tour de table *nm* pool, backers

trader *nm Bourse* trader

traite *nf (lettre de change)* (banker's) draft, bill (of exchange); **encaisser/tirer une traite** to collect/draw a bill; **escompter une traite** to discount a bill; **présenter une traite à l'acceptation** to present a bill for acceptance

◇ **traite contre acceptation** acceptance bill

◇ **traite en l'air** fictitious bill, kite

◇ **traite avalisée** guaranteed bill

◇ **traite bancaire** bank *or* banker's draft

◇ **traite de complaisance** accommodation bill

◇ **traite à courte échéance** short-dated bill

◇ **traite à date fixe** time bill

◇ **traite documentaire** documentary bill

◇ **traite domiciliée** domiciled bill

◇ **traite sur l'extérieur, traite sur l'étranger** foreign bill

◇ **traite sur l'intérieur** inland bill

- ◇ *traite libre* clean bill
- ◇ *traite à longue échéance* long-dated bill
- ◇ *traite de plaisance* accommodation bill
- ◇ *traite pro forma* pro forma bill
- ◇ *traite 'sans frais'* bill 'without protest'
- ◇ *traite à terme* term draft
- ◇ *traite à vue* sight draft

traitement nm *(rémunération des fonctionnaires)* pay, salary; **sans traitement** unsalaried
- ◇ *traitement de base* basic pay or salary
- ◇ *traitement fixe* fixed salary
- ◇ *traitement initial* starting salary

tranche nf *(de chiffres)* group, block; *(d'actions)* block, tranche; *(d'un crédit, d'un emprunt)* instalment; *(d'assistance financière internationale)* tranche; *Admin* **par tranche de 1000 francs ou fraction de 1000 francs** for every complete sum of 1,000 francs or part thereof
- ◇ *tranche d'imposition* tax bracket or band
- ◇ *tranche de revenus* income bracket or group

┌ **"** ─────────────

Le directeur général du FMI, Michel Camdessus, a rendu public un communiqué insistant sur la nécessité de mener à bien les réformes économiques afin que le fonds puisse débloquer en septembre la seconde **tranche** de son aide financière de 11,2 milliards de dollars

───────────── **"** ┘

transaction nf *(opération)*

transaction, deal; **transactions** transactions, dealings
- ◇ *transaction bancaire* bank transaction
- ◇ *transactions bancaires en ligne* on-line banking
- ◇ *transaction boursière* stock exchange transaction
- ◇ *Banque* **transaction par carte** card transaction
- ◇ *Bourse* **transactions de clôture** closing transactions or trade
- ◇ *transaction commerciale* business transaction
- ◇ *Bourse* **transaction au comptant** spot or cash transaction
- ◇ *transaction à crédit* credit transaction
- ◇ *transactions hors Bourse* after-hours or street dealing
- ◇ *Bourse* **transactions à terme** futures

transcrire vt *(recopier)* to transcribe; *Compta* **transcrire le journal au grand-livre** to transfer journal entries into the ledger

transférer vt *(argent, actions, effets)* to transfer; **transférer un billet par voie d'endossement** to transfer a bill by endorsement; **il a transféré son argent sur un compte suisse** he's transferred his money into a Swiss account

transfert nm *(d'argent, d'actions, d'effets)* transfer
- ◇ *Banque* **transfert par CCP** giro transfer
- ◇ *Compta* **transfert de charges** transfer of charges
- ◇ *Compta* **transfert de compte à compte** book entry transfer
- ◇ *Compta* **transfert de cré-**

ances assignment of accounts receivable *or* of debts

◇ **transfert de devises** currency transfer

◇ **transfert de fonds électronique** electronic funds transfer

◇ *Banque* **transfert télégraphique** telegraphic transfer

transfert-paiement   *nm* transfer of account *(from one savings bank to another)*

transmissible *adj* **transmissible par endossement** transferable by endorsement

transmission *nf* transfer

◇ **transmission par endossement** transfer by endorsement

transport *nm* (**a**) *Banque (de fonds)* transfer *(from one account to another)* (**b**) *Compta* transfer

transporter *vt* (**a**) *Banque (fonds)* to transfer *(from one account to another)* (**b**) *Compta* to transfer

treizième mois *nm* = extra month's salary paid as an annual bonus

trésor *nm* treasury; **le Trésor (public)** *(institution)* = department dealing with the State budget, *Br* ≃ the Treasury, *Am* ≃ the Treasury Department; *(finances publiques)* public funds *or* finances

trésorerie *nf* (**a**) *(fonction de trésorier)* treasurership (**b**) *(bu-*

reau) (gouvernemental) public revenue office; *(d'une entreprise)* accounts department (**c**) *(ressources)* funds, finances; **avoir des problèmes de trésorerie** to have cash flow problems (**d**) *(gestion)* accounts

trésorier, -ère *nm,f* treasurer

◇ **trésorier de banque** bank treasurer

tribunal de commerce *nm* commercial court

trimestre *nm* *(période)* quarter, three months; **premier/deuxième trimestre** first/second quarter; **par trimestre** quarterly

trop-perçu *nm* *(d'impôts)* excess payment; **rembourser le trop-perçu** to refund the excess payment

trust *nm* trust

◇ **trust commercial** commercial monopoly

◇ **trust industriel** industrial monopoly

◇ **trust de placement** investment trust

◇ **trust de valeurs** holding company

◇ **trust vertical** vertical trust

truster **1** *vt* to monopolize, to form into a monopoly
2 *vi* to form a monopoly

TVA *nf* (*abrév* **taxe à la valeur ajoutée**) *Br* VAT, *Am* sales tax; **soumis à la TVA** subject to *Br* VAT *or Am* sales tax

UEM *nf UE (abrév* **union économique et monétaire**) EMU

UME *nf UE (abrév* **union monétaire européenne**) EMU

unification *nf* (**a**) *(des crédits)* consolidation (**b**) *(fusion d'entreprises)* merger

unifié, -e *adj (crédits)* consolidated

unifier *vt (crédits)* to consolidate

union monétaire européenne *nf UE* European monetary union

unité *nf (étalon)* unit

◊ *Écon* **unité de compte** unit of account

◊ *UE* **unité de compte européenne** European currency unit

◊ **unité de coût** cost unit

◊ **unité monétaire** monetary unit, unit of currency

◊ *UE* **unité monétaire européenne** European currency unit

◊ *Bourse* **unité de transaction** lot size

URSSAF *nf (abrév* **Union de recouvrement des cotisations de Sécurité sociale et d'Allocations familiales**) = organization which collects social security and family allowance payments

valable *adj* valid; *Bourse* **valable jusqu'à nouvel ordre** good until cancelled

valeur *nf* (a) *(prix)* value, worth (b) *Bourse (titre)* security, share (c) **valeurs** *(capital)* assets

◇ **valeur d'achat** purchase value

◇ *Compta* **valeur de l'actif** asset value

◇ *Compta* **valeur d'actif net** net asset value

◇ *Compta* **valeur actionnariale** shareholder value

◇ **valeurs actives** assets

◇ *Compta* **valeur actualisée** discounted (present) value

◇ *Compta* **valeur actualisée nette** discounted cash flow

◇ *Compta* **valeur actuelle** current value

◇ *Compta* **valeur actuelle nette** current net value, net present value

◇ *Écon* **valeur ajoutée** added value

◇ *Compta* **valeur amortie** written-down cost *or* value

◇ **valeur assurable** insurable value

◇ **valeur assurée** insured value

◇ **valeur attendue** expected value

◇ *Bourse* **valeurs aurifères** gold shares

◇ **valeurs bancaires** bank shares

◇ *Compta* **valeur de bilan, valeur bilantielle** book value

◇ *Bourse* **valeurs de bourse** quoted securities

◇ **valeur boursière** *(d'une action)* market value; *(action cotée à la Bourse)* trading security

◇ **valeur brute** gross value

◇ **valeur en capital** capital assets

◇ **valeur capitalisée** capitalized value

◇ *Compta* **valeur à la casse** break-up value

◇ **valeurs classées** investment stock

◇ **valeur compensée** cleared value

◇ *Compta* **valeur comptable** book value

◇ *Compta* **valeur comptable nette** net book value

◇ *Bourse* **valeurs au comptant** securities dealt in for cash

◇ *Banque* **valeur en compte** value in account

◇ *Compta* **valeurs de croissance** growth shares *or* stocks

◇ *Compta* **valeur cyclique** cyclical stock

◇ **valeur déclarée** declared value

◇ **valeur de départ** initial value

◇ **valeurs disponibles** available or liquid or current assets

◇ **valeur d'échange** exchange value

◇ **valeur à l'échéance** maturity value

◇ **valeur effective** real value

◇ **valeur à l'encaissement** value for collection

◇ **valeur d'émission** issue price

◇ **valeur en espèces** cash, bullion

◇ **valeur extrinsèque** extrinsic value; *(d'une monnaie)* legal or fictitious value

◇ *Bourse* **valeur faciale** *(d'une action)* face or nominal value

◇ **valeur de facture** invoice value

◇ **valeur fictive** *(de la monnaie fiduciaire)* face value

◇ **valeur future** prospective value

◇ **valeurs immatérielles** fixed assets

◇ **valeurs immobilières** property shares

◇ **valeurs immobilisées** fixed assets

◇ **valeurs incorporelles** intangible assets, intangibles

◇ *Bourse* **valeurs industrielles** industrial shares, industrials

◇ **valeur initiale** original value

◇ *Bourse* **valeurs à intérêt fixe** fixed-interest securities

◇ **valeur intrinsèque** intrinsic value

◇ *Compta* **valeur d'inventaire** balance sheet value, break-up value

◇ *Compta* **valeur de liquidation, valeur liquidative** value at liquidation, scrap or cash-in value

◇ **valeurs liquides** liquid assets or securities

◇ **valeur locative** rental value

◇ **valeur locative imposable** rateable value

◇ *Bourse* **valeurs à lot** lottery or prize bonds

◇ **valeur marchande** commercial or marketable value

◇ **valeur marginale** marginal value

◇ **valeurs matérielles** tangible assets, tangibles

◇ *Bourse* **valeurs mobilières** stocks and shares, transferable securities

◇ **valeurs mobilières de placement** marketable securities

◇ **valeur monétaire escomptée** expected monetary value

◇ *Bourse* **valeurs nanties** pledged securities

◇ **valeur négociable** market or commercial value

◇ *Bourse* **valeurs négociables** marketable securities

◇ **valeur nette** net value or worth

◇ **valeur à neuf** replacement value

◇ *Bourse* **valeur nominale** *(d'une obligation)* par value; *(d'une action)* nominal or face value

◇ *Bourse* **valeurs nominatives** registered securities

◇ *Bourse* **valeur non cotée** unlisted security

◇ **valeur numéraire** legal-tender value

◇ **valeur à l'origine, valeur d'origine** original value

◇ **valeur au pair** par value

◇ **valeurs passives** liabilities

◇ **valeur perçue** perceived value

◇ *Bourse* **valeurs de père de famille** blue chip stocks or shares

◇ *Bourse* **valeurs de placement** marketable or investment securities

◇ *Bourse* **valeurs de portefeuille** portfolio securities

◇ *Bourse* **valeurs au porteur** bearer securities *or* bonds

◇ *Bourse* **valeurs de premier choix, valeurs de premier ordre** blue chip stocks *or* shares

◇ *Bourse* **valeur de rachat** redemption value

◇ **valeur réalisable nette** net realizable value

◇ *Bourse* **valeurs réalisables** realizable *or* marketable securities

◇ **valeur réelle** real *or* actual value

◇ **valeur de remboursement** redemption value

◇ **valeur de remplacement** replacement value

◇ **valeur de rendement** *(d'une entreprise)* profitability value

◇ *Bourse* **valeurs de rendement** income bonds

◇ **valeur résiduelle nette** net residual value

◇ *Bourse* **valeurs de retournement** recovery shares

◇ **valeur à la revente** resale value

◇ *Bourse* **valeurs à revenu fixe** fixed-income securities

◇ *Bourse* **valeurs à revenu variable** floating-rate *or* variable-rate securities

◇ *Bourse* **valeurs du second marché** unlisted securities

◇ *Bourse* **valeurs des sociétés industrielles** industrials

◇ *Bourse* **valeurs spéculatives, valeurs de spéculation** speculative securities

◇ *Bourse* **valeur temporelle** time value

◇ *Bourse* **valeurs à terme** futures

◇ *Bourse* **valeurs de tout repos** gilt-edged securities

◇ **valeur transactionnelle** settlement value

◇ **valeur d'usage** value as a going concern, value in use

◇ *Bourse* **valeur vedette** equity leader, glamour stock

◇ **valeur vénale** fair market value

"

Les sociétés cotées utilisent de plus en plus des indicateurs de performance financière qui sont dérivés de la notion de '**valeur actionnariale**' ... Les dirigeants de la BNP expliquent volontiers que les OPE qu'ils ont lancées sur la Société Générale et Paribas ayant fait monter leurs cours, elles ont donc déjà "créé de la valeur pour leurs actionnaires'. En fait la '**valeur actionnariale**' est créée par l'entreprise, pas par la Bourse: elle se calcule à partir de ses comptes (bénéfice par action, rentabilité des capitaux, etc.) et non du cours de Bourse. Une société qui crée de la valeur peut voir son cours baisser.

"

"

Mais, de fait, la Bourse de New York a à nouveau perdu du terrain cette semaine. L'indice Dow Jones des **valeurs vedettes** a cédé 4,85 % à 10 279,33 points, le plus important recul sur la semaine parmi les grandes places boursières.

"

valeur-or *nf* value in gold currency

valoir *vi* (**a**) *(avoir comme valeur)* to be worth; **valoir cher** *(objet en* *vente)* to be expensive; *(objet précieux)* to be worth a lot

(b) *(fructifier)* **faire valoir son argent** to invest one's money profitably

(c) à valoir *(paiement, somme)* to be deducted, on account; **payer 200 francs à valoir** to pay 200 francs on account; **verser un acompte à valoir sur une somme** to pay a deposit to be set off against *or* deducted from a sum

valorisation *nf (augmentation de la valeur)* increase in value, valorization; *Compta (d'un inventaire)* valuation

> Un nouvel avis de tempête a été déclenché, jeudi 23 septembre, sur les valeurs technologiques américaines. … Le facteur déclenchant de cette panique a été un jugement sans appel de Steven Ballmer, le président de Microsoft, sur la **valorisation** des actions de haute technologie.

valoriser 1 *vt* to valorize
2 se valoriser *vpr (portefeuille, valeur)* to gain *or* increase in value

VAN *nm Compta (abrév* **valeur actuelle nette)** current net value

vendeur, -euse *nm,f Bourse* seller; *(d'une prime)* giver
◇ **vendeur à découvert** short *or* bear seller

vendre *vt* to sell; *Bourse* **vendre à découvert** to sell short, to go a bear; *Bourse* **vendre à terme** to sell forward

vente *nf Compta* **ventes** sales, turnover

◇ **vente au comptant** cash sale
◇ *Bourse* **vente à découvert** short *or* bear sale
◇ *Bourse* **vente nue** naked sale
◇ *Bourse* **vente spéculative** speculative selling
◇ *Bourse* **vente à terme** forward sale

vérificateur, -trice *nm,f* inspector
◇ **vérificateur de comptes** auditor
◇ **vérificateur externe** external auditor
◇ **vérificateur interne** internal auditor

vérification *nf (de déclarations)* checking, verification
◇ *Compta* **vérification de comptes** audit(ing) of accounts
◇ *Compta* **vérification d'écritures** audit(ing) of accounts
◇ **vérification externe** external auditing
◇ **vérification fiscale** tax audit
◇ **vérification interne** internal auditing
◇ *Compta* **vérification à rebours** audit trail

vérifier *vt* to check; *(comptes)* to audit

versement *nm (paiement)* payment; *(paiement partiel)* instalment; **en plusieurs versements** by *or* in instalments; **premier versement** down payment
◇ **versement annuel** yearly payment
◇ **versement à la commande** down payment
◇ **versement comptant** cash payment
◇ **versements échelonnés** staggered payments, instalments

◇ *versement d'espèces* cash deposit

◇ *versement libératoire* final instalment

◇ *versement en numéraire* payment in cash

◇ *versement partiel* instalment

verser *vt (argent, intérêt)* to pay; *(sur un compte)* to deposit; **verser qch au crédit de qn** to credit sb with sth; **verser un acompte** to make a down payment; **verser de l'argent sur son compte** to pay money into one's account; *Bourse* **verser un premium** to pay *or* deposit a premium

verso *nm (d'un effet, d'un chèque)* back

VI *nf Compta (abrév* **valeur d'inventaire***)* balance sheet value, break-up value

viager, -ère 1 *adj (rente)* life **2** *nm* life annuity; **placer son argent en viager** to invest one's money in a life annuity; **acheter une propriété en viager** = to acquire a property by paying pre-determined instalments until the death of the owner(s)

virement *nm Banque* (credit) transfer

◇ *virement automatique* automatic transfer, standing order

◇ *virement bancaire* bank transfer

◇ *virement par courrier* mail transfer

◇ *virement de crédit* credit transfer

◇ *Admin virement de fonds* = transfer (often illegal) of funds from one article of the budget to another

◇ *virement interbancaire* inter-bank transfer

◇ *virement postal* post office transfer

◇ *virement télégraphique* cable transfer

◇ *virement par télex* telex transfer

virer *vt Banque (somme)* to transfer; *(chèque)* to clear; **je vire 1 000 francs tous les mois sur son compte** I transfer *or* pay 1,000 francs into his account every month

visa *nm* **(a)** *(de chèque)* certification **(b)** *Bourse* **visa de la COB** ≃ permission to deal

viser *vt (chèque)* to certify; *Compta* **viser des livres de commerce** to certify the books

vitesse *nf (rapidité)* speed, rate; **être en perte de vitesse** *(monnaie)* to be losing ground

◇ *Écon vitesse de transformation des capitaux* income velocity of capital

VMP *nfpl (abrév* **valeurs mobilières de placement***)* marketable securities

volant *nm* **(a)** *(d'argent)* reserve **(b)** **talon et volant** *(de chèque)* counterfoil and leaf

◇ *volant de sécurité* reserve fund

◇ *volant de trésorerie* cash reserve

volatil, -e *adj Bourse (option)* volatile

volatilité *nf Bourse (d'une option)* volatility

volet *nm (d'un chèque)* tear-off portion

vue *nf* **à sept jours de vue** seven days after sight

warrant *nm* warrant
◇ *warrant à l'achat* call warrant
◇ *warrant à la vente* put warrant

X-Dax *n Bourse* **le X-Dax** the X-Dax (index)

Xetra-Dax *n Bourse* **le Xetra-Dax** the Xetra-Dax (index)

yen *nm* yen

zinzin *nm Fam* institutional investor

zone *nf* area, zone
◇ *zone dollar* dollar area
◇ *zone euro* euro zone
◇ *zone franc* franc area

◇ *zone monétaire* monetary area
◇ *zone sterling* sterling area

> **❝**
>
> En définitive, la croissance économique de la zone pour les années 90 devrait être bien médiocre : de 1991 à 1999, le PIB réel des Onze ne devrait pas avoir progressé de plus de 1,8% l'an en moyenne … Mais c'est une note d'espoir qui ressort des tendances économiques récentes de la **zone euro**. Tout d'abord, parce que la plupart des indicateurs conjoncturels des Onze sont repassés au vert depuis le printemps.
>
> **❞**

RAPPORTS FINANCIERS BRITANNIQUES ET AMÉRICAINS

En ce qui concerne la présentation et le calcul des données financières, les différences entre les pays dans le monde se sont réduites avec le temps, mais les bases historiques n'en sont pas moins différentes.

- La comptabilité française est réglementée par l'Etat depuis le XVIIe siècle, et avec pour objectif d'aider au calcul de l'impôt et à la gestion de l'économie.

- A l'intérieur d'un cadre statutaire, les comptabilités britannique et américaine ont été réglementées en détail par la profession comptable; elles tirent leur origine de la révolution industrielle, époque à laquelle il devint nécessaire de réunir des fonds pour financer et contrôler les programmes industriels.

Historiquement, le bilan est le plus ancien rapport financier. Il s'agissait à l'origine pour l'entreprise d'établir un inventaire annuel de tous ses biens tout en décomptant les dettes afin d'estimer la valeur de son patrimoine. La différence de la valeur entre deux inventaires annuels représente la perte ou le gain sur l'année écoulée.

La comptabilité moderne, elle, se passe de la réévaluation annuelle, mais elle garde une base de données des transactions financières dans le grand livre, base qui sert à établir les états financiers. Il s'agit (a) du bilan, (b) du compte de résultat, (c) du tableau des flux de trésorerie, et (d) de l'annexe.

- Le bilan montre d'une part, les modes de financement de l'entreprise, lesquels se répartissent entre le capital non remboursable (les fonds souscrits par les actionnaires), et la dette ou emprunt qui doit être remboursé; d'autre part, l'actif – les équipements de production et les éléments courants d'exploitation que le passif a financés. L'actif est normalement divisé entre l'actif immobilisé (la capacité de production à long terme) et l'actif circulant (éléments d'exploitation tels que le stock de marchandises et les montants dus par les clients, ainsi que les liquidités).

- Le compte de résultat donne une présentation détaillée des produits et des dépenses de l'année.

- Le tableau des flux de trésorerie analyse les changements dans la structure financière de l'entreprise au cours d'une même année, c'est-à-dire les sommes rapportées par les différentes opérations, la part des fonds investis et les conséquences de ces deux flux sur l'endettement de l'entreprise.

- L'annexe a le même statut réglementaire que les états financiers et sert en principe d'outil pour une analyse complémentaire.

La comptabilité s'établit sur une base qu'on appelle "comptabilité d'engagement". Elle essaie de saisir toutes les opérations contractuelles (par exemple la livraison de produits aux clients), plutôt que de se limiter à un traitement des flux de trésorerie. En conséquence le compte d'exploitation est une estimation économique, ce qui explique l'intérêt d'un tableau des flux de trésorerie qui examine ceux-ci séparément.

Si les rapports financiers de différents pays donnent à peu près les mêmes informations, la présentation diverge quelque peu. Cependant les éléments fondamentaux du bilan que représentent le capital, la dette, l'actif immobilisé, l'actif circulant, existent bien et sont facilement identifiables. Le bilan fonctionne sur le fait que la totalité des sources de financement (dettes et capital, le passif) est toujours égal à la globalité de l'utilisation du financement (actifs immobilisé et circulant).

- Si l'Union européenne a été une force majeure d'harmonisation dans la présentation des états financiers, elle en admet encore plusieurs formats différents. La France et le Royaume-Uni ont fait un choix différent, leurs états financiers ne se ressemblent donc pas dans tous les détails.

- La France permet aux grandes entreprises d'utiliser un format international, par conséquent tous les bilans ne sont pas faits de façon identique.

- En Europe, la tradition veut que bien que les entreprises doivent respecter les formats admis, elles peuvent néanmoins fournir des renseignements complémentaires.

- Aux Etats-Unis, bien qu'il n'y ait pas de formats spécifiques, il y a un minimum de catégories d'informations à respecter. Si les pratiques des entreprises américaines varient, le format utilisé par une majorité d'entre elles est celui donné dans l'exemple.

- En général les autorités ne limitent pas l'utilisation de l'annexe. Les entreprises américaines et britanniques ont donc tendance à offrir une présentation très simple du bilan, en utilisant des chiffres en agrégat, et à garder le détail pour l'annexe.

Modèles de Rapports Financiers Britanniques

Profit and loss account ← Présentation reconnue par la 4ème Directive de l'UE

for the year ended 30 June

(in thousands of pounds)

	20X2	20X1
Turnover	50,925	46,543
Costs ← Charges analysées par fonction		
Cost of Sales	15,342	13,467
Marketing expenses ← Faux ami: catégorie de charge courante qui est anormale mais pas "exceptionnelle"	8,843	6,923
Administration costs	18,261	18,236
Exceptional items	30	38
Operating profit before finance costs ← Détails des charges et produits en annexe	8,449	7,879
Finance costs (net)	(3,054)	(2,652)
Profit on ordinary activities before taxation	5,395	5,227
Tax on profit on ordinary activities	(1,356)	(1,369)
Profit attributable to shareholders	4,039	3,858
Dividends	(1,903)	(1,808)
Retained profit	2,136	2,050
Earnings per ordinary share	2.1p	2.0p

Balance sheet

Formule utilisée parfois par des sociétés américaines

at 30 June

(in thousands of pounds)

	20X2	20X1
Fixed assets		
Tangible assets	109,703	102,805
Investments	5,000	5,000
	114,703	107,805
Current assets		
Stocks	276	298
Debtors	4,087	4,592
Cash at bank and in hand	3,086	6,818
	7,449	11,708
Creditors		
Amounts falling due within one year	14,006	13,870
Net current liabilities	(6,557)	(2,162)
Total assets less current liabilities	108,146	105,643
Creditors		
Amounts falling due after more than one year	(41,199)	(40,792)
Provision for liabilities and charges	(236)	(306)
Net assets	66,711	64,545
Capital and reserves		
Share Capital	19,032	19,032
Share premium	43,321	43,321
Revenue reserves	4,358	2,192
	£66,711	£64,545

Tangible assets — Analyse des immobilisations dans l'annexe

Net assets — La présentation montre: actif moins dettes = capitaux propres

Statement of cash flows

for the year ended 30 June	20X2	20X1
(in thousands of pounds)		
Operating profit	8,479	7,917
Depreciation	3,136	2,870
Movement on stock	22	219
Movement on debtors	558	(537)
Movement on creditors	(150)	(556)
Provisions	(70)	(360)
Net cash flow from operating activities	11,975	9,553
Interest received	303	429
Interest paid	(4,029)	(3,417)
Dividends paid	(1,827)	(1,693)
Net cash flow from returns on investments and servicing finance	(5,553)	(4,681)
Tax paid	(1,166)	(1,465)
Investing activities		
Purchase of tangible fixed assets	(9,543)	(11,373)
Sale of tangible fixed assets	210	783
Investment in shares	(1,000)	(1,395)
Net cash flow from investing activities	(10,333)	(11,985)
Financing activities		
Issue of shares	—	22
Increase in debt	1,345	9,610
Net cash flow from financing activities	1,345	9,632
Net increase (decrease) in cash	(3,732)	1,054
Cash at beginning of period	£6,818	£5,764
Cash at end of period	£3,086	£6,818

L'exercice comptable n'est pas forcément l'année civile

Catégories spécifiques à la version britannique

Modèles de rapports financiers américains

Statement of earnings

Deux exercices précédents doivent être montrés

for the years ended March 31

(in millions of dollars except per share amounts)	20X2	20X1	20X0
Net revenue			
Sales	24,991	20,317	16,410
Costs and expenses			
Cost of goods sold	15,490	12,123	9,158
Research and development	2,027	1,761	1,620
Selling, general and administrative	4,925	4,554	4,228
	22,442	18,438	15,006
Earnings from operations	2,549	1,879	1,404
Interest income and other, net	29	25	17
Interest expense	155	121	96
Earnings before taxes	2,423	1,783	1,325
Provision for taxes	824	606	444
Net Earnings	1,599	1,177	881
Earnings per share *(in dollars)*	$6.14	$4.65	$3.49

Les charges sont ventilées par destination plutôt que par nature

Les charges de recherche sont souvent mises en évidence

Information obligatoire

business@harrap.fr

Balance sheet

March 31 *(in millions of dollars)*	20X2	20X1
Assets		
Current assets		
Cash and cash equivalents	1,357	890
Short-term investments	1,121	755
Accounts & notes receivable	5,028	4,208
Inventories		
Finished goods	2,466	2,121
Purchased parts and fabricated assemblies	1,807	1,570
Other current assets	730	693
Total current assets	12,509	10,237
Property, plant & equipment		
Land	508	504
Buildings & leasehold improvements	3,472	3,264
Machinery & equipment	3,958	3,759
	7,938	7,527
Accumulated depreciation	(3,610)	(3,347)
	4,328	4,180
Long-term receivables and other assets	2,730	2,320
	19,567	16,736
Liabilities and shareholders' equity		
Current liabilities:		
Notes payable and short-term borrowings	2,469	2,190
Accounts payable	1,466	1,223
Employee compensation and benefits	1,256	1,048
Taxes on earnings	1,245	922
Deferred revenues	598	507
Other accrued liabilities	1,196	978
Total current liabilities	8,230	6,868
Long-term debt	547	667
Other liabilities	864	690
Shareholders' equity		
Common stock	1,186	1,090
less Treasury stock	(153)	(153)
Retained earnings	8,893	7,574
Total shareholders' equity	9,926	8,511
Total liabilities and equity	$19,567	$16,736

L'actif est présenté avec les éléments à court terme en tête

Détails fournis dans l'annexe

Détails fournis dans l'annexe

Sociétés américaines peuvent racheter leurs propres actions

Consolidated statement of cash flows

Présentation américaine
ressemble beaucoup
aux autres pays

for the years ended March 31
(in millions of dollars)

	20X2	20X1	20X0
Cash flows from operating activities:			
Net earnings	$1,599	$1,177	$881
Adjustments to reconcile net earnings to cash provided by operating activities:			
Depreciation and amortization	1,006	846	573
Deferred taxes on earnings	(156)	(137)	(35)
Changes in assets & liabilities:			
Accounts and notes receivable	(848)	(709)	(380)
Inventories	(582)	(1,056)	(399)
Accounts payable	243	283	226
Taxes on earnings	320	452	163
Other current assets and liabilities	585	200	328
Other, net	57	86	(69)
	2,224	1,142	1,288
Cash flows from investing activities:			
Investment in property, plant & equipment	(1,257)	(1,405)	(1,032)
Disposal of property plant & equipment	291	215	183
Purchase of short-term investments	(2,758)	(1,634)	(782)
Maturities of short-term investments	2,392	1,283	883
Purchase of long-term investments	(332)	(22)	(53)
Maturities of long-term investments	47	22	4
Acquisitions, net of cash	(62)	(86)	(411)
Other, net	69	23	(58)
	(1,610)	(1,604)	(1,266)
Cash flows from financing activities:			
Increase in notes payable and short-term borrowings	250	815	186
Issuance of long-term debt	64	387	309
Payment of current maturities of long-term debt	(159)	(228)	(79)
Dividends	(305)	(242)	(213)
Other, net	4	(22)	(209)
	(146)	710	(6)
Increase in cash and cash equivalents	468	248	16
Cash and cash equivalents at beginning of year	889	641	625
Cash and cash equivalents at end of year	$1,357	$889	$641

L'UNION EUROPÉENNE ET LA MONNAIE UNIQUE

La construction de l'Union économique et monétaire (UEM) a atteint un stade déterminant en janvier 1999 quand onze membres de l'Union européenne ont lancé une monnaie unique: l'euro. A partir de cette date, les états membres ont bloqué le taux de change de leurs monnaies respectives par rapport à l'euro, ce dernier devenant la monnaie officielle de l'Union européenne. Les organismes financiers se sont alors mis à traiter en euros sur les marchés internationaux. Les onze états membres pratiquent le même taux d'intérêt, établi par la Banque centrale européenne (BCE), et un taux de change unique. Cependant les habitants des pays de l'Union européenne auront le temps de s'accoutumer à l'euro étant donné que les billets et les pièces de chaque pays continueront à circuler jusqu'en 2002; ils seront alors remplacés par l'euro. Durant la période de transition, le double affichage des prix donnera aux populations le temps de s'habituer à cette nouvelle monnaie.

La France fut l'un des fondateurs de l'euro, bien que les mesures prises pour que l'inflation et les dépenses publiques répondent aux critères de convergence aient suscité des difficultés d'ordre social et peut-être même entraîné la défaite de la droite aux élections législatives en 1997.

L'euro: la fixation des taux de change

Taux de conversion irrévocables de l'euro par rapport aux monnaies nationales des pays participants au 31 décembre 1998:

Allemagne	= 1,95583 marks
Autriche	= 13,7603 schillings
Belgique	= 40,3399 francs belges
Espagne	= 166,386 pesetas
Finlande	= 5,94573 marks finlandais
France	= 6,55957 francs
Irlande	= 0,787564 livre irlandaise
Italie	= 1 936,27 lires
Luxembourg	= 40,33399 francs luxembourgeois
Pays-Bas	= 2,20371 florins
Portugal	= 200,482 escudos

Historique de l'Union européenne et de l'Union économique et monétaire

Mars 1957	Le traité de Rome établit la Communauté économique européenne (CEE)
1971	Pour parvenir à l'UEM le rapport Werner présente un projet en trois étapes
Jan 1973	Adhésion de la Grande-Bretagne, de l'Irlande et du Danemark à la CEE
Mars 1979	Création du SME: le système monétaire européen (accord sur le rétrécissement des marges) avec huit monnaies et introduction de l'ECU comme moyenne pondérée de toutes les monnaies européennes
1987	Entrée en vigueur de l'Acte unique européen. Publication du rapport Delors sur l'union économique et monétaire: il définit les étapes concrètes de la mise en œuvre de l'UEM
Juil 1990	Étape 1 de l'UEM: abolition de la réglementation des changes en Europe, ainsi que celle des contrôles des capitaux
Fév 1992	Traité de Maastricht: il précise les modalités de l'union monétaire et prescrit les critères de convergence pour les états membres candidats à la monnaie unique
Nov 1993	Le Traité de Maastricht entre en vigueur; la composition du panier de devises est gelée
Jan 1994	Étape 2 de l'UEM: l'Institut monétaire européen (IME) est fondé en précurseur de la Banque centrale européenne
Déc 1995	La nouvelle monnaie est officiellement baptisée l'euro lors de la réunion du Conseil européen à Madrid
Mars 1996	Début de la conférence inter-gouvernementale (CIG) à Turin: discussion des réformes institutionnelles de l'UE et préparations à un élargissement de l'UE
Déc 1996	Pacte de stabilité et de croissance pour assurer le maintien d'une discipline économique
Oct 1997	Signature du traité d'Amsterdam
Mai 1998	Début officiel de l'UEM: les chefs d'état de l'UE décident quels états peuvent prétendre à l'adhésion à la monnaie unique, fixent le taux de conversion entre les devises et s'accordent à maintenir leurs économies respectives en conformité avec les critères de convergence
Juin 1998	Inauguration de la Banque centrale européenne (BCE)
Jan 1999	L'euro devient la monnaie officielle des états de l'UEM: le taux de conversion de leur monnaie est figé par rapport à l'euro
Jan 2002	Introduction des billets et pièces en euros
Juil 2002	Étape 3 de l'UEM: retrait des billets et des pièces des pays participant à l'UEM

Le monnaie unique et ses implications pour la France

Pour la France, comme pour les autres pays qui participent à l'union monétaire, la nouvelle monnaie a des conséquences directes:

- la suppression des coûts de transaction sur les devises
- l'élimination des risques de change
- la transparence des prix

L'introduction de la monnaie unique est une source de défis et d'opportunités. Puisque la France partage désormais la même monnaie que les autres pays de la zone euro, elle n'a plus à se soucier des coûts de transaction liés aux opérations de change entre les différentes monnaies; de plus, de tels échanges sont désormais facilités par la plus grande transparence des prix à travers la zone euro, puisque la monnaie unique permet une meilleure comparaison des prix, ce qui devrait intensifier la concurrence et accroître, par voie de conséquence, l'efficacité économique dans toute la zone. L'adoption de la nouvelle monnaie signifie également que la France ne sera plus vulnérable aux fluctuations des taux de change lors des transactions transfrontalières effectuées au sein de la zone. Du point de vue de tous les partisans de l'union monétaire, la stabilité économique procurée par l'utilisation, à travers l'Europe, d'une monnaie unique sera favorable à la croissance des économies, à l'investissement et donc à la création d'emplois.

Pour les entreprises françaises, ainsi que pour les particuliers, quelques points saillants relatifs aux domaines principaux qui les concernent peuvent être résumés sous les rubriques suivantes:

- Comptes et opérations bancaires: dès le 1er janvier 1999, les banques françaises proposaient des comptes en euros et les banques proposaient à leurs clients des chèques libellés en euros. Du 1er janvier 1999 au 31 décembre 2001, c'est-à-dire pendant la période de double circulation, les banques qui reçoivent des paiements en euros devront convertir automatiquement les sommes concernées en monnaie de tenue de compte. Les salariés qui sont payés en euros peuvent donc continuer d'avoir leur compte en francs: le traitement en euros y sera déposé sans que le titulaire du compte ait à acquitter des frais supplémentaires.

- Comptabilité: les règlements européens ont fixé le principe de l'absence d'interdiction comme de l'absence d'obligation d'usage de l'euro dans la période transitoire. Les entreprises sont donc libres de choisir le moment du passage à l'euro de leur comptabilité, mais elles la convertiront de préférence au début d'un exercice comptable (à partir de tout exercice comptable débutant à partir du 1er janvier 1999). Dans ce contexte, certaines entreprises auront rapidement intérêt à tenir leur comptabilité en euros (membres de groupes européens, de multinationales, d'entreprises qui interviennent sur le marché européen... Il incombe à chaque entreprise de définir sa stratégie générale en fonction de sa situation commerciale: l'euro sera-t-il la seule monnaie utilisée à l'extérieur et à l'intérieur de l'entreprise ou est-ce que l'entreprise prévoit d'adopter une double comptabilité? Les systèmes de comptabilité devraient aussi permettre aux entreprises de faire des écritures en euros.

- Facturation: une entreprise pourra établir indifféremment ses factures en francs ou en euros, pourvu qu'elle respecte les règles générales de facturation posées en matière de TVA. L'intégralité de la facture sera donc établie dans l'une ou l'autre des monnaies. Néanmoins, le double affichage, en bas de facture, des prix en francs et en euros est également possible. Ceci dit, les entreprises ont intérêt à faire en sorte de pouvoir régler les factures en euros afin d'éviter les pertes sur arrondis s'ils doivent les convertir en monnaie locale et inversement.

- Fiscalité: dès le 1er janvier 1999, tous les impôts peuvent être payés en euros par les particuliers et les entreprises. Par ailleurs, les entreprises ayant basculé leur comptabilité en euros pouvaient dès 1999 souscrire leurs déclarations en euros. Pour les particuliers, les déclarations fiscales restent en francs jusqu'en 2002.

- Contrats: à partir de 2002, tous les contrats seront convertis en euros. Pendant la période de double circulation des monnaies, les contrats peuvent être libellés en francs ou en euros indifféremment.

- Les marchés et les investissements: en favorisant le développement et l'intégration des marchés de capitaux, la monnaie unique devrait faire baisser les taux à long terme, du fait de la plus forte liquidité des marchés. En outre, un marché financier plus important et plus liquide dans la zone euro facilitera l'intermédiation entre les épargnants et les investisseurs.

- Commerces: jusqu'au 31 décembre 2001, en accord avec le principe selon lequel il n'y a ni obligation ni interdiction d'utiliser l'euro, les commerçants sont en droit de refuser d'être réglés en euros. Cependant, s'ils affichent leurs prix en euros - démarche qui reste facultative pendant cette période - ils peuvent y être contraints, à moins qu'un affichage n'indique clairement que les paiements en euros ne sont pas acceptés.

En France, la transition vers l'euro se passe sans douleur pour le moment, grâce à des conditions économiques propices. Au moment du vrai passage à l'euro et de l'abandon du franc, des oppositions au sacrifice de la souveraineté nationale sont susceptibles de se manifester. Si l'abandon du franc, symbole fort, devait coïncider avec une récession économique, on se rendrait alors compte que le gouvernement français n'a plus autant de marge de manœuvre que par le passé dans la conduite des affaires économiques.

Toujours est-il que l'économie française est actuellement en expansion et que les partisans de l'euro espèrent que la nouvelle monnaie sera un vecteur de croissance économique et de prospérité pour la France et pour l'Europe.

Les sites Internet ci-après contiennent des informations sur l'euro:

www.finances.gouv.fr/euro (site de la ministère des finances)
www.banque-france.fr/actu/europe (site de la Banque de France)
www.euro.fee.be (site de la Fédération des experts comptables européens)

Billets et pièces en euros

Tout comme la livre sterling ou le dollar, la nouvelle monnaie a son propre symbole: €.

Les billets en euros seront disponibles en sept valeurs: 5€, 10€, 20€, 50€, 100€, 200€ et 500€. Chaque valeur a une couleur dominante particulière et une taille différente afin d'éviter toute confusion. Quelques prototypes sont présentés ci-dessous. Les motifs ont été sélectionnés par concours à l'échelle européenne, le thème d'inspiration étant l'histoire de l'architecture européenne.

Le billet de 5€ représente l'architecture classique, le billet de 10€ l'art roman, celui de 50€ la Renaissance, celui de 100€ le Baroque, celui de 200€ représente l'âge du fer et du verre dans l'architecture, enfin le billet de 500€ illustre la période de l'architecture moderne.

Fenêtres et arches sont les motifs principaux du dessus des billets, symboles de l'esprit d'ouverture et de coopération au sein de l'UE. Des ponts ornent l'envers des billets, métaphores de la communication entre les peuples d'Europe, et de l'Europe avec le reste du monde.

Les caractéristiques des billets sont les suivantes:

- un logo des douze étoiles du drapeau européen au recto des billets, et ce même drapeau en miniature au verso

- les initiales de la Banque centrale européenne dans les cinq variantes linguistiques (BCE, ECB, EZB, EKT et EKP)

- le nom de la monnaie en grec surmonté de son équivalent en latin (EURO); près des initiales de la BCE, la signature de son président

- un hologramme au recto des billets de valeur (50€, 100€, 200€ et 500€)

- un fil d'aluminium sur celui des billets de moindre valeur (5€, 10€ et 20€)

Recto d'un billet de €20

Verso d'un billet de €20

- la valeur des billets imprimée en caractères gras en haut à droite pour aider les mal-voyants.

Les pièces en euros ont une face européenne commune, et l'autre propre à chaque pays. La face européenne (choisie après concours à l'échelle européenne) représente une carte de l'Europe sur un fond de lignes parallèles sur chacune desquelles apparaissent les étoiles du drapeau européen. Le dessin de la face spécifique à chaque pays a été sélectionné sur la base d'un concours national. Les pièces seront disponibles en huit valeurs allant de 1 cent à 2 euros.

Pièce de 1 euro: recto   Verso: face belge   Verso: face espagnole

Pièce de 50 cents: recto   Verso: face française   Verso: face irlandaise

L'euro et le dollar américain

Aujourd'hui, le dollar est incontestablement la monnaie dominante (il est utilisé dans 50% des transactions commerciales et dans plus de 80% des transactions sur les marchés financiers), mais sa position pourrait être remise en question par la venue de l'euro.

Si la monnaie unique est un succès, la domination de l'économie mondiale par le dollar pourrait être remplacée par un système où les deux monnaies représenteraient chacune 40% des échanges à l'échelle mondiale. A titre d'exemple, l'euro pourrait se substituer au dollar dans les échanges commerciaux pour les pays ayant des liens géographiques, économiques et monétaires avec l'UE. Il pourrait s'ensuivre d'importantes répercussions sur les marchés financiers mondiaux et sur l'économie globale.

Pourtant, d'autres analystes prévoient un avenir beaucoup moins rose pour l'euro. Une telle analyse est fondée sur une évaluation pessimiste de l'économie européenne (surtout si l'on compare avec la croissance rapide de l'économie américaine ces dernières années). Les tenants de ce point de vue soutiennent que l'euro sera gravement compromis par ce qu'ils perçoivent comme des faiblesses dans la structure économique des pays membres de l'UEM. D'après eux, la livre sterling, et non l'euro, s'avérera être la monnaie forte capable de rivaliser avec le dollar, dans le cas où la Grande-Bretagne n'adhérerait pas à la monnaie unique.

Mais les partisans de la monnaie unique espèrent que la création de l'euro finira par supprimer le fossé qui existe actuellement entre le rôle monétaire des États-Unis et celui de l'Europe. Ils soutiennent que la transformation des marchés financiers européens provoquée par l'euro jouera un rôle primordial dans ce processus.

Cependant, même si selon certains analystes l'euro pourrait concurrencer le dollar comme monnaie de réserve dès 2003, il est encore trop tôt pour savoir quelle en sera la trajectoire, son destin étant au bout de compte étroitement lié à la conjoncture économique des pays qui l'auront adopté.

Sources of English Quotes

ACCRUED *Accountancy* London: Institute of Chartered Accountants, 1992

AFTER-HOURS *Wall St Journal* [Online highlights]1999

AIM *The Guardian* 1999

AMERICAN DEPOSITARY RECEIPT *Irish Times* 1999

ARBITRAGE *Computergram International* Date and publisher unknown

A-SHARE *The Economist* 1999

AVC *Moneywise* 1999

BAD *South China Morning Post* 1999

BANCASSURANCE *The Observer* 1999

BOLSTER *The Financial Times* 1999

BOOM *The Financial Times* 1999

BULL *Bloomberg Money* 1999

BUY-BACK *The Observer* 1999

CAPITAL *Bloomberg Money* 1999

CHAEBOL *Korea Times* 1999

CHURNING *Public Order and Private Lives* Brake, M. & Hale, C. London: Routledge & Kegan Paul plc, 1992

COMMODITY *Bloomberg Money* 1999

COMPOSITE INDEX *The Guardian* 1999

CONVERTIBLE *Bloomberg Money* 1999

COUNTERBID *Investors Chronicle* 1999

CREDIT *The Scotsman* 1999

CROSS-HOLDING *The Guardian* 1999

DEBENTURE *Law for the Haulier* Brown, Largent. London: Kogan Page Ltd, 1987

DEBT-EQUITY *South China Morning Post* 1999

DEEP-DISCOUNT BOND *Accountancy* London: Institute of Chartered Accounts, 1993

DELINQUENT *South China Morning Post* 1999

DEMUTUALIZE *The Guardian* 1999

DIGITAL SIGNATURE *The Irish Times* 1999

DIVERSIFY *The Financial Times* 1999

DOLLAR *Twentieth Century British History* Oxford: Oxford University Press, 1999

DRAWDOWN *The Financial Times* 1999

DUAL *The Irish Times* 1999

EARNED *What Every Woman Should Know About Retirement* Donald, V.; Orton, C.; Dudley, C.; Ward, S. Mitcham: Age Concern England, 1987

EBRD *Kessings Contemporary Archives* Harlow: Longman Group UK Ltd, 1990

E-BROKING *The Economist* 1999

ELECTRONIC *The Economist* 1997

ENDOWMENT *Bloomberg Money* 1999

EQUITY *Investors Chronicle* 1999

EURO *The Financial Times* 1999

EURO-CURRENCY *International Finance and Developing Countries* Leslie, James. Harlow: Longman Group UK Ltd, 1987

EXIT CHARGES *The Financial Times* 1999

FACTORING [Financial leaflets], Date and publisher unknown

FED *The Daily Telegraph* 1992

FEDERAL *The Economist* 1993

FIAT *Involuntary Employment* Trevithick, J.A. Hemel Hempstead: Harvester & Wheatsheaf, 1992

FLOOR *Moneywise* 1999

FOREIGN *International Finance and Developing Countries* Leslie, James. Harlow: Longman Group UK Ltd, 1987

FOREX *The Observer* 1999

FREE *The Scotsman* 1999

FRONT-END *The Scotsman* Date unknown

GEARING *The Independent* 1989

GILT-EDGED *The Independent* 1989

GO-GO STOCK *The Observer* 1999

GOODWILL *The Independent*

HEDGE *Investors Chronicle* 1999

HIGHLY-GEARED *Takeovers* Stedman, Graham. Harlow: Longman Group UK Ltd, 1993

HOLDING *The Economist* 1991

HOSTILE TAKEOVER BID *Competition and Business Regulation in the Single Market* S.J. Berwin & co, Date and publisher unknown

IFA *Ideal Home* 1991

IMF *The Independent* 1989

IMPREST *The Hotel Receptionist* Paige, Jane & Paige, Grace. London: Cassell Educational, 1992

INDEX *The Irish Times* 1999

INSIDER *The Economist* 1999

INSTANT-ACCESS *Economics* Date and publisher unknown

INTERIM *The Financial Times* 1999

IPO *The Times* 1999

ISA *Moneywise* 1999

JUNK BOND *Financial Market Analysis* Blake, David. Maidenhead: McGraw-Hill Book Company, 1990

KEY-ESCROW *The Irish Times* 1999

LAUNDER *The Daily Telegraph* 1992

LEVERAGED *The Independent* 1989

LIFFE *Financial Market Analysis* Blake, David. Maidenhead: McGraw-Hill Book Company, 1990

LIQUIDITY *Economics* Date and publisher unknown

MARGINAL *R&D Management: Managing Projects and Accounting* Glynn, J. Oxford: Basil Blackwell Ltd, 1990

MARKET *Financial Conglomerates and the Chinese Wall* McVea, H. New York: Oxford University Press, 1993

MBI *The Alton Herald* 1992

MERCANTILE *Sale of Goods and Consumer Credit* Dobson, A.P. London: Sweet and Maxwell Ltd, 1989

MEZZANINE *The Independent* 1989

MIRAS *Accountancy* London: Institute of Chartered Accountants, 1992

MONEY *The Guardian* 1999

MORTGAGE *The Financial Times* 1999

MPC *The Guardian* 1999

NEGATIVE *The Scotsman* Date unknown

NET *Investors Chronicle* 1999

NON-CONTRIBUTORY PENSION *Accountancy* London: Institute of Chartered Accountants, 1993

OCCUPATIONAL PENSION SCHEME *Accountancy* London: Institute of Chartered Accountants, 1993

OFFSHORE *Accountancy* London: Institute of Chartered Accountants, 1992

ON-LINE *The Economist* 1999

OVERBOUGHT *The Guardian* 1999

OVERDRAFT *Accountancy* London: Institute of Chartered Accountants, 1993

OVER-THE-COUNTER *UK Financial Institutions and Markets* Pawlet, Michael; Bentley, Patrick; Winstone, David. London: MacMillan Press Ltd, 1991

PAID-UP *Principles of Hotel and Catering Law* Pannet, A. London: Cassell, 1992

PAPER *The Guardian* 1999

PARI PASSU [Dawson International plc: Notice of annual general meeting], Date unknown

PAYE *The Rock File* York, Norton. Oxford: Oxford University Press, 1991

PENSION *The Economist* 1991

PIBOR *Markets and Dealers* Leslie, James. Harlow: Longman Group UK Ltd, 1992

PORTFOLIO *The Irish Times* 1999

PRICE *The Observer* 1999

PROFIT *The Guardian* 1999

PRUDENCE CONCEPT *Public Sector Accounting* Pendlebury, Maurice & Jones, Rowan. London: Pitman Publishing, 1992

RECAPITALIZE *Investors Chronicle* 1999

REDEMPTION *Investors Chronicle*

REMUNERATION *Introductory Sociology* Sheard, K.; Stanworth, M.; Buton, T.; Jones, P.; Bonnet, K. Basingstoke: MacMillan Publishers Ltd, 1992

RESERVE *Applied Economics in Banking and Finance* Partington. New York: Oxford University Press, 1989

REVOLVING *Consumers and Credit* London National Consumer Council, 1980

SEAQ *The Economist* 1998

SECURITY *The Economist* 1991

SELF-LIQUIDATING *International Finance and Developing Countries* Leslie, James. Harlow: Longman Group UK Ltd, 1987

SET *.net magazine* 1998

SHAREHOLDER *State and Society in Post-war Japan* Eccleston, Bernard. Cambridge: Polity Press, 1989

SHORT-TERM *Kessings Contemporary Archives* Harlow: Longman Group UK Ltd, 1990

SINGLE *The Economist* 1998

SLUSH FUND *Kessings Contemporary Archives* Harlow: Longman Group UK Ltd, 1991

SPECIAL *Capitalism since 1945* Harrison, John; Glyn, Andrew; Armstrong, Philip. Oxford: Blackwell, 1991

SPEND *The Scotsman* 1999

SRO *UK Financial Institutions and Markets* Pawlet, Michael; Bentley, Patrick; Winstone, David. London: MacMillan Press Ltd, 1991

STAKEHOLDER *The Observer* 1999

STOCK [Dawson International plc: Notice of annual general meeting], Date unknown

STRADDLE *Financial Market Analysis* Blake, David. Maidenhead: McGraw-Hill Book Company, 1990

SUBSIDY *Kessings Contemporary Archives* Harlow: Longman Group UK Ltd, 1991

SWAPTION *The Guardian* 1999

AKEOVER *The Independent* 1989
AX *The Guardian* 1999
AXMAN *Investors Chronicle* 1999
ESSA *The Economist* 1990
IGER ECONOMY *The Economist* 1998
OP-HEAVY *Managing Innovation* Date
 and Publisher unknown
RANCHE *The Independent* 1989
REASURY *The Economist* 1990
RUSTED THIRD PARTY *The Economist*
 1998
UMBRELLA FUND *The Financial Times*

1999
UNDERLYING *Investors Chronicle* 1999
UNLISTED *The Daily Telegraph* 1992
UNSECURED *Principles of Modern
 Contemporary Law* Gower, London: Sweet
 & Maxwell Ltd, 1992
VENTURE *The Financial Times* 1999
WASTING ASSET *Drafting Business Leases*
 Lewison, Kim. Harlow: Longman Group
 UK Ltd, 1993
WINDFALL *The Guardian* 1999
WRITE-DOWN *The Scotsman* 1999

Sources de Citations Françaises

ABATTEMENT *L'Entreprise* 1994
ABONDEMENT *Le Revenu* 1999
ACTIF *Le Revenu Français* 1994
ACTIONNARIAT *Le Monde* 1999
AFFLUX *Le Monde* 1999
ANNÉE *L'Expansion* 1994
APPORT *L'Expansion* 1994
ARGENT *Le Figaro* 1994
ASSAINIR *Le Figaro* 1994
AUTOFINANCEMENT *La Tribune des
 Fossés* 1994
AVOIR *Mieux Vivre Votre Argent* 1999
BAISSE *Libération* 1998
BAISSIER *Libération* 1998
BANCASSURANCE *Le Monde* 1999
BANQUE *L'Expansion* 1999
BÉNÉFICE *Courrier International* 1994
BLOC *Libération* 1999
BON *Le Monde* 1999
BONIFICATION *L'Expansion* 1994
BULLE *Mieux Vivre Votre Argent* 1999
BUSINESS ANGEL *Le Revenu* 1999
CAC *La Vie Française* 1999
CAPITAL *Libération* 1998
CAPITALISATION *Libération* 1999 •
CAPITAL-RISQUEUR *Le Revenu* 1999
CARTE *L'Expansion* 1994
CASH-FLOW *La Vie Française* 1999
CESSION *Le Monde* 1999
CHÈQUE *Le Revenu Français* 1994
CHEVALIER *Le Monde* 1999
CHIFFRE *Le Revenu Français* 1994

CODEVI *Le Monde* 1999
COMPTE *L'Expansion* 1994
COMPTE-TITRES *Mieux Vivre Votre
 Argent* 1999
CONTRE-OFFRE *Le Monde* 1999
CONTRIBUABLE *L'Expansion* 1994
CONTRÔLE *Libération* 1998
CONVERTIBLE *Le Revenu Français* 1994
COTÉ *Libération* 1998
COUPURE *L'Expansion* 1994
COURTIER *Le Monde* 1999
CRÉANCE *L'Expansion* 1994
CRÉDIT *Le Revenu Français* 1994
CRÉDIT-BAIL *La Vie Française* 1999
CSG *Le Nouvel Observateur* 1994
DÉBIT *Le Revenu Français* 1994
DÉCOTE *Le Journal des Finances* 1999
DÉFICIT *L'Expansion* 1994
DÉGRÈVEMENT *Le Revenu Français* 1994
DÉLIT *Le Point* 1999
DÉPÔT *Le Monde* 1999
DÉSINDEXATION *L'Expansion* 1994
DÉTENTE *Le Revenu Français* 1994
DÉTENTEUR *Le Revenu Français* 1994
DOTATION *L'Expansion* 1994
DOUBLE *Les Echos* 1999
DROIT *Libération* 1998
ÉMETTRE *Le Monde/Sélection
 hebdomadaire* 1998
ENCOURS *La Vie Française* 1999
ENVELOPPE *Le Figaro* 1994, *Mieux Vivre
 Votre Argent* 1999
ÉPARGNE *L'Expansion* 1994

Sources de Citations Françaises

ÉVASION *L'Expansion* 1994

EXERCICE *Courrier International* 1994, *Le Monde/Sélection hebdomadaire* 1998

FISCALITÉ *Les Echos* 1999

FLOTTER *Libération* 1998

FONDS *Libération* 1999, *Courrier Cadres* 1994

FOURNISSEUR *Libération* 1999

FRAIS *Professions et Entreprises* 1994

FRUCTIFIER *L'Expansion* 1994

GESTION *Courrier Cadres* 1994

HAUTEUR *Libération* 1998

IMPAYÉ *Courrier Cadres* 1994

IMPÔT *L'Expansion* 1994

INDEXATION *L'Expansion* 1994

INTERDIT *Le Revenu Français* 1994

KRACH *L'Expansion* 1994

LIQUIDATION *L'Expansion* 1994

LIQUIDITÉ *L'Expansion* 1994

LIVRET *Mieux Vivre Votre Argent* 1999

LOYER *Le Nouvel Observateur* 1994

MAJORATION *l'Expansion* 1994

MARCHÉ *Le Monde* 1999

MARGE *L'Expansion* 1999

MENSUALITÉ *L'Expansion* 1994

MOINS-VALUE *Le Revenu Français* 1994

MONNAIE *Le Monde* 1999

OAT *Mieux Vivre Votre Argent* 1999

OBLIGATION *Le Revenu Français* 1994

OPÉABLE *Mieux Vivre Votre Argent* 1999

OPÉRATION *L'Expansion* 1994

PEE *Le Revenu* 1999

PLACE *Le Monde/Sélection hebdomadaire* 1998

PLACEMENT *L'Express* 1999

PLUS-VALUE *L'Expansion* 1994

PORTEFEUILLE *L'Expansion* 1994

PORTE-MONNAIE ÉLECTRONIQUE *Mieux Vivre Votre Argent* 1999

PORTEUR *L'Expansion* 1994

PRÉLÈVEMENT *L'Expansion* 1994

PRIX *L'Expansion* 1994

PRODUIT *Libération* 1999

PROVISION *L'Expansion* 1994

QUOTE-PART *Le Monde/Sélection hebdomadaire* 1998

RAFFERMIR *Le Figaro* 1994

RECAPITALISER *Le Monde* 1999

RECETTE *L'Expansion* 1994

REDRESSEMENT *Le Monde/Sélection hebdomadaire* 1998

REFLUER *Le Monde* 1999

RÉGIME *Le Revenu Français* 1994

RELUTIF *La Vie Française* 1999

RENCHÉRIR *Libération* 1998

RENTE *Mieux Vivre Votre Argent* 1999

RÉSERVE *Le Figaro* 1994

REVENU *Les Cahiers Français* 1994

SICAV *L'Expansion* 1994

SICOVAM *La Vie Française* 1999

SOCIÉTÉ *Le Revenu* 1999, *L'Événement du Jeudi* 1998

SOLVABILITÉ *Les Echos* 1999

SOULTE *La Vie Française* 1999

SOUTENIR *Libération* 1998

STOCK-OPTION *L'Expansion* 1999

SURENCHÈRE *Le Monde/Sélection hebdomadaire* 1999

SURVALEUR *Mieux Vivre Votre Argent* 1999

TAUX *Le Revenu* 1999, *L'Expansion* 1994

TITRE *Le Figaro* 1994

TRANCHE *Libération* 1998

VALEUR *Le Revenu* 1999, *Le Monde* 1999

VALORISATION *Le Monde* 1999

ZONE *Le Monde* 1999